D1609931

THE HIDDEN PLACES OF

EAST ANGLIA

Including Norfolk, Suffolk, Essex and Cambridgeshire

By Kate Daniel

C153930203

Regional Hidden Places

Cornwall
Devon
Dorset, Hants & Isle of Wight
East Anglia
Lake District & Cumbria
Lancashire & Cheshire
Northumberland & Durham
Peak District and Derbyshire
Yorkshire

National Hidden Places

England
Ireland
Scotland
Wales

Country Living Rural Guides

East Anglia
Heart of England
Ireland
North East of England
North West of England
Scotland
South
South East
Wales
West Country

Other Guides

Off the Motorway
Garden Centres and Nurseries
of Britain

Published by: Travel Publishing Ltd, Airport Business Centre,
10 Thornbury Road, Estover, Plymouth, Devon PL6 7PP

ISBN13   9781904434894

© Travel Publishing Ltd

First published 1989, second edition 1993,
third edition 1994, fourth edition 1996,
fifth edition 1999, sixth edition 2001,
seventh edition 2003, eighth edition 2005,
ninth edition 2007, tenth edition 2010

Printing by: Latimer Trend, Plymouth

Maps by: ©MAPS IN MINUTES/Collins Bartholomew (2010)

Editor: Kate Daniel

Cover Design: Lines and Words, Aldermaston

Cover Photograph: Sailing boats at High Tide, Blakeney
© Rod Edwards/ Alamy www.alamy.com

Text Photographs:
© Bob Brooks, Weston-super-Mare
www.britainhistoricsites.co.uk
and
© Pictures of Britain www.picturesofbritain.co.uk

All advertisements in this publication have been accepted in
y Travel Publishing and have not necessarily
een endorsed by the company.

n is included by the publishers in good faith
l to be correct at the time of going to press.
ponsibility can be accepted for errors.

old subject to the condition that it shall not by
or otherwise be lent, re-sold, hired out, or
ulated without the publisher's prior consent in
binding or cover other than that which it is
nd without similar condition including this
eing imposed on the subsequent purchase.

KENT LIBRARIES AND ARCHIVES

C 153930203	
Askews	

Foreword

This is the 10th edition of *The Hidden Places of East Anglia* taking you on a relaxed but informative tour of **Norfolk, Suffolk, Essex and Cambridgeshire.** The guide has been fully updated and in this respect we would like to thank the Tourist Information Centres in East Anglia for helping us update the editorial content. The guide is packed with information on the many interesting places to visit in these predominantly rural counties. In addition, you will find details of places of interest and advertisers of places to stay, eat and drink included under each village, town or city, which are cross referenced to more detailed information contained in a separate, easy-to-use section to the rear of the book. This section is also available as a free supplement from the local Tourist Information Offices.

East Anglia offers plenty for the visitor to explore in real *Hidden Places* country. *Norfolk* is rightly famous for the Norfolk Broads, but also possesses gentle rolling hills, delightful pastoral scenes and a beautiful coastline rich in wildlife. *Suffolk* is blessed with incomparable rural beauty. Meandering tidal rivers and numerous streams, brooks and gullies intersect a land blended with low hills and vast open spaces. Suffolk was made famous by the brush of John Constable and his paintings reflect the sheer beauty and tranquility of this attractive county. *Essex* with its large estuaries and fishing communities, has a rich maritime tradition going back as far as Roman times. The county is equally well endowed with pretty stone-built villlages and contains the oldest recorded town in England, namely Colchester. *Cambridgeshire* is most famous for its ancient university as well as being the birthplace of Oliver Cromwell and Samuel Pepys. The county offers a wealth of peaceful and attractive countryside with many towns and villages steeped in history and tradition.

The Hidden Places of East Anglia contains a wealth of interesting information on the history, the countryside, the towns and villages and the more established places of interest. But it also promotes the more secluded and little known visitor attractions and places to stay, eat and drink many of which are easy to miss unless you know exactly where you are going.

We include hotels, bed & breakfasts, restaurants, pubs, bars, teashops and cafes as well as historic houses, museums, gardens and many other attractions throughout the area, all of which are comprehensively indexed. Many places are accompanied by an attractive photograph and are easily located by using the map at the beginning of each chapter. We do not award merit marks or rankings but concentrate on describing the more interesting, unusual or unique features of each place with the aim of making the reader's stay in the local area an enjoyable and stimulating experience.

Whether you are travelling around East Anglia on business or for pleasure we do hope that you enjoy reading and using this book. We are always interested in what readers think of places covered (or not covered) in our guides so please do not hesitate to use the reader reaction form provided to give us your considered comments. We also welcome any general comments which will help us improve the guides themselves. Finally if you are planning to visit any other corner of the British Isles we would like to refer you to the list of other **Hidden Places** titles to be found to the rear of the book and to the Travel Publishing website.

Travel Publishing

Did you know that you can also search our website for details of thousands of places to see, stay, eat or drink throughout Britain and Ireland? Our site has become increasingly popular and now receives over **500,000** visits annually. Try it!

website: www.findsomewhere.co.uk

Location Map

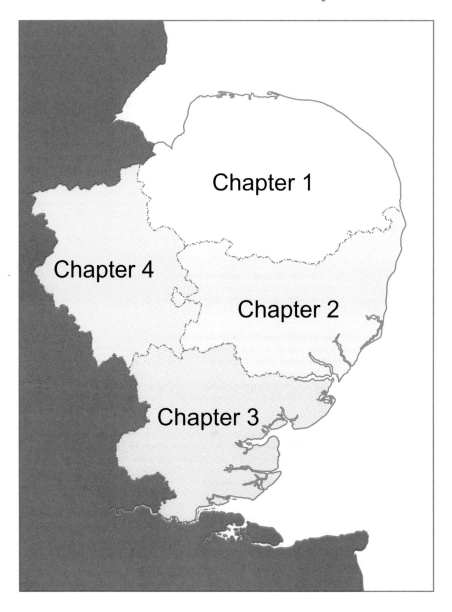

Chapter 1

Chapter 4

Chapter 2

Chapter 3

Contents

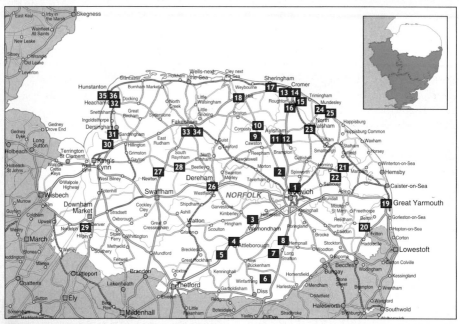

Norfolk

A journey through the area between the county capital of Norwich and the border with Suffolk, consisting mainly of flat farmland, takes you through some beautiful scenery with quiet villages and handsome old farmhouses – punctuated by the charming spires and towers of churches. One such church can be found at Cawston, boasted as being one of the finest examples of Gothic parish churches in England. Possibly the most enchanting backdrop in the county can be experienced in the valleys of Rivers Nar and Wensum.

The major centres of population include Diss, an old market town with a mix of Tudor, Georgian and Victorian houses, and Wymondham with its timber-framed buildings, picturesque market place and an Abbey church that can compare even with the majestic Norwich Cathedral. Norwich has a wealth of heritage, once an important centre of the worsted trade, which has been retained in many medieval buildings, some of which now serve as museums relating the fascinating history of the region.

The unique Norfolk Broads, to the east of the fine city of Norwich, contains beautiful stretches of shallow water, most of them linked by navigable rivers and canals. This is Britain's finest wetland area, a National Park in all but name. Broadland covers some 220 square miles in a rough oval to the northwest of Great Yarmouth. Three main rivers – the Ant, the Thurne and the Bure – thread their way through the marshes, providing some 120 miles of navigable waterways. The Broads have long provided a restful and relaxing holidaying destination for both human and feathered visitors – with a whole host of migrating birds favouring this spot during spring and autumn seasons for a respite on their lengthy journey. This area also supplies a more permanent refuge for many species of endangered birds and plants – making it quite a bustling hive of wildlife activity.

On the coast due east of Norwich is the old port and modern holiday resort of Great Yarmouth. Here it is the miles of sandy beaches, beautiful breezy promenade, two grand old traditional piers and all the fun of the fair, that attracts the huge number of visitors every year – but it is also home to a rich and just as fascinating marine heritage that lives on to this day. Stretching from Great Yarmouth in the east up to Cromer and west to Sheringham, Hunstanton and beyond are rewarding miles of quiet sandy beaches, spectacular sea views and the exhilarating, bracing sea air. The northeast coast includes what are sometimes known as 'the Highlands of Norfolk' – the Cromer Ridge, which rises to the not-so-dizzy heights of 330 feet above sea level. The most important town on the northwest coast is the busy seaside resort of Hunstanton, which has cliffs comprising red, white and brown geological layers. Another curious thing about Hunstanton: it is the only east-coast resort that actually faces west!

King's Lynn, on the Great Ouse three miles inland from The Wash, was one of England's most important ports in medieval times, sitting at the southern end of an underwater maze of sandbanks. To the northeast of King's Lynn is the prosperous market town of Fakenham, around which lie a remarkable variety of places of interest. To the north, in the valley of the River Stiffkey, the shrine of Our Lady of Walsingham was in medieval times second only to that of St Thomas à Becket at Canterbury as a pilgrim destination.

Breckland, which extends for more than 360 square miles in southwest Norfolk and northwest Suffolk, is underlain by chalk with only a light covering of soil. The name 'Breckland' comes from the dialect word breck, meaning an area of land cultivated for a while and then allowed to revert to heath after the soil has become exhausted. This quiet corner of the county is bounded by the Rivers Little Ouse and Waverney, which separate Norfolk from Suffolk.

NORWICH

Norwich castle, the most famous landmark in Norwich, with its impressive façade and beautiful views of the city from the keep and roof, is a must for any visitors. Built over 900 years ago by the Normans as a Royal Place – the first castle structure, in wood, was replaced in the late 1100s by a mighty fortress in stone which, unlike most blank-walled castles of the period, is decorated with a rich façade of blind arcades and ornamental pilasters.

Providing a great introduction to much of the regions history, culture and wildlife is the **Norwich Castle Museum and Art Gallery**, housed within the castle walls. It contains some of the most outstanding regional collections of fine art, archaeological exhibits and natural history displays. The rather gory history of the castle is explored in the dungeons, with a forbidding display of instruments of torture, along with the death masks of some of the prisoners who were executed here. Among the countless other fascinating exhibits are those devoted to Queen Boudica (Boadicea), which features the life of the Iceni tribe with an interactive chariot ride, the Egyptian gallery with its mummy Ankh Hor, and interactive displays in the Castle keep and keep basement.

The Art Gallery has an incomparable collection of paintings by the celebrated Norwich artist, John Sell Cotman (1782-1842), and others in the group known as the Norwich School. Their subjects were mostly landscape scenes, such as John Crome's The Poringland Oak. Quite apart from the artistic quality of their works, they have left a fascinating pictorial record of early 19th century Norfolk.

The **Bulwer and Miller** collection of more than 2,600 English china teapots makes its home in the Twinings Gallery, while the museum's Langton collection of around 100 cats fashioned in porcelain, ivory, bronze, glass and wood, originating from anywhere between Derbyshire and China, and Margaret Elizabeth Fountaine's mind-boggling accumulation of 22,000 butterflies which she had personally netted during her travels around the world, are available to view by appointment at the **Shirehall Study Centre**, next door to the Royal Norfolk Regimental Museum

Norwich Cathedral, Norfolk

on Market Avenue.

Down the road from the castle you can find **Strangers' Hall**, a grand building dating back to 1320, where a selection of costumed guides and informative exhibits bring the lives of Tudor and Stuarts to life. See the Tudor Great Hall where you can find a dining table set for a feast, the Great Chamber which now provides business quarters for the Lord Mayor of Norwich and a beautiful walnut panelled bedroom once belonging to Lady Paine in the 17th century.

The great open space of the Market Square, where every weekday a colourful jumble of traders' stalls can be found, offers just about every conceivable item for sale. Dominating the western side of the Market Square is **City Hall**, modelled on Stockholm City Hall and opened by King George VI in 1938. Opinions differ about its architectural merits, but there are no such doubts about the nearby Guildhall, a fine example of 15th century flintwork that now houses a tea room.

An interesting museum/shop, located in the Royal Arcade, a tiled riot of Art Nouveau fantasy, celebrates the county's great contribution to world cuisine: mustard. Back in the early 1800s, Jeremiah Colman perfected his blend of mustard flours and spice to produce a condiment that was smooth in texture and tart in flavour. Together with his nephew James he founded J & J Colman in 1823; 150 years later **The Mustard Shop** was established to commemorate the company's history. The shop sells, of course, a large range of mustard including some specialties made uniquely for the shop, as well as a wide selection of mustard pots and spoons, together with tea towels and Colman's memorabilia. On display are some fascinating artifacts covering all aspects of the history and production on loan from the archives.

In addition to Colman, other notable sons of Norwich include Matthew Parker, first Anglican Archbishop of Canterbury, nicknamed Nosey by Queen Elizabeth because he had a big nose and was prying by nature; Luke Hansard (1752-1828), Printer to the House of Commons, who gave his name to the official report of parliamentary proceedings; and the actor Rupert Everett.

Millennium Plain just off Theatre Street is where visitors will find **The Forum**, an architecturally stunning modern building designed by Sir Michael Hopkins. Combining

The Assembly House in Theatre Street is one of the city's finest historical houses and also a leading venue for the arts. It contains two concert halls, three galleries featuring changing exhibitions and a restaurant and tea rooms, as well as lovely tranquil gardens; a magnificent Georgian home which must be included in any visit to the city.

Elm Hill, Norwich

•

Norwich is home to some 32 medieval churches in all, every one of them worth attention, although many are now used for purposes other than worship. Outstanding among them are St Peter Mancroft, a masterpiece of Gothic architecture built between 1430-55 (and the largest church in Norwich), and St Peter Hungate, a handsome 15th century church standing at the top of Elm Hill, a narrow, unbelievably picturesque lane where in medieval times the city's wool merchants built their homes, close to their warehouses beside the River Wensum.

•

a unique horseshoe shape with an all-glass façade, this spectacular structure has, at its heart, the Atrium and Bridge, meeting places where you can enjoy a meal or drink anytime through to midnight, seven days a week. Inside The Forum can be found Fusion – Europe's largest permanent digital screen gallery with free public access – which is utilized in many weird and wonderful ways to the benefit of the community. Also The Curve in The Forum, designed by technology, lighting and acoustics specialists, is a perfect space for conferences, lectures and other presentation needs. Here can also be found the Tourist Information Centre, and the **Norfolk & Norwich Millennium Library** which houses 120,000 books and offers the best in information and communication technology – including 90 computers with free internet access.

Dragon Hall, on King Street a mere 10 minute walk from the city centre and railway station, is a breath-taking medieval merchant's trading hall lovingly restored for the enjoyment of the many visitors which frequent its Great Hall each year. Though the Great Hall dates from around 1430, there has been evidence of 1000 years of human habitation on the site found from archaeological excavations in its cellars – quite a history! The centre provides a really great visit, with much to explore under its spectacular timber crown-posted roof. Children will have much fun

being wealthy medieval merchants in dressing-up costumes, and exploring the many hands-on activities and exhibits. Open Mon – Fri 10am to 5pm and Sun 11am to 4pm, Bank holiday Mondays have Sunday opening times, and the centre is closed to the public (excluding special and private events) from Nov to Jan.

While Norwich Castle has been used for many purposes over the years, the **Cathedral** remains what it has always been: the focus of ecclesiastical life in the county. It's even older than the castle, its service of consecration taking place over 900 years ago, in 1101. This peerless building, its flint walls clad in creamy-white stone from Caen is, after Durham, the most completely Norman cathedral in England, its appeal enhanced by later Gothic features such as the flying buttresses. The Norman cloisters are the largest in the country and notable for the 400 coloured and gilded bosses depicting scenes from medieval life. Another 1,200 of these wondrous carvings decorate the glorious vaulted roof of the nave.

It's impossible to list all the Cathedral's treasures here, but do seek out the Saxon **Bishop's Throne** in the Presbytery, the lovely 14th century altar painting in St Luke's Chapel, and the richly carved canopies in the Choir.

Outside, beneath the slender 315-feet spire soaring heavenwards, the **Cathedral Close** is timeless in its tranquility. In the words of the former Dean Alan Webster, this is no longer a 'Close' but an 'Open' – extending the warmest of welcomes and engaging with the thousands of pilgrims and visitors who venture here every year. There are some 80 houses inside the Close, some medieval, many Georgian, their residents enjoying an idyllic refuge free from cars, with beautiful stretching greens and a backdrop of the cathedral reaching into the sky. At peace here lie the remains of Nurse Edith Cavell. A daughter of the rector of Swardeston, a few miles south of Norwich, Nurse Cavell worked at a Red Cross hospital in occupied Brussels during the First World War. She helped some 200 Allied soldiers to escape to neutral Holland before being detected and court-martialled by the Germans. As she faced execution by firing squad on 12 October 1915, she spoke her own resonant epitaph: 'Standing as I do, in the view of God and eternity, I realise that patriotism is not enough. I must have no hatred or bitterness towards anyone.'

A stroll around the Close will take you to **Pull's Ferry** with its picturesque flint gateway fronting the River Wensum. In medieval times a canal ran inland from here so that provisions, goods and, in the earliest days, building materials, could be moved direct to the Cathedral. Along the riverside walk is **Cow Tower**, built around 1378 and the most massive of the old city towers.

At the western end of the Cathedral Close is the magnificent

Erpingham Gate, presented to the city in 1420 by a hero of the Battle of Agincourt, Sir Thomas Erpingham.

Beyond this gate, in Tombland (originally Toom or wasteland), is **Samson and Hercules House**, its entrance flanked by two 1674 carvings of these giants. Diagonally opposite stands the 15th century Maid's Head Hotel.

Based in St Peter Hungate Church is the new **Hungate Medieval Art** exhibit, which

I CATTON OLD HALL

Norwich

A family run, private boutique B&B, ideal for those wanting to get away from the hustle and bustle of city life.

🛏 *see page 222*

Pulls Ferry, Norwich

2 BECKLANDS GUEST HOUSE

Horsford
A quality guest house offering a warm welcome and a high standard of quality and attentive service.

see page 223

•

Brown tourist signs from the A140 lead to the City of Norwich Aviation Museum at Horsham St Faiths, dedicated to keeping Norfolk's aviation heritage alive. The most impressive craft on display is a massive Avro Vulcan bomber that saw service in the 1982 Falklands conflict, but there are several other aircraft as well as displays showing the development of flying in Norfolk. The major roles played by Norfolk-based aircraft during the Second World War are remembered by exhibitions on the RAF and USAAF. The museum is open all year round, excluding December and the beginning of January, and under 8 year olds have free admission.

•

showcases all of the beauty of Medieval art in Norfolk and can give some amazing insight into the period. It demonstrates the development of design and processes in stained glass over the medieval period, by displaying detailed and illuminated images from around the county and through the church's own 15th and 16th century windows. A giant light-box with hands-on activities for children can also be found here. Open Thurs – Sat 10am to 4pm, free family art and craft activity is run on Saturdays.

St Gregory's Church in Pottergate is another Norwich church to have been deconsecrated. When the basic structure of the present St Gregory's was built in the late 14th century, the general rule seems to have been that any parish of around 1,000 people would have its own place of worship. St Gregory's was founded on the site of a Saxon church in 1210 and rebuilt in its present form in 1394. The church takes it name from Gregory the Great, the 6th century Pope best known for his campaign to convert the heathen Anglo-Saxons of 'Angle-land' to Christianity, despatching a party of 40 monks to Angle-land in AD 596, led by Augustine, whom the Pope consecrated as the first Archbishop of Canterbury.

The **Inspire Discovery Centre**, housed in the medieval church of St Michael in Coslany Street, just across the Wensum, northeast of the city centre, is full of exciting hands-on displays and

activities that make scientific enquiry come to life. These fun, fully interactional, displays explore the properties of gravity, the effects of light and risk taking in mathematical problems, as well as Medieval engineering. It is also open all year around – the perfect fun activity to amuse young ones on a rainy day!

To the south of Norwich in the village of Caistor St Edmund are the remains of **Venta Icenorum**, the Roman town established here after Boudica's rebellion in AD 61. Unusually, this extensive site has not been disturbed by later developments, so archaeologists have been able to identify the full scale of the original settlement. Most of the finds discovered during excavations in the 1920s and 1930s are now in Norwich Castle Museum, but the riverside site still merits a visit.

AROUND NORWICH

HORSHAM ST FAITHS

1 mile N of Norwich on the A140

This pretty green village, rich with a welcoming community spirit, has many amenities including a restaurant, two public hostelries, two post offices and function rooms available for hire. In addition a wealth of activities can be enjoyed from the community centre during your visit, such as tennis, badminton, archery and football, whilst the centre also has a gymnasium, sauna & swimming pool, play area and pleasant woodland walks.

WYMONDHAM

9 miles SW of Norwich off the A11

The exterior of **Wymondham Abbey** – two impressive towers which can be seen for miles around - presents one of the oddest ecclesiastical buildings in the county; the interior reveals one of the most glorious. The Abbey was founded in 1107 by the Benedictines - or Black Monks, as they were known because of the colour of their habits. The richest and most aristocratic of the monastic orders, the Black Monks apparently experienced some difficulty in respecting their solemn vows of poverty and humility. Especially the latter. Constantly in dispute with the people of Wymondham, the dissension between them grew so bitter that in 1249 Pope Innocent IV himself attempted to reconcile their differences. When his efforts failed, a wall was built across the interior of the Abbey, dividing it into an area for the monks and another for the parishioners. Even this drastic measure failed to bring peace, however. Both parties wanted to ring their own bells, so each built a tower. The townsfolk erected a stately rectangular tower at the west end; the monks an octagonal one over the crossing, thus creating the Abbey's curious exterior appearance.

Step inside and you find a magnificent Norman nave, 112 feet long (it was originally twice as long, but the eastern end, along with most of the Abbey buildings, was

Norwich Aviation Museum, Horsham St Faiths

demolished after the Dissolution of the Monasteries). The superb hammerbeam roof is supported by 76 beautifully carved angels. There's also an interesting 16th century tomb, of the last Abbot, in delicate terracotta work, and a striking modern memorial: a gilded and coloured reredos and tester commemorating the local men who lost their lives in the First World War.

Sadly many of Wymondham's oldest houses were lost in the fire of 1615, when some 300 dwellings were destroyed, so there are few surviving buildings pre-dating this fire – despite this however, the heart of the town still retains an attractive antiquity. The Market Place is given dignity by the picturesque octagonal **Market Cross**, rebuilt two years after the fire, and since 1990 has housed the welcoming Tourist Information Centre (Tel: 01953 604721). The Central Hall will be closed for major refurbishment for much of

3   THE HEART OF WYMONDHAM

Wymondham

A family run establishment offering the very best in fine pub cuisine.

see page 222

9

Wymondham Abbey

2010, but the weekly general **Market** and monthly **Farmers Market** (held the third Saturday of each month) are still going to continue as usual. Unfortunately the twice annually Sunday Antiques and Collectors Fair will be postponed while this work is done, but Wymondham has such a wealth of interesting antiques outlets and treasure-troves it is still assured to satisfy any visiting enthusiast.

A place of some interest is **Becket's Chapel**, founded in 1174 and restored in 1559. In its long history it has served as a pilgrim's chapel, grammar school, and coal store. In the recent past this building was home to the town's library, but this has now been moved to a different location, and (continuing the trend of amazing versatility) the chapel is now home to a successful Arts Centre which hopes to be permanently settled here. **The Bridewell**, or House of Correction, on Norwich Road was built as a model prison in 1785 along lines recommended by the

prison reformer, John Howard, who had condemned the earlier gaol on the site as 'one of the vilest in the country'. Wymondham's The Bridewell is said to have served as a model for the penitentiaries established in the United States. Now owned by the town's Heritage Society, Bridewell is home to several community projects, including the **Wymondham Heritage Museum**. The museum provides some delightful exhibits looking into daily life, heroes and villains in Wymondham's past, as well as housing a tea room, gift shop and beautiful courtyard garden which was once used as an exercise yard for the inmates at Bridewell.

Railway buffs will want to visit the historic **Railway Station** at Wymondham, built in 1845 on the Great Eastern's Norwich-Ely line. At its peak, the station and its section employed over 100 people. Still providing a rail link to Norwich, London and the Midlands, the station has been restored, and its buildings house a railway museum and restaurant. Also the completely volunteer-run **Mid-Norfolk Railway,** which runs some 11 miles (the longest heritage railway in East Anglia) through gorgeous countryside between Wymondham and Dereham, has proven to be a favourite attraction for all visitors to the town, not just those with interests in trains. One cannot imagine any better way to soak in the beauty of this area than this most elegant transport – particularly on one of their very popular

"Santa's specials" during the festive season, when the landscape is glittering with frost (or even snow!).

ATTLEBOROUGH

14 miles SW of Norwich off the A11

The greatest glory of this pleasant market town is to be found in its **Church of St Mary**. Here, a remarkable 15th century chancel screen stretches the width of the church and is beautifully embellished with the arms of the 24 bishoprics into which England was divided at that time. The screen is generally reckoned to be one of the most outstanding in the country, a remarkable survivor of the Reformation purging of such beautiful creations from churches across the land.

BANHAM

18 miles SW of Norwich on the B1114

Banham Zoo provides the opportunity to come face to face with some of the world's rarest wildlife - many of the animals who find a home here otherwise face extinction. In the 25 acres of landscaped gardens you'll find a fascinating array of animals in vast enclosures emulating their natural habitats, including many cheeky monkeys and apes, elegant tigers, cheetahs, lemurs, penguins, and one of the largest birds of prey exhibits in the UK. There are educational talks and displays, a children's play area, various eateries including a restaurant and more informal cafes and al fresco eating areas throughout the park (some with seasonal open times).

BRESSINGHAM

22 miles SW of Norwich off the A1066

Bressingham Steam and Gardens has plenty to interest the visitor. The Museum boasts one of the world's finest collections of British and Continental locomotives, housed under cover in the museum's extensive locomotive sheds; they also contain many steam-driven industrial engines, traction engines, a Victorian steam roundabout, and The Fire Museum, whose collection of fire engines and fire-fighting equipment could form a complete museum in its own right. Visitors can view the interior of the Royal Coach, ride on a narrow-gauge railway and experience the renowned special 'Steam Days' when the engines can be seen in full steam on the three narrow-gauge lines, with talks and footplate rides given on the standard-gauge locomotives. It is also home to the **National Dads Army Collection**. The gardens here are simply divine – with over 8000 species on display, the two six acre gardens provide delightful walks and will be a paradise for gardening enthusiasts. The rich colours and wonderfully maintained flower beds run through the grounds, with highlights for every season. This is definitely a tranquil haven away from the bustling cities and tourist crowds.

DISS

20 miles S of Norwich on the A1066/A140

The past Poet Laureate, John Betjeman, voted Diss his favourite

4 SHERBOURNE COUNTRY HOUSE AND HOLLY'S RESTAURANT

Attleborough

Located in a historic market town, the high standard of food served at Sherbourne House matches the quality of the accommodation.

🛏 🍴 see page 224

5 WHITE LODGE TRADITIONAL COACHING INN

Attleborough

A great 14th century thatched family pub serving fine real ale and food with a large garden, play area and campsite for all the family to enjoy.

🍴 🛏 see page 225

6 GISSING CROWN

Gissing

A popular and friendly pub offering great food and drink in a peaceful location.

 see page 226

7 WILDERNESS HOUSE

Wacton

A secluded 16th century farmhouse in large grounds offering the ideal get-away for those wanting to explore Norfolk

see page 227

8 BARN LODGE

Tasburgh

An attractive Victorian barn conversion offering a relaxing and comfortable get-away.

see page 227

Norfolk town, and it's easy to understand his enthusiasm. At the heart of this attractive old market town is **The Mere** and park, which houses many ducks and is fished upon by the locals. The town is a pleasing mixture of Tudor, Georgian and Victorian houses grouped around this pretty little sanctuary, and the River Waveney running alongside forms the boundary between Norfolk and Suffolk. Winner of "Best Kept Market Town in Norfolk", the town centre is now a designated conservation area, and keeps itself firmly on the northern bank of the river. The old town grew up on the hill above The Mere, perhaps because, as an 18th century resident observed, 'all the filth of the town centring in the Mere, beside the many conveniences that are placed over it, make the water very bad and altogether useless ... it stinks exceedingly, and sometimes the fish rise in great numbers, so thick that they are easily taken; they are chiefly roach and eels.' A proper sewerage system was finally installed in 1851. The traditional vocation of farming remains an important industry in the area.

The public park beside the six-acre Mere is lovely for gentle walks and from it leads a narrow street to the small Market Place. This former poultry market is dominated by **St Mary's Church**. The oldest parts date back some 700 years, and the St Nicholas Chapel is particularly enjoyable with its wonderful corbels, angels in the roof, and gargoyles. Not far from this church is the delightful Victorian **Shambles** with a cast-iron veranda and a small museum inside. This award-winning museum is packed with memorabilia and information about 'the town's past, its trade, famous people and 'orrible murders'.

SCOLE

2 miles E of Diss on the A140

Scole's history goes back to Roman times, since it grew up alongside the Imperial highway from Ipswich to Norwich at the point where it bridged the River Waveney. Traffic on this road (the A140) became unbearable in the 1980s, but a bypass has now mercifully restored some peace to the village. There are two hostelries of note: a coaching inn of 1655, built in an extravagant style of Dutch gables, giant pilasters and towering chimney stacks, and the Crossways Inn, which must have a good claim to being the prettiest pub in the county.

LANGMERE

6 miles NE of Diss on minor road off the A140 (through Dickleburgh)

Veterans of the Second World War and their families and friends will be interested in the **100th Bomb Group Memorial Museum**, a small museum on the edge of Dickleburgh Airfield (now disused). The Museum is the 'Bloody Hundredths' tribute to the US 8th Air Force, which was stationed here during the war, and includes displays of USAAF decorations and uniforms, equipment, combat records and other memorabilia and photographs. Facilities include refreshments, a museum shop, visitor centre and a picnic area. The Museum is open Saturdays, Sundays and Bank Holidays, also on Wednesdays between May and September. Closed November, January and February.

HARLESTON
7 miles NE of Diss off the A143

This pretty market town with some notable half-timbered and Georgian houses, and a splendid 12th century coaching inn, was a favourite of the renowned architectural authority, Nikolaus Pevsner. Another writer has described the area around the marketplace as 'the finest street scene in East Anglia'. The town of Harleston lies in the heart of the Waveney Valley, a lovely area which inspired many paintings by the locally-born artist, Sir Alfred Munnings.

Harleston is home to many specialist independent shops, which offer visitors a really friendly welcome. Market days are held every Wednesday, and there are other delightful attractions.

PORINGLAND
6 miles S of Norwich on the B1332

The name of this sizable village will be familiar to those who love the paintings of the Norwich artist John Crome (1794-1842) whose Arcadian painting of The Poringland Oak hangs in the Tate Gallery.

GREAT WITCHINGHAM
11 miles NW of Norwich off the A1067

The Animal Ark & Country Park is home to an interesting collection of rare, or ancient, breeds of farm livestock such as Highland cattle, white-faced woodland and Shetland sheep, pygmy goats and Exmoor ponies. Set in 20 acres of peaceful parkland, the Centre also has reindeer, llamas, wallabies, polecats, parakeets, otters and badgers, pools teeming with wildfowl and a huge colony of wild herons nesting in the trees. There is quite an interest taken in domestic pets also, such as rabbit, chinchilla and ferrets, and an importance is stressed on their care with pet care sheets available for anyone who owns or are thinking of keeping any of these adorable species as pets. For children there are 'Commando' and Adventure Play Areas to explore and play in, as well as one of the finest collections of trees and flowering shrubs in the county, a café and gift shop. Open Easter to the end of October. For more details and special events call 01603 872274.

Anyone who has ever read Parson Woodforde's enchanting Diary of a Country Parson will want to make a short diversion to the tiny village of **Weston Longville**, a mile or so south of the Dinosaur Park. The Revd James Woodforde was vicar of this remote parish from 1774 until his death in 1803, and throughout that time he conscientiously maintained a daily diary detailing a wonderful mixture of the momentous and the trivial. 'Very great Rebellion in

Eye Castle in Harleston, started life 900 years ago as a Mott and Bailey castle, and now stands as the ruins of a Victorian folly on top of a mount, which has lovely views of the town and surrounding countryside. In summer months the castle ruins are used for events including theatrical productions of Shakespeare. To learn more about Harleston's interesting history there is a Discovery Trail around the town, with an audio CD and player available from the tourist information centre for a small returnable deposit to talk you through the different buildings and sites of interest. Also the Harleston Museum at King Georges Hall has some fascinating artifacts and displays.

Heydon

A 16th century, former coaching house nestled in the pretty, privately owned, village of Heydon offering fine food and a varied selection of cask ales.

🍴 see page 228

Corpusty

A great village pub in an ideal location between Norwich and the coast.

🍴 see page 229

France' he notes when, ten days after the fall of the Bastille, the dramatic news eventually arrived at Weston Longville. More often he records his copious meals ('We had for dinner a calf's head, boiled fowl and tongue, a saddle of mutton roasted on the side table, and a fine swan roasted with currant jelly sauce for the first course. The second course a couple of wild fowl, larks, blamange, tarts etc. etc.'), the weather (during the winter of 1785, for example, the frost was so severe that it froze the chamberpots under the beds), and his frequent dealings with the smuggler Andrews, who kept the good parson well-supplied with contraband tea, gin and cognac. Inside the simple village church there's a portrait of Parson Woodforde, painted by his nephew, and across the road the inn has been named after this beguiling character.

SWANNINGTON

11 miles NW of Norwich off the A1067/B1149

The gardens of **Swannington Manor** are famous for the 300-year-old yew and box topiary hedge. Other features of this small town are the 13th century St Margaret's church, Swannington Hall – where can be seen the remains of the former moat – and the charming thatched village water pump. Preserving and taking a joy in their heritage is of great importance here, and in 2009 Swannington Heritage Trust won an achievement award from the

Leicestershire and Rutland Heritage Awards for their consistent and passionate efforts.

REEPHAM

12 miles NW of Norwich on the B1145

Reepham is an attractive spot set in the rich countryside between the Wensum and Bure Valleys. Lovely 18th century houses border the Market Place, and there is delightful walking along the Marriott's Way cycle path. Market day is Wednesday, and regular antiques fairs are held at the Old Reepham Brewery.

CAWSTON

12 miles NW of Norwich on the B1145

Cawston, a large village in an easy access position to both the city of Norwich and the coastal road to Great Yarmouth, has some great features. **St Agnes Church**, among many other treasures, boasts a magnificent double hammerbeam roof, where angels with protective wings 8 feet across float serenely from the roof, and a gorgeous 15th century rood screen embellished with lovely painted panels of saints and Fathers of the Church. The Oakes family field is a real testament to the strong community spirit here - once a crop field, recent developments with the help and support of the community has built a lovely space which is enjoyed by everyone from toddlers and teenagers to the elderly. Quite unusually, Cawston is home to **Broadland Wineries**, which has been making and bottling wines for over 40 years now. They offer wine bottling services for your own wine, but it is very much worth savoring their delightful range of fruit and country wines including delicious apricot, blackcurrant and elderflower, as well as traditional Norfolk mead.

AYLSHAM

14 miles N of Norwich on the A140

The attractive market town of Aylsham is set beside the River Bure, the northern terminus of the **Bure Valley Railway**. This 15" gauge railway was built in 1990 and is operated mainly by steam locomotives. It runs for nine miles between Aylsham and Wroxham, with intermediate stations at Brampton, Buxton and Coltishall. There are several Days Out with Thomas the Tank Engine during the year, and one- and two-day steam driving courses available during off-peak periods are aimed at everyone from the absolute beginner upwards. Aylsham's unspoilt Market Place is surrounded by late 17th and early 18th century houses, reflecting the prosperity the town enjoyed in those years from the cloth trade, and a 14th/15th century church, **St Michael's**, said to have been built by John O'Gaunt. In the churchyard is the tomb of one of the greatest of the 18th century landscape gardeners, Humphry Repton, the creator of some 200 parks and gardens around the country.

One of Repton's many commissions was to landscape the grounds of **Blickling Hall** (National Trust), a 'dream of architectural beauty' which stands a mile or so outside Aylsham. Many visitors have marvelled at their first sight of the great Hall built for Sir Henry Hobart in the 1620s. 'No-one is prepared on coming downhill past the church into the village, to find the main front of this finest of Jacobean mansions, actually looking upon the road, unobstructed, from behind its velvet lawns' enthused Charles Harper in 1904. 'No theatrical manager cunning in all the artful accessories of the stage could devise anything more dramatic.'

From the outside, Sir Henry's house fully satisfied the contemporary architectural vogue for perfect symmetry. Four towers topped with lead-covered turret-caps rise at each corner, there are lines of matching Dutch gables and mullioned windows, and even the chimneys were placed in corresponding groups of twos, threes or fours.

Inside, the most spectacular feature is the Long Gallery, which extends for 135 feet and originally provided space for indoor exercise in bad weather. Its glory is the plaster ceiling, an intricately patterned expanse of heraldic panels bearing the Hobart arms, along with others displaying bizarre and inscrutable emblems such as a naked lady riding a two-legged dragon.

Other treasures at Blickling include a dramatic double-flight carved oak staircase, the Chinese Bedroom lined with 18th century

11 THE OLD PUMP HOUSE

Aylsham

A warm, welcoming Georgian House, with surrounding unspoilt countryside, offering five ensuite bedrooms

see page 230

12 BURE VALLEY RAILWAY

Aylsham

Norfolk's longest narrow gauge heritage railway, a 15" gauge line operating between the old market town of Aylsham and Wroxham, a distance of nine miles.

see page 231

15

Just north of Mannington Hall stands the village of Little Barningham, where St Mary's Church is a magnet for collectors of ecclesiastical curiosities. Inside, perched on the corner of an ancient box pew, stands a remarkable wood-carved skeletal figure of the Grim Reaper. Its fleshless skull stares hollow-eyed at visitors with a defiant, mirthless grin: a scythe gripped in one clutch of bones, and an hour-glass in the other, symbolise the inescapable fate that awaits us all. This gruesomely powerful memento mori was donated to the church in 1640 by one Stephen Crosbie who, for good measure, added the inscription: 'As you are now, even so was I, Remember death for ye must dye.' Those words were a conventional enough adjuration at that time, but what is one supposed to make of Stephen's postscript inscribed on the back of the pew: 'For couples joined in wedlock this seat I did intend'?

hand-painted wallpaper, a library of over 12,000 books, an exhibition on the RAF at Blickling and the dazzling Peter the Great Room. A descendant of Sir Henry Hobart, the 2nd Earl of Buckinghamshire, was appointed Ambassador to Russia in 1746, and he returned from that posting with a magnificent tapestry, the gift of Empress Catherine the Great. This room was redesigned so as to display the Earl's sumptuous souvenir to its full effect, and portraits of himself and his Countess by Gainsborough were added later.

The Earl was a martyr to gout, and his death in 1793 at the age of 50 occurred when, finding the pain unbearable, he thrust his bloated foot into a bucket of icy water, and suffered a heart attack. He was buried beneath the idiosyncratic Egyptian Pyramid in the grounds, a 45-feet high structure designed by Ignatius Bonomi that combines Egyptian and classical elements to create a mausoleum which, if nothing else, is certainly distinctive.

Blickling also offers its visitors miles of footpaths through extensive parkland, a formal woodland wilderness garden, a Victorian parterre and a dry moat with scented plants, a plant centre, a picnic area, a superb restaurant, a shop and cycle hire.

Within a few miles of Blickling Hall are two other stately homes, both the properties of Lord and Lady Walpole. **Mannington** is a 15th century moated manor house whose grounds feature a wide variety of plants, trees and shrubs, including thousands of roses. The Heritage Rose Garden and Twentieth century Rose Garden are set in small gardens reflecting their period of origin; the gardens contain more than 1,500 varieties of roses. In 2003 a sensory garden was created, with plants chosen for scent, touch, sight, taste and hearing. There are also garden shops, with plants, souvenirs and crafts, and tea rooms. The grounds are open Sundays May to September and also Wednesday to Friday June to August.

Wolterton Park is a stately 18th century Hall built for Horatio Walpole, brother of Sir Robert, England's first Prime Minister. The grounds, landscaped by Humphry Repton, contain walks and trails, orienteering and an adventure playground, and various special events are held throughout the year here and at Mannington. The Hall is open for tours every Friday from April to late October.

Over 20 miles of waymarked public footpaths and permissive paths around Mannington and Wolterton link into the Weavers Way long-distance footpath and Holt circular walk.

CROMER

As you enter a seaside town, what more reassuring sight could there be than to see the pier still standing? **Cromer Pier** is the genuine article, complete with Lifeboat Station and the Pavilion Theatre, which still stages

Cromer Pier and Beach

traditional end-of-the-pier shows. The Pier's survival is all the more impressive since it was badly damaged in 1953 and 1989, and in 1993 it was sliced in two by a drilling rig which had broken adrift in a storm.

Cromer has been a significant resort since the late 1700s and in its early days even received an unsolicited testimonial from Jane Austen. In her novel *Emma* (1816), a character declares that 'Perry was a week at Cromer once, and he holds it to be the best of all the sea-bathing places.' A succession of celebrities, ranging from Lord Tennyson and Oscar Wilde to Winston Churchill and the German Kaiser, all came to see for themselves.

The inviting sandy beach remains much as they saw it (horse-drawn bathing machines aside), as does the **Church of St Peter & St Paul**, which boasts the tallest tower

in Norfolk, 160 feet high. And then as now, Cromer Crabs were reckoned to be the most succulent in England. During the season, between April and September, crab-boats are launched from the shore (there's no harbour here), sail out to the crab banks about 3 miles offshore, and there the two-man teams on each boat deal with some 200 pots. The fresh days catch can be enjoyed at many small fish restaurants on the waterfront and through the town.

Housed in the former Lifeboat Station, the **RNLI Henry Blogg Museum** tells the dramatic story of the courageous men who manned the town's rescue service. Pre-eminent among them was Henry Blogg, who was coxswain of the lifeboat for 37 years, from 1910 to 1947. During those years his boat, the *H F Bailey*, was called out 128 times and saved 518 lives. In 1991, the *H F Bailey* was purchased

13 BON VISTA GUESTHOUSE

Cromer

This stunning Victorian building has been tastefully refurbished to provide outstanding comfort in a great location.

see page 231

14 RUMBLETUMS RESTAURANT

Cromer

Homely and friendly eatery just a two minute walk from the famous Cromer pier and beach.

see page 232

15 THE FOUNDRY ARMS

Northrepps

A terrific traditional pub just three miles from the seaside town of Cromer

see page 232

17

Beached boats, Cromer

**16 NEW INN AND
SEREMBAN
RESTAURANT**

Roughton

A fine, family-friendly
establishment offering the
very best in oriental and
British cuisine

🍴 *see page 233*

by Peter Cadbury of the chocolate manufacturing family and presented to the Museum as its prime exhibit.

After enjoying the beautiful beach and pier, it is nice to see the independent retailers operating here just off the seafront. There are many interesting and welcoming shops to enjoy, as well relaxing cafes and the aforementioned seafood restaurants. Wednesday is traditionally an early closing day for shops in the town – though more shops are now staying open.

AROUND CROMER

AYLMERTON

*3 miles W of Cromer on minor road
off the A148*

Aylmerton is home to one of Norfolk's grandest houses, **Felbrigg Hall** (National Trust).

Thomas Windham began rebuilding the old manor house at Felbrigg in the 1620s, erecting in its place a grand Jacobean mansion with huge mullioned windows, pillared porch, and at roof-level a dedication in openwork stone: *Gloria Deo in Excelsis*, 'Glory to God in the Highest'. Later that century, Thomas's grandson William Windham I married a wealthy heiress and added the beautifully proportioned Carolean West Wing, where visitors can see portraits of the happily married couple painted by Sir Peter Lely. Their son, William Windham II, returning from his four-year-long Grand Tour, filled the house with treasures he had collected - so many of them that he had to extend the Hall yet again. The Windham family's ownership of Felbrigg Hall came to a tragi-comic end in the 1860s when William Frederick Windham inherited the estate. William was one of the great English eccentrics. He loved uniforms. Dressed in the Felbrigg blue and red livery, he would insist on serving at table; in guard's uniform he caused chaos on the local railway with his arbitrary whistle-blasts; dressed as a policeman, he sternly rounded up the ladies of easy virtue patrolling London's Haymarket. Inevitably, 'Mad' Windham fell prey to a pretty fortune-hunter and Felbrigg was only saved from complete bankruptcy by his death at the age of 26.

The Hall was acquired by the National Trust in 1969, complete with its 18th century furnishings, collection of paintings by artists such as Kneller and van der Velde, and a wonderful Gothic library. The items on display throughout the house, from the vastly unseen collection in the National Trust's possession, are changed on a regular basis so there is always a wealth of interest even on repeat visits. The 1,750-acre estate includes a traditional working walled garden containing an elegant octagonal dovecote, an orangery of 1707, a 500-acre Great Wood and a restaurant, tea room, gift shop and plant shop. Admission is charged for access to the house and gardens, although the estate itself is free to the public and open dawn to dusk all year round. The house is only open to the public for visiting between April and November, but the gardens are open 11am to 5pm most of the year.

WEST RUNTON

3 miles W of Cromer on the A149

The parish of West Runton can boast that within its boundaries lies the highest point in Norfolk - **Beacon Hill**, which was the perfect strategic site of a signal station and watch tower during the Napoleonic era. This eminence is 330 feet high, so you won't need any oxygen equipment to reach the summit, but there are some excellent views. Nearby is the Roman Camp (National Trust), a misleading name since there's no evidence that the Romans ever occupied this 70-acre stretch of heathland. Excavations have shown, however, that in Saxon and medieval times this was an iron-working settlement.

SHERINGHAM

5 miles W of Cromer on the A149

Sheringham has made the transition from fishing village to popular seaside resort with grace and style. There are plenty of activities on offer, yet Sheringham has managed to avoid the brasher excesses of many English seaside towns. The beach here is among the cleanest in England, and markedly different from the shingle beaches elsewhere on this part of the coast. Consisting mainly of gently sloping sand, it is excellent for bathing and the team of lifeguards makes it ideal for families with children. Rainfall at Sheringham is one of the lowest in the county, and the bracing air has also recommended the town to sufferers from rheumatism and respiratory problems.

Like so many other former fishing villages in England, Sheringham owes its transformation into a resort to the arrival of the railway. During the Edwardian peak years of rail travel, some 64 trains a day steamed into the station but the line became yet another victim of the Beeching closures of the 1960s. Devotees of steam trains joined together and, by dint of great effort and enthusiasm, managed to re-open the line in 1975 as the **North Norfolk Railway**, better known as "The Poppy Line".

West Runton's major tourist attraction is undoubtedly the Hillside Animal and Shire Horse Sanctuary (previously the Hillside Shire Horse Centre); founded in 1995 by Wendy Valentine, they endeavor to help and campaign for animals in need and most importantly, to bring public awareness to the millions of animals suffering every day in the intensive factory farming industry. Although Hillside has given sanctuary to 300 horses, ponies and donkeys, most of the resident animals have been rescued from the farming industry. The heavy horses are still a great attraction – with demonstrations and talks about the five different breeds living here at the sanctuary running through the season on open days. There are also outdoor and indoor play areas for children, a delightful gift shop and cafe where you can enjoy some refreshments. Dogs are welcome (on a lead) and open days run from the start of April to the start of November from 10am to 5pm (closed Saturdays June, July and August, closed Friday and Saturday April, May, September and October).

•

A small fleet of fishing boats still operates from the beach at Sheringham, mostly concentrating on crabs and lobsters, but also bringing in catches of cod, skate, plaice, mackerel and herring. Several original fishermen's cottages remain, some with lofts where the nets were mended. Sheringham has never had a harbour, so boats are launched from the shore where stacks of creels stand as they have for generations. A 'golden lobster' in the town's coat of arms celebrates this traditional industry.

•

17 NORTH NORFOLK RAILWAY

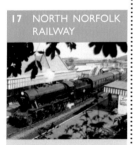

Sheringham

The "Poppy Line", successor to the M&GN, carries thousands of visitors each year on one of the most scenic steam heritage railways in Britain

 see page 232

The name refers to 'Poppyland', a term given to the area by the Victorian journalist Clement Scott who visited in pre-herbicide days when the summer fields were ablaze with poppies. In 1883, Scott travelled to Cromer on the newly-opened Great Eastern Railway's extension from Norwich. Walking out of the town, he was entranced by the tranquillity of the countryside. In his dispatch to the Daily Telegraph he wrote: 'It is difficult to convey an idea of the silence of the fields through which I passed, or the beauty of the prospect that surrounded me - a blue sky without a cloud across it, a sea sparkling under a haze of heat, wild flowers in profusion around me, poppies predominating everywhere ...' Spurred by Scott's enthusiasm, a succession of notable Victorians made their way here - painters, writers, actors, even a youthful Winston Churchill. Although greatly diminished in number, plenty of brilliant poppies can still be seen as you travel the scenic five-mile journey, steam or diesel operated, from Sheringham to Holt via Weybourne.

Nearby to Sheringham Station (the smallest terminal on the National Rail network) is the tranquil **Sheringham Park** (National Trust). The Park was landscaped by the hand of famous 18th Century landscape gardener Humphry Repton, who declared it to be his 'favourite and darling child in Norfolk', and offers one of the finest examples of his design legacy. The many miles of walks though the park hold many marvels; including many varied species of trees and shrubs within mature woodland, banks of rhododendrons which are at their most dazzling from May to early June, and of course beautiful coastal views from gazebos and viewing towers. The park is open to the public all year round, with a visitors centre open on weekends throughout the year and during the week in the summer months when there is also a refreshments kiosk in operation.

Another delightful walk, and a real hidden gem, can be found just outside of Sheringham towards Cromer at the **Priory Maze and Gardens**. "Away from the sterile formality of most gardens, we could relax and enjoy an unbelievably atmospheric experience" said one visitor of this tranquil haven. The natural beauties of these gardens, which have been so lovingly grown, have attracted numerous birds, insects and mammals which have made it their home. And it is not hard to see why; with the dramatic backdrop of Beeston Bump cliffs, and the ruins of Beeston Priory, the gardens range from the elegant grasses and flowers in the meadow stream gardens to the deliciously fragrant herb and aromatic gardens, with the constant tinkling music of water running down the gentle streams and waterfalls throughout. The microclimate of this particular part of Norfolk has allowed a wondrous variety of rare and exotic plants to flourish, many of which are available to buy from the plant centre, with the help of passionate and experienced staff. The hedge maze, designed on the ruins of the adjacent Beeston Priory with copper beech and hornbeam trees, will be a joy for both children and adults alike, and holds some intriguing treasures within its leafy walls. The Foxglove Tea Room serves a delicious menu of local home-cooked food in a log cabin based on Scandinavian design. Dogs are allowed into the gardens on a short leash. The maze and gardens are open 10am – 5pm everyday from April until October, 10am – 4pm Wednesday to Sunday from November to March and everyday in December from the 1st to the 21st.

WEYBOURNE

9 miles W of Cromer on the A149

Here, the shingle beach known as **Weybourne Hope** (or Hoop) slopes so steeply that an invading fleet could bring its ships right up to the shore. Which is exactly what the Danes did many times during the 9th and 10th centuries. A local adage states that 'He who would Old England win, Must at Weybourne Hoop begin,' and over the centuries care has been taken to protect this stretch of the coast. A map dated 1st May 1588 clearly shows 'Waborne Fort', and Holt's Parish Register for that year of the Armada notes that *'in this yeare was the town of Waborne fortified with a continuall garrison of men bothe of horse and foote with sconces (earthworks) ordinaunce and all manner of appoyntment to defend the Spannyards landing theare.'*

As it turned out, the 'Spannyards' never got close, but during both World Wars the same concern was shown for defending this vulnerable beach. The garrison then became the Anti-Aircraft Permanent Range and Radar Training Wing, providing instruction for National Servicemen until the camp finally closed in 1959. It was reckoned that by then some 1,500,000 shells had been fired out to sea. The site has since been returned to agricultural use, but the original NAAFI building remains and now houses the **Muckleburgh Collection**, a fascinating museum of military vehicles, weapons and equipment, most of which have seen action in battlefields all over the world. All the tanks, armoured cars and amphibious vehicles on display at the Muckleburgh Collection can be inspected at close quarters, and there are regular tank demonstrations. Meals and snacks are available - served in a NAAFI-style canteen, and there is a gift shop selling a great range of collectables, toys, clothing and gifts. The Muchleburgh Collection is open from 4th April until 1st November 10am to 5pm (last admission is at 4pm) and there are full disabled facilities. You can contact the museum on Tel: 01263 588210.

Weybourne is the middle station on the "Poppy Line" (see under Sheringham) and alongside the station are the line's locomotive and carriage & wagon workshops.

18 LETHERINGSETT WATERMILL

Letheringsett, Holt

In the attractive village of Letheringsett is a fully functional water powered Flour Mill generally accepted to be the only producing one in Norfolk

 see page 234

HOLT

10 miles W of Cromer on the A148

A perennial finalist in the 'Anglia in Bloom' competition, Holt's town centre always looks a picture, with hanging baskets and flowers everywhere. Back in 1892, a guide-book to the county described Holt as '*A clean and very prettily situated market town, being planted in a well undulating and very woody neighbourhood.*' More than a century later, one can't quarrel with that characterisation. The worst day in Holt's history was May 1st, 1708, when a raging fire consumed most of the town's ancient houses. The consequent rebuilding replaced them with some elegant Georgian houses, gracious buildings which played a large part in earning the town its designation as a Conservation Area.

There is a real sense of community spirit and a lovely atmosphere in Holt, with a great wealth of pretty individual shops ranging from antiques and pottery, to arts and books, as well as many cafes and restaurants with outdoor seating perfect for soaking up the sun and ambience in the summer months.

CLEY-NEXT-THE-SEA

12 miles W of Cromer on the A149

Cley's name is no longer appropriate. Cley-a-mile-away-from-the-Sea would be more truthful. But in early medieval times, Cley (pronounced Cly, and meaning clay) was a more important port than King's Lynn, with a busy trade exporting wool to the Netherlands. In return, Cley imported a predilection for houses with curved gables, Flemish bricks and pantiles. The windmill overlooking the harbour adds to the sense that a little piece of Holland has strayed across the North Sea. This is the famous **Cley Mill**, the subject of thousands of paintings. Built in 1713 and in use until 1921, the now beautifully restored mill is a bed and breakfast and open to the public, the owners usually allowing visitors to climb to the top for breath-taking views of the marshes and town.

Half a mile east of Cley on the A149 coast road, the Norfolk Wildlife Trust's **Cley Marshes** have a well-earned reputation as one of the UK's premier birdwatching sites. The pools and scrapes attract water birds in their thousands, so there is something interesting to see whatever the season. From Cley it's possible to walk westward along the shoreline to Blakeney Point, the most

Windmill, Cley-next-the-Sea

northerly extremity of East Anglia. This spit of land that stretches three miles out into the sea is another twitcher's paradise. Over 250 species of birds have been spotted here, and the variety of flora is scarcely less impressive. On the edge of the marshes is the **Cley Nature Reserve,** on which the environmentally friendly visitors centre is situated. This welcoming centre contains a gift shop and café, as well as serving as an observation area where you may catch glimpses of avocet, bearded tit or even the extremely rare bitten enjoying the patchwork of reedbeds, freshwater pools, dykes, grazing marshes and saline lagoons within the nature reserve.

GLANDFORD

12 miles W of Cromer off the B1156

Near this delightful village, the **Natural Surroundings Wild Flower Centre** is dedicated to gardening with a strong ecological emphasis. There are wild flower meadows and gardens, organic vegetable and herb gardens, nurseries, a nature trail alongside the unspoilt River Glaven, and the Centre also organises a wide range of events with a conservation theme. There is a delightful giftshop where you can purchase all you need for a wildlife garden, as well as a tea or coffee and snack. From the nurseries there are hundreds of varieties of plants available to buy.

A short walk down the valley from the Centre is the **Glandford Shell Museum**, a lovely Dutch-style building which houses the private collection of Sir Alfred Jodrell, a unique accumulation of sea shells gathered from beaches all around the world, together with a fascinating variety of artifacts made from them. In addition to shells, the museum has some other fascinating artifacts including fragments of old pottery, a piece of Pompeii, a sugar bowl used by Queen Elizabeth 1, some very fine specimens of agate ware, and an evocative tapestry executed by a local fisherman, John Craske, depicting the North Norfolk Coast. The museum is open from Easter Saturday to the end of October Tuesday to Saturdays 10am – 12.30pm and 2pm – 4.30pm, and it is open on Bank Holidays.Located nearby is the river Glaven, with a picturesque ford, wild ducks and a foot bridge which provides a delightful stroll.

MORSTON

13 miles W of Cromer on the A149

Great stretches of salt marshes (a spectacular blaze of purple sea lavender in the summer months) and mud flats lie between this pleasant village and the sea, which is reached by way of a tidal creek that almost disappears at low tide. It is a popular place for boating enthusiasts, who sail the local waters from the quay. The puzzle of creeks and pools of salt marsh that make up Morston Marsh, are under the care of the National Trust. Boats can be caught from Morston to visit the seal population at Blakeney Point (see Blakeney).

•

Cley-next-the-Sea's prosperity in the past is reflected in the enormous scale of its 14th/15th century parish church, St Mary's, whose south porch is particularly notable for its fine stonework and 16 armorial crests. The gorgeous fan-vaulted roof is decorated with bosses carved with angels, flowers, and a lively scene of an old woman throwing her distaff at a fox running away with her chickens.

•

•

Morston is a particularly pleasing village with quiet lanes and clusters of cottages built from local flint cobbles. If the church tower looks rather patched-up, that's because it was struck by lightning in 1743. It's said that local people took this as a sign that the Second Coming of Christ was imminent, and that repairing their church was therefore pointless. It was many years before restoration work was finally undertaken, by which time the fabric of the tower had deteriorated even further.

•

The beautifully restored Church of St Nicholas, set on a hill overlooking Blakeney village and marshland, has a lovely Early English chancel, built in 1220, and a magnificent west tower, 100 feet high, a landmark for miles around. In a small turret on the northeast corner of the chancel a light would once burn as a beacon to guide ships safely into Blakeney Harbour.

LANGHAM

14 miles W of Cromer off the A149/A148

The minor road leading south from Morston will bring visitors, after a mile or so, to **Langham Glass & Rural Crafts** where, in a wonderful collection of restored 18th century barn workshops, a variety of craftspeople can be seen practising their traditional skills. There is a lovely array of glassware; beautiful and delicate creations made by glass craftsmen from a furnace which burns at a scorching 1100 degrees, as well as the opportunity to see demonstrations (runs Oct to Easter) and even make your own piece of glass art. In the churchyard of St Andrew and St Mary is the grave of the novelist Captain Marryat, who wrote Mr Midshipman Easy and devised a signalling code for the Merchant Navy.

BLAKENEY

14 miles W of Cromer on the A149

One of the most enchanting of the North Norfolk coastal villages, Blakeney was a commercial port until the beginning of the 20th century, when silting up of the estuary prevented all but pleasure craft from gaining access. The silting has left a fascinating landscape of serpentine creeks and channels twisting their way through mud banks and sand hills. In a side street off the quay is the 14th century **Guildhall** (English Heritage), which was probably a private house and contains an interesting undercroft, or cellar, which is notable as an early example of a brick-built vaulted ceiling. The **Blakeney Hotel** has a marvelous location on the quay, with dramatic views across the estuary and salt flats all the way to **Blakeney Point**, which has been designated an Area of Outstanding Natural Beauty owned by the National Trust and part of the Heritage Coastline. As previously mentioned, Blakeney Point has a fascinating population of around 500 Common and Grey seals, which can be visited by boat on one of the purpose-run trips with knowledgeable professionals from Blakeney village. Visitors can have a real close encounter with these playful and inquisitive animals as they lie on the sands of Blakeney point, or swim out in the waters alongside the boats as they sail past. For a real special experience, seal pups can be seen between November and January for the Grey Seals and June and August for the Common seals. Boat trips are reliant on the tides, so times change daily, the season runs from 1st April – 31st October, but there are also weather permitting trips regularly throughout the winter. Also the bird life thrives here, enticing enthusiasts with the populations of Common, Sandwich and Little Terns and Arctic Terns being seen at the point, as well as shorebirds such as Oyster Catcher, Ringed Plover, Turnstone, and Dunlin, and during winter a large number of geese and ducks.

STIFFKEY

16 miles W of Cromer on the A149

Regarded as one of the prettiest villages in the county, Stiffkey lies beside the little river of the same name. Pronounced 'Stewkey', the name means 'island of tree stumps' and is most likely derived from the marshy river valley of reed beds and fallen trees, which indeed gives the village the appearance of an island. At the east end of the village is the church of St John the Baptist; from the churchyard there are fine views of the river and of **Stiffkey Hall** to the south. All that now remains of this once-impressive building, built by the Bacon family in 1578, are the towers, one wing of the house, and the 17th century gatehouse. The stately ruins of the great hall have been transformed into a rose terrace and sunken garden and are open to the public.

The former Rectory is a grand Georgian building, famous as the residence of the Revd Harold Davidson, Rector of Stiffkey during the 1920s and 1930s. This gentleman launched a personal crusade to save the fallen women of London, and caused much gossip and scandal by doing so. Despite the fact that his notoriety regularly filled the church to capacity, he constantly fell foul of the ecclesiastical authorities and eventually lost his living. There is a rather bizarre ending to his story. After handing over the keys of Stiffkey Rectory, Harold joined a travelling show and was later killed by a lion whose cage he was sharing. A couple of miles south of Stiffkey stand the picturesque ruins of **Binham Priory** (English Heritage), its magnificent nave still serving as the parish church. This represents only about one-sixth of the original Priory, founded in 1091 by a nephew of William the Conqueror. The church is well worth a visit to see its unusually lofty interior with a Monk's Walk at roof level, its Seven Sacraments font, and noble west front.

GREAT YARMOUTH

The topography of Great Yarmouth is rather curious. Back in Saxon times, it was actually an island, a large sandbank dotted with fishermen's cottages. Later, the narrow estuary of the River Bure at the northern end was blocked off, causing it to flow down the western side of the town. It runs parallel to the sea for two miles before joining the larger River Yare, and then their united waters curve around the southern edge of the town for another three miles before finally entering the sea.

So Yarmouth is now a promontory, its eastern and western sides displaying markedly different characters. The seaward side is a 5-mile stretch of sandy beaches, tourist attractions and countless amusements, with a breezy promenade from which one can watch the constant traffic of ships in Yarmouth Roads. There

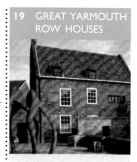

19 GREAT YARMOUTH ROW HOUSES

Great Yarmouth

Experience the sights and sounds of yesterday's Great Yarmouth. Visit these unique and vividly-presented houses

 see page 234

In Victorian times the whole town of Great Yarmouth was pervaded with the aroma of smoked herring, the silvery fish that were the basis of Yarmouth's prosperity. Around the time of Dickens' stay here, the author of the town's directory tried to pre-empt any discouraging effect this might have on visitors by claiming that 'The wholesome exhalations arising from the fish during the operation of curing are said to have a tendency to dissipate contagious disorders, and to be generally beneficial to the human constitution which is here sometimes preserved to extreme longevity.'

are two fine old traditional piers, the Britannia (810 feet long) and the Wellington (600 feet long), as well as The Jetty, first built in the 16th century for landing goods and passengers. A host of activities are on offer for families: the **Sealife Centre** with many kinds of marine life including octopus and seahorses, and an underwater viewing channel passing through shark-infested 'oceans'; **Amazonia**, an indoor tropical paradise featuring the largest collection of reptiles in Britain; **Merrivale Model Village** which offers an acre of attractive landscaped gardens with over 200 realistic models of town and country in miniature, which are illuminated at dusk, and the **Pleasure Beach**, featuring over 70 rides and attractions combining all the thrills of modern high-tech amusement park rides with the fun of traditional fairground attractions.

Guided heritage walks are run from April to October, covering a variety of topics including the history of Great Yarmouth as a holiday destination, a walk to recover the remains of Great Yarmouth's medieval town wall, much of which has been 'recycled' into other accommodation and building work and, for the brave, an eerie walk exploring the dark side of Great Yarmouth during July and August.

For heritage enthusiasts, Great Yarmouth has a rich and proud maritime history. The **Norfolk Nelson Museum** on South Quay features displays, paintings and

contemporary memorabilia relating to the life and times of Horatio Lord Nelson. Also on South Quay is the **Elizabethan House Museum**, built by a wealthy merchant and now a museum of domestic life, with 16th century panelled rooms and a functional Victorian kitchen. In Row 117, South Quay, the Old Merchant's House is an excellent example of a 17th century dwelling and a showplace for local wood and metalwork. Nearby is **The Tollhouse**, originally built in 1262 as a gaol and later used as a courthouse. It is now a museum with original dungeons. Nearby is the exciting **Time and Tide, Museum of Great Yarmouth Life**, where visitors can find out all about the town's fishing and maritime heritage.

Most of Yarmouth's older buildings are concentrated in the western, or riverside, part of the town. Here you will find **The Quay**, which moved Daniel Defoe, in 1724, to describe it as 'the finest quay in England, if not Europe'. It is more than a mile long and in places 150 yards wide. The **Town Hall** is well known for its grand staircase, Court Room and Assembly Room; the building itself is in use by the Local Authority. **The Rows**, a medieval network of tiny courtyards and narrow alleys, are a mere 2 feet wide in places. Badly damaged during a bombing raid in 1942, enough remains to show their unique character. There were originally 145 of these rows, about 7 miles in total, all of them built at right angles to the sea and therefore freely ventilated by onshore breezes which, given the urban sanitary conditions of those times, must have been extremely welcome.

The bombing raid of 1942 also completely destroyed the interior of **St Nicholas' Church**, but left its walls standing. Between 1957 and 1960 this huge building - the largest parish church in England - was completely restored and furnished in traditional style largely by using pieces garnered from redundant churches and other sources. The partly Norman font, for example, came from Highway church in Wiltshire, the organ from St Mary-the-Boltons in Kensington.

Great Yarmouth Toll House

Just south of the church, off the Market Place, is the half-timbered **Anna Sewell House**, built in 1641, in which the author of *Black Beauty* lived. Sewell was born in the town in 1820, but it was only when she was in her late fifties that she transmuted her concern for the more humane treatment of horses into a classic and seemingly timeless novel. Anna was paid just £20 for the rights to a book which, in the five months that elapsed between its publication and her death in 1878, had already sold an incredible 100,000 copies. (Anna Sewell, who died in 1878, is buried in the Quaker burial ground in Lamas, a village between Coltishall and Aylsham.)

Across the town, some 60 curing houses were busy gutting, salting and spicing herrings to produce Yarmouth's great contribution to the English breakfast, the kipper. The process had been invented by a Yarmouth man, John Woodger: a rival of his, a Mr Bishop, developed a different method which left the fish wonderfully moist and flavoursome, and so created the famous Yarmouth bloater.

For centuries, incredible quantities of herring were landed, nearly a billion in 1913 alone. In earlier years the trade had involved so many fishermen that there were more boats (1,123) registered at Yarmouth than at London. The scale of over-fishing produced the inevitable result: within the space of two decades Yarmouth's herring industry foundered, and by the late 1960s found itself dead in the water. Luckily, the end of that historic trade coincided with the beginning of North Sea oil and gas exploitation, a business which has kept the town in reasonably good economic health up to the present day.

27

Fritton

Fritton Lake, with fishing and boating both available, is one of the loveliest stretches of water in East Anglia.

 see page 235

AROUND GREAT YARMOUTH

FRITTON

6 miles SW of Great Yarmouth off the A143

Fritton Lake is one of the most beautiful stretches of water in East Anglia, extending two and a quarter miles from end to end and covering 150 acres. Visitors to **Fritton Lake Countryworld** can explore the lake in rowing boats and pedaloes. There is a special boat for disabled visitors, in addition to other disabled facilities throughout. You can also take a 25 minute guided tour of the lake in an electric powered launch, The Bittern, and learn about the history and wildlife of the lake. There is a large adventure playground offering children an assault course, aerial slides and more. The marked trail along the lakeside takes walkers through acres of natural woodland where at certain times of the season you will see the rhododendrons, bluebells and other wild flowers. The lake is part of the Somerleyton Hall estate which is about four miles away. The centre is open 10am to 5pm through the summer months, as well as all of October half term.

BURGH CASTLE

4 miles W of Great Yarmouth off the A12 or A143

When the Romans established their fortress of Garionnonum, now known as **Burgh Castle**, the surrounding marshes were still under water. The fort then stood on one bank of a vast estuary, commanding a strategic position at the head of an important waterway running into the heart of East Anglia. The ruins are impressive, with walls of alternating flint and brick layers rising 15 feet high in places (thought to be the full original height), and spreading more than 11 feet wide at their base; a remarkable survival, nearly unrivaled by other Roman ruins in Britain. The Romans abandoned Garionnonum around AD 408 and some two centuries later the Irish missionary St Fursey (or Fursa) founded a monastery within its walls. Later generations cannibalised both his building, and much of the crumbling Roman castle, as materials for their own churches and houses.

CAISTER-ON-SEA

3 miles N of Great Yarmouth off the A149

In Boudica's time, this modern holiday resort with its stretch of fine sands was an important fishing port for her people, the Iceni. After the Romans had vanquished her unruly tribe, they settled here sometime in the 2nd century and built a castra, or castle, or Caister, of which only a few foundations and remains have yet been found. **Caister Castle**, which stands in a picturesque setting about a mile to the west of the town, is a much later construction, built between 1432 and 1435 by Sir John Fastolf with his spoils from the French wars in which he had served, very profitably, as Governor of

Normandy and also distinguished himself leading the English bowmen at the Battle of Agincourt. Academics have enjoyed themselves for centuries disputing whether this Sir John was the model for Shakespeare's immortal rogue, Falstaff. Certainly the real Sir John was a larger-than-life character, but there's no evidence that he shared Falstaff's other characteristics of cowardliness, boastfulness or general over-indulgence.

Caister Castle was the first in England to be built of brick, and is in fact one of the earliest brick buildings in the county. The 90-feet tower remains, together with much of the moated wall and gatehouse, now lapped by still waters and with ivy relentlessly encroaching. The castle is open daily from May to September and, as an additional attraction, there is an impressive collection of veteran and vintage cars. About three miles west of Caister Castle, the pleasantly landscaped grounds surrounding an 1876 Victorian mansion have been transformed into the **Thrigby Hall Wildlife Gardens**, home for a renowned collection of Asian mammals, birds and reptiles. There are snow leopards and rare tigers; gibbons and crocodiles; deer and otters; and other attractions include a tropical house, aviaries, waterfowl lake, willow pattern garden, gift shop and café. The Gardens are open every day, all year round from 10am, the café from 10.30am during the summer months, and unfortunately dogs are not allowed on the premises.

THE NORFOLK BROADS

REEDHAM

8 miles SW of Great Yarmouth off the B1140

Here in Reedham is the single remaining car and passenger ferry in the Broads. There's also an interesting craft showroom at the Old Brewery, and a great pub in The Reedham Ferry Inn.

ACLE

10 miles W of Great Yarmouth off the A47

A thousand years ago, this small market town, now 10 miles inland, was a small fishing port on the coast. Gradually, land has been reclaimed from the estuaries of the Rivers Bure, Waveney and Yare, so that today large expanses of flat land stretch away from Acle towards the sea. The town's importance as a boating centre began in the 19th century with boat-building yards springing up beside the bridge. When Acle's first Regatta was held in 1890, some 150 yachts took part. The town became known as the 'Gateway to the Broads' and also as the gateway to 'Windmill Land', a picturesque stretch of the River Bure dotted with windmills. The medieval bridge that formerly crossed the Bure at Acle has less agreeable associations, since it was used for numerous executions with the unfortunate victims left to dangle over the river.

•

Acle was granted permission for a market in 1272, and it's still held every Thursday, attracting visitors from miles around. Others come to see the unusual Church of St Edmund with its Saxon round tower, built some time around AD 900, crowned with a 15th century belfry from which eight carved figures look down on the beautifully thatched roof of the nave. The treasures inside include a superbly carved font, 6 feet high, and inscribed with the date 1410, and a fine 15th century screen.

•

21 THE KINGS ARMS

Ludham

A warm and friendly place to enjoy a fine meal and drink.

see page 235

22 FAIRHAVEN WOODLAND AND WATER GARDEN

South Walsham

This beautiful woodland and garden boasts the UK's finest naturalised collection of Candelabra primulas, a 950 year old oak tree (home to a family of ducks), and 130 acres of natural woodland and water garden.

see page 237

SOUTH WALSHAM

10 miles NW of Great Yarmouth on the B1140

This small village is notable for having two parish churches built within yards of each other; something not completely uncommon in Norfolk. The village has some picturesque thatched and red brick cottages, a pretty green and two pubs. Just to the north of the village is the **Fairhaven Woodland and Water Garden**, an expanse of delightful water gardens lying beside the private South Walsham Inner Broad. Its centrepiece is the 900-year-old King Oak, lording it over the surrounding displays of rare shrubs and plants, native wildflowers, rhododendrons and giant lilies. There are tree-lined walks, a bird sanctuary, plants for sale, and a restaurant. A vintage-style riverboat takes visitors around the Broad where you can see Kingfishers, Grebe and Swans or maybe even catch sight of an Otter, and this makes for an interesting way to visit the magnificent ruins of St Benet's Abbey, the service runs from April to the end of October; the gardens are open all year around excluding Christmas Day.

The best way to see the remains of **St Benet's Abbey** is from a boat along the River Bure (indeed, it's quite difficult to reach it any other way). Rebuilt in 1020 by King Canute, after the Vikings had destroyed an earlier Saxon building, St Benet's became one of the richest abbeys in East Anglia. When Henry VIII closed it down in 1536 he made an unusual deal with its last Abbot. In return for creating the Abbot Bishop of Norwich, the Cathedral estates were to be handed over to the King, but St Benet's properties could remain in the Abbot/Bishop's possession. Even today, the Bishop of Norwich retains the additional title of Abbot of St Benet's, and on the first Sunday in August each year travels the last part of the journey by boat to hold an open-air service near the stately ruins of the Abbey gatehouse.

RANWORTH

14 miles NW of Great Yarmouth off the B1140

This beautiful Broadland village is famous for its church and its position on Ranworth Broad. From the tower of **St Helen's** church it is possible to see five Norfolk Broads, Horsey Mill, the sea at Great Yarmouth and, on a clear day, the spire of Norwich Cathedral. Inside, the church houses one of Norfolk's greatest ecclesiastical treasures, a breathtaking early 15th century Gothic choir screen, the most beautiful and the best preserved in the county. In glowing reds, greens and golds, gifted medieval artists painted a gallery of more than 30 saints and martyrs, inserting tiny cameos of such everyday scenes as falcons seizing hares, dogs chasing ducks and, oddly for Norfolk, lions. Cromwell's men, offended by such idolatrous images, smothered them with brown paint - an ideal preservative for these wonderful paintings, as became apparent when they were once again revealed during the course of a 19th century restoration of the church. The Norfolk Wildlife Trust's **Ranworth Broad** is a popular family destination where interpreted boardwalks promote an understanding of Broads ecology. The **Norfolk Wildlife Trust Information Centre** at Ranworth is delightful; a floating thatched building reached on a path winding through a nature reserve of woodland and reeds. It really is quite magical.

HORNING

12 miles NW of Great Yarmouth off the A1062

The travel writer Arthur Mee described Horning as 'Venice in Broadland', where 'waterways wandering from the river into the gardens are crossed by tiny bridges.' With its pretty reed-thatched cottages lining the bank of the River Bure and its position in the heart of the Broads, there are few more attractive places from which to explore this magical area.

POTTER HEIGHAM

13 miles NW of Great Yarmouth off the A149

Modern Potter Heigham has sprung up around the medieval bridge over the River Thurne, a low-arched structure with a clearance of only 7 feet at its highest, a notorious test for novice sailors. The Thurne is a major artery through the Broads, linking them in a continuous waterway from Horsey Mere in the east to Wroxham Broad in the west. Potter Heigham is the major boating centre on the Norfolk Broads, with many boating holidays and day trips starting from here.

A pleasant excursion from Potter Heigham is a visit to **Horsey Mere**, about six miles to the east, and **Horsey Windpump** (both National Trust). From this early 20th century drainage mill, now restored and fully working, there are lovely views across the Mere. A circular walk follows the north side of Horsey Mere, passes another windmill, and returns through the village. There's a small shop at the Windpump, and light refreshments are available.

STALHAM

18 miles NW of Great Yarmouth on the A149 (or 13 miles NE of Norwich)

At the Staithe, Stalham, on the opposite side of the A149 from Stalham centre, lies the **Museum of the Broads,** a delightful

Horsey Windpump

Wroxham is also the southern terminus of the Bure Valley Railway, a nine-mile long, narrow-gauge (15-inch) steam train service that closely follows the course of the River Bure through lovely countryside to the market town of Aylsham.

museum which won the "Best Water-Based Attraction" in 2008. Open for the season just before Easter from 10.30am to 4.30pm (last entry) Monday to Friday and also during the local school summer holidays, the Museum has boats, displays, exhibits and videos telling the story of life in the Broads. **Stalham Fire Museum**, next to the church on the main street, houses the town's original fire engine. Four miles southeast of Stalham, the Norfolk Wildlife Trust's **Hickling Broad** is the largest Norfolk Broad and is home to a spectacular variety of wildlife that includes swallowtail butterflies, bitterns, marsh harriers and other rare Broadland species. The Water Trail takes visitors by boat through the quiet backwaters to the tree Tower, with its breathtaking views of the Broads.

WROXHAM

8 miles NE of Norwich on the A1151

This riverside village, linked to its twin, Hoveton, by a hump-backed bridge over the River Bure, is the self-styled 'capital' of the Norfolk Broads and as such gets extremely busy during the season. The banks of the river are chock-a-block with boatyards full of cruisers of all shapes and sizes; there's a constant traffic of boats making their way to the open spaces of Wroxham Broad, and in July the scene becomes even more hectic when the annual Regatta is under way. For those staying in Wroxham for the boating, there is some great two, three or four bedroom

accommodation with gardens which back directly onto the water; so you needn't wrestle your way through crowds to reach your vessel in high season!

A couple of miles north of Wroxham is **Wroxham Barns**, a delightful collection of beautifully restored 18th century barns set in 10 acres of countryside, and housing a community of craftspeople. There are 13 workshops, producing between them a wide range of crafts, from stained glass to woodturning, stitchcraft to handmade children's clothes, pottery to floral artistry, and much more. The complex also includes a cider-pressing centre, a junior farm with lots of hands-on activities, a traditional Family Fair (with individually priced rides), a gift and craft shop, and a tearoom.

Anyone interested in dried flower arrangements should make their way to the tiny hamlet of **Cangate**, another couple of miles to the east, where **Willow Farm Flowers** provides an opportunity of seeing the whole process, from the flowers in the field to the final colourful displays. The farm shop has an abundance of dried, silk, parchment and wooden flowers, beautifully arranged, and more than 50 varieties of dried flowers are available in bunches or made into arrangements of all shapes and sizes, or to special order. Willow Farm also has a picnic and play area, a guided farm walk, lays on flower arranging demonstrations and also runs one-day classes.

COLTISHALL

8 miles N of Norwich on the B1150/B1354

This charming village beside the River Bure captivates visitors with its riverside setting, leafy lanes, elegant Dutch-gabled houses, village green and thatched church. Coltishall has a good claim to its title of 'Gateway to Broadland', since for most cruisers this is the beginning of the navigable portion of the Bure. Anyone interested in Norfolk's industrial heritage will want to seek out the **Ancient Lime Kiln**, next door to the Railway Tavern in Station Road. Lime, formerly an important part of Norfolk's rural economy, is obtained by heating chalk to a very high temperature in a kiln. Most of the county sits on a bed of chalk, but in the area around Coltishall

and Horstead it is of a particularly high quality.

WORSTEAD

12 miles NE of Norwich off the A149 or B1150

Hard to imagine now, but Worstead was a busy little industrial centre in the Middle Ages. The village lent its name to the hard-wearing cloth produced in the region, and many of the original weavers' cottages can still be seen in the narrow side-streets. Worsted cloth, woven from tightly-twisted yarn, was introduced by Flemish immigrants and became popular throughout England from the 13th century onwards. The Flemish weavers settled happily into the East Anglian way of life and seem to have influenced its architecture almost as strongly as its weaving industry.

NORTH WALSHAM

This busy country town with its attractive Market Cross of 1600 has some interesting historical associations. Back in 1381, despite its remoteness from London, North Walsham became the focus of an uprising in support of Wat Tyler's Peasants' Rebellion. These North Norfolk rebels were led by John Litester, a local dyer, and their object was the abolition of serfdom. Their actions were mainly

The lovely 14th century Church of St Mary provides ample evidence of Worstead's former prosperity. Its many treasures include a fine hammerbeam roof, a chancel screen with a remarkable painted dado, and a magnificent traceried font complete with cover. The village stages an annual weekend festival in July to raise money for the restoration of the church. The Festival, which has been running near-on 40 years now, has a range of events from traditional crafts like sheep shearing to modern local bands and a classic car exhibition. The memory of Worstead's days of glory is kept alive by a still-functioning Guild of Weavers. The Guild has placed looms in the north aisle of St Mary's, and from time to time there are demonstrations of the ancient skill of weaving.

Worstead Church

symbolic: invading manor houses, monasteries and town halls and burning the documents that recorded their subservient status. In a mass demonstration they gathered on Mousehold Heath outside Norwich, presented a petition to the King, and then retreated to North Walsham to await his answer. It came in the form of the sanguinary Bishop of Norwich, Henry Despenser, who, as his admiring biographer recorded, led an assault on the rebels, 'grinding his teeth like a wild boar, and sparing neither himself nor his enemies ... stabbing some, unhorsing others, hacking and hewing'. John Litester was captured, summarily executed and, on the orders of the Bishop, 'divided into four parts, and sent throughout the country to Norwich, Yarmouth, Lynn and to the site of his own house.'

A more glorious fate awaited the town's most famous resident, Horatio Nelson, who came to the **Paston School** here in 1768 as a boy of ten. Horatio was already dreaming of a naval career and, three years later when he read in the county newspaper that his Uncle Maurice had been appointed commander of a warship, he prevailed on his father to let him join the *Raisonnable*.

The Paston School had been founded in 1606 by Sir William Paston. His ancestors were the writers of the extraordinary collection of more than a thousand letters, written between 1422 and 1509, which present an astonishingly vivid picture of East Anglian life at the end of the turbulent Middle Ages. Sir William himself is buried in the parish church where he personally supervised (and paid for) the construction of the impressive marble and alabaster monument he desired to be erected in his memory.

The ruins of the town **tower** can be seen next to the **Church of St Nicholas**; in the early 18th century, the church was given the soaring tower, its height only beaten by Norwich cathedral. However, in 1724, a rather heavy set of bells was rung for a lengthy period and the following day two sides of the steeple collapsed in front a horrified town. It was never repaired, and now has been quite weakened by weathering but is still a very impressive sight. The town holds some interesting individual shops, and pretty white washed houses.

About four miles east of North Walsham, near the village of Erpingham on the A140, **Alby Crafts & Gardens** has a Crafts Gallery promoting the excellence of mainly East Anglian and British craftsmanship - lacework, woodturning, jewellery, canework and much more. The 'Plantsman's Garden' displays a fine collection of unusual shrubs, plants and bulbs in a 4-acre site; there are also workshops where you can watch craftsmen at work, a Bottle Museum and a tearoom. Open 10am to 5pm until Christmas, Mondays it is closed except for

Bank holidays and summer school holiday.

AROUND NORTH WALSHAM

MUNDESLEY

5 miles NE of North Walsham on the B1159

'The finest air in the kingdom has been wasted for centuries,' said a speaker celebrating the arrival of the railway at Mundesley in 1898, 'because nobody had the courage to bring the people to the district.' The railway has been and gone, but the fresh breezes off the North Sea remain as invigorating as ever.

After the hazards of the coastline immediately to the north where cliffs, fields and houses have all been eroded by the relentless sea, it's a pleasure to arrive at this unassuming holiday resort with its superb sandy beach, lined with colourful beach huts, considered by many the very best in Norfolk. Mundesley village is quite small (appropriately, its **Maritime Museum** is believed to be the smallest museum in the country), but it provides all the facilities conducive to a relaxing family holiday. Best of all, there is safe swimming in the sea, and when the tide is out children can spend many a happy hour exploring the 'lowes', or shallow lagoons, left behind.

PASTON

5 miles NE of North Walsham on the B1159

It was in this small village that the Paston family entered historical record. The vivid collection of letters they wrote to each other

Paston Tithe Barn

during the years that England was being racked by the Wars of the Roses has already been mentioned, and the village boasts another magnificent legacy from this remarkable family.

In 1581, Sir William Paston built a cavernous **Tithe Barn** here with flint walls and a thatched roof. It still stands, its roof still thatched: 160 feet long, almost 60 feet high - the longest, most imposing barn in Norfolk. In the nearby church, the most striking of the family memorials is the one dedicated to Katherine Paston. Sculpted in alabaster by Nicholas Stone in 1628, Katherine lies dressed to kill in her Jacobean finery of starched ruff, embroidered bodice, puffed sleeves and pearl necklaces. The monument cost £340, a staggering sum of money at that time.

Just outside of Paston on the road from Mundesley you will find Stow Mill; a beautifully restored windmill built in 1825, which was an operational corn mill until 1930. Here you can find about the

24 BREAKAWAY HOLIDAYS

Mundesley

A group of well equipped self-catering chalets and cottages for those wishing to enjoy a peaceful break.

see page 238

25 CASTAWAYS HOLIDAY PARK

Bacton

Perfect for a family holiday on the North Norfolk coast.

see page 237

35

history of this elegant building, and even buy a miniature version for your garden from their gift shop! The mill is open all year round from 10am until the evening, and the shop is open 10am to 5.30pm (unless weather permits an early close) Easter to Christmas although is closed most Saturdays.

HAPPISBURGH
6 miles E of North Walsham on the B1159

The seafront of this pretty coastal village has, in recent years, fallen victim to erosion and the man-made problem of offshore "dredging" (about 10 million tonnes of sand and gravel are dredged off the East Anglian coast each year for projects like road building). The wooden defenses built in the 1950's have been failing over several years and causing the sandy cliffs to start falling in chunks into the sea (in 2003 including a 30 meter strip of Happisburgh). The lifeboat service here has been re-located to nearby Sea Palling. Long and short term plans to conserve this beautiful stretch of coast have since been put in motion.

The coastal waters off Happisburgh (or 'Hazeborough', to give the village its correct pronunciation), have seen many a shipwreck over the centuries, and the victims lie buried in the graveyard of **St Mary's Church**. The large grassy mound on the north side of the church contains the bodies of the ill-fated crew of HMS *Invincible*, wrecked on the

treacherous sandbanks here in 1801. The ship was on its way to join up with Nelson's fleet at Copenhagen when the tragedy occurred, resulting in the death of 119 sailors. Happisburgh's distinctive Lighthouse, built in 1791 and striped like a barber's pole, certainly proved ineffectual on that occasion, as did the soaring 110-feet tower of the church itself, which could normally be relied on as a 'back-up' warning to mariners. Visitors can have the opportunity to climb the 133 steps of the tower in high season and get a glimpse of the breathtaking views available from its summit; on a good day you can see 30 churches, 2 lighthouses, 7 water towers, 5 corn mills, 5 drainage mills, 2 wind farms, and even the Cathedral spire in Norwich over 16 miles away.

Inside the Church is a splendid 15th century octagonal font carved with the figures of lions, satyrs and 'wild men'; embedded in the pillars along the aisle are the marks left by shrapnel from German bombs dropped on the village in 1940.

LESSINGHAM
7 miles SE of North Walsham off the B1159

From this small village a lane winds down through spectacular dunes to the sands at Eccles Beach and, a little further north, to Cart Gap with its gently sloping beach and colourful lines of beach huts. About four miles south of Lessingham stands a windmill that is not just the tallest in Norfolk, but in the whole of England. Eighty feet high and covering nine storeys, **Sutton Windmill** was built in the year of the French Revolution, 1789, and its millstones only finally ground to a halt in 1940. Unfortunately, as of September 2008, the Sutton Windmill and Yesterday's world museum on the site have been closed; the structure's continued deterioration has caused it to be deemed unsafe for visitors. No plans have presently been made to begin the massive and expensive task of restoring the windmill, or to relocate the collection contained in the museum. However, this still remains an impressive structure to visit while in the village of Lessingham, and all are hopeful that the future will hold the much needed restoration of this treasured historic building.

SEA PALLING

12 miles SE of North Walsham on the B1159

This pretty seaside village has a lovely sandy beach backed by sand dunes of marram grasses and, with its off-shore man-made reefs, calm waters perfect for safe swimming and bathing (particularly for young children). There is a section of the beach which welcomes dogs, even in the summer. The village contains a pub, a very picturesque old church, as well as various stores, cafes and amusement arcades. You can holiday in one of the picturesque cottages, stay in a caravan or take your own tent/ trailer. It can become busy in the height of summer.

KING'S LYNN & WEST NORFOLK

THETFORD

Some 2,000 years ago, Thetford may well have been the site of Boudica's Palace. In the 1980s, excavations for building development at Gallows Hill, north of the town, revealed an Iron Age enclosure. It is so extensive it may well have been the capital of the Iceni tribe which gave the Romans so much trouble. Certainly, the town's strategic location at the meeting of the Rivers Thet and Little Ouse made it an important settlement for centuries. At the time of the Domesday Book, 1086, Thetford was the sixth-largest town in the country and the seat of the Bishop of East Anglia, with its own castle, mint and pottery.

Of **Thetford Castle**, only the 80-feet motte remains, but it's worth climbing to the top of this mighty mound for the views across the town. An early Victorian traveller described Thetford as 'An ancient and princely little town ... one of the most charming country towns in England.' Despite major development all around, the heart of the town still fits that description, with a goodly number of medieval and Georgian houses presenting an attractive medley of flint and half-timbered buildings. Perhaps the most striking is the **Ancient House Museum of Thetford Life** in White Hart

Just down the coast from Sea Palling on the B1159 are Waxham (also with stretches of sandy beaches) and the 16th Century Grade I listed Waxham Great Barn. The barn was built in around 1570 as a display of wealth and, at 180 feet long, is the biggest in Norfolk. The building includes materials from three local dissolved and disintegrating priories following the Dissolution in the 1530s. Its roof features tie beams and hammer beams and the walls have coursed flint decorated with diamond patterned brickwork. A wing of the barn was converted into a lovely little café in 2003. The whole complex is open to the public during the summer, though it is also available for hire through the year. Phone 01603 629048 for full information on opening times.

On the edge of Thetford forest, about two miles west of Thetford, are the ruins of Thetford Warren Lodge, built around 1400. At that time a huge area here was preserved for farming rabbits, a major element of the medieval diet. The vast warren was owned by the Abbot of Thetford Priory, and it was he who built the Lodge for his gamekeeper.

Street, a magnificent 15th century timber-framed house with superb carved oak ceilings. Some of the most interesting exhibits are replicas of the Thetford Treasure, a 4th century hoard of gold and silver jewellery discovered as recently as 1979 by an amateur archaeologist with a metal detector. The originals of these sumptuous artefacts are housed in the British Museum in London. There is a new museum in an oak pavilion, and also a re-planted garden. The museum is open April – October 10am-5pm and November – March 10am-4pm (closed 24th-28th Dec and 1st Jan) and you should allow for an hour and a half for your visit.

Even older than the Ancient House is the 12th century **Cluniac Priory** (English Heritage), now mostly in ruins but with an impressive 14th century gatehouse still standing. During the Middle Ages, Thetford could boast 24

churches; today, only three remain. It is open daily April to September 10:00-6:00pm and Wednesday to Sunday October to March 10:00-4:00pm.

While in Thetford it is worth going on one of the **Trails** to get a taste of an aspect of the multi-faceted history of the town. There are trails covering the history of Duleep Singh (the last Maharajah of the Punjab and first Sikh settler in Britain), Thomas Paine (a hugely influential figure in the American and French Revolutions) and also for the long-running popular TV program Dad's Army which was filmed in Thetford.

Thetford's industrial heritage is vividly displayed in the **Burrell Steam Museum**, in Minstergate, which has full-size steam engines regularly 'in steam', re-created workshops and many examples of vintage agricultural machinery. The Museum tells the story of the Burrell Steam Company, which formed the backbone of the town's industry from the late 18th to the early 20th centuries, their sturdy machines famous around the world. Open every Tuesday April - October 10am to 2pm, and every last Saturday of the month March - October 10am to 4pm.

To the west of Thetford stretches the 90 square miles of **Thetford Forest**, the most extensive lowland forest in Britain. The Forestry Commission began planting in 1922, and although the woodland is largely given over to conifers, with Scots and Corsican Pine and Douglas Fir

Charles Burrell Museum, Thetford

predominating, oak, sycamore and beech can also be seen throughout. There is a particularly varied trail leading from the Forestry Commission Information Centre which has detailed information about this and other walks through the area.

Still in the forest, reached by a footpath from the village of Santon Downham, are **Grimes Graves** (English Heritage), the earliest major industrial site to be discovered in Europe. At these unique Neolithic flint mines, Stone Age labourers extracted the materials for their sharp-edged axes and knives. It's a strange experience entering these 4,000 year old shafts which descend some 30 feet to an underground chamber. The experience is even better if you bring your own high-powered torch. Opening times are Thursday to Monday in March and October, daily from April to September. Tel: 01842 810656

Thetford Forest

AROUND THETFORD

MUNDFORD

8 miles NW of Thetford on the A1065/A134

Mundford is a large Breckland village of flint-built cottages, set on the northern edge of Thetford Forest and with the River Wissey running by. If you ever watch television, you've almost certainly seen **Lynford Hall**, a mile or so northwest of Mundford. It has provided an impressive location for scenes in Dad's Army; Allo, Allo; You Rang My Lord? and Love on a Branch Line, as well as featuring in numerous television commercials. The Hall is a superb Grade II listed mansion, built for the Lyne-Stevens family in 1885 (as a hunting-lodge, incredibly) and designed in the Jacobean Renaissance style by William Burn.

THOMPSON

10 miles NE of Thetford on a minor road off the A1075

This is a quiet village with a marshy man-made lake, Thompson Water, and a wild common. **The Peddars Way** long-distance footpath passes about a mile to the west and, about the same distance to the northeast, the Church dedicated to St Martin is a splendid early 14th century building notable for its fine carved screen and choice 17th century fittings. The church also contains an amazing parish register which

39

dates back to 1538 with very few gaps; quite a feat of bookkeeping. There are a number of 17th century thatched cottages through Thompson, leading to its charm, including the Chequers Inn which has been an inn for at least 300 years and still serves up a great Sunday lunch!

WATTON

14 miles NE of Thetford on the A1075

Watton's striking town sign depicts the 'Babes in the Wood' of the famous nursery story. The story, which was already current hereabouts in the 1500s, relates that as Arthur Truelove lay dying he decided that the only hope for his two children was to leave them in the care of their uncle. Unfortunately, the uncle decided to help himself to their inheritance and paid two men to take the children into nearby **Wayland Wood** and kill them. In a moment of unexpected compassion, one of the men decided that he could not commit the dastardly act. He disposed of his accomplice instead, and abandoned the children in the wood to suffer whatever fate might befall them. Sadly, unlike the nursery tale in which the children find their way back home and live happily ever after, this unfortunate brother and sister perished. Their ghosts are said to wander hand in hand through the woods to this day.

Watton boasts an unusual Clock Tower, dated 1679, standing at the centre of its long main street.

EAST HARLING

8 miles E of Thetford on the B1111

This attractive little town boasts a beautiful 15th century parish church of **St Peter and St Paul** in a pastoral location beside the River Thet, which was mentioned in the Domesday Book during the reign of William the Conqueror. Inside, a magnificent hammerbeam roof crowns the lofty nave, there's some outstanding 15th century glass and, in the Harling Chapel, the fine marble **Tomb of Robert Harling**. Harling was one of Henry V's knights, who met his death at the siege of Paris in 1435. Since this was long before the days of refrigeration, the knight's body was instead stewed, then stuffed into a barrel and brought back to East Harling for a ceremonious burial.

Harling's church houses another equally sumptuous memorial, the **Tomb of Sir Thomas Lovell**. Sculpted in alabaster, Sir Thomas is an imposing figure, clad in armour with a long sword, his head resting on a helmet, his feet on a spray of peacock's feathers. He and his wife lie beneath a wondrously ornamented canopy, decorated with multi-coloured shields and pinnacles.

DEREHAM

One of the most ancient towns in the county, Dereham has a recorded history stretching back to AD 654 when St Withburga founded a Nunnery here. Her name lives on at **St Withburga's Well**, just to the west of the church. This is where she was laid to rest but, some 300 years later, the Abbot and monks of Ely robbed her grave and ensconced the precious, fundraising relic in their own Cathedral. In the saint's desecrated grave a spring suddenly bubbled forth, its waters possessed of miraculous healing properties, and St Withburga's shrine attracted even more pilgrims than before. Some still come.

In the **Church of St Nicholas**, the second largest in Norfolk, there are features from every century from the 12th to the 16th: a magnificent lantern tower, a lofty Bell Tower, painted roofs, and a Seven Sacrament Font. This is the largest of these notable fonts, of which only 30 have survived - 28 of them in Norfolk and Suffolk.

In the northeast transept is buried a poet, some of whose lines have become embedded in the language:

"Variety's the very spice of life, that gives it all its flavour"

"I am the monarch of all I survey"

"God made the country and man made the town"

They all came from the pen of William Cowper who, despite being the author of such cheery poems as John Gilpin ("A citizen of credit and renown"), suffered grievously from depression, a condition not improved by his association with John Newton, a former slave-trader who had repented and become 'a man of gloomy piety'. The two

St Withburga's Well, Dereham

men collaborated on a book of hymns that included such perennial favourites as *"Oh! for a Closer Walk with God"*, *"Hark, my soul, it is the Lord"* and *"God moves in a mysterious way"*. Cowper spent the last four years of his life at Dereham, veering in and out of madness. In a late-flowering romance he had married the widow Mary Unwin, but the strain of caring for the deranged poet drove her in turn to insanity and death. She, too, is buried in the church.

William Cowper died four years

26 HILL HOUSE HOTEL

Dereham

A handsome Queen Anne hotel in the heart of Dereham, luxuriously and stylishly decorated with fantastic facilities and a large carvery restaurant attached.

see page 239

41

after Mary, in 1800. Three years later, another celebrated writer was born at the quaintly named hamlet of **Dumpling Green** on the edge of the town. George Borrow was to become one of the great English travel writers, producing books full of character and colour such as Wild Wales and The Bible in Spain. In his autobiographical novel Lavengro he begins with a warm recollection of the town where he was born:

"I love to think on thee, pretty, quiet D[ereham], thou pattern of an English market town, with thy clean but narrow streets branching out from thy modest market place, with thine old-fashioned houses, with here and there a roof of venerable thatch."

The house in which George Borrow was born, Borrow's Hall, still stands in Dumpling Green.

A character much less attractive than George Borrow connected with Dereham is Bishop Bonner, the enthusiastic arsonist of Protestant 'heretics' during the unhappy reign of Mary Tudor. He was rector of the town before being appointed Bishop of London, and he lived in the exquisite thatched terrace now called **Bishop Bonner's Cottage Museum**. The exterior is ornamented with delightful pargeting, a frieze of flower and fruit designs below the eaves, a form of decoration which is very unusual in Norfolk. The museum contains displays of local archaeology and the history of the town, including photos and memorabilia of a by-gone

Dereham. Open May-September Tues and Thurs 2pm to 4.30pm, Fri and Sat 11am to 4pm, October Saturdays 11am to 4pm (October half term has May-Sept opening times).

AROUND DEREHAM

GRESSENHALL

3 miles NW of Dereham off the B1146

The **Gressenhall Farm and Workhouse** rural life museum is housed in an impressive late 18th century former workhouse built in rose-red brick. Gressenhall Workhouse was designed to accommodate some 700 unfortunates, so it was built on a very grand scale indeed. Now one of the UK's leading rural life museums and among Norfolk's top family attractions, there's ample room for the many exhibits illuminating the working and domestic life of Norfolk people over the last 150 years. Farming the old-fashioned way is there to be discovered on Union Farm, where heavy animals still work the fields, and visitors can ride a cart through the fairy-talesque farmland. A stroll along the 1930s village high street takes in the grocer's, post office and schoolroom. The surrounding 50 acres of unspoilt countryside are perfect for walking. The site hosts numerous special events during the season, ranging from Steam Days to an international folk dance festival with more than 200 dancers taking part.

A mile or so south of Gressenhall, the tiny community of

Dillington is worth seeking out for **Norfolk Herbs** at Blackberry Farm, a specialist herb farm located in a beautiful wooded valley. Visitors are invited to browse through a vast collection of aromatic, culinary and medicinal herb plants, and to learn all about growing and using herbs.

NORTH ELMHAM

6 miles N of Dereham off the B1110

Near the village of North Elmham stand the sparse remains of a Saxon Cathedral. North Elmham was the seat of the Bishops of East Anglia until 1071, when they moved to Thetford (and then, 20 years later, to Norwich). Although there had been a cathedral here since the late 7th century, what has survived is mostly from the 11th century. Despite its grand title, the T-shaped ground plan reveals that the cathedral was no larger than a small parish church.

BRISLEY

7 miles N of Dereham on the B1145

Brisley village is well known to local historians and naturalists for its huge expanse of heathland, some 170 acres of it. It's reckoned to be the best example of unspoilt common in Norfolk, and at its centre are scores of pits that were dug out in medieval times to provide clay for the wattle-and-daub houses of the period. Another feature of interest in the village is Gately Manor (private), an Elizabethan manor house standing within the remains of a medieval moat, and yet another moated

house at Old Hall Farm in the southwest corner of the green.

SWAFFHAM

Swaffham's one-time claim to be the 'Montpellier of England' was justified by the abundance of handsome Georgian houses that used to surround the large, wedge-shaped market place. A good number still survive, along with the **Assembly Room** of 1817 where the quality would foregather for concerts, balls and soirees. The central focus of the market square is the elegant **Butter Cross**, presented to the town by the Earl of Orford in 1783. It's not a cross at all, but a classical lead-covered dome standing on eight columns and surmounted by a life-size statue of Ceres, the Roman goddess of agriculture - an appropriate symbol for this busy market town, from which ten roads radiate out across the county.

The market is held every Saturday in the town centre; a very

•

Howard Carter, the man who discovered the tomb of Tutankhamen, was born at Swaffham in 1874; his death in 1939 was attributed by the popular press to 'the Curse of Tutankhamen'. If so, it must have been an extremely slow-acting curse. Some 17 years had elapsed since Carter had knelt by a dark, underground opening, swivelled his torch and found himself the first human being in centuries to gaze upon the astonishing treasures buried in the tomb of the teenage Pharaoh.

•

Swaffham Museum

At Cockley Cley Iceni Village and Museums, three miles southwest of Swaffham off the A1065, archaeologists have reconstructed a village of Boudica's time, complete with wooden huts, moat, drawbridge and palisades. Reconstruction though it is, the village is remarkably effective in evoking a sense of what daily life entailed more than 1,900 years ago. The exhibits cover many centuries, up to the Second World War.

popular and colourful array of stalls which attracts people from the surrounding areas here every week to pick up some "knick-knacks" or delicious local produce.

From the market place an avenue of limes leads to the quite outstanding **Church of St Peter & St Paul**, a 15th century masterpiece with one of the very best double hammerbeam roofs in the county, strikingly embellished with a host of angels, their wings widespread. The unknown mason who devised the church's harmonious proportions made it 51 feet wide, 51 feet high and 102 feet long. Carved on a bench-end here is a man in medieval dress accompanied by a dog on a chain. The same two figures are incorporated in the town's coat of arms, and also appear in the elegantly designed town sign just beyond the market place.

Swaffham Museum in the Town Hall, recently fully refurbished, is the setting for the story of the town's past. Visitors can follow Howard Carter's road to the Valley of the Kings including an interactive Egyptian gallery with tomb reconstruction, see the Symonds Collection of handmade figurines, and admire the Sporle collection of locally-found artefacts. Presently the museum is closed Sunday and Mondays, though you can phone or fax (01760) 721 230 Mon – Thurs 9am to 4pm to make opening time enquiries or book group visits.

Move on some 1,400 years

from the death of Tutankhamen to Norfolk in the 1st century AD. Before a battle, members of the Iceni tribe, led by Boudica, would squeeze the blue sap of the woad plant onto their faces in the hope of frightening the Roman invaders (or any other of their many enemies).

Another Swaffham attraction is the **EcoTech Discovery Centre**, opened in 1998. Through intriguing interactive displays and hands-on demonstrations, visitors can discover what startling innovations, current and possible, technology may have in store for us during the next millennium.

AROUND SWAFFHAM

CASTLE ACRE

4 miles N of Swaffham off the A1065

Set on a hill surrounded by water meadows, Castle Acre seems still to linger in the Middle Ages. William de Warenne, William the Conqueror's son-in-law, came here very soon after the Conquest and built a Castle that was one of the first, and largest, in the country to be built by the Normans. Of that vast fortress, little remains apart from the gargantuan earthworks and a squat 13th century gateway.

Much more has survived of **Castle Acre Priory**, founded in 1090 and set in fields beside the River Nar. Its glorious West Front gives a powerful indication of how majestic a triumph of late Norman architecture the complete Priory must have been. With five apses and twin towers, the ground plan was modelled on the Cluniac mother church in Burgundy, where William de Warenne had stayed while making a pilgrimage to Rome. Despite the Priory's great size, it appears that perhaps as few as 25 monks lived here during the Middle Ages - and in some comfort, judging by the well-preserved Prior's House, which has its own bath and built-in wash-basin.

Castle Acre Priory

Castle Acre Priory lay on the main route to the famous Shrine at Walsingham, with which it tried to compete by offering pilgrims a rival attraction in the form of an arm of St Philip.

Today the noble ruins of the Priory are powerfully atmospheric, a brooding scene skilfully exploited by Roger Corman when he filmed here for his screen version of Edgar Allan Poe's ghostly story, *The Tomb of Ligeia*. The walled herb garden is divided into four sections containing medicinal, decorative, culinary and strewing herbs.

Castle Acre village is extremely picturesque, the first place in Norfolk to be designated a Conservation Area, in 1971. Most of the village, including the 15th century parish church, is built in traditional flint, with a few later houses of brick blending in remarkably happily.

LITCHAM

11 miles NE of Swaffham on the B1145

Small though it is, this village strung alongside the infant River Nar can boast an intriguing **Village**

Museum, with displays of local artefacts from Roman times to the present, an extensive collection of photographs, some of which date back to 1865, and an underground lime kiln.

KING'S LYNN

John Betjeman famously stated "This town probably has what is the most beautiful walk in England – from St. Nicholas Chapel across the Tuesday Market Place, down King's Street and Queen's Street to St Margaret's Church." It seems, though, that word of this ancient sea-port's many treasures has not yet been widely broadcast, so most visitors to the area tend to stay on the King's Lynn bypass while making their way to the better-known attractions of the north Norfolk coast. They are missing a lot.

Following Betjeman's beautiful walk, we can start at the light and vast **St Nicholas Chapel** – the largest parochial chapel in England – with a two storey porch and a

27 LODGE FARM

Castle Acre

A charming farmhouse providing B & B or camping sites in the heart of beautiful Norfolk countryside.

see page 240

28 THE BULL INN

Litcham

This great Inn dates in part back to the 14th century and has lost none of its charm and hospitality.

see page 241

45

beautiful angel roof. Through the **Tuesday Market Place** (markets are held here, believe it or not, on Tuesdays) and down King's Street will bring you to the Purfleet Quay and dramatic views over the River Great Ouse.

Standing proudly by itself at the Quay overlooking the River, is the handsome **Custom House** of 1685, designed by the celebrated local architect Henry Bell with very fine carving of garlands and grotesques, and a statue of Charles II over the entrance.

Queen's Street leads past **Clifton House** – an early 18th century merchant house with a five storey Elizabethan watchtower as well as an entrance flanked with barley-sugar columns and a magnificent Queen Anne staircase rising up to elegant rooms. It is open from 11am and numbers into the house and tower are restricted. The **Town House Museum** is also on Queen's Street and has a delightful garden in addition to the interesting displays which explores

King Lynn's social history through period rooms from Medieval to the 1950's.

At the end of the road, beside the also aptly-named Saturday Market Place, is the **Town Hall** and **Guildhall** – a striking group of buildings. The Guildhall of the Holy Trinity has a distinctive chequerboard design of black flint and white stone. The Guildhall was built in 1423, extended in Elizabethan times, and its Great Hall is still used today for wedding ceremonies and various civic events. Behind it is a fine **Assembly Room** of 1767 with distinguished portraits, fine mirrors and the original chandeliers.

At the aforementioned Saturday Market Place is the **Old Gaol House**, an experience complete with the sights and sounds of the ancient cells. You can also admire the municipal regalia. The greatest treasure in this collection is King John's Cup, a dazzling piece of medieval workmanship with coloured enamel scenes set in gold. The Cup was supposed to be part of King John's treasure which had been lost in 1215 when his overburdened baggage train was crossing the Nene Estuary and sank into the treacherous quicksands. This venerable legend is sadly undermined by the fact that the Cup was not made until 1340, more than a century after John's death.

King's Lynn Arts Centre, housed in St George's Guildhall is active all year round with events and exhibitions. Since 1951 it has been the force behind an annual Arts

Kings' Lynn Tudor Guildhall

46

Festival in July with concerts, theatre and a composer in residence (some of the concerts are held in St Nicholas' Chapel, whose acoustics outmatch those of many a modern concert hall). **St George's Guildhall** was built around 1406 and is reputedly the largest civic hall in England. The Hall was from time to time also used as a theatre; it's known that Shakespeare's travelling company played here, and it is considered highly likely that the Bard himself trod the boards.

Also well worth mentioning is the curious octagonal red-brick **Red Mount Chapel** in the middle of the park in Kings Lynn. This building dates back to the late 15th Century and served as a shelter to pilgrims heading to the shrine of Our Lady of Walsingham. Inside it has a glorious fan vaulted roof at the top of its three floors, and visitors now have a chance to see inside this most unusual of structures, which previously had remained locked to prevent damage, in limited openings on Saturday and Wednesdays from May until Sept 11am – 3pm. On St James Street you will find **Greyfriars Tower** – part of a Franciscan friary founded in the 1230's, the bell tower of which (dating a later 15th century) features many fine carved bosses and corbels.

This, however, just scratches the surface of all there is to see in King's Lynn; among other important buildings are the Hanseatic Warehouse (1475), the South Gate (1440), and the Greenland Fishery Building (1605).

At **Caithness Crystal Visitor Centre**, you can watch craftsmen at close quarters as they shape and manipulate glass into beautiful objets d'art.

AROUND KING'S LYNN

TERRINGTON ST CLEMENT

5 miles W of King's Lynn off the A17

Terrington St Clement is a sizable village notable for its superb church, a 14th century Gothic masterwork more properly known as **St Clement's Church**, and for the **African Violet and Garden Centre**, where some quarter of a million violets are grown each year, in a wide range of colour and species. This unique working nursery, an all-seasons attraction, has earned many awards since opening in 1987, including Gold Medals at the Chelsea Flower Show. The centre contains a café, shop and children's play area and is open all year round.

STOW BARDOLPH

8 miles S of King's Lynn off the A10

Holy Trinity Church at Stow Bardolph houses one of the oddest memorials in the country. Before her death in 1744, Sarah Hare, youngest daughter of the Lord of the Manor, Sir Thomas Hare, arranged for a life-sized effigy of herself to be made in wax. It was said to be an exceptionally good likeness: if so, Sarah appears to have been a rather uncomely

The beautiful Church of St Margaret in King's Lynn, was founded in 1101 and has a remarkable leaning arch of that original building still intact. The architecture is impressive, but the church is especially famous for its two outstanding 14th century brasses, generally reckoned to be the two largest and most monumental in the kingdom. Richly engraved, one shows workers in a vineyard, the other, commemorating Robert Braunche, represents the great feast which Robert hosted at King's Lynn for Edward III in 1364. Marks on the tower doorway indicate the church's, and the town's, vulnerability to the waters of the Wash and the River Great Ouse. They show the high-water levels reached during the great floods of 11 March 1883 (the lowest), 31 January 1953 and 11 January, 1978.

47

29 DENVER WINDMILL

Denver

Built in 1835, Denver Windmill produced flour for over a hundred years until it was struck by lightening in 1941. It has now been restored and is open to the public.

 see page 240

maiden, and afflicted with boils to boot. Her death was attributed to blood poisoning after she had pricked her finger with a needle, an act of Divine retribution, apparently, for her sin of sewing on a Sunday. Sarah was then attired in a dress she had chosen herself, placed in a windowed mahogany cabinet, and the monument set up in the Hare family's chapel, a grandiose structure which is larger than the chancel of the church itself.

Just off the A10 from Stow Bardolph is the **Church Farm Rare Breeds Centre** – the perfect place to spend a day if you have young ones. They will be thrilled by the indoor and outdoor playgrounds, tractor rides, and not to mention an opportunity to have close-up encounters with numerous tame farmyard animals including goats, pigs and sheep. The range of breeds they have here is quite impressive, and definitely worth a visit even if you don't have children, you can enjoy the nature walks, tea room and a piece of tranquility in the gorgeous mature garden at Stow Hall. Dogs are not allowed in the centre, but can be walked on a lead around the tractor area. The rare breeds centre is open in the summer March until the start of November daily 10am-5pm; winter Thursday to Sunday 10am-5pm (is only closed Christmas day and New Year's Day. Father Christmas is at the farm all through December). The gardens at Stow Hall are open every Wednesday until 28th October 10.00am – 4.00pm.

DOWNHAM MARKET

10 miles S of King's Lynn off the A10/A1122

Once the site for a major horse fair, this compact little market town stands at the very edge of the Fens, with the River Great Ouse and the New Bedford Drain running side by side at its western edge. Many of its houses are built in the distinctive brick and carrstone style of the area. One of the finest examples of this traditional use of local materials can be seen at Dial House in Railway Road, built in the late 1600s.

The parish church has managed to find a small hill on which to perch. It's an unassuming building with a rather incongruously splendid glass chandelier from the 1730s. The town square has recently been regenerated and in it stands the elegant, riotously decorated cast-iron Clock. This was erected in 1878 at a cost of £450 and now chimes on the hour. The clock tower's backdrop of attractive cottages provides a charming setting for a holiday snap.

DENVER

2 miles S of Downham Market off the A10/A1122

Denver Sluice was originally built in 1651 by the Dutch engineer, Cornelius Vermuyden, as part of a scheme to drain 20,000 acres of land owned by the Duke of Bedford. Various modifications were made to the system over the years, but the principle remains the same, and the oldest surviving sluice, built in 1834, is still in use today. Running parallel with it is the modern Great Denver Sluice, opened in 1964; together these two sluices control the flow of a large complex of rivers and drainage channels, and are able to divert floodwaters into the Flood Relief Channel that runs alongside the Great Ouse.

The two great drainage cuts constructed by Vermuyden are known as the Old and New Bedford rivers, and the strip of land between them, never more than 1,000 yards wide, is called the Ouse Washes. This is deliberately allowed to flood during the winter months so that the fields on either

side remain dry. The drains run side by side for more than 13 miles, to Earith in Cambridgeshire, and this has become a favourite route for walkers, with a rich variety of bird, animal and insect life to be seen along the way.

Denver Windmill, built in 1835 but put out of commission in 1941 when the sails were struck by lightning, re-opened in 2000. This wonderful working mill set on the edge of the Fens has been carefully restored. On-site attractions include a visitor centre, craft workshops, bakery and tea shop. Holiday accommodation is also available. Open 7 days a week (excluding Christmas Day) 10am-5pm.

HILGAY

3 miles S of Downham Market off the A10

When the *Domesday Book* was written, Hilgay was recorded as one of only two settlements in the Norfolk fens. It was then an island, its few houses planted on a low hill rising from the surrounding marshland. The village is scarcely any larger today, and collectors of unusual gravestones make their way to **All Saints** churchyard seeking the last resting place of George William Manby. During the Napoleonic wars, Manby invented a rocket-powered life-line that could be fired to ships in distress. His gravestone is carved with a ship, an anchor and a depiction of his rocket device, and the inscription that ends with the reproachful words, 'The public should have paid this tribute.'

Denver Windmill

49

30 CASTLE RISING CASTLE

Castle Rising

Explore the imposing keep and vast earthworks of this Norman castle.

 see page 240

OXBOROUGH

10 miles SE of Downham Market off the A134

How many hamlets in the country, one wonders, can boast two such different buildings of note as those to be seen at Oxborough? First there's the **Church of St John the Evangelist**, remarkable for its rare brass eagle lectern of 1498 and its glorious Bedingfeld Chapel of 1525, sheltering twin monuments to Sir Edmund Bedingfeld and his wife fashioned in the then newly popular material of terracotta.

It was Sir Edmund who built **Oxburgh Hall** (National Trust), a stunning moated house built of pale-rose brick and white stone. Sir Edmund's descendants still live in what a later architect, Pugin, described as 'one of the noblest specimens of domestic architecture of the 15th century.' Henry VII and his Queen, Elizabeth of York, visited in 1497 and lodged in the splendid State Apartments which form a bridge between the glorious gatehouse towers, and which ever since have been known as the King's Room and the Queen's Room. These rooms also house some magnificent period furniture, a collection of royal letters to the Bedingfelds, and the huge Sheldon Tapestry Map of 1647 showing Oxfordshire and Berkshire. Another more poignant tapestry, known as the Marian Needlework, was the joint handiwork of Bess of Hardwick and Mary, Queen of Scots, during the latter's captivity here in 1570. Though National Trust owned, the Bedingfeld family still reside here as they have done for 500 years. The hall is open on weekends year round 11am-4pm, and weekdays at certain times in the year, the phone number is (01366) 328258.

CASTLE RISING

5 miles NE of King's Lynn off the A148/A149

As the bells ring for Sunday morning service at Castle Rising, a group of elderly ladies leave the mellow redbrick Bede House and walk in procession to the church. They are all dressed in long scarlet cloaks, emblazoned on the left breast with a badge of the Howard family arms. Once a year, on Founder's Day, they add to their regular Sunday costume a tall-crowned hat typical of the Jacobean period, just like those worn in stereotypical pictures of broomstick-flying witches.

These ladies are the residents of the almshouses founded by Henry Howard, Earl of Northampton in 1614, and their regular Sunday attendance at church was one of the conditions he imposed on the original 11 needy spinsters who were to enjoy his beneficence. Howard also required that each inmate of his 'Hospital of the Holy and Undivided Trinity' must also 'be able to read, if such a one may be had, single, 56 at least, no common beggar, harlot, scold, drunkard, haunter of taverns, inns or alehouses'.

The weekly *tableau vivant* of this

procession to the church seems completely in keeping with this picturesque village, which rates high on any 'not to be missed' list of places to visit in Norfolk. The church to which the women make their way, St Lawrence's, is an outstanding example of Norman and Early English work, even though much of it has been reconstructed. But overshadowing everything else in this pretty village is the massive **Castle Keep**, its well-preserved walls rising 50 feet high, and pierced by a single entrance. The Keep's towering presence is made even more formidable by the huge earthworks on which it stands. The Castle was built in 1150, guarding what was then the sea approach to the River Ouse. (The marshy shore is now some three miles distant and still retreating.)

Despite its fortress-like appearance, Castle Rising Castle was much more of a residential building than a defensive one. In 1331, when Edward III found it necessary to banish his ferocious French-born mother, Isabella, to some reasonably comfortable place of safety, he chose this far-from-London castle. She was to spend some 27 years here before her death in 1358. How could Edward treat his own mother in such a way? Her crime, in his view, was that the 'She-Wolf of France', as all her enemies and many of her friends called Isabella, had joined forces with her lover Mortimer against her homosexual husband Edward II (young Edward's father)

and later colluded in the king's grisly murder at Berkeley Castle. For three years after that loathsome assassination, Isabella and Mortimer ruled England as Regents. The moment Edward III achieved his majority, he had Mortimer hung, drawn and quartered. His mother he despatched to a lonely retirement at Castle Rising.

The spacious grounds around the castle provide an appropriate backdrop for an annual display by members of the White Society. Caparisoned in colourful medieval garments and armed with more-or-less authentic replicas of swords and halberds, these modern White Knights stage a battle for control of the castle. The castle is open to the public 1st April to 1st November: 10:00am to 6:00pm daily (or dusk if earlier in October), 2nd November to 31st March: Wed to Sun 10:00am to 4:00pm daily, and it is closed 24th to 26th Dec.

SANDRINGHAM

8 miles NE of King's Lynn off the A149/B1140

A couple of miles north of Castle Rising is the entrance to **Sandringham**, the Royal Family's charming country retreat. Unlike the State Rooms at Windsor Castle and Buckingham Palace, where visitors marvel at the awesome trappings of majesty, at Sandringham they can savour the atmosphere of a family home. The rooms the visitor sees at Sandringham are those used by the royal family when in residence,

31 SANDRINGHAM HOUSE

Sandringham

Sandringham House is the charming country retreat of Her Majesty The Queen hidden in the heart of sixty acres of beautiful wooded gardens.

 see page 242

complete with family portraits and photographs, and comfy armchairs. Successive royal owners have furnished the house with an intriguing medley of the grand, the domestic and the unusual. Entering the principal reception room, The Saloon, for example, you pass a weighing-machine with a leather-covered seat, apparently a common amenity in great houses of the 19th century. In the same room, with its attractively carved Minstrels' Gallery, hangs a fine family portrait by one of Queen Victoria's favourite artists, Heinrich von Angeli. It shows the Prince of Wales (later Edward VII), his wife Alexandra and two of their children, with Sandringham in the background. The Prince first saw Sandringham on 4th February 1862. At Victoria's instigation, the 20-year-old heir to the throne had

been searching for some time for a country property, a refuge of the kind his parents already enjoyed at Balmoral and Osborne. A courtier accompanying the Prince reported back that although the outside of house was ugly, it was pleasant and convenient within, and set in pretty grounds. The surrounding countryside was plain, he went on, but the property was in excellent order and the opportunity of securing it should not be missed. Within days, the purchase was completed.

Most of the 'ugly' house disappeared a few years later when the Prince rebuilt the main residence; the 'pretty grounds' have matured into one of the most beautiful landscaped areas in the country. And the 'plain' countryside around - open heath and grassland overrun by rabbits - has been transformed into a wooded country park, part of the coastal Area of Outstanding Natural Beauty.

One of the additions the Prince made to the house in 1883 was a Ballroom, much to the relief of Princess Alexandra. 'It is beautiful I think & a great success.' she wrote, '& avoids pulling the hall to pieces each time there is a ball or anything'. This attractive room is now used for cinema shows and the estate workers' Christmas party. Displayed on the walls is a remarkable collection of Indian weapons, presented to the Prince during his state visit in 1875-6; hidden away in a recess are the two flags planted at the South Pole by the Shackleton expedition.

Sandringham House

The grounds of Sandringham House are host to the Sandringham Flower Show in July each year; one of the most prestigious horticultural events in the East of England which has been running now for 128 years. With some amazing horticultural displays, some 200 trade stands, craft marquee and competitions in fruit and veg, flowers, and floral art. The royal patrons of the show often make an appearance.

DERSINGHAM
9 miles NE of King's Lynn off the A149

This large village just north of Sandringham was actually the source of the latter's name: in the *Domesday Book*, the manor was inscribed as 'Sant-Dersingham'. Norfolk tongues found 'Sandringham' much easier to get around. Dersingham village has expanded greatly in recent years and modern housing has claimed much of Dersingham Common, although there are still many pleasant walks here through Dersingham Wood and the adjoining Sandringham Country Park.

SNETTISHAM
11 miles N of King's Lynn off the A149

Snettisham is best known nowadays for its spacious, sandy beaches and the **RSPB Bird Sanctuary**, both about two miles west of the village itself. But for centuries Snettisham was much more famous as a prime quarry for carrstone, an attractive soft-red building-block that provided the 'light relief' for the

walls of thousands of Georgian houses around the country, and for nearby Sandringham House. The carrstone quarry is still working, its product now destined mainly for 'goldfish ponds and the entrance-banks of the more pretentious types of bungalow'. Unfortunately, one has to go to the British Museum in London to see Snettisham's greatest gift to the national heritage: an opulent collection of gold and silver ornaments from the 1st century AD, the largest hoard of treasure trove ever found in Britain, discovered here in 1991.

HEACHAM
13 miles N of King's Lynn off the A149

Heacham Park Fishery on Pocahontas Lake is set within the original boundary of Heacham Hall. This three-and-a-half acre freshwater lake was re-established in 1996. Spring 1997 saw the introduction to the lake of specimen carp, to be followed in 1998 by rudd, bream, perch and roach. The lake takes its name from the renowned Native American princess, who married into the Rolfe family, owners of Heacham Hall, and lived here in the 1600s.

FAKENHAM

Fakenham is a busy and prosperous-looking market town, famous for its National Hunt Racecourse, antique & bric-a-brac markets and auctions, and as a major agricultural centre for the region. Straddling the River

Just outside the charming village of Heacham is the famous Norfolk Lavender, the largest lavender-growing and distilling operation in the country. Established in 1932, it is also the oldest. The information point at the western entrance is sited in an attractive listed building, a Victorian watermill that has become something of a Norfolk landmark. On entering the site, visitors instinctively breathe in, savouring the unmistakable aroma that fills the air. The centre is open all year round, and guided tours of the grounds run throughout the day in the summer; and during the lavender harvest, visitors can tour the distillery and see how the wonderful fragrance is made. Among other attractions at Norfolk Lavender are a Fragrant Meadow Garden, Fragrant Plant Centre, Herb Garden, a gift shop selling a wide variety of products, and a tearoom serving cream teas and even lavender-and-lemon scones! Norfolk Lavender is open April-October: 9:00am - 5:00pm and November-March: 9:00am - 4:00pm, admission is free all year.

32 FRANS PANTRY FAYRE

Heacham

Quaint tearoom style restaurant offering bags of character to go with the delicious home made food.

see page 242

33 THE BULL

Fakenham

A light and modern pub with quality B&B attached, ideal for light lunches and quality steaks on Wednesdays.

see page 243

34 CAFÉ COFFEEHOLICS

Fakenham

The ideal spot to indulge in your coffee habit and relax over a light lunch in the ancient market town of Fakenham.

see page 243

Wensum, this attractive country town has a number of fine late-18th and early-19th century brick buildings in and around the Market Place. And it must surely be one of the few towns in England where the former gasworks (still intact) have been turned into the **Museum of Gas & Local History**, housing an impressive historical display of domestic gas appliances of every kind. **Fakenham Church** also has an unusual feature, a powder room - a room over the large porch, built in 1497, used for storing gunpowder. Even older than the church is the 700-year-old hunting lodge, built for the Duchy of Lancaster, which is now part of the Crown Hotel. As an antidote to the idea that Norfolk is unremittingly flat, reinforced by Noel Coward in his Private Lives, take the B1105 north out of Fakenham and after about half a mile take the first minor road to the left. This quiet road loops over and around the rolling hills, a 10-mile drive of wonderfully soothing countryside that ends at Wells-next-the-Sea.

AROUND FAKENHAM

A mile southeast of Fakenham, on the A1067, lies **Pensthorpe, the Natural Centre of Norfolk**. The aim of its owners is to combine world-class wildlife conservation, fabulous gardens, sustainable farming and fantastic food in a truly memorable visitor experience. The multi-award-winning attraction really does provide a wonderful day out at any time of the year. More than 70 species of birds breed here in the spring and summer, while autumn and winter see hundreds of migratory birds. The Conservation centre has the largest collection of cranes in the UK and works with other organisations on the 'Great Crane Project', which aims to accelerate the re-establishment of the European crane into the British countryide. The site includes wonderful gardens, beautiful lakes, tranquil woodland, nature trails, water meadows, wild flowers, birds, bees, butterflies and dragonflies, a café and a gift shop. The centre is open from 10 to 5 (till 4 between January and March).

One mile off the A148, halfway between Fakenham and Holt (or about two minutes' walk from Thursford Green), you will find an unusual and visceral treat at **Thursford Collection Sight and Sound Spectacular,** which holds the world's largest collection of steam engines and organs. The museum here is a world away from the pale and hush of other museums, with its beautiful displays of lights, colour and jaunty organ music emanating from the many magnificent machines on show. The show is really stolen by the two large rides, however, an ornate 1896 Carousel and beautiful Venetian Gondola Switchback ride, both the creations of Frederick Savage who settled with his wife in 1850's King's Lynn to become famous for his beautifully crafted roundabouts. George Cushing began this extraordinary collection of steam-powered traction engines, fairground organs and carousels back in 1946 when 'one ton of tractor cost £1'. Another astonishing exhibit is a 1931 Wurlitzer organ whose 1,339 pipes can produce an amazing repertoire of sounds - horses' hooves, fire engine sirens, claps of thunder, waves crashing on sand, and the toot-toot of an old railway engine are just some of the Wurlitzer's marvellous effects. There are regular live music shows when the Wurlitzer displays its virtuosity. This is a particular stunning sight through November and December, where the museum holds the largest and most spectacular Christmas show in England, as well as other festive treats for young and old. There are also shops selling a wide variety of goods, many of them locally made, and a tearoom. The Collection is open from 12 to 5 every day except Saturday.

EAST RAYNHAM

3 miles SW of Fakenham, on the A1065

Raynham Hall is another superb Palladian mansion, designed by Inigo Jones and with magnificent rooms created a century later by William Kent. The house is only open to the public by appointment since it is the private residence of the 7th Marquess of Townshend. It was his 18th century ancestor,

the 2nd Viscount (better known as 'Turnip' Townshend), who revolutionised English agriculture by promoting the humble turnip as an effective means of reclaiming untended land for feeding cattle in winter, and along with wheat, barley and clover, as part of the four-year rotation of crops that provided a cycle of essential nutrients for the soil. The Townshend family have owned extensive estates in this area for centuries, and in **St Mary's Church** there are some fine monuments to their ancestors, the oldest and most sumptuous of which commemorates Sir Roger, who died in 1493.

TATTERFORD

5 miles SW of Fakenham off the A148 or A1065

This tiny village is well known to botanists for **Tatterford Common**, an unspoilt tract of rough heathland with tiny ponds, some wild apple trees and the River Tat running through it to join the River Wensum about a mile away.

About four miles west of Tatterford stands **Houghton Hall**, home of the Marquess of Cholmondely and one of the country's most magnificent buildings. This glorious demi-palace was built in the Palladian style during the 1720s by Sir Robert Walpole, England's first Prime Minister. The Walpoles had been gentlemen of substance here since the 14th century. With his family revenues augmented by the

55

considerable profits Sir Robert extracted from his political office, he was in a position to spend lavishly and ostentatiously on his new house. The first step was to destroy completely the village of Houghton (it spoilt the view), and re-house the villagers a mile away at New Houghton.

Although Sir Robert deliberately cultivated the manner of a bluff, down-to-earth Norfolk squire, the personal decisions he made regarding the design and furnishings of the house reveal a man of deep culture and refined tastes. It was he who insisted that the Hall could not be built in homely Norfolk brick, and took the expensive decision to use the exceptionally durable stone quarried at Aislaby in North Yorkshire and transport it by sea from Whitby to King's Lynn. More than two and a half centuries later, the Aislaby stone is still flawless, the only sign of its age a slight weathering that has softened its colour to a creamy gold.

Visitors to this beautiful and extravagant (the interior is just as lavish) building can explore its many aspects, including the extensive gardens, 5-acre walled garden (which won "Garden of the Year" from Christies and the Historic Houses Association), catch sight of the splendid white deer which roam the park, and even stay in accommodation on and near the estate. The hall is open for public visits April – September Wed, Thur, Sun and Bank Holiday Mondays 11.30am – 5.30pm (the house is only open between 1.30pm and 5pm on these days, with last admission at 4.30).

LITTLE WALSINGHAM

5 miles N of Fakenham on the B1105

Every year, some half a million pilgrims make their way to this little village of just over 500 souls, noted for its impressive timber-framed buildings and fine Georgian façades, to worship at the **Shrine of Our Lady of Walsingham**. In 1061 the Lady of the Manor of Walsingham, Lady Richeldis de Faverches, had a vision of the Holy Virgin in which she was instructed to build a replica of the Holy House in Nazareth, the house in which the Archangel Gabriel had told Mary that she would be the mother of Christ. Archaeologists have located the original house erected by Lady Richeldis. It was just 13 feet by 23 feet and made of wood, later to be enclosed in stone.

These were the years of the Crusades, and the **Holy House** at Walsingham soon became a major centre of pilgrimage, because it was regarded by the pious as an authentic piece of the Holy Land. Around 1153, an **Augustinian Priory** was established to protect the shrine, now encrusted with jewels, gold and silver, and to provide accommodation for the pilgrims. The Priory is in ruins now but the largest surviving part, a stately Gatehouse on the east side of the High Street, is very impressive.

For almost 500 years, Walsingham prospered. Erasmus of Rotterdam visited in 1511 and was critical of the rampant commercialisation of the Shrine with its plethora of bogus relics and religious souvenirs for sale. He was shown a gigantic bone, 'the finger-joint of St Peter' no less, and in return for a small piece of translation was presented with a highly aromatic fragment of wood - a sliver of a bench on which the Virgin had once seated herself.

Little Walsingham itself is an exceptionally attractive village, set in the midst of parks and woodlands, with the interesting 16th century octagonal **Clink in Common Place**, used in medieval times as a lock-up for petty offenders, and the scant ruins of Walsingham's **Franciscan Friary** of 1347. In the 1770s the friary was converted into the shire hall for the quarter sessions, a role it filled until 1861; the petty sessions continued until 1971. The early-16th century building that now houses the **Walsingham Shirehall Museum** was once used as a hostel for visitors to the Priory Church. In the 1770s it was converted in to the shirehall for the quarter and petty sessions; the courtroom has survived unaltered and is now part of the museum that includes a display of Walsingham as a place of pilgrimage since 1061. It is also the entrance to the Abbey grounds.

GREAT WALSINGHAM

5 miles N of Fakenham on the B1388

English place names observe a logic of their own, so Great Walsingham is of course smaller than Little Walsingham. The two villages are very different in atmosphere and appearance, Great Walsingham displaying the typical layout of a rural Norfolk settlement, with attractive cottages set around a green watered by the River Stiffkey, and dominated by the fine 14th century **Church of St Peter**, noted for its superb window tracery, wondrously carved Norman font, and perfectly preserved 15th century carved benches.

WIGHTON

7 miles N of Fakenham, on the B1105

Just outside the village, the **Wells to Walsingham Light Railway** trundles its way between Little Walsingham and Wells-next-the-Sea. The longest 10¼-inch narrow-gauge steam railway in the world, it runs throughout the summer along a 20-minute scenic journey through the North Norfolk countryside.

GREAT SNORING

5 miles NE of Fakenham off the A148

The names of the twin villages, Great and Little Snoring, are such a perennial source of amusement to visitors it seems almost churlish to explain that they are derived from a Saxon family called Snear. At Great Snoring the main street rises from a bridge over the River Stiffkey and climbs up to St Mary's Church.

35 HUNSTANTON SEALIFE SANCTUARY

Hunstanton

Every year, many sick and abandoned seals are rescued and brought to the Hunstanton Sea Life Sanctuary to be nursed back to health.

see page 244

36 FISHERS OF HUNSTANTON

Hunstanton

A traditional fish & chip shop and restaurant with licensed bar, equally popular with visitors and locals.

see page 245

•

Hunstanton town is a comparative newcomer, developed in the 1860s by Mr Hamon L'Estrange of nearby Hunstanton Hall to take advantage of the arrival of the railway here, and to exploit the natural appeal of its broad, sandy beaches. The centre is well-planned with mock-Tudor houses grouped around a green that falls away to the shore.

•

THE NORTHWEST COAST

Although the whole of Norfolk lies on a foundation of chalk, 1,000 feet deep in places, it is only in this northwest corner that it lies close enough to the surface to have been used as a building material. Once exposed to the air, the chalk, or 'clunch' as it's known, becomes a surprisingly durable material. It was widely used in medieval buildings and can still be found in many barns, farmhouses and cottages in the area. Chalk was also quarried and then burnt to produce lime, prodigious quantities of which were used in building the sublime churches of the Middle Ages.

HUNSTANTON

The busy seaside resort of Hunstanton can boast two unique features: one, it has the only cliffs in England made up of colourful levels of red, white and brown strata, and two, it is the only east coast resort that faces west, looking across The Wash to the Lincolnshire coast and the unmistakeable tower of the 272-feet high Boston Stump (more properly described as the Church of St Botolph).

Hunstanton's social standing was assured after the Prince of Wales, later Edward VII, came here to recover from typhoid fever. He stayed at the Sandringham Hotel which, sadly, has since been demolished, along with the grand

Victorian pier and the railway. But Hunston, as locals call the town, still has a distinct 19th century charm about it and plenty to entertain visitors.

The huge stretches of sandy beach, thought to be one of the best beaches in Norfolk, framed by those multi-coloured cliffs, are just heaven for children who will also be fascinated by the **Sea Life Sanctuary**, on Southern Promenade, where an underwater glass tunnel provides a fascinating opportunity to watch the varied and often weird forms of marine life that inhabit Britain's waters. There are also attractions along the seafront promenade, including a funfair, pitch'n'putt course and donkey rides – as well as lots of shops selling everything sweet and colourful. A popular excursion from Hunstanton is the boat trip to Seal Island, a sandbank in The Wash where seals can indeed often be seen sunbathing at low tide.

AROUND HUNSTANTON

HOLME NEXT THE SEA

3 miles NE of Hunstanton, off the A149

This village is at the northern end of the **Peddars Way**, the 50-mile pedestrian trail that starts at the Suffolk border near Thetford and, almost arrow-straight for much of its length, slices across northwest Norfolk to Holme, with only an occasional deviation to negotiate a necessary ford or bridge. This determinedly straight route was already long-trodden for centuries before the Romans arrived, but they incorporated long stretches of it into their own network of roads. It was from the Latin word pedester that the route takes its name. With few gradients of any consequence to negotiate, the Peddars Way is ideal for the casual walker.

RINGSTEAD

3 miles E of Hunstanton off the A149

Another appealing village, with pink and whitewashed cottages built in wonderfully decorative Norfolk carrstone. A rare Norman round tower, all that survives of St Peter's church, stands in the grounds of the former Rectory and adds to the visual charm. In a region well provided with excellent nature reserves, the one on Ringstead Downs is particularly attractive, and popular with picnickers. The chalky soil of the valley provides a perfect habitat for the plants that thrive here and for the exquisitely marked butterflies they attract.

DOCKING

9 miles SE of Hunstanton, on the B1454 & B1153

One of the larger inland villages, Docking was at one time called Dry Docking because, perched on a hilltop 300 feet above sea level, it had no water supply of its own. The nearest permanent stream was at Fring, almost three miles away, so in 1760 the villagers began boring for a well. They had to dig some 230 feet down before they finally struck water, which was then sold at a farthing (0.1p) per bucket. A pump was installed in 1928, but a mains supply didn't reach Docking until the 1930s.

GREAT BIRCHAM

7 miles SE of Hunstanton off the B1153

A couple of miles south of Docking stands the five-storey **Great Bircham Windmill**, one of the few in Norfolk to have found a hill to perch on, and it's still working. If you arrive on a day when there's a stiff breeze blowing, the windmill's great arms will be groaning around; on calm days, content yourself with tea and home-made cakes in the tearoom, and take home some bread baked at the Mill's own bakery, and a look at the unique gift shop. There is also opportunity to stay in this glorious location, in a self catering cottage actually attached to the windmill (Dogs are welcome to stay too by prior arrangement). The windmill, shop and bakery are open every day from April until Sept 10am-5pm, and 'Humphrey Cottage' can be hired from March until Oct.

TITCHWELL

7 miles E of Hunstanton, on the A149

Perhaps in keeping with the village's name, the church of **St Mary at Titchwell** is quite tiny - and very pretty indeed. Its circular, probably Norman tower is topped by a little 'whisker' of a spire, and inside is some fine late 19th century glass.

Just to the west of Titchwell is a path leading to **Titchwell Marsh**,

•

At Holme, the Peddars Way meets with the Norfolk Coastal Footpath, a much more recent creation. Starting at Hunstanton, it closely follows the coastline all the way to Cromer. Holme next the Sea is famous in part as the site of 'Sea Henge', a 4,500-year-old Bronze Age tree circle discovered on Holme Beach. This early religious monument was removed by English Heritage for study and preservation to Flag Fen, Peterborough, though after its restoration it is hoped that it will be returned to Holme.

•

a nationally important RSPB reserve comprising some 420 acres of shingle beach, reed beds, freshwater and salt-marsh. These different habitats encourage a wide variety of birds to visit the area throughout the year, and many of them breed on or around the reserve. Brent geese, ringed plovers, marsh harriers, terns, waders and shore larks may all be seen, and two of the three hides available are accessible to wheelchairs.

BRANCASTER STAITHE

9 miles NE of Hunstanton, on the A149

In Roman times a castle was built near Brancaster to try and control the Iceni, Boudica's turbulent tribe. Nothing of it remains, although a Romano-British cemetery was discovered nearby in 1960. In the 18th century, this delightful village was a port of some standing, hence the 'Staithe', or quay, in its name. The waterborne traffic in the harbour is now almost exclusively pleasure craft, although whelks are still dredged from the sea bed, 15 miles out, and mussels are farmed in the harbour itself.

From the harbour a short boat trip will take you to **Scolt Head Island** (National Trust), a three-and-a-half mile sand and shingle bar separated from the mainland by a narrow tidal creek. It was originally much smaller, but over the centuries deposits of silt and sand have steadily increased its size, and continue to do so. Scolt Head is home to England's largest colony of Sandwich terns, which flock here to breed during May, June and July.

BURNHAM MARKET

9 miles E of Hunstanton, on the B1155

There are seven Burnhams in all, strung along the valley of the little River Burn. Burnham Market is the largest of them, its past importance reflected in the wealth of Georgian buildings surrounding the green

Brancaster Straithe

and the two churches that lie at each end of its broad main street, just 600 yards apart. In the opinion of many, Burnham Market has the best collection of small Georgian houses in Norfolk, and it's a delight to wander through the yards and alleys that link the town's three east-west streets.

Burnham Market also boasts two excellent bookshops and probably the best hat shop in the county. Auctions are held on the village green every other Monday in summer.

BURNHAM THORPE
11 miles E of Hunstanton off the B1355

From the tower of All Saints' Church, the White Ensign flaps in the breeze, and the only pub in the village is the *Lord Nelson*, and the shop next door is called the Trafalgar Stores. No prizes for deducing that Burnham Thorpe was the birthplace of **Horatio Nelson**. His father the Revd Edmund Nelson was the rector here for 46 years; Horatio was the sixth of his eleven children.

Parsonage House, where Horatio was born seven weeks' premature in 1758, was demolished during his lifetime, but the pub (one of more than 200 hostelries across the country bearing the hero's name) has become a kind of shrine to Nelson's memory, its walls covered with portraits, battle scenes and other marine paintings.

There are more Nelson memorabilia in the church, among them a crucifix and lectern made with wood from HMS *Victory*, a

great chest from the pulpit used by the Revd Nelson, and two flags from HMS *Nelson*.

A little over a mile to the south of Burnham Thorpe stand the picturesque ruins of **Creake Abbey** (English Heritage), an Augustinian monastery founded in 1206. The Abbey's working life came to an abrupt end in 1504 when, within a single week, every one of the monks died of the plague. At Creake Abbey you will also find **Creake Abbey Studios** – recognized as the centre for artistic talent in north Norfolk, there is an amazing array of oil paintings and watercolours, jewellery made with semi precious stones, oriental rugs, fabulous home décor, painted furniture, antiques and objects d'art, as well as Provencal foods and home ware pieces. The café here specializes in locally sourced food – the cakes in particular are sublime. The first Saturday of every month (excluding January) you will find a delightful Farmers Market stocked with much quality local produce, which runs from 9.30am to 1pm. The studios have free admission and are open Tues - Sun 11am to 4.30pm (and Bank Holiday Mondays).

HOLKHAM
16 miles E of Hunstanton, on the A149

If the concept of the Grand Tour ever needed any justification, **Holkham Hall**, seat of eight generations of the Earls of Leicester, amply provides it. For six years, from 1712 to 1718, young Thomas Coke (pronounced Cook) travelled extensively in Italy, France and Germany, studying and absorbing at first hand the glories of European civilisation. And, wherever possible, buying them. When he returned to England, Coke realised that his family's modest Elizabethan manor could not possibly house the collection of treasures he had amassed. The manor would have to be demolished and a more worthy building erected in its place. Building began in 1734 but was not completed until 1762, three years after Coke's death.

The completed building, its classical balance and restraint emphasised by the pale honey local brick used throughout, has been described as 'the ultimate achievement of the English Palladian movement'. As you step into the stunning entrance hall, the tone is set for the rest of the

house. Modelled on a Roman Temple of Justice, the lofty coved ceiling is supported by 18 huge fluted columns of pink Derbyshire alabaster, transported to nearby Wells by river and sea.

Each room reveals new treasures: Rubens and Van Dyck in the Saloon (the principal reception room), the Landscape Room with its incomparable collection of paintings by Lorrain, Poussin and other masters, the Brussels tapestries in the State Sitting Room and, on a more domestic note, the vast, high-ceilinged kitchen that remained in use until 1939 and still displays the original pots and pans. Historically the most important room at Holkham is the Statue Gallery, which contains one of the finest collections of classical sculpture still in private ownership. In this sparsely furnished room there is nothing to distract one's attention from the sublime statuary that has survived for millennia, among it a bust of Thucydides (one of the earliest portrayals of man) and a statue of Diana, both of which have been dated to the 4th Century BC.

Astonishingly, the interior of the house remains almost exactly as Thomas Coke planned it, his descendants having respected the integrity of his vision. They concentrated their reforming zeal on improving the enormous estate. It was Coke's great-nephew, Thomas William Coke (1754-1842), in particular who was responsible for the elegant layout of the 3,000-acre park visitors see today.

Holkham Hall

Universally known as 'Coke of Norfolk', Thomas was a pioneer of the Agricultural Revolution, best known for introducing the idea of a four-crop rotation. William Coke, son of Thomas William, was the first man in England to wear a bowler hat, made specially for him by the Bowler firm of London hatters. Among some more traditionalist hat-makers a bowler hat is still apparently known as a Coke. As well as the Pottery in the former brickworks and its associated shop, Holkham's other attractions include an 18th century walled garden, a fascinating Bygones Museum and a History of farming Exhibition with thousands of domestic and agricultural artefacts. Gwyneth Paltrow walked on the lovely sands of Holkham Beach in the closing scenes of the film *Shakespeare in Love*.

WELLS-NEXT-THE-SEA
17 miles E of Hunstanton, on the A149

There's no doubt about the appeal of the picturesque quayside, narrow streets and ancient houses of Wells. It has been a working port since at least the 13th century, but over the years the town's full name of Wells-next-the-Sea has become increasingly inapt – its harbour now stands more than a mile from the sea. In 1859, to prevent the harbour silting up altogether, Lord Leicester

of Holkham Hall built an Embankment cutting off some 600 acres of marshland. This now provides a pleasant walk down to the sea.

The Embankment gave no protection, however, against the great floods of 1953 and 1978. On the 11th January 1978 the sea rose 16 feet 1 inch above high tide, a few inches less than the 16 feet 10 inches recorded on the 31st January 1953, when the floodwaters lifted a ship on to the quay. A silo on the harbour is marked with these abnormal levels.

Running alongside the Embankment in Wells-next-the-Sea is the **Harbour Railway**, which trundles from the quay to the lifeboat station by the beach. The nearby narrow-gauge Wells to Walsingham Light Railway carries passengers on a particularly lovely ride along the route of the former Great Eastern Railway to Little Walsingham. The four-mile journey takes about 30 minutes with stops at Warham St Mary and Wighton. Both the WWR and the Harbour Railway services are seasonal.

In a curious change of function, the former GER station at Wells is now home to the Old Station Pottery & Bookshop, the former signal box is now the station, while the old station at Walsingham is now a church!

63

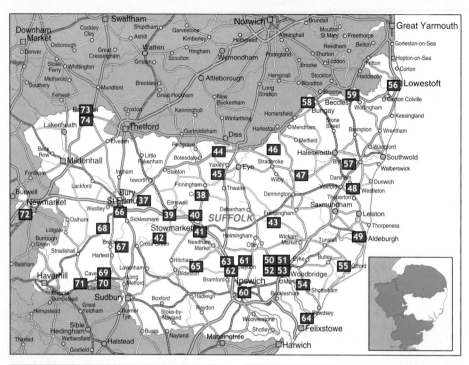

Suffolk

Suffolk is known for its lovely countryside but is also very every much a maritime county, with over 50 miles of coastline. The whole coast is a conservation area, which the 50-mile Suffolk Coastal Path makes walkable throughout. Watery pursuits are naturally a popular pastime, and everything from sailing to scuba diving, angling to powerboat racing is available. Many of the museums also have a nautical theme, and the coast has long been a source of inspiration for artists, writers and composers. The sea brings its own dangers, even in human form, and it was against the threat of a Napoleonic invasion that Martello Towers were built in southeastern Suffolk, in the tradition of Saxon and Tudor forts and the precursors of concrete pillboxes. Starting just before the end of the 18th century, over 100 of these sturdy circular fortified towers were built along the coast from Suffolk to Sussex. Aldeburgh's at Slaughden is the most northerly (and the largest), while the tower at Shoreham in Sussex the southernmost. The whole of this coastal stretch is known as the "Sunrise Coast", due to its easterly facing direction (those eager enough can rise early to witness some of the most beautiful sunrises to be seen in England).

Inland Suffolk has few peers in terms of picturesque countryside and villages, and the area of central Suffolk between the heathland and the coast is a delightful place to get away from it all to the real countryside, with unspoilt ancient villages, gently flowing rivers and rich farmland. The Rivers Deben and Gipping run through much of the region, which also boasts a generous share of churches, museums, markets, fairs and festivals. The little market towns of Stowmarket and Needham Market are full of interest, and in this part of the county some of the best-preserved windmills and watermills are to be found. Southeast of Ipswich, the peninsula created by the Deben and the Orwell is one of the prettiest areas in Suffolk, its winding lanes leading through quiet rural villages and colourful riverside communities. John Constable, England's greatest landscape painter, was born at East Bergholt in 1776 and remained at heart a Suffolk man throughout his life. The Suffolk tradition of painting continues to this day, with many artists drawn particularly to Walberswick as well as what is known as Constable Country. Cambridgeshire, Norfolk, the A134 and the A14 frame the northern part of West Suffolk, which includes Bury St Edmunds, a pivotal player in the country's religious history, and Newmarket, one of the major centres of the horseracing world. Between and above them are picturesque villages, bustling market towns, rich farming country, the fens and the expanse of sandy heath and pine forest that is Breckland. The area south and west of Bury towards the Essex border contains some of Suffolk's most attractive and peaceful countryside. The visitor will come upon a succession of picturesque villages, historic churches, remarkable stately homes, heritage centres and nature reserves. In the south, along the River Stour, stand the historic wool towns of Long Melford, Cavendish and Clare.

37 THE GRANGE COUNTRY HOUSE HOTEL

Thurston

A magnificent Tudor style country house providing three star accommodation and superb food, perfect for those special occasions.

 see page 246

CENTRAL AND EASTERN SUFFOLK

NORTH AND EAST OF BURY ST EDMUNDS

PAKENHAM

4 miles NE of Bury St Edmunds off the A143

On a side road just off the A143 (turn right just north of Great Barton) lies the village of Pakenham; known as the "Village of Two Mills" because it, uniquely, has both a working windmill and watermill. **Pakenham Watermill** is still a working mill, kept that way by a group of dedicated volunteers who work on Thursday mornings to stone grind the wheat into wholemeal flour – visitors always receive a warm welcome and are able to purchase the flour. The mill is open from April until the start of November on Sat, Sun and Bank Holidays 1.30pm – 5pm and on Thurs from 10am to 4pm. (There are milling demonstrations until 11am on the first Thursday of the month). The quaint café is open during these times, and on Thursdays they serve light lunches.

Elsewhere in Pakenham is the 17th century **Nether Hall**, from whose lake in the park the village stream flows through the fen into the millpond. From the same period dates **Newe House**, a handsome Jacobean building with Dutch gables and a two-storey

porch. Pakenham's **Church of St Mary** has an impressive carved Perpendicular font, and in its adjacent vicarage is the famous Whistler Window - a painting by Rex Whistler of an 18th century parish priest. The fens were an important source of reeds, and many of Pakenham's buildings show off the thatcher's art.

IXWORTH

5 miles NE of Bury St Edmunds on the A143

Ixworth played its part as one of the Iceni tribe's major settlements, with important Roman connections and, in the 12th century, the site of an Augustinian priory. The remains of the priory were incorporated into a Georgian house known as **Ixworth Abbey**, which stands among trees by the River Blackbourne. Ixworth is home to the most glorious church – the much understated **All Saints Church**. Sitting on a rise on the busy Ixworth to Thetford road, it would be possible to dismiss this delightful thatched church as a barn or farmhouse, were it not for the little bellcote at its end. To gain entry you will need to get the key from the farm office opposite, which is only possible on weekdays, but it is well worth the visit. Inside is as beautifully simple and patchwork-like as the exterior; three-sided 17th century communion rails, an 18th century pulpit, a 15th century statue (described as both a "thatcher" and "harvester") which is an amazing example of East Anglian art of that period, and 19th century benches.

A variety of circular walks take in lovely parts of Ixworth, which is also the starting point of the Miller's Trail cycle route.

A little way north of the village, on the A1088, is a nature trail and bird reserve at **Ixworth Thorpe Farm**. At this point a brief diversion northwards up the A1088 is very worth while.

BARDWELL

7 miles NE of Bury St Edmunds just off the A1088

Bardwell offers another **Tower Windmill**. This one dates from the 1820s and was worked by wind for 100 years, then by an oil engine until 1941. It was restored in the 1980s, only to suffer severe damage in the great storm of October 1987, when its sails were torn off. Stoneground flour is still produced by an auxiliary engine. Also in this delightful village are a 16th century inn and the **Church of St Peter and St Paul**, known particularly for its medieval stained glass.

HONINGTON

7 miles NE of Bury St Edmunds on the A1088

Back on the A1088, the little village of Honington was the birthplace of the pastoral poet Robert Bloomfield (1766-1823), whose best known work is *The Farmer's Boy*. The house where he was born is now divided, one part called Bloomfield Cottage, the other Bloomfield Farmhouse. A brass plaque to his memory can be seen in **All Saints Church**, in the graveyard of which his parents are buried.

Ixworth Abbey, Ixworth

EUSTON

9 miles N of Bury St Edmunds on the A1088

Euston Hall, on the A1088, has been the seat of the Dukes of Grafton for 300 years. It's open to the public on Thursday afternoons and is well worth a visit, not least for its portraits of Charles II and its paintings by Van Dyck, Lely and Stubbs. In the colourful landscaped grounds is an ice-house disguised as an Italianate temple, the distinguished work of John Evelyn and William Kent. The beautiful garden and grounds for the hall, also open to the public, provide some lovely walks. It is worth visiting the recently restored watermill, which has been located here in the grounds since 1670 (and was rebuilt in 1730 in the style of a Gothic church).

Euston's church, also in the grounds of the Hall, is the only one in the county dedicated to **St Genevieve**. It's also one of only two Classical designs in the county, being rebuilt in 1676 on part of the

67

If visiting Walsham-le-Willows on the Sunday and Bank Holiday Monday of August, you will not want to miss the garden open day. About 30 village residence participate in opening their gardens up for your pleasure each year - a tradition which is now 30 years strong. This event has a wonderful atmosphere, with live music and tea, cakes and light lunches being served at the Priory Room and Memorial Hall – in addition to seeing all those lovingly tendered gardens!

original structure. The interior is richly decorated, with beautiful carving on the hexagonal pulpit, panelling around the walls and a carved panel of the Last Supper. Parts of this lovely wood carving are attributed by some to Grinling Gibbons. Behind the family pew is a marble memorial to Lord Arlington, who built the church.

STANTON

7 miles NE of Bury St Edmunds on the A143

Stanton is mentioned in the *Domesday Book*; before that, the Romans were here. A double ration of medieval churches - **All Saints** and **St John the Baptist** - will satisfy the ecclesiastical scholar, while for more worldly indulgences **Wyken Vineyards** will have a strong appeal, as well as a delightful weekly farmers market held on Saturday mornings. The four acres of grounds around the Elizabethan **Wyken Hall** include herb, knot, rose, kitchen, edible and woodland gardens, a water garden, a nuttery, a gazebo and a hornbeam maze planted in 1991. The gardens are open from April to September.

BARNINGHAM

8 miles NE of Bury St Edmunds on the B1111

Near the Norfolk border, Barningham was the first home of the firm of Fisons, which started in the late 18th century. Starting with a couple of windmills, they later installed one of the earliest steam mills in existence. The engine saw service for nearly 100 years and is now in an American museum; the

mill building exists to this day, supplying animal feed.

WALSHAM-LE-WILLOWS

9 miles NE of Bury St Edmunds off the A143

A pretty name for a pretty village, with weather-boarded and timber-framed cottages along the willow-banked river which flows throughout its length. **St Mary's Church** is no less pleasing to the eye, with its sturdy western tower and handsome windows in the Perpendicular style. Of particular interest inside is the superb tie and hammerbeam roof of the nave, and (unique in Suffolk, and very rare elsewhere) a tiny circular medallion which hangs suspended from the nave wall, known as a 'Maiden's Garland' or 'Virgin's Crant'. These marked the pew seats of unmarried girls who had passed away, and the old custom was for the young men of the village to hang garlands of flowers from them on the anniversary of a girl's death. This particular example celebrates the virginity of one Mary Boyce, who died (so the inscription says) of a broken heart in 1685, just 20 years old.

RICKINGHALL

12 miles NE of Bury St Edmunds on the A143

More timber-framed buildings, some thatched, are dotted along the streets of the two villages, Superior and Inferior, which follow an underground stream running right through them. Each has a church dedicated to St Mary and featuring fine flintwork and tracery. The upper church, now closed, was used as a school for London evacuees during the Second World War.

REDGRAVE

13 miles NE of Bury St Edmunds on the B1113

Arachnophobes beware! Redgrave and Lopham Fens form a 360-acre reserve of reed and sedge beds where one of the most interesting inhabitants is the Great Raft Spider. The village is the source of the Little Ouse and Waveney rivers, which rise on either side of the B1113 and set off on their seaward journeys in opposite directions.

THELNETHAM

12 miles NE of Bury St Edmunds off the B111

West of Redgrave between the B1113 and the B1111 lies Thelnetham – which boasts a windmill of its own. This one is a tower mill, built in 1819 to replace a post mill on the same site, and worked for 100 years. It has now been lovingly restored. Stoneground flour is produced and sold at the mill.

COTTON

16 miles E of Bury St Edmunds off the B1113

South of Finningham, where Yew Tree House displays some fine pargeting, and just by Bacton, a lovely village originally built round seven greens, lies the village of Cotton, which should be visited for several reasons, one of which is to see the splendid 14th century flint church of St Andrew, impressive in its dimensions and notable for its

double hammerbeam roof with carved angels.

Cotton's **Mechanical Music Museum & Bygones** has an extensive collection that includes gramophones, music boxes, street pianos, fairground organs and polyphons, as well as the marvellous Wurlitzer Theatre pipe organ. Tel: 01449 613876

HESSETT

4 miles E of Bury St Edmunds off the A14

Dedicated to St Ethelbert, King of East Anglia, **Hessett's Church** has many remarkable features, particularly some beautiful 16th century glass and wall paintings, both of which somehow escaped the Puritan wave of destruction. Ethelbert was unlucky enough to get on the wrong side of the mighty Offa, King of the Mercians, and was killed by him at Hereford in AD794.

WOOLPIT

6 miles E of Bury St Edmunds on the A14

The **Church of St Mary the Virgin** is Woolpit's crowning glory,

38 MECHANICAL MUSIC MUSEUM & BYGONES

Cotton

The place for music enthusiasts, with a unique collection of music boxes, polyphons, street pianos, pianolas and organs.

 see page 244

Mechanical Music Museum & Bygones, Cotton

Near Woolpit is a moated site known as Lady's Well, a place of pilgrimage in the Middle Ages. The water from the spring was reputed to have healing properties, most efficacious in curing eye troubles.

39 KILN FARM GUESTHOUSE

Elmswell

A quiet and comfortable guesthouse, ideally situated for touring many of Suffolk's main attractions.

see page 247

40 RED HOUSE FARM

Haughley

An extremely comfortable and welcoming old building featuring B & B, caravan pitches and self catering accommodation.

see page 247

with a marvellous porch and one of the most magnificent double hammerbeam roofs in the county. Voted winner of Suffolk Village of the Year in 2000, the village was long famous for its brick industry, and the majority of the old buildings are faced with 'Woolpit Whites'. This yellowish-white brick looked very much like more expensive stone, and for several centuries was widely exported. Some was used in the building of the Senate wing of the Capitol Building in Washington DC. Red bricks were also produced, and the village Museum, open in summer, has a brick-making display and also tells the story of the evolution of the village. Woolpit also hosts an annual music festival.

ELMSWELL

7 miles E of Bury St Edmunds off the A14

Clearly visible from the A14, the impressive church of St John the Baptist with its massive flint tower stands at the entrance to the village, facing Woolpit across the valley. A short drive north of Elmswell lies **Great Ashfield**, an unspoilt village whose now disused airfield played a key role in both World Wars. In the churchyard of the 13th century **All Saints** is a memorial to the Americans who died during the Second World War, as attested to by the commemorative altar. Some accounts say that Edmund was buried here in AD 903 after dying at the hands of the Danes; a cross was put up in his memory. The cross was replaced in the 19th

century and now stands in the garden of Ashfield House.

HAUGHLEY

12 miles E of Bury St Edmunds off the A14

On the run into Stowmarket, Haughley once had the largest motte-and-bailey castle in Suffolk. All that now remains is a mound behind the church. **Haughley Park** is a handsome Jacobean redbrick manor house set in gardens, parkland and surrounding woodland featuring ancient oaks and splendid magnolias. Woodland paths take the visitor past a half-mile stretch of rhododendrons, and in springtime the bluebells and lilies of the valley are a magical sight. The gardens are open on Tuesdays between May and September, the house by appointment only.

HARLESTON

9 miles E of Bury St Edmunds off the A14

The churches of Shelland and Harleston lie in close proximity on a minor road between Woolpit and Haughley picnic site. At Shelland, the tiny church of **King Charles the Martyr** is one of only four in England to be dedicated to King Charles I. The brick floor is laid in a herringbone pattern, there are high box pews and a triple-decker pulpit, but the most unusual feature is a working barrel organ dating from the early 19th century.

The church of **St Augustine** at Harleston stands all alone among pine trees and is reached by a track across a field. It has a thatched roof, Early English windows and a tower with a single bell.

STOWMARKET

The largest town in the heart of Suffolk, Stowmarket enjoyed a period of rapid growth when the River Gipping was still navigable to Ipswich and when the railway arrived.

Much of the town's history and legacy are brought vividly to life in the splendid **Museum of East Anglian Life**, situated in the centre of town to the west of the marketplace (where markets are held twice a week), in a 70-acre meadowland site on the old Abbot's Hall Estate (the aisled original barn dates from the 13th century). Part of the open-air section features several historic buildings that have been moved from elsewhere in the region and carefully re-erected on site. These include an engineering workshop from the 1870s, part of a 14th century farmhouse, a watermill from Alton and a wind pump which was rescued in a collapsed state at Minsmere in 1977. There's also a collection of working steam engines, farm animals and year-round demonstrations of all manner of local arts and crafts, from coopering to chandlery, from sheep shearing to saddlery.

Stowmarket's church of St Peter and St Mary acquired a new spire in 1994, replacing the 1715 version (itself a replacement) which was dismantled on safety grounds in 1975.

The town certainly merits a leisurely stroll, while for a peaceful picnic the riverbank beckons.

Serious scenic walkers should make for the **Gipping Valley River Park Walk**, which follows the former towpath all the way to Ipswich.

The **Mid-Suffolk Leisure Centre** in Stowmarket provides some great facilities; including pools, tennis and squash courts, fitness suite, climbing wall and 'PlayWorld' – a large indoor playground which will keep young ones entertained for hours.

AROUND STOWMARKET

BUXHALL

3 miles W of Stowmarket just off the B1115

The village church here is notable for its six heavy bells, but the best-known landmark in this quiet village is undoubtedly the majestic tower mill, without sails since a gale removed them in 1929 but still standing as a silent, sturdy reminder of its working days. This is good walking country, with an ancient wood and many signposted footpaths.

NEEDHAM MARKET

4 miles SE of Stowmarket off the A14

A thriving village whose greatest glory is the wonderful carvings on the ceiling of the **Church of St John the Baptist**. The church's ornate double hammerbeam roof is nothing short of remarkable, especially when bathed in light from the strategically placed skylight. The roof is massive, as high as the walls of the church itself; the renowned authority on

41   MUSEUM OF EAST ANGLIAN LIFE

Stowmarket

The Museum of East Anglian Life occupies a 75-acre site in the heart of Stowmarket.

 see page 248

42   THE SIX BELLS

Felsham

An excellent pub that caters for both locals and visitors to the area.

see page 248

71

The Stonham Barns leisure and rural pursuits complex in Stonham Aspal, has a golf course, fishing lake and local arts and crafts shops – as well as being the base for the Suffolk Owl Sanctuary. The Sanctuary, which is home to some 60 owls and birds of prey kept in spacious aviaries, is a completely volunteer-run establishment which relies on visitor donations. As well as the fascinating birds themselves here, you will find a sensory garden, an information centre about Owls, a woodland walk with bird hide, picnic areas and plenty of activities for children including a mini-maze & adventure frame. It is open in summer Easter – late Sept and in winter late Sept – early March, 10am until late afternoon everyday, and flying demonstrations and talks are held in the summer throughout the day.

Suffolk churches, H Munro Cautley, described the work at Needham as 'the culminating achievement of the English carpenter'. The village also boasts some excellent examples of Tudor architecture.

The River Gipping flows to the east of the High Street and its banks provide miles of walks: the towpath is a public right of way walkable all the way from Stowmarket to Ipswich. **Fen Alder** Local Nature Reserve consists of meadow, fen and alder carr – boggy areas, with a canopy of alder trees, a network of ditches and a pond. Together they support an abundance of wildlife.

Monthly farmers' markets are held at **Alder Carr Farm**, where there is also a pottery, crafts centre and farm shop.

Barking, on the B1018 south of Needham, was once more important than its neighbour, being described in 1874 as 'a pleasant village ... including the hamlet of Needham Market'. This explains the fact that Barking's church is exceptionally large for a village house of worship: it was the mother church to Needham Market and was used for Needham's burials when Needham had no burial ground of its own.

EARL STONHAM
6 miles E of Stowmarket on the A1120

A scattered village set around three greens in farming land, Earl Stonham's church of **St Mary the Virgin** boasts one of Suffolk's finest single hammerbeam roofs, and is also notable for its Bible scene

murals, the 'Doom' (Last Judgement scene) over the chancel arch and a triple hour-glass, presumably to record just how protracted were some of the sermons.

STONHAM ASPAL
7 miles E of Stowmarket on the A1120

On the other side of the A140 lies Stonham Aspal, where in 1962 the remains of a Roman bath-house were unearthed. The parish church has an unusual wooden top to its tower, a necessary addition to house the ten bells that a keen campanologist insisted on installing.

EARL SOHAM
12 miles E of Stowmarket on the A1120

Earl Soham comprises a long, winding street that was once part of a Roman road. It lies in a valley, and on the largest of its three greens the village sign is a carved wooden statue of a falconer given as a gift by the Women's Institute in 1953. The 13th century church of St Mary is well worth a visit.

SAXTEAD GREEN
14 miles E of Stowmarket off the A1120

One of the prettiest sights in Suffolk is the white 18th century **Mill** that stands on the marshy green in Saxtead. This is a wonderful example of a post mill, perhaps the best in the world, dating back to 1796 and first renovated in the 19th century. It worked until 1947 and has since been kept in working order, with the sails turning even though the mill no longer grinds. In summer, visitors can climb into the buck (body) of this elegant weather-boarded construction and explore its machinery.

FRAMLINGHAM

18 miles NE of Stowmarket on the B1119

The marvellous **Castle**, brooding on a hilltop, dominates this agreeable market town, as it has since Roger Bigod, 2nd Earl of Norfolk, built it in the 12th century (his grandfather built the first castle a century earlier, but this wooden construction was soon demolished). The Earls and Dukes of Norfolk, the Howards, were here for many generations before moving to Arundel in 1635. The castle is in remarkably good condition, partly because it was rarely attacked – though King John put it under siege in 1215. Its most famous occupant was Mary Tudor, who was in residence when proclaimed Queen in 1553. During the reign of Elizabeth I it was used as a prison for defiant priests and, in the 17th century after being bequeathed to Pembroke College, Cambridge, it saw service as a home and school for local paupers. Nine of the castle's 13 towers are accessible - the climb up the spiral staircase and walk round the battlements are well worth the effort. On one side the view is of the Mere, managed by the Suffolk Wildlife Trust and home to a diversity of wildlife, from marsh marigolds and ragged robin to water voles, kingfishers and barn owls. In the north wing is the **Lanman Museum**, devoted to agricultural, craftsman's tools and domestic memorabilia.

DENNINGTON

2 miles N of Framlingham on the B1116

The pretty little village of Dennington boasts one of the oldest post offices in the country,

•

The Castle brought considerable prestige and prosperity to Framlingham, evidence of which can be found in the splendid Church of St Michael, which has two wonderful works of art. One is the tomb of Henry Fitzroy, bastard son of Henry VIII and Elizabeth Blount, a lady-in-waiting to Catharine of Aragon, beautifully adorned with scenes from Genesis and Exodus and in a superb state of repair. The other is the tomb of the 3rd Duke, with carvings of the apostles in shell niches. Also of note is the Carolean organ of 1674, a gift of Sir Robert Hitcham, to whom the Howards sold the estate. Cromwell and the Puritans were not in favour of organs in churches, so this instrument was lucky to have escaped the mass destruction of organs at the time of the Commonwealth. Sir Robert is buried in the church.

•

Framlingham Castle

43 THE CRETINGHAM BELL

Cretingham

A family run inn just steeped in history offering accommodation and great food.

see page 249

this one having occupied the same site since 1830. The **Village Church** has a some very unusual features, none more so than the hanging 'pyx' canopy above the altar. A pyx served as a receptacle for the Reserved Sacrament, which would be kept under a canopy attached to weights and pulleys so that the whole thing could be lowered when the sacrament was required for the sick and the dying. In the chapel at the top of the south aisle stands the tomb of Lord Bardolph, who fought at Agincourt, and of his wife, their effigies carved in alabaster. The most remarkable carving is that of a skiapod, the only known representation in this county of a mythical creature of the African desert, humanoid but with a huge boat-shaped foot with which it could cover itself and its family against the sun. This curious beast was 'known' to Herodotus and to Pliny, who remarked that it had 'great pertinacity in leaping'.

CHARSFIELD

5 miles S of Framlington off the B1078

A minor road runs from Framlingham through picturesque Kettleburgh and Hoo to Charsfield, best known as the inspiration for Ronald Blyth's book Akenfield, later memorably filmed by Sir Peter Hall. A cottage garden in the village displays the Akenfield village sign and is open to visitors in the summer.

OTLEY

7 miles SW of Framlingham on the B1079

The sumptuously decorated 15th century **Moated Hall** in Otley is open to the public at certain times of the year. Standing in ten acres of gardens that include a canal, a nuttery and a knot garden, the hall was long associated with the Gosnold family, whose coat of arms is also that of the village. The best-known member of that family was Bartholomew Gosnold, who sailed to the New World, coined the named 'Martha's Vineyard' for the island off the coast of Massachusetts, discovered Cape Cod and founded the settlement of Jamestown, Virginia. The 13th century church of **St Mary** has a remarkable baptistry font measuring 6 feet in length and 2 feet 8 inches in depth. Though filled with water, the font is not used and was only discovered in 1950 when the vestry floor was raised. It may have been used for adult baptisms.

FRAMSDEN

7 miles SW of Framlingham on the B1077

The scenery in these parts is real picture-postcard stuff, and in the village of Framsden the picture is completed by a fine **Post Mill**, built high on a hill in 1760, refitted and raised in 1836 and in commercial use until 1934. The milling machinery is still in place and the mill is open for visits (at weekends, by appointment only).

CRETINGHAM

4 miles SW of Framlingham off the A1120

The village sign is the unusual item here, in that it has two different panels: one shows an everyday

Anglo-Saxon farming scene, the other a group (possible Danes) sailing up the River Deben, with the locals fleeing. The signs are made from mosaic tiles.

BRANDESTON

3 miles SW of Framlingham off the A1120

A further mile to the east, through some charming countryside, Brandeston is another delightful spot, with a row of beautiful thatched cottages and the parish **Church of All Saints** with its 13th century font.

DEBENHAM

10 miles E of Stowmarket on the B1077

Debenham is a sizable village of architectural distinction, with a profusion of attractive timber-framed buildings dating from the 14th to the 17th centuries. The River Deben flows beside and beneath the main street. There is also a pottery centre. **St Mary's Church** is unusual in having an original Saxon tower, and the roof alternates hammerbeams with crested tie beams.

MENDLESHAM

6 miles NE of Stowmarket off the A140

On the green in Old Market Street, Mendlesham, lies an enormous stone which is said to have been used as a preaching stone, mounted by itinerant Wesleyan preachers. In the **Church of St Mary** there is a collection of parish armour assembled some 400 years ago, and also some fine carvings. The least hidden local landmark is a 1,000-feet TV mast put up by the IBA in

1959. The 34th Bomb Group operated from Mendlesham airfield, and an impressive memorial to personnel lost over the airfield was built in 1949.

WETHERINGSETT

7 miles NE of Stowmarket off the A140

On the other side of the A140, Wetheringsett is where visitors will find the **Mid-Suffolk Light Railway Museum** (affectionately known by the nickname – 'The Middy'); the museum endeavors to preserve the hardware and documents of this beautiful railway with its history in the Edwardian era, as well as educating visitors. Open on Sundays and Bank Holidays from Easter to September. Tel: 01449 766899

THORNHAM MAGNA & PARVA

10 miles N of Stowmarket off the A140

The **Thornham Walks and Field Centre**, with 12 miles of walks and a herb garden and nursery, cater admirably for hikers, horticulturists and lovers of the countryside. The tiny thatched **Church of St Mary** at Thornham Parva houses a considerable treasure in the shape of an exquisite medieval altar painting, known as a retable, with a central panel depicting the Crucifixion and four saints on each side panel. Its origins are uncertain, but it was possibly the work of the Royal Workshops at Westminster Abbey and made for Thetford Priory, or for a nearby Dominican monastery. When conservation work was urgently needed, the

44 ROOKERY FARM

Wortham
Straddling the border between Norfolk and Suffolk, this Georgian farmhouse supplies excellent accommodation in beautiful surroundings.

◨ see page 250

45 THORNHAM HALL

Thornham Magna
A delightful country house offering comfortable accommodation in beautiful surroundings.

◨ see page 251

75

villagers of Thornham Parva managed to raise the money needed to save this national treasure; their successful efforts were rewarded when the work, carried out by the Hamilton Kerr Institute, part of the Fitzwilliam Museum in Cambridge, earned an allocation of funds from the Heritage Lottery Fund. Also to be admired is the 14th century octagonal font and a series of fascinating wall paintings. In the churchyard are the grave and monument of Sir Basil Spence (1907-76), architect of Coventry Cathedral.

YAXLEY

12 miles N of Stowmarket on the A140

Yaxley's **Church of St Mary** offers up more treasures. One is an extremely rare sexton's wheel, which hangs above the south door and was used in medieval times to select fast days in honour of the Virgin. When a pair of iron wheels were spun on their axle, strings attached to the outer wheel would catch on the inner, stopping both and indicating the chosen day. The

17th century pulpit is one of the finest in the country, with the most glorious, sumptuous carvings.

EYE

13 miles NE of Stowmarket on the B1117

The name of this excellent little town is derived from the Saxon for an island, as Eye was once surrounded by water and marshes. The **Church of St Peter and St Paul** stands in the shadow of a mound on which a castle once stood (the remains are worth visiting and the mound offers a panoramic view of the town – almost a bird's eye view, in fact). The church's 100-feet tower was described by Pevsner as 'one of the wonders of Suffolk' and the interior is a masterpiece of restoration, with all the essential medieval features in place. The rood screen, with painted panels depicting St Edmund, St Ursula, Edward the Confessor and Henry VI, is particularly fine.

Other interesting Eye sights are the ornate redbrick Town Hall; the timbered Guildhall, with the archangel Gabriel carved on a corner post; a crinkle-crankle wall fronting Chandos Lodge, where Sir Frederick Ashton once lived; and a tiny but thriving theatre.

HOXNE

4 miles NE of Eye on the B1118

Palaeolithic remains indicate the exceptionally long history of Hoxne (pronounced Hoxon), which stands along the banks of the River Waveney near the Norfolk border. It is best known for its links with

Eye Castle

King Edmund, who was reputedly killed here, though Bradfield St Clare and Shottisham have rival claims to this distinction. The Hoxne legend is that Edmund was betrayed to the Danes by a newlywed couple who were crossing the Goldbrook bridge and spotted his golden spurs reflected from his hiding place below the bridge. Edmund put a curse on all newlyweds crossing the bridge, and to this day some brides take care to avoid it.

The story continues that Edmund was tied to an oak tree and killed with arrows. That same oak mysteriously fell down in 1848 while apparently in good health, and a monument at the site is a popular tourist attraction. In the church of St Peter and St Paul an oak screen (perhaps that very same oak?) depicts scenes from the martyr's life. A more cheerful event is the Harvest Breakfast on the village green that follows the annual service. The East Anglian bishops once had their seat at Hoxne, and the moated vicarage beside the church may have been the original location of the Bishops Palace.

HORHAM
6 miles E of Eye on the B1117

Three distinct musical connections distinguish this dapper little village. The Norman church has had its tower strengthened for the rehanging of the peal of eight bells, which is believed to be the oldest in the world. Benjamin Britten, later associated with the Aldeburgh Festival, lived and composed in Horham for a time. On a famous day during the Second World War, Glenn Miller brought his band to Horham to celebrate the 200th flying mission to set out from the American aerodrome. The 95th Bomb Group Hospital Museum contains some wonderful wartime paintings, and a memorial in Horham Church remembers the airfield's personnel.

WORLINGWORTH
8 miles SE of Eye off the B1118

It's well worth taking the country road to Worlingworth, a long, straggling village whose **Church of St Mary** has a remarkable font cover reaching up about 30 feet. It is brilliantly coloured and intricately carved, and near the top is an inscription in Greek which translates as 'wash my sin and not my body only.' Note, too, the Carolean box pews, the carved pulpit and an oil painting of Worlingworth's Great Feast of 1810 to celebrate George III's jubilee. The village is surrounded by farmland which produces many crops including wheat, barley, sugar beet and oil seed rape. As the year passes the landscape changes from shades of brown to green, yellow and gold. Harvest time for the wheat and barley in the summer provides wonderful photo opportunities.

WINGFIELD
6 miles E of Eye off the B1118

Wingfield College is one of the country's most historic seats of

46 GABLES FARM B&B

Wingfield

This beautiful 16th century comes with landscaped gardens and a moat, great for short breaks to somewhere special.

see page 153

The village sign of Fressingfield is a pilgrim and a donkey, recording that Fressingfield was a stopping place on the pilgrim route from Dunwich to Bury St Edmunds.

47 THE KINGS HEAD (THE LOW HOUSE)

Laxfield

A 16th century inn oozing with charm and character offering fine food, drink and accommodation.

🍴 🛏 see page 252

A couple of miles east of Laxfield, Heveningham Hall is a fine Georgian mansion, a model of classical elegance designed by James Wyatt with lovely grounds by Capability Brown. As it runs through the grounds, the River Blyth widens into a lake.

learning, founded in 1362 as a college for priests with a bequest from Sir John de Wingfield, Chief Staff Officer to the Black Prince. Sir John's wealth came from ransoming a French nobleman at the Battle of Poitiers in 1356. Surrendered to Henry VIII at the time of the Dissolution, the college became a farmhouse and is now in private hands. The façade is now Georgian, but the original medieval Great Hall still stands, and the college and its three acres of gardens are open to the public at weekends in summer. Attractions include regular artistic events and printing demonstrations.

On a hill outside the village are the imposing remains of a castle built by the 1st Earl.

FRESSINGFIELD

10 miles E of Eye on the B1116

Fressingfield's first spiritual centre was the **Church of St Peter and St Paul**. It has a superb hammerbeam roof and a lovely stone bell tower that was built in the 14th century. On one of the pews the initials A P are carved. These are believed to be the work of Alice de la Pole, Duchess of Norfolk and grand-daughter of Geoffrey Chaucer. Was this a work of art or a bout of vandalism brought on by a dull sermon?

LAXFIELD

12 miles E of Eye on the B1117

Laxfield & District Museum, in the 16th century Guildhall, gives a fine insight into bygone ages with geology and natural history

exhibits, agricultural and domestic tools, a Victorian kitchen, a village shop and a costume room. The museum is open on Saturday and Sunday afternoons in summer.

All Saints Church is distinguished by some wonderful flint 'flushwork' (stonework) on its tower, roof and nave. In the 1808 Baptist church is a plaque remembering John Noyes, burnt at the stake in 1557 for refusing to take Catholic vows. History relates that the villagers - with a single exception - dowsed their fires in protest. The one remaining fire, however, was all that was needed to light the stake.

The **Country Fair** (the beginning of July) at the hall has been running a mere 5 years and yet has proved amazingly popular, with around 7000 people attending the 2009 event to see the jousting reconstructions, shop at the huge range of stalls, take a ride in a helicopter and take part in the many activities for all ages.

ALONG THE COAST

DUNWICH

4 miles SW of Southwold off the B1105

Surely the hidden place of all hidden places, Dunwich was once the capital of East Anglia, founded by the Burgundian Christian missionary St Felix and for several centuries a major trading port (wool and grain out; wine, timber and cloth in) and a centre of fishing and shipbuilding. The records show that in 1241 no fewer than 80 ships were built here for the king. By the middle of the next century, however, the sea attacked from the east and a vast bank of sand and shingle silted up the harbour. The course of the river was diverted, the town was cut off from the sea and the town's trade was effectively killed off. For the next 700 years the relentless forces of nature continued to take their toll, and of the six churches, monasteries, mills and hospitals all that remains now of ancient Dunwich are the ruins of the Norman **Leper Hospital of St James**, the ruins of a clifftop **Friary** that was home to the Greyfriars, and a buttress of one of the nine churches which once served the community. The last church succumbed to the waves in 1920, but local legend says that the church bells can be heard beneath the waves on stormy nights. Other tales tell of strange lights in the ruined priory and the eerie chanting of long-dead monks.

Today's village comprises a 19th century church and a row of Victorian cottages, one of which houses the **Dunwich Museum**. Local residents set up the museum in 1972 to tell the Dunwich story; the historical section has displays and exhibits from Roman, Saxon and medieval times, the centrepiece being a large model of the town at its 12th century peak. There are also sections devoted to natural history, social history and the arts. Extended and refurbished in 1998 after a generous grant from the national Lottery, Dunwich Museum has won numerous awards,

including the coveted Gulbenkian Award. It is open March Sat/Sun 2-4:30pm, 1st April - 30th September 11:30-4:30pm daily, and daily through October 12-4pm.

Dunwich Forest, immediately inland from the village, is one of three – the others are further south at Tunstall and Rendlesham – named by the Forestry Commission as **Aldewood Forest**. Work started on these in 1920 with the planting of Scots pine, Corsican pine and some Douglas fir; oak and poplar were tried but did not thrive in the sandy soil. The three forests, which between them cover nearly 9,000 acres, were almost completely devastated in the hurricane of October 1987, Rendlesham alone losing more than a million trees. Currently the forest is undergoing a "rewilding" to restore the natural heathland habitat, which is a rare and vital habitat for many rare species of birds, reptiles and butterflies. The forest provides a peaceful walking environment for visitors, and is far from the crowds,

•

South of Dunwich lies Dunwich Heath, one of Suffolk's most important conservation areas, comprising the beach, splendid heather, a field study centre, a public hide and an information centre and restaurant in converted coastguard cottages.

•

Dunwich Medieval Friary

Around Dunwich Heath are the attractive villages of Westleton, Middleton, Theberton and Eastbridge. During the First World War, German airships were used to spy on and bomb England. In the porch of Theberton church are remains of a Zeppelin that crashed in a nearby field in 1917.

48 THE WHITE HORSE INN

Westleton, nr Saxmundham

A friendly ambience, Adnams ales, good food and B&B rooms in a delightful village inn.

¶ ⊨ see page 253

often just leaving you and the Dartmoor ponies that graze here, in this beautiful landscape.

In Westleton, the 14th century thatched **Church of St Peter**, built by the monks of Sibton Abbey, has twice seen the collapse of its tower. The first fell down in a hurricane in 1776; its smaller wooden replacement collapsed when a bomb fell during the Second World War. The village is also the main route of access to the RSPB-managed **Minsmere Bird Sanctuary**, the most important sanctuary for wading birds in eastern England. The marshland was flooded during the Second World War, and nature and this wartime emergency measure created the perfect habitat for innumerable birds. More than 100 species nest here, and a similar number of birds visit throughout the year, making it a birdwatcher's paradise. Minsmere is rich in other kinds of wildlife, and one of the best ways of discovering more is to join one of the guided walks. The

Suffolk Coastal Path runs along the foreshore. Within the sanctuary is a visitors centre, where you can find out more about the wildlife, pick up a trail booklet to help you find your way around and a tearoom where you can enjoy a delicious meal. The reserve is open daily all year round, during daylight hours. The visitors centre 9am-5pm, shop 10am-5pm, tearoom 10am-4.30pm (hot food served 11.30am-2.30pm); all of which are closed from the start of November until the end of January.

A little way inland from Westleton lies **Darsham**, where another nature reserve is home to many varieties of birds and flowers.

YOXFORD

10 miles SW of Southwold on the A12

Once an important stop on the London-to-Yarmouth coaching route, Yoxford now attracts visitors with its pink-washed cottages and its arts and crafts, antiques and food shops. Look for the cast-iron signpost outside the church, with hands pointing to London, Yarmouth and Framlingham set high enough to be seen by the driver of a stagecoach.

SAXMUNDHAM

12 miles SW of Southwold off the A12

A little town that was granted its market charter in 1272. On the font of the church in Saxmundham is the carving of a 'woodwose' - a tree spirit or green man. He, and others like him, have given their name to a large number of pubs in Suffolk and elsewhere. A major

Dunwich Heath, Saxmundham

attraction is the **Saxmundham Museum**, housed in a former bakehouse. Among the many fascinating displays are a scale model of Saxmundham railway station as it was in the 1930s, complete with working trains; a recreation of Saxmundham Playhouse; replicas of shops; costumes and dolls; and various memorabilia relating to the town. The museum is open from the start of April until the end of September, Monday to Saturday including Bank Holidays but excluding Sundays and Good Friday, from 10:00am until 1:00pm. In addition the Museum will be open each day of the Arts Festival Week in October, including Sundays. There is no admission charge – though donations are welcomed.

BRUISYARD

4 miles NW of Saxmundham off the B1119

Just west of this village is the **Bruisyard Vineyard, Winery and Herb Centre**, a complex of a 10-acre vineyard with 13,000 Müller Thurgau grape vines, a wine-production centre, herb and water gardens, a tea shop and a picnic site.

PEASENHALL

6 miles NW of Saxmundham on the A1120

A little stream runs along the side of the main street in Peasenhall, whose buildings present several styles and ages. Most distinguished is the old timbered **Woolhall**, splendidly restored to its 15th century grandeur.

LEISTON

4 miles E of Saxmundham off the B1119

For 200 years the biggest name in Leiston was that of Richard Garrett, who founded an engineering works here in 1778 after starting a business in Woodbridge. In the early years ploughs, threshers, seed drills and other agricultural machinery were the main products, but the company later started one of the country's first production lines for steam machines. The Garrett works are now the **Long Shop Museum**, the factory buildings having been lovingly restored, and many of the Garrett machines are now on display, including traction engines, a steam-driven tractor and a road roller. There's also a section where the history and workings of steam engines are explained. A small area of the museum recalls the USAAF's 357th fighter group, who flew from an airfield outside Leiston during the Second World War. One of their number, a Captain Chuck Yeager, was the first man to fly faster than the speed of sound. It is open from the end of March until the end of October, Mondays to Saturdays 10am - 5pm and Sundays 11am - 5pm.

The Garrett works closed in 1980, but what could have been a disastrous unemployment situation was alleviated to some extent by the nuclear power station at **Sizewell**. The coast road in the centre of Leiston leads to this establishment, where visitors can take tours - on foot with access to

The first Leiston Abbey was built on Nunsmere marshes in 1182, but in 1363 the Earl of Suffolk rebuilt it on its present site away from the frequent floods. It became one of the largest and most prestigious monasteries in the country, and its wealth probably spelled its ruin, as it fell within Henry VIII's plan for the Dissolution of the Monasteries. The visible ruins are of a chapel built on the site of the monastic church. A new abbey was built using stone from the first abbey site, and the restored old hall is used as a base for PROCORDA, a group promoting musical excellence.

Aldeburgh's maritime connections remain very strong. There has been a lifeboat station here since 1851, when the RNLI took over from the Suffolk Shipwreck Association; it was the last station to operate the traditional 'double-ended' design of lifeboat. The very modern lifeboat station on Crag Path is one of the town's chief attractions for visitors, open daily from 10 to 4, and there are regular practice launches from the shingle beach. A handful of fishermen still put out to sea from the beach, selling their catch from their little wooden huts, while a thriving yacht club is the base for sailing on the river and the sea.

buildings at Sizewell A or by minibus, with a guide and videos, round Sizewell B.

ALDRINGHAM

4 miles E of Saxmundham on the B1122

Aldringham's church is notable for its superb 15th century font, and the village inn was once a haunt of smugglers. It now helps to refresh the visitors who flock to the **Aldringham Craft Market**, founded in 1958 and extending over three galleries, with a serious selection of arts and crafts, clothes and gifts, pottery, basketry, books and cards.

THORPENESS

6 miles E of Saxmundham on the B1353

Thorpeness is a unique holiday village with mock-Tudor houses and the general look of a series of eccentric film sets. Buying up a considerable packet of land called the Sizewell estate in 1910, the architect, barrister and playwright Glencairn Stuart Ogilvie created what he hoped would be a fashionable resort with cottages, some larger houses and a 65-acre shallow boating and pleasure lake called the Meare. Every August, following the Aldeburgh Carnival, a regatta takes place on the Meare, culminating in a splendid fireworks display. The 85-feet water tower, built to aid in the lake's construction, looked out of place, so Ogilvie disguised it as a house. Known ever since as the **House in the**

Clouds, it is now available to rent as a holiday home. The neighbouring **Watermill**, moved lock, stock and millstones from Aldringham, stopped pumping in 1940 but has been restored and now houses a visitor centre. Thorpeness is very much a one-off, not at all typical Suffolk but with a droll charm that is all its own.

ALDEBURGH

6 miles SE of Saxmundham on the A1094

And so down the coast road to Aldeburgh, another coastal town that once prospered as a port with major fishing and shipbuilding industries. Drake's *Greyhound* and *Pelican* were built at Slaughden, now taken by the sea, and during the 16th century some 1,500 people were engaged in fishing. Both industries declined as shipbuilding moved elsewhere and the fishing

Aldeburgh Beach

boats became too large to be hauled up the shingle.

Suffolk's best-known poet, George Crabbe, was born at Slaughden in 1754 and lived through the village's hard times. He reflected the melancholy of those days when he wrote of his fellow townsmen:

Here joyless roam a wild
amphibious race,
With sullen woe displayed in every face;
Who far from civil arts and social fly,
And scowl at strangers with
suspicious eye.

He was equally evocative concerning the sea and the river, and the following lines written about the River Alde could apply to several others in the county:

With ceaseless motion comes
and goes the tide
Flowing, it fills the channel
vast and wide;
Then back to sea,
with strong majestic sweep
It- rolls, in ebb yet terrible and deep;
Here samphire-banks
and salt-wort bound the flood
There stakes and seaweed
withering on the mud;
And higher up, a ridge of all things base,
Which some strong tide
has rolled upon the place.

It was Crabbe who created the character of the solitary fisherman Peter Grimes, later the subject of an opera composed by another Aldeburgh resident, **Benjamin Britten**. Britten lived in the **Red House**, off the B1122 Leiston road opposite the golf course, from 1957 until hid death in 1976.

Here he composed many of his greatest works, including the *War Requiem* and *Death in Venice*. Guided tours of the house take place on certain days in the summer; for details call 01728 451700.

Aldeburgh's role gradually changed into that of a holiday resort, and the Marquess of Salisbury, visiting early in the 19th century, was one of the first to be attracted by the idea of sea-bathing without the crowds. By the middle of the century the grand houses that had sprung up were joined by smaller residences, the railway had arrived, a handsome water tower was put up (1860) and Aldeburgh prospered once more. There were even plans for a pier, and construction started in 1878, but the project proved too difficult or too expensive and was halted, the rusting girders being removed some time later.

One of the town's major benefactors was Newson Garrett, a wealthy businessman who was the first mayor under the charter of the Local Government Act of 1875. This colourful character also developed the Maltings at Snape, but is perhaps best remembered through his remarkable daughter Elizabeth, who was the first woman doctor in England (having

49 THE RAILWAY INN

Aldeburgh

A great local inn, full of community spirit and the perfect place to stay a night or two.

see page 254

Moot Hall, Aldeburgh

•

In Aldeburgh there are several interesting buildings, notably the Moot Hall, which is a 16th century timber-framed building that was built in what was once the centre of town. It hasn't moved, but the sea long ago took away several houses and streets. Inside the Hall is a museum of town history and finds from the nearby Snape burial ship. The museum also recounts the story of the Aldeburgh lifeboat's rescue on the second Sunday of the Second World War of sailors from the SS Magdapur. Benjamin Britten set the first scene of Peter Grimes in the Moot Hall. A sundial on the south face of the Hall proclaims, in Latin, that it only tells the time when the sun shines.

•

qualified in Paris at a time when women could not qualify here) and the first woman mayor (of Aldeburgh, in 1908). This lady married the shipowner James Skelton Anderson, who established the golf club in 1884.

If Crabbe were alive today he would have a rather less cantankerous opinion of his fellows, especially at carnival time on a Monday in August when the town celebrates with a colourful procession of floats and marchers, a fireworks display and numerous other events. As for the arts, there is, of course, the **Aldeburgh Festival**, started in 1948 by Britten and others; the festival's main venue is **Snape Maltings**, but many performances take place in Aldeburgh itself. **Suffolk Summer Theatres**, which runs during the season, has a fabulous variety of plays from drama to comedy, and was described as "... the Rolls-Royce of Summer repertory" in *The Observer*.

The parish church of **St Peter and St Paul**, which stands above the town as a very visible landmark for mariners, contains a memorial to George Crabbe and a beautiful stained-glass window, the work of John Piper, depicting three Britten parables: *Curlew River*, *The Burning Fiery Furnace* and *The Prodigal Son*. Britten, his companion Peter Pears and the musician Imogen Holst are buried in the churchyard, part of which is set aside for the benefit of wildlife. Elizabeth Garrett Anderson (see above) is also buried in the churchyard, so too George

and Mary Crabbe, the poet's parents.

The latest of the many tributes in Aldeburgh to Britten is a giant metal **Clam Shell** (about 12-14 ft high and the 20 ft wide) designed by Maggie Hambling. It stands on the beach at the north end of town, and the words on its rim – 'I hear those voices that will not be drowned' – are taken from Britten's opera *Peter Grimes*.

FRISTON
3 miles SE of Saxmundham off the A1094

Friston's **Post Mill**, the tallest in England, is a prominent sight on the Aldeburgh-Snape road, moved from Woodbridge in 1812 just after its construction. It worked by wind until 1956, then by engine until 1972.

SNAPE
3 miles S of Saxmundham on the A1094

This 'boggy place' has a long and interesting history. In 1862 the remains of an Anglo-Saxon ship were discovered here, and since that time regular finds have been made, with some remarkable cases of almost perfect preservation. Snape, like Aldeburgh, has benefited over the years from the philanthropy of the Garrett family, one of whose members built the primary school and set up the Maltings, centre of the Aldeburgh Music Festival.

The last 30-odd years have seen the development of the **Snape Maltings Riverside Centre**, a group of shops and galleries located in a complex of restored Victorian granaries and malthouses that is also the setting for the renowned Aldeburgh festival. The Maltings began their designated task of converting grain into malt in the 1840s, and continued thus until 1965, when the pressure of modern techniques brought them to a halt. There was a real risk of the buildings being demolished, but George Gooderham, a local farmer, bought the site to expand his animal feeds business and soon saw the potential of the redundant buildings.

The Concert Hall came first, in 1967, and in 1971 the Craft Shop was established as the first conversion of the old buildings for retail premises. Conversion and expansion continue to this day, and in the numerous outlets visitors can buy anything from fudge to country-style clothing, from herbs to household furniture, silver buttons to top hats. Plants and garden accessories are also sold, and art galleries feature the work of local painters, potters and sculptors. The Centre hosts regular painting, craft and decorative art courses, and more recent expansion saw the creation of an impressive country-style store.

WOODBRIDGE

Udebyge, Wiebryge, Wodebryge, Wudebrige ... just some of the ways of spelling this splendid old market town since it was first mentioned in writing in AD 970. As to what the name means, it could simply be 'wooden bridge' or 'bridge by the wood', but the most likely and most interesting explanation is that it is derived from Anglo-Saxon words meaning 'Woden's (or Odin's) town'. Standing at the head of the Deben estuary, it is a place of considerable charm with a wealth of handsome, often historic buildings and a considerable sense of history, as both a market town and a port.

The shipbuilding and allied industries flourished here, as at most towns on the Suffolk coast, and it is recorded that both Edward III, in the 14th century, and Drake in the 16th sailed in Woodbridge ships. There's still plenty of activity on and by the river, though nowadays it is all leisure-orientated. The town's greatest benefactor was Thomas Seckford, who rebuilt the abbey, paid for the chapel in the north aisle of St Mary's Church and founded the original almshouses in Seckford Street. In 1575 he gave the town the splendid Shire Hall on Market Hill. Originally used as a corn exchange, it now houses the **Suffolk Punch Heavy Horse Museum**, with an

50 THE ANCHOR INN

Woodbridge

A pretty pub serving Malaysian cuisine with great service and atmosphere.

see page 255

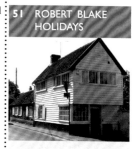

51 ROBERT BLAKE HOLIDAYS

Woodbridge

This family run business offers various accommodations in the style of refurbished properties of varying ages.

see page 255

River Deben, Woodbridge

85

52 THE CHERRY TREE

Woodbridge

A flagship pub in Woodbridge, with a good choice of real ales, popular pub dishes and quiet, comfortable accommodation.

see page 256

exhibition devoted to the Suffolk Punch breed of heavy working horse, the oldest such breed in the world. The breed dates from the 16th century, but all animals alive today trace the male line back to one stallion called Crisp's Horse of Ufford, foaled in 1768. The history of the breed and its rescue from near-extinction in the 1960s is covered in fascinating detail, and a small section relates to other famous Suffolk breeds – the Red Poll cattle, the Suffolk sheep and the Large Black pigs. The opening times for the museum are subject to change so it is best to phone them to confirm the present times. Tel: 01394 380643. Please note that there are stairs into the Museum, so for those with mobility restrictions it is recommended that you contact the museum before you visit.

Opposite the Shire Hall is **Woodbridge Museum**, a treasure trove of information on the history of the town and its more notable

residents (again it is best to phone for opening times before you visit Tel: 01394 380502); from here it is a short stroll down the cobbled alleyway to the magnificent parish church of St Mary, where Seckford was buried in 1587.

Seckford naturally features prominently in the museum, along with the painter Thomas Churchyard, the map-maker Isaac Johnson and the poet Edward Fitzgerald. 'Old Fitz' was something of an eccentric and, for the most part, fairly reclusive. He loved Woodbridge and particularly the River Deben, where he often sailed in his little boat Scandal.

Woodbridge is lucky enough to have two marvellous mills, both in working order, and both great attractions for the visitor. The **Tide Mill**, on the quayside close to the town centre, dates from the late 18th century (though the site was mentioned 600 years previously) and worked by the power of the tide

Woodbridge Tide Mill

until 1957. It has been meticulously restored and the waterwheel still turns, fed by a recently created pond which replaced the original huge mill pond when it was turned into a marina. **Buttrum's Mill**, named after the last miller, is a tower mill standing just off the A12 bypass a mile west of the town centre. A marvellous sight, its six storeys make it the tallest surviving tower mill in Suffolk. There is a ground-floor display of the history and workings of the mill.

AROUND WOODBRIDGE

WICKHAM MARKET
5 miles N of Woodbridge off the A12

Places to see in this straggling village are the picturesque watermill by the River Deben and All Saints Church, whose 137-feet octagonal tower has a little roof to shelter the bell. In the little country churchyard at **Boulge**, a couple of miles southwest of Wickham Market, is the grave of Edward Fitzgerald (1809-1883), whose free translation of *The Rubaiyat of Omar Khayyam* is an English masterpiece. Tradition has it that on his grave is a rose bush grown from one found on Omar Khayyam's grave in Iran.

EASTON
5 miles N of Woodbridge off the B1078

A scenic drive leads to the lovely village of Easton, one of the most colourful, flower-bedecked places in the county.

Tucked away three miles off the A12 in the beautiful Deben Valley, **Easton Park Farm** is one of Suffolk's greatest attractions. Since it opened in 1973, more than a million visitors have passed through the gates to have a great day out; they leave knowing a lot more about the ways of the countryside than when they arrived. It's a marvellous place to bring the family, as the children can have endless fun feeding and making friends with the animals in Pets Paddock, riding ponies, seeing the Suffolk Punches or simply running around in the adventure playground. The showpiece of the park is the Victorian dairy, an ornate octagonal building, while the Dairy Centre is contrastingly modern, with walkways over the top of the stalls and a viewing gallery over the milking parlour. Tel: 01728 746475.

PARHAM
8 miles N of Woodbridge on the B1116

Parham Airfield is now agricultural land, but in the museum in the control tower and an adjacent hut can be found memorabilia of the 390th Bomb Group of the USAAF. The airfield was built in 1942 for the RAF, but it was taken over by the USAAF in 1943. From here they flew Flying Fortresses on many successful missions, and the museum is a memorial to all the airmen who flew from here. It is open Sunday and Summer School Holiday Monday, from first Sunday in April to last Sunday in October from 11am-5pm, and Wednesdays from June - September from 11am-4pm.

• *Many of Woodbridge's streets are traffic-free, so shopping is a real pleasure. If you should catch the Fitzgerald mood and feel like 'a jug of wine and a loaf of bread', Woodbridge can oblige with a good variety of pubs and restaurants.*

•

UFFORD

4 miles N of Woodbridge off the A12

Pride of place in a village that takes its name from Uffa (or Wuffa), the founder of the leading Anglo-Saxon dynasty, goes to the 13th century **Church of the Assumption**. The font cover, which telescopes from 5 feet to 18 feet in height, is a masterpiece of craftsmanship, its elaborate carving crowned by a pelican. Many 15th century benches have survived, but William Dowsing (a government commissioner responsible for demolishing monuments of idolatry) smashed the organ and most of the stained glass in 1644 – what's there now is mainly Victorian, some of it a copy of 15th century work at All Souls College, Oxford. Ufford is where the Suffolk Punch originated, Crisp's 404 being, in 1768, the progenitor of this distinguished breed of horses.

BREDFIELD

3 miles N of Woodbridge off the A12

There's a plaque on the wall of the village pub in Bredfield commemorating a day in 1742 on which nothing at all happened. On a day in 1809, however, something did happen: Edward Fitzgerald, who translated a selction of Persian poems by Omar Khayyam and published the Rubaiyat of Omar Khayyam, was born. Something else happened in 1953: a wrought-iron canopy with a golden crown, made at the village forge, was put on the crossroads pump to celebrate Queen Elizabeth II's coronation.

CAMPSEA ASHE

6 miles NE of Woodbridge on the B1078

On towards Wickham Market the road passes through Campsea Ashe in the parish of Campsey Ashe. The 14th century church of St John the Baptist has an interesting brass showing one of its first rectors in full priestly garb.

RENDLESHAM

5 miles NE of Woodbridge on the A1152

The **Church of St Gregory the Great** dates from the 14th century, but there is evidence (not physical, unfortunately) of an earlier Christian presence in the shape of Raedwald's palace.

The only part still standing of **Rendlesham Hall**, built in 1871 and demolished in 1949, is the Gothic folly of Woodbridge Lodge, a remarkable edifice which loses little in comparison with some of the more extraordinary buildings designed by Gaudi in Barcelona.

BUTLEY

5 miles NE of Woodbridge on the B1084

At the northern edge of Rendlesham Forest, the village of Butley has a splendid 14th century gatehouse, all that remains of **Butley Priory**, an Augustinian priory founded by Ranulf de Glanville in 1171. The gatehouse is, by itself, a fairly imposing building, with some interesting flintwork on the north façade (1320) and baronial carvings. Butley still has a working mill, remarkable for its fine Regency porch, and the parish church is Norman, with a 14th century tower.

There are some splendid country walks around Butley, notably by **Staverton Thicks**, which has a deer park and woods of oak and holly. The oldest trees date back more than 400 years – some of the oldest oaks in East Anglia. Butley Clumps is an avenue of beech trees planted in fours, with a pine tree at the centre of each clump – the technical term for such an arrangement is a quincunx. Butley has long been renowned for its oysters – and there are many great places to eat which specialize in oysters in the area

SUTTON HOO
1 mile E of Woodbridge off the B1083

A mile or so east of Woodbridge on the opposite bank of the Deben is the **Sutton Hoo Burial Site**, a group of a dozen grassy barrows which hit the headlines in 1939 and are sometimes known as 'page one of the history of England'. Excavations, which initially unearthed ship's rivets, brought to light the outline of an 80-feet long Anglo-Saxon ship, filled with one of the greatest hoards of treasure ever discovered in Britain. The priceless find, which eluded grave robbers and lay undisturbed for over 1,300 years, includes gold coins and ornaments, silverware, weapons and armoury, drinking horns and leather cups; it is housed in the British Museum in London, but there are exhibitions, replicas and plenty of other items of interest

at the site, along with special events throughout the year. Research continues, and it is now believed that the ship was the burial place of Raedwald, of the Wuffinga dynasty, King of East Anglia from about AD 610 to AD 625. Access to the site is on foot from the B1083; the Sutton Hoo Society conduct informative guided tours, details of which are available from the National Trust.

CHILLESFORD
6 miles E of Woodbridge on the B1084

Brick was once big business here, and while digging for clay the locals made many finds, including hundreds of varieties of molluscs and the skeleton of an enormous whale. Chillesford supplies some of the clay for Aldeburgh brickworks.

ORFORD
12 miles E of Woodbridge at the end of the B1084

Without doubt one of the most charming and interesting of all the places in Suffolk, Orford has something to please everyone. The ruins of **Orford Castle**, one of the most important in medieval England, are a most impressive sight, even though the keep is all that remains of the original building commissioned by Henry II in 1165. The walls of the keep are 90 feet high and 10 feet deep, and behind them are many rooms and passages in a remarkable state of preservation. A climb up the spiral staircase to the top provides splendid views over the surrounding countryside and to the sea.

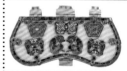

53 SUTTON HOO

Sutton Hoo

Sutton Hoo kept its secret for more than 1300 years, until, on the very brink of war in 1939, an incomparable buried treasure was discovered here.

 see page 256

54 THE PLOUGH INN

Sutton

A fantastic old pub, offering food, drink and accommodation for 500 years has led to it's unbeatable reputation.

see page 257

•

In the market square of Orford are a handsome town hall, two pubs with a fair quota of smuggling tales, and the well-loved and delightfully named 'Butley Orford Oysterage' restaurant serving Butley oysters which has been grown in the same way from Butley Creek since the 1950's. They also have a smokehouse where kippers, salmon, trout, ham, sausages, chicken and even garlic are smoked over Suffolk oak.

•

55 THE JOLLY SAILOR

Orford

A real smugglers haven on the Suffolk heritage coast providing comfortable accommodation and fine food.

🍴 🛏 *see page 258*

St Bartholomew's Church was built at the same time, though the present church dates from the 14th century. A wonderful sight at night when floodlit, the church is regularly used for the performance of concerts and recitals, and many of Benjamin Britten's works were first heard here. At the east end lie the still-splendid Norman remains, all that is left of the original chancel.

These two grand buildings indicate that Orford was a very important town at one time. Indeed it was once a thriving port, but the steadily growing shingle bank of Orford Ness gradually cut it off from the sea, and down the years its appeal has changed.

The sea may have gone from Orford but the river is still there, and in summer the quayside is alive with yachts and pleasure craft. On the other side of the river is **Orford Ness**, the largest vegetated shingle spit in England which is home to a variety of rare flora and fauna. The lighthouse marks the most easterly point (jointly with Lowestoft) in Britain.

Access to the 10-mile spit, which is in the hands of the National Trust, is by ferry from Orford Quay. For many years the Ness was out of bounds to the public, being used for various military purposes, including pre-war radar research under Sir Robert Watson-Watt. Trails pass through the varied habitats found on the Ness, as well as areas and buildings of historic interest such as the First World War airfield site, firing ranges and the lighthouse. Boat trips also leave Orford Quay for the RSPB reserve at **Havergate Island**, haunt of avocet and tern (the former returned in 1947 after being long absent).

The **Dunwich Underwater Exploration Exhibition** in Front Street features exhibits on marine archaeology, coastal erosion and more, gleaned from the exploration of the ruins of the former town of Dunwich, now largely claimed by the sea. This exhibition is not suitable for young children.

Orford Castle

BAWDSEY

7 miles SE of Woodbridge on the B1083

The B1083 runs from Woodbridge through farming country and several attractive villages (Sutton, Shottisham, Alderton) to Bawdsey, beyond which lies the mouth of the River Deben, the end of the Sussex Coastal Path, and the ferry to Felixstowe. The late-Victorian **Bawdsey Manor** was taken over by the Government and became the centre for radar development when Orford Ness was deemed unsuitable. By the beginning of the Second World War there were two dozen secret radar stations in Britain, and radar HQ moved from Bawdsey to Dundee. The manor is now a leisure centre.

RAMSHOLT

7 miles SE of Woodbridge off the B1083

Ramsholt is a tiny community on the north bank of the Deben a little way up from Bawdsey. The pub is a popular port of call for yachtsmen, and half a mile from the quay, in quiet isolation, stands the Church of All Saints with its round tower. Road access to Ramsholt is from the B1083 just south of Shottisham.

HOLLESLEY

5 miles SE of Woodbridge off the B1083

The Deben and the Ore turn this part of Suffolk almost into a peninsula, and on the seaward side lie Hollesley and Shingle Street. The latter stands upon a shingle bank at the entrance to the Ore and comprises a row of little houses, a coastguard cottage and a Martello tower. Its very isolation is an attraction, and the sight of the sea rushing into and out of the river is worth the journey.

Brendan Behan did not enjoy his visit. Brought here on a swimming outing from the Borstal at Hollesley, he declared that the waves had 'no limit but the rim of the world'. Looking out to the bleak North Sea, it is easy to see what he meant.

LOWESTOFT

The most easterly town in Britain had its heyday as a major fishing port during the late 19th and early 20th centuries, when it was a mighty rival to Great Yarmouth in the herring industry. That industry has been in major decline since the First World War, but Lowestoft is still a fishing port and the trawlers still chug into the harbour in the early morning with the catches of the night.

The **"Mincarlo"** - the last surviving Lowestoft built and engined side-fishing trawler - was built in 1960, and after a varied history including conversion to an oil rig standby vessel, is now fully restored and on display in the harbour, where visitors have a chance to step aboard and talk to knowledgeable guides about the marvellous history of this interesting trawler. Tel: 01502 565234 for availability.

Lowestoft is also a popular holiday resort, the star attraction being the lovely South Beach with

•

Poplar Park Equestrian Centre, located about 3 minutes from the centre of Hollesley, offer visitors lessons and, for those competent on horseback, hire of their horses to ride through their beautiful park (what could be better than going on one of their 'pub runs' – hacking through miles of unspoilt countryside with a few welcome stops at pubs on the way!). Saturday afternoons they run a Pony Club for children (2pm-5pm in the summer, 1pm-4pm in the winter), and in August they run the annual three-day Pony Club Camp – which includes sleepovers. Tel: 01394 411023.

•

91

56 LOWESTOFT MARITIME MUSEUM

Lowestoft

Open daily from May to September, Lowestoft Maritime Museum specialises in the history of the Lowestoft fishing fleet, from early sail to steam and through to the modern diesel-powered vessels.

 see page 257

its golden sands, safe swimming, two piers and all the expected seaside amusements and entertainments. **Claremont Pier**, over 600 feet in length, was built in 1902, ready to receive day-trippers on the famous Belle steamers. The buildings near the pier were developed in mid-Victorian times by the company of Sir Samuel Morton Peto, also responsible for Nelson's Column, the statues in the Houses of Parliament, the Reform Club and Somerleyton Hall.

At the heart of the town is the old harbour, home to the Royal Norfolk & Suffolk Yacht Club and the Lifeboat Station. Further upriver is the commercial part of the port, used chiefly by ships carrying grain and timber. The history of Lowestoft is naturally tied up with the sea, and much of that history is recorded in fascinating detail in the **Lowestoft & East Suffolk Maritime Museum** with model boats, fishing gear, a lifeboat cockpit, paintings and shipwrights' tools. The setting is a flint-built fisherman's cottage in Sparrow's Nest Gardens. The **Royal Naval Patrol Museum** nearby remembers the minesweeping service in models, photographs, documents and uniforms. Lowestoft had England's first lighthouse, installed in 1609. The present one dates from 1874. Also in Sparrow's Nest Gardens is the **War Memorial Museum**, dedicated to those who served during the Second World War. There's a chronological photographic collection of the

bombing of the town, aircraft models and a chapel of remembrance.

St Margaret's Church, notable for its decorated ceiling and copper-covered spire, is a memorial to seafarers, and the north aisle has panels recording the names of fishermen lost at sea from 1865 to 1923.

Just north of town, with access from the B1385, **Pleasurewood Hill** is the largest theme park in East Anglia.

Oulton Broad, on the western edge of Lowestoft, is a major centre of amusements afloat, with boats for hire and cruises on the Waveney. It also attracts visitors to Nicholas Everitt Park to look around **Lowestoft Museum**, housed in historic Broad House. Opened by the Queen and Prince Philip in 1985, the museum displays archaeological finds from local sites, some now lost to the sea, costumes, toys, domestic bygones and a fine collection of Lowestoft porcelain. (The porcelain industry lasted from about 1760 to 1800, using clay from the nearby Gunton Hall Estate. The soft-paste ware, resembling Bow porcelain, was usually decorated in white and blue.)

AROUND LOWESTOFT

CARLTON COLVILLE

3 miles SW of Lowestoft on the B1384

Many a transport enthusiast has enjoyed a grand day out at the **East**

Carlton Colville Transport Museum

Anglia Transport Museum, where children young and old (and even very old!) can climb aboard wide-eyed to enjoy rides on buses, trams and trolleybuses (one of the resident trolleybuses was built at the Garrett works in Leiston). The East Suffolk narrow-gauge railway winds its way around the site, and there's a 1930s street with all the authentic accessories, plus lorries, vans and steamrollers.

Carlton Marshes is Oulton Broad's nature reserve, with grazing marsh and fen, reached by the Waveney Way footpath.

BLUNDESTON
4 miles N of Lowestoft off the A12

Known chiefly as the village used by Charles Dickens as the birthplace of that writer's 'favourite child', David Copperfield, the morning light shining on the sundial of **St Mary's Church** – which has the tallest, narrowest Saxon round tower of any in East Anglia – greeted young David as he looked out of his bedroom window in the nearby Rookery. He said of the churchyard: *"There is nothing half so green that I know anywhere, as the grass of that churchyard, nothing half so shady as its trees; nothing half so quiet as its tombstones."*

LOUND
5 miles N of Lowestoft off the A1

Lound's parish **Church of St John the Baptist**, in the very north of the county, is sometimes known as the 'golden church'. This epithet is the result of the handiwork of designer/architect Sir Ninian Comper, seen most memorably in the gilded organ-case with two trumpeting angels, the font cover and the rood screen. The last is a very elaborate affair, with several heraldic arms displayed. The surprise package here is the modern St Christopher mural on the north wall. It includes Sir Ninian at the wheel of his Rolls Royce – and in 1976 an aeroplane was added to the scene!

93

Herringfleet Windmill

•

Kessingland's major tourist attraction is the Africa Alive! Wildlife Park, 100 acres of coastal parkland that are home to the exotic animals of Africa; giraffes, lions, meerkats and rhinos to name a few, as well as a petting area with tame farmyard animals, reptile and bat house and a great train ride which takes you around the park with a commentary of what animals it is you are seeing. In addition there are many opportunities to see demonstrations, have guided talks and even go into some enclosures with the keepers in high season. Also there is a children's adventure play area, gift shop, and restaurant (as well as other places to stop and have a snack throughout the park). The park is open daily 10am-4pm (last admission 3pm).

•

SOMERLEYTON

5 miles NW of Lowestoft on the B1074

Somerleyton Hall, one of the grandest and most distinctive of stately homes, is a splendid Victorian mansion built in Anglo-Italian style by Samuel Morton Peto. The Oak Room, with 17th century panelling from the original Jacobean house, some outstanding wood carvings and an exquisite silver and gilt mirror made for the Doge's Palace in Venice, is one of several superb rooms in this most magnificent of houses; others include the elegant Library, its walls lined with over 3,500 books, the Dining Room and the sumptuous Ballroom. The grounds include a renowned yew-hedge maze, where people have been going round in circles since 1846, walled and sunken gardens, and a 300-feet pergola. There's also a sweet little miniature railway, and **Fritton Lake Countryworld**, part of the Somerleyton Estate, is a 10-minute drive away. At Fritton Lake

guests can stay in eco-friendly self-contained lodges, dotted among the mature woodland on the edge of East Anglia's most beautiful stretch of water. The Hall is open to the public on most days in summer.

HERRINGFLEET

5 miles NW of Lowestoft on the B1074

Standing above the River Waveney, the parish **Church of St Margaret** is a charming sight with its Saxon round tower, thatched roof and lovely glass. **Herringfleet Windmill** is a beautiful black-tarred smock mill in working order, the last survivor of the Broadland wind pump, whose job was to assist in draining the marshes. This example was built in 1820 and worked regularly until the 1950s. It contains a fireplace and a wooden bench, providing a modicum of comfort for a millman on a cold night shift. To arrange a visit call 01473 583352.

KESSINGLAND

3 miles S of Lowestoft off the A12

The tower of the church of St Edmund reaches up almost 100 feet – not unusual on the coast - where it provides a conspicuous landmark for sailors and fishermen. Most of Kessingland's maritime trappings from its prosperous past have now disappeared: the lighthouse on the cliffs was scrapped 100 years ago, the lifeboat lasted until 1936 (having saved 144 lives), and one of the several former coastguard stations was purchased by the writer Rider

Haggard as a holiday home. However, it has once again become quite prosperous, but now it is people rather than fish that are bringing in wealth. The holiday village and chalets greatly increases the population of Kessingland during the summer months, with tourists yearning for a piece of sand, sea and beautiful Suffolk countryside.

COVEHITHE

7 miles S of Lowestoft off the A12

Leave the A12 at Wrentham and head for the tiny coastal village of Covehithe, remarkable for its 'church within a church'. The massive **Church of St Andrew**, partly funded by the Benedictine monks at Cluniac, was left to decline after being laid waste by William Dowsing's men. The villagers could not afford a replacement on the same grand scale, so in 1672 it was decided to remove the roof and sell off some of the material. From what was left a small new church was built within the old walls. The original tower still stands, spared by Cromwell for use as a landmark for sailors.

SOUTHWOLD

A town full of character and interest for the holidaymaker and for the historian. Though one of the most popular resorts on the east coast, Southwold has very little of the kiss-me-quick commercialism that spoils so many seaside towns. It's practically an island, bounded by creeks and marshes, the River Blyth

and the North Sea, and has managed to retain the genteel atmosphere of the 19th century. There are some attractive buildings, from pink-washed cottages to elegant Georgian town houses, many of them ranged around a series of open spaces – the 'Southwold Greens' – which were left undeveloped to act as firebreaks after much of the town was lost in the great fire of 1659.

In a seaside town whose buildings present a wide variety of styles, shapes and sizes, William Denny's **Buckenham House** is among the most elegant and interesting. On the face of it a classic Georgian town house, it's actually much older, dating probably from the middle of the 16th century. Richard Buckenham, a wealthy Tudor merchant, was the

Southwold, which was granted its charter by Henry VII in 1489, once prospered, like many of its neighbours, through herring fishing, and the few remaining fishermen share the harbour on the River Blyth with pleasure craft. Also adding to the period atmosphere is the recently renovated 1900 pier, which was once named Pier of the Year by the National Piers Society; as a result of storm damage this is much shorter than in the days when steamers from London called in on their way up the east coast.

The Beach, Southwold

- At Wangford is the Perpendicular Church of St Peter and St Paul, built on the site of a Benedictine priory. Even closer to Southwold is Reydon Wood Nature Reserve, which is run by the Suffolk Wildlife Trust and famous for its bluebells in the Spring.

-

man who had it built and it was truly impressive in size, as can be deduced from the dimensions of the cellar (now the Buckenham Coffee House). Many fine features survive, including moulded cornices, carefully restored sash windows, Tudor brickwork and heavy timbers in the ceilings.

There are also bathing huts, and a brilliant white **Lighthouse** that's over 100 years old. It stands 100 feet tall and its light can be seen 17 miles out to sea. Guided tours of the lighthouse culminate in unrivalled views over the town and out to sea. Beneath the lighthouse stands a little Victorian pub, the **Sole Bay Inn**, whose name recalls a battle fought off Southwold in 1672 between the British and French fleets and the Dutch. This was an episode in the Third Anglo-Dutch War, when the Duke of York, Lord High Admiral of England and later to be crowned James II, used Sutherland House in Southwold as his headquarters and launched his fleet (along with that of the French) from here. One distinguished victim of this battle was Edward Montagu, 1st Earl of Sandwich, great-grandfather of the man whose gambling mania did not allow him time for a formal meal. By inserting slices of meat between slices of bread, the 4th Earl ensured that his name would live on.

Southwold's maritime past is recorded in the **Museum** set in a Dutch-style cottage in Victoria Street – the small cottage has by no means restricted the scope of subjects covered and displays on show however; they have made the

very best of every bit of space! Open daily in the summer months, it records the famous battle and also features exhibits on local archaeology, geology and natural history, the history of the Southwold railway, and the history of the town's tourism. An interactive section has been added recently, as well as enhanced displays. From the museum you can purchase one of the booklets the Southwold Historical Society publishes itself on different aspects of the town's rich history. The **Southwold Sailors' Reading Room** contains pictures, ship models and other items, and at Gun Hill the Southwold **Lifeboat Museum** has a small collection of RNLI-related material with particular reference to Southwold. The main attraction at **Gun Hill** is a set of six 18-pounder guns, captured in 1746 at the Battle of Culloden and presented to the town (hitherto more or less undefended) by the Duke of Cumberland. Amber has been found on the beaches of Southwold for many years, and at the back of the Amber Shop in the market place is an **Amber Museum** with a large number of amber pieces, some in original form, others carved into beautiful pieces of jewellery.

AROUND SOUTHWOLD

WANGFORD

2 miles NW of Southwold off the A12

There's some great walking in the country around Southwold, both along the coast and inland. At Wangford, a mile or so inland, **Henham Walks** are waymarked paths through Repton Park, lake and woods. A splendid place for a ramble or a picnic, or to see the wildlife, rare-breed sheep and Highland cattle, the paths are open only on specific dates, and there's an entry fee.

BLYTHBURGH

2 miles SW of Southwold, A1095 then A12

Blythburgh's **Church of Holy Trinity** is one of the wonders of Suffolk, a stirring sight as it rises from the reed beds, visible for miles around and floodlit at night to spectacular effect. This 'Cathedral of the Marshes' reflects the days when Blythburgh was a prosperous port with a bustling quayside wool trade. With the silting up of the river, trade rapidly fell off and the church fell into decay. In 1577 the steeple of the 14th century tower was struck by lightning in a severe storm; it fell into the nave, shattering the font and took two lives. The scorch marks visible to this day on the north door are said to be the claw marks of the Devil in the guise of hellhound Black Shuck, left as he sped towards Bungay to terrify the congregation of St Mary's.

Disaster struck again in 1644, when Dowsing and his men smashed windows, ornaments and statues, blasted the wooden angels in the roof with hundreds of bullets and used the nave as a stable, with tethering rings screwed into the pillars of the nave. Luckily, the bench-end carvings escaped the desecration, not being labelled idolatrous. These depict the Labours of the Months, and the Seven Deadly Sins. Blythburgh also has a Jack o'the Clock, a brother of the figure at Southwold, and the priest's chamber over the south porch has been lovingly restored complete with an altar made with wood from HMS *Victory*. The angels may have survived, but the font was defaced to remove the signs of the sacraments.

Another angel worth mentioning in Blythburgh comes in the form of their beautiful and unique village sign, constructed lovingly by Suffolk artist Graham Chaplin who works in metals from his forge near Stowmarket. This amazing (and large!) sign, made to commemorate the millennium, has become known as "The Angel of the East" and makes a nice start or finish to a walk around the village.

The **Norman Gwatkin Nature Reserve** is an area of marsh and fen with two hides, walkways and a willow coppice.

WENHASTON

5 miles W of Southwold off the A12

The **Church of St Peter** is well worth a detour. Saxon stones are embedded in its walls, but the most remarkable feature is the Doom (Last Judgement scene), said to

Blythburgh Church of Holy Trinity

57 THE STAR INN

Wenhaston

Surrounded by rolling countryside The Star Inn is a cosy and traditional village pub close to the five heaths of Wenhaston Commons.

see page 259

97

have been painted around 1500 by a monk from Blythburgh.

When the rood was ordered to be taken down during the reign of Edward VI, the doom painting was covered with whitewash and not rediscovered until 1892.

WALBERSWICK

1 mile SW of Southwold on the B1387

The story is familiar: flourishing fishing port; grand church; changing of the coastline due to erosion and silting; decline of fishing and trading; no money to maintain the church; church falls into disrepair. Towards the end of the 16th century, a smaller church was built within the original St Andrew's, by then in ruins through neglect. The situation in Walberswick had also been exacerbated by the seizing of church lands and revenues by the King, and by a severe fire.

Fishing hardly exists today, and boating in Walberswick is almost entirely a weekend and holiday activity. The tiny 'church within a church' is still in use, its churchyard a nature reserve. South of the village is the bird sanctuary of **Walberswick & Westleton Heaths**.

HALESWORTH

16 miles SW of Lowestoft on the A144

Granted a market in 1222, Halesworth reached the peak of its trading importance when the River Blyth was made navigable as far as the town in 1756. A stroll around the streets reveals several buildings of architectural interest. The Market Place has a handsome

Elizabethan timber-framed house, but the chief attraction for the visitor is the **Halesworth and District Museum** at the railway station, in Station Road, where exhibits feature local geology and archaeology, with various fossils and flints on display, and there's also a fascinating account of the Halesworth witchcraft trials of 1645. A new exhibit plots the heart-warming story of resident Fred Knights; a tailor who worked from his home, with the front room being the fitting room, and cutting out and machining took place in the back room, which has been recreated in the museum.

Halesworth Gallery, at Steeple End, holds a collection of contemporary paintings, sculpture and other artwork in a converted row of 17th century almshouses.

BRAMFIELD

3 miles S of Halesworth on the A144

The massive Norman round tower of **St Andrew's Church** is separate from the main building and was built as a defensive structure, with walls over 3 feet thick. Dowsing ran riot here in 1643, destroying 24 superstitious pictures, one crucifix, a picture of Christ and 12 angels on the roof. The most important monument is one to Sir Arthur Coke, sometime Lord Chief Justice, who died in 1629, and his wife Elizabeth. Arthur is kneeling, resplendent in full armour, while Elizabeth is lying on her bed with a baby in her arms. This monument is the work of Nicholas Stone, the most important English mason and sculptor of his day. The Cokes at one time occupied Bramfield Hall, and another family, in residence for 300 years, were the Rabetts, whose coat of arms in the church punningly depicts rabbits on its shield.

BUNGAY

9 miles N of Halesworth on the A144

"Old Bungay's a wonderful town" goes the chorus to the town song, which accurately describes this ancient fortress town on the River Waveney. The river played an important part in Bungay's fortunes until well into the 18th century, with barges laden with coal, corn, malt and timber plying the route to the coast. The river is no longer navigable above Geldeston, but is a great attraction for anglers and yachtsmen.

Bungay is best known for its **Castle**, built in its original form by Hugh Bigod, 1st Earl of Norfolk, as a rival to Henry II's castle at Orford. In 1173 Hugh took the side of the rebellious sons of Henry, but this insurrection ended with the surrender of the castle to the King. Hugh was killed not long after this episode while on the Third Crusade; his son Roger inherited the title and the castle, but it was another Roger Bigod who came to Bungay in 1294 and built the round tower and mighty outer walls that stand today.

To the north of the castle are Bungay's two surviving churches of note (the *Domesday Book* records five). The Saxon round tower of **Holy Trinity Church** is the oldest

complete structure in the town, and a brass plate on the door commemorates the church's narrow escape from the fire of 1688 that destroyed much of the town (similar disasters overtook many other towns with close-set timber-and-thatch buildings). The **Church of St Mary** - now deconsecrated - was not so lucky, being more or less completely gutted. The tower survives to dominate the townscape, and points of interest in the church itself include a woodcarving of the Resurrection presented by Rider Haggard, and a monument to General Robert Kelso, who fought in the American War of Independence.

A century before the fire, the church received a visit, during a storm, from the devilish Black Shuck, a retriever-like hound who, hot from causing severe damage at Blythburgh, raced down the nave and killed two worshippers. A weather vane in the market place puts the legend into verse:

All down the church in midst of fire
The Hellish Monster Flew
And Passing onwards to the Quire
He many people slew.

Bungay Butter Cross

58 THE CHEQUERS INN

Bungay

A traditional pub serving homemade food in the thriving country market town of Bungay

‖ see page 259

99

59 THE SWAN HOUSE

Beccles

Specialising in modern Anglo and international cuisine, The Swan House is cosy, slightly eccentric and highly popular.

see page 260

FLIXTON

2 miles SW of Bungay on the B1062

Javelin, Meteor, Sea Vixen, Avro Anson C19, Dassault Mystère IVA, Westland Whirlwind: names that evoke earlier days of flying, and just four of more than 25 aircraft on show at the **Norfolk and Suffolk Aviation Museum**, on the site of a USAAF Liberator base during the Second World War. There's a lot of associated material, both civil and military, covering the period from the First World War to the present day. The museum incorporates the Royal Observer Corps Museum, RAF Bomber Command Museum, and the Museum and Memorial of the 446th Bomb Group - the Bungay Buckeroos. The museum has easy-access slopes to all parts not on ground level, and it has facilities for refreshments as well as a shop. Dogs are allowed in most parts of the museum, on a short leash. Last admission is one hour before closing. Tel: 01986 896644. American airmen presented the gates into Flixton churchyard.

MENDHAM

6 miles SW of Bungay off the A143

This pretty little village on the Waveney was the birthplace of Sir Alfred Munnings RA, who was born at Mendham Mill, where his father was the miller. Sir Alfred's painting *Charlotte and her Pony* was the inspiration for the village sign, which was unveiled by his niece Kathleen Hadingham.

BECCLES

9 miles W of Lowestoft on the A146

The largest town in the Waveney district at the southernmost point of the Broads, Beccles has in its time been home to Saxons and Vikings, and at one time the market here was a major supplier of herring (up to 60,000 a year) to the Abbey at Bury St Edmunds. At the height of its trading importance Beccles must have painted a splendidly animated picture, with wherries constantly on the move transporting goods from seaports to inland towns. The same stretch of river is still alive, but now with the yachts and pleasure boats of the holidaymakers and weekenders who fill the town in summer. The regatta in July and August is a particularly busy time.

Fire, sadly such a common part of small-town history, ravaged Beccles at various times in the 16th and 17th centuries, destroying much of the old town. For that reason the dwellings extant today are largely Georgian in origin, with handsome redbrick facades. One that is not is **Roos Hall**, a gabled building dating from 1583. Just outside the town, far enough away to escape the great fire of 1586, it was built to a Dutch design, underlining the links between East Anglia and the Low Countries forged by the wool and weaving trades. Elizabeth I stayed at the Hall just after it was completed, when she visited Beccles to present the town's charter; the occasion is depicted in the town sign. One of the hall's owners was Sir John Suckling (later to become Controller of the Household to James I), one of whose descendants was Lord Nelson. Any old hall worth its salt has ghosts, and the Roos has its fair share; a headless coachman who is said to appear on Christmas Eve; an oak tree in the grounds named after Nelson which is said to be haunted by those once hanged from its branches, including a woman in white; and on an inside wall, within a bedroom cupboard, is said to be the imprint of the Devil's hoof print burned into solid brick.

Down the A145 from Beccles, near Brampton, is the **Moo Play Farm** – an attraction which proves endlessly delightful for children up to 12 years old. Here they have everything you need for a great day out; indoor soft play area (with underfloor heating, perfect for those cold rainy days), and outdoor adventure play area, tractor rides, animal petting sections, alpacas, picnic areas and for adults there is a bistro café, as well as morning yoga and pilates sessions (which your young ones can join in too!). Tel: 01502 575841.

RINGSFIELD

2 miles SW of Beccles off the A146

In a wooded valley away from the main village, Ringfield's parish **Church of All Saints** has a dual appeal: the marvellous array of spring flowers in the churchyard and the story of the robins. A pair nested in the lectern 50 years ago and raised a family, an event recalled in carvings on the new lectern and on the porch gates. The original nest, in the old lectern, can still be found in the church.

SOUTH AND WEST SUFFOLK

IPSWICH

History highlights Ipswich as the birthplace of Cardinal Wolsey in 1475, but the story of Suffolk's county town starts very much earlier than that. It has been a port since the time of the Roman occupation, and by the 7th century the Anglo-Saxons had expanded it into the largest port in the country. King John granted a civic charter in 1200, confirming the townspeople's right to their own laws and administration, and for several centuries the town prospered as a port, exporting wool, textiles and agricultural products.

When the cloth market fell into decline in the 17th century, a respite followed in the following century, when the town was a food-distribution port during the Napoleonic Wars. At the beginning of the 19th century the risk from silting was becoming acute at a time when trade was improving and industries were springing up. The Wet Dock, constructed in 1842, solved the silting problem and, with the railway arriving shortly after, Ipswich could once more look forward to a safe future. The Victorians were responsible for considerable development: symbols

•

A fine building with Dutch-style gables houses the Beccles and District Museum, whose contents include 19th century toys and costume, farm implements, items from the old town gaol and memorabilia from the sailing wherries, including a wealth of old photographs. It is open from 1st April until 1st November, 2.15pm to 5.00pm daily except Mondays, when it is closed. Open on Bank Holidays during these months. There is great disabled access, as well as a small 'hands on' section for those with sight difficulties. Entry is free, but donations are gratefully received.

•

101

Christchurch Mansion is a beautiful Tudor home standing in 65 acres of attractive parkland a short walk from Ipswich town centre. Furnished as an English country house, it contains the biggest collection of works by Constable and Gainsborough outside of London, as well as many other paintings, prints and sculptures by Suffolk artists from the 17th century onwards.

of their civic pride include the handsome **Old Custom House** by the Wet Dock, the **Town Hall**, and the splendid **Tolly Cobbold** brewery, rebuilt at the end of the 19th century, 150 years after brewing started on the site. Victorian enterprise depleted some of the older buildings, but a number survive, notably the house where Wolsey was born, and the **Ancient House** (also called Sparrowe's House) with its wonderful pargeting and Royal Arms of Charles II – perhaps painted after the King hid here after the Battle of Worcester.

Fine former Tudor merchants' houses grace the town's historic waterfront, such as Isaac Lord's and **The Neptune** (the latter was once home of Thomas Eldred, who circumnavigated the world with Thomas Cavendish shortly after Drake). A dozen medieval churches remain, of which **St Margaret's** is the finest, boasting some very splendid flintwork and a double hammerbeam roof. Another, St Stephen's, today houses the town's Tourist Information Centre.

Wolsey Art Gallery is a purpose-built space entered through Christchurch Mansion which features changing displays including touring and national exhibitions. **Ipswich Museum** is in a Victorian building in the High Street. Displays include a natural history gallery, a wildlife gallery complete with a model of a mammoth, a reconstruction of a Roman villa, replicas of Sutton Hoo treasures and a display of elaborately carved timbers from the homes of wealthy 17th century merchants. There is also a rolling programme of exciting temporary exhibitions, events and displays. It is open Tuesday to Saturday 10am-5pm all year round, excluding Christmas and New Year.

Outside of the town centre, on Cobham Road, is the **Ipswich Transport Museum** (bus service 2 from the town centre runs every 30mins Mon-Sat from the town centre and stops right at the museum's doorstep). Preserving the transport heritage of Ipswich since 1965, it contains the largest

Wolsley's Gate, Ipswich

The Marina, Ipswich

60 THE ROYAL OAK

Ipswich

The Royal Oak is heralded as the place to be in Ipswich for live music.

see page 260

collection of transportation items dedicated to one town in Britain. The extensive collection includes horse and electric trams, trolleybuses and Ipswich buses (one of the few bus services in the UK still owned by the council), as well as aviation displays from Ipswich Airport which was closed in 1996 to make way for a housing estate. Their shop is stocked with all of the fascinating books on Ipswich transport you will ever find, as well as gifts, DVDs, toys suitable for children and some great accurate models. Tel: 01473 715666.

Ipswich's position at the head of the River Orwell has always influenced the town's fortunes; today, a stroll along the waterfront should be included in any visit. Tudor houses and medieval churches stand alongside stylish new apartments which overlook the new marinas. An art gallery and choice of eateries enhance the experience, and there are regular pub cruises, leaving the Ipswich waterfront and travelling the pretty River Orwell as far as Felixstowe harbour.

Notables from the world of the arts with Ipswich connections include Thomas Gainsborough, who got his first major commissions here to paint portraits of local people; David Garrick, the renowned actor-manager, who made his debut here in 1741 as Aboan in Thomas Southerne's *Oroonoko*; and the peripatetic Charles Dickens, who stayed at the Great White Horse while still a young reporter with the Morning Chronicle. Soon afterwards, he featured the tavern in *The Pickwick Papers* as the place where Mr Pickwick wanders inadvertently into a lady's bedroom. Sir V S Pritchett was born in Ipswich, while Enid Blyton trained as a kindergarten teacher at Ipswich High School.

61 DAMERONS FARM HOLIDAYS

Henley

A complex of five self catering cottages with many facilities for all of the family.

see page 261

62 THE GREYHOUND PUBLIC HOUSE

Claydon

A grade II listed, 15th century and thoroughly pink pub offering excellent food and drink all week long.

 see page 261

63 THE SORRELL HORSE INN

Barham

A 17th century inn offering real ales, home cooking and accommodation in a converted barn.

  see page 262

AROUND IPSWICH

BRAMFORD

2 miles NW of Ipswich off the A14

Bramford has a pretty little church, St Mary's, with a 13th century stone screen. It was once an important spot on the river route, when barges from Ipswich stopped to unload corn; the walls of the old lock are still visible. In the vicinity is **Suffolk Water Park**, which offers superb fishing for anglers, and lessons with experienced professionals for beginners, on a day-ticket basis. It has all the ingredients for a peaceful trip; scenic views, large platforms with plenty of space from other anglers, nearby parking, and a café and bait shop within the park. Open 7 days a week from 7am. Dogs are not allowed in the park. Tel: 01473 832327.

BAYLHAM

5 miles NW of Ipswich off the B11130

The Roman site of Combretrovium is home to the small **Baylham House Rare Breeds Farm**, and visitors (April-early October) will find displays and information relating to both Rome and rare animals. The farm's chief concern is the survival of rare breeds, and there are breeding groups of cattle, sheep, pigs, goats and poultry; including foreign breeds Kune Kune pigs and Ouessant sheep. There is a visitor's centre with a shop, which serves refreshments and light lunches, and there is a picnic area in the grounds. Tel: 01473 830264.

NACTON

4 miles SE of Ipswich off the A14

South of Nacton's medieval church lies **Orwell Park House**, which was built in the 18th century by Admiral Edward Vernon, sometime Member of Parliament for Ipswich. The admiral, who had won an important victory over the Spanish in the War of Jenkins Ear, was known to his men as 'Old Grog' because of his habit of wearing a cloak of coarse grogram cloth. His nickname passed into the language when he ordered that the rum ration dished out daily to sailors should be diluted with water to combat the drunkenness that was rife in the service. That was in 1740, but this allotted ration of 'grog' was officially issued to sailors right up until 1970.

Nacton Picnic Site in Shore Lane (signposted from the village) commands wonderful views of the Orwell and is a prime spot in winter for birdwatchers. The birds feed very well off the mud flats.

LEVINGTON

5 miles SE of Ipswich off the A14

A pretty village on the banks of the Orwell. Fisons established a factory here in 1956, and developed the now famous Levington Compost. On the foreshore below the village is an extensive marina which has brought a bustling air to the area. The coastal footpath along the bank of the Orwell leads across the nature reserve of **Trimley Marshes** and on to Felixstowe.

TRIMLEY ST MARY & TRIMLEY ST MARTIN

6 miles SE of Ipswich off the A14

Twin villages with two churches in the same churchyard, famous Trimley residents have included the Cavendish family, whose best-known member was the adventurer Thomas Cavendish. In 1590 he became the second man to sail round the world. Two years later he died while embarked on another voyage. He is depicted on the village sign.

NEWBOURNE

7 miles E of Ipswich off the A12

A small miracle occurred here on the night of the hurricane of October 1987. One wall of the ancient **St Mary's Church** was blown out, and with it the stained glass, which shattered into fragments. One piece, showing the face of Christ, was found undamaged and was later incorporated into the rebuilt wall.

Two remarkable inhabitants of Newbourne were the Page brothers, who both stood over 7 feet tall; they enjoyed a career touring the fairs, and are buried in Newbourne churchyard.

WALDRINGFIELD

7 miles E of Ipswich off the A12

Waldringfield lies on a particularly beautiful stretch of the Deben estuary, and the waterfront is largely given over to leisure boating and cruising. The quay was once busy with barges, many of them laden with coprolite. This fossilised

dung, the forerunner of today's fertilisers, was found in great abundance in and around Waldringfield, and a number of exhausted pits can still be seen.

FELIXSTOWE

12 miles SE of Ipswich off the A14

Until the early 17th century, Felixstowe was a little-known village - but it was the good Colonel Tomline of Orwell Park who put it on the map by creating a port to rival its near neighbour Harwich. He also started work on the Ipswich-Felixstowe railway (with a stop at Nacton for the

Felixstowe Museum

64 FISHERMANS HALL

Felixstowe Ferry

A quality bed and breakfast in a sleepy hamlet that provides the perfect base for those exploring the area.

see page 261

Felixstowe Museum is actually housed in the Ravelin Block (1878), which was used as a mine storage depot by the army when a mine barrier was laid across the Orwell during the First World War. A fascinating variety of exhibits includes local history, model aircraft and model paddle steamers, Roman coins and the history of the fort itself, which was the scene of the last invasion of English soil. In 1667 Captain Nathaniel Darell and 500 men defeated Admiral de Ruyter's Dutch force. The fort is open daily from May to October. Beyond the fort is an excellent viewing point for watching the comings and goings of ships.

guests of his grand parties), and 1887 saw the completion of both projects. Tomline also developed the resort aspects of Felixstowe, rivalling the amenities of Dovercourt, and when he died in 1887 most of his dreams had become reality. (He was, incidentally, cremated, one of the first in the county to be so disposed of in the modern era.) The town has suffered a number of ups and downs since that time, but continues to thrive as one of England's busiest ports, having been much extended in the 1960s. The resort is strung out round a wide, gently curving bay, where the long seafront road is made even prettier with trim lawns and gardens.

All kinds of attractions are provided for holidaymakers, including indoor and outdoor adventure golf, miniature train rides and a boating lake – as well as traditional seaside amusement arcades which line the seafront.

The Martello Tower in Felixstowe is a noted landmark, as is the Pier, which was once long enough to merit an electric tramway. It was shortened as a security measure during the Second World War, and sadly has never quite recovered; despite plans over the years to restore the pier it is now closed to the public and seemingly doomed by a demolition order (the unfortunate fate of many piers around Britain).

At the southernmost tip of the peninsula is **Landguard Point**, where a nature reserve supports rare plants and migrating birds. From this end of Felixstowe is a foot ferry which links to Shotley and Harwich.

Just north on this shingle bank is **Landguard Fort**, built in 1718 to protect Harwich harbour and replacing an earlier construction ordered by Henry VIII. It is now home to **Felixstowe Museum**.

FRESTON

3 miles S of Ipswich off the B1080

Freston is an ancient village on the south bank of the Orwell, worth visiting for some fine old buildings and some curiosities. The most curious and best known of these buildings is **Freston Folly**, a six-storey Tudor tower by the river in **Freston Park** (it's actually best viewed from across the river). This redbrick house, built around 1570, has just six rooms, one per storey. It might be a folly, but it was probably put up as a lookout tower

Freston Folly

to warn of enemies sailing up the river. The nicest theory is that it was built for Ellen, daughter of Lord Freston, to study a different subject each day, progressing floor by floor up the tower (and with Sundays off, presumably). Studies started with charity at 7 am, and continued onwards and upwards with tapestry, music, painting, literature and astronomy. On the south side of **St Peter's Church** grounds in Freston is a wonderful wooden statue of Peace holding a laurel wreath high, a fitting memorial for the war.

WOOLVERSTONE

4 miles S of Ipswich on the B1456

Dating back to the Bronze Age, Woolverstone has a large marina along the banks of the Orwell. One of the buildings in the complex is **Cat House**, where it is said that a stuffed white cat placed in the window would be the all-clear sign for smugglers. **Woolverstone House** was originally St Peter's Home for 'Fallen Women', run by nuns. It was designed by Sir Edwin Lutyens and has its own chapel and bell tower.

TATTINGSTONE

4 miles S of Ipswich off the A137

The **Tattingstone Wonder**, on the road between Tattingstone and Stutton, looks like a church from the front, but it isn't. It is a folly, built by a local landowner to provide accommodation for estate workers. He presumably preferred to look at a church from his mansion than some plain little

cottages. Tattingstone lies at the western edge of Alton Water, a vast man-made lake created as a reservoir in the late 1970s. A footpath runs round the perimeter, and there's a wildlife sanctuary. On the water itself all sorts of leisure activities are on offer, including angling, sailing and windsurfing.

STUTTON

6 miles S of Ipswich on the B1080

The elongated village of Stutton lies on the southern edge of Alton Water. The *Domesday Book* records six manor houses standing here, and there are still some grand properties down by the Stour. **St Peter's Church** stands isolated overlooking Holbrook Bay, and a footpath from the church leads all the way along the river to Shotley Gate. A little way north, on the B1080, Holbrook is a large village with a brook at the bottom of the hill. Water from the brook once powered Alton Mill, a weather-boarded edifice on a site occupied by watermills for more than 900 years. The mill is now a restaurant.

CHELMONDISTON

5 miles SE of Ipswich on the B1456

The church here is modern, but incorporates some parts of the original, which was destroyed by a flying bomb in 1944. In the same parish is the tiny riverside community of **Pin Mill**, a well-known beauty spot and sailing centre. The river views are particularly lovely at this point, and it's also a favourite place for woodland and heathland walks.

107

Orwell Estuary

Pin Mill was once a major manufacturer of barges, and those imposing craft can still be seen, sharing the river with sailing boats and pleasure craft. Each year veteran barges gather for a race that starts here, at Buttermans Bay, and ends at Harwich. It is also said that Pin Mill was once a haven for smugglers, presumably for its sheltered position tucked into a bend on the River Orwell. Arthur Ransome, author of *Swallows and Amazons*, stayed here and had boats built to his specifications. His *We*

Didn't Mean to Go to Sea starts aboard a yacht moored here.

ERWARTON
6 miles SE of Ipswich off the B1456

An impressive redbrick Jacobean gatehouse with a rounded arch, buttresses and pinnacles is part of **Erwarton Hall**, the family home of the Calthorpes. Anne Boleyn was the niece of Philip Calthorpe, and visited as a child and as queen. Just before her execution Anne apparently requested that her heart be buried in the family vault at St Mary's Church. A casket in the shape of a heart was found there in 1836, but when opened contained only dust that could not be positively identified. The casket was resealed and laid in the Lady Chapel.

SHOTLEY
8 miles SE of Ipswich on the B1456

Right at the end of the peninsula, with the Orwell on one side and the Stour on the other, Shotley was the home of HMS *Ganges*, where generations of sailors received their training. In the parish of Shotley there are several listed buildings and recently Napoleonic era buildings and fortifications have been discovered. At the very tip of the Shotley Peninsula is a large marina where a classic boat festival is an annual occasion.

HINTLESHAM
7 miles W of Ipswich on the A1071

Hintlesham's glory is a magnificent hall dating from the 1570s, when it was the home of the Timperley family. It was considerably altered during the 18th century, when it acquired its splendid Georgian façade. For some years the hall was owned by the celebrated chef Robert Carrier, who developed it into the county's leading restaurant. It still functions as a high-class hotel and restaurant.

HADLEIGH

10 miles W of Ipswich on the A1071

The name Hadleigh is believed to derive from the Norse Haethlega (a heath-covered place). The old and not-so-old blend harmoniously in a variety of architectural styles in Hadleigh. Timber-framed buildings, often with elaborate plasterwork, stand in the long main street as a reminder of the prosperity generated by the wool trade in the 14th to 16th centuries, and there are also some fine houses from the Regency and Victorian periods. The 15th century **Guildhall** has two overhanging storeys, and together with the **Deanery Tower** and the church makes for a magnificent trio of huge appeal and contrasting construction – timber for the Guildhall, brick for the tower and flint for the church.

KERSEY

12 miles W of Ipswich off the A1141

The ultimate Suffolk picture-postcard village, Kersey boasts a wonderful collection of timbered merchants' houses and weavers' cottages with paint and thatch. The main street has a **Water Splash**, which, along with the 700-year-old Bell Inn, has featured in many films and travelogues. The **Church of St**

Mary, which overlooks the village from its hilltop position, is of massive proportions, testimony to the wealth that came with the wool and cloth industry. Kersey's speciality was a coarse twill broadcloth much favoured for greatcoats and army uniforms. Headless angels and mutilated carvings are reminders of the Puritans' visit to the church, though some treasures survive, including the ornate flintwork of the 15th century south porch. Traditional craftsmanship can still be seen in practice at the **Kersey Pottery**, which sells many items of stoneware plus paintings by Suffolk artists.

CHELSWORTH

14 miles W of Ipswich off the A1141

Chelsworth is an unspoilt delight in the lovely valley of the River Brett, which is crossed by a little double hump-backed bridge. The timbered houses and thatched cottages look much the same as when they were built, and every year the villagers open their gardens to the public.

MONKS ELEIGH

16 miles W of Ipswich on the A1141

The picture-postcard setting of thatched cottages, a 14th century church and a pump on the village green is so traditional that Monks Eleigh was regularly used on railway posters as a lure to this wonderful part of the country.

BILDESTON

14 miles W of Ipswich on the B1115

More fine old buildings here, including timber-framed cottages

65 RIVERSIDE COTTAGE & HORNES B&B

Great Bricett, nr Ipswich

Two thatched cottages and an adjoining studio provide a choice of quiet B&B and self-catering accommodation.

⊨ *see page 263*

•

The beautiful St Mary's Church in Hadleigh must be quite a rousing sight - impressively it has been painted by no less than four great artists; Morris, Constable, Turner and Gainsborough. In the south chapel of the church is a 14th century bench-end carving depicting the legendary scene of the wolf guarding the head of St Edmund. The wolf is wearing a monk's habit, indicating a satirical sense of humour in the carpenter. Also of interest is the Clock Bell, which stands outside the tower.

•

More than 350 of Lavenham's buildings are officially listed as being of architectural and historical interest, and none of them is finer than the Guildhall (National Trust). This superb 16th century timbered building was originally the meeting place of the Guild of Corpus Christi, an organisation that regulated the production of wool. It now houses exhibitions of local history and the wool trade, and has a walled garden with a special area devoted to dye plants. Tel: 01787 247646.

John Constable went to school in Lavenham, where one of his friends was Jane Taylor, who wrote the words to 'Twinkle Twinkle Little Star'.

with overhanging upper floors. The **Church of St Mary** has a superb carved door and a splendid hammerbeam roof. A tablet inside the church commemorates Captain Edward Rotherham, Commander of the Royal Sovereign at the Battle of Trafalgar. He died in Bildeston while staying with a friend, and is buried in the churchyard. The local manor was once a royal estate owned by Queen Edith, consort of Edward the Confessor. The only trace of the manor is an ancient manorial wood, enclosed by a deep ditch.

BRENT ELEIGH

17 miles W of Ipswich off the A1141

The **Church of St Mary**, on a side road off the A1141, is remarkable for a number of quite beautiful ancient wall paintings, discovered during maintenance work as recently as 1960. The most striking and moving of the paintings is one of the Crucifixion.

LAVENHAM

18 miles W of Ipswich on the A1141

An absolute gem of a town, the most complete and original of the medieval 'wool towns', with crooked timbered and whitewashed buildings lining the narrow streets from the 14th to the 16th centuries, Lavenham flourished as one of the leading wool and cloth-making centres in the land. With the decline of that industry, however, the prosperous times soon came to an end. It is largely due to the fact that Lavenham found no replacement industry that so much of its medieval character remains:

there was simply not enough money for the rebuilding and development programmes that changed many other towns, often for the worse. The medieval street pattern still exists, complete with market place and market cross.

Little Hall is a 15th century hall house with a superb crown post roof. It was restored by the Gayer Anderson brothers, and has a fine collection of their furniture. It is now a museum which mirrors the history of the town over the centuries, open from Easter until the end of summer.

The **Church of St Peter and St Paul** dominates the town from its elevated position. It's a building of great distinction, perhaps the greatest of all the 'wool churches', and declared by the 19th century architect August Pugin to be the finest example of late-Perpendicular style in the world. It was built, with generous help from wealthy local families (notably the Spryngs and the de Veres) in the late 15th and early 16th centuries to celebrate the end of the Wars of the Roses. Its flint tower is a mighty 140 feet in height, and it's possible to climb to the top to take in the glorious views over Lavenham and the surrounding countryside. Richly carved screens and fine (Victorian) stained glass are eye-catching features within.

Set in 3 acres of grounds in the centre of Lavenham is **The Priory**; a Grade I listed building, which originated in the 13th century as a farm for Benedictine monks, the present beautiful timber-framed house dating from about 1600. In the original hall, at the centre of the building, is a striking stained-glass window. It is now an award winning 5 star bed and breakfast. The beautiful **Swan Hotel** in Lavenham played a key role in the wool trade in the 15th century, and is now a 4 star hotel with a relaxed, traditional atmosphere and original oak beams and inglenook fireplaces.

To get a real feel for Lavenham there are guided walks through the town, starting from the tourist Information Centre. They run from mid June to end of October, Saturdays at 2.30pm and Sundays at 11am. On the 13th June and 4th October special walks are run, with the guides in medieval dress. There is no need to book – just turn up.

SUDBURY

Sudbury is another wonderful town, the largest of the 'wool towns' and still home to a number of weaving concerns.

Sudbury boasts three medieval churches, but what most visitors make a beeline for is **Gainsborough's House** in Gainsborough Street. The painter Thomas Gainsborough was born here in 1727 in the house built by his father John. Around 25 oil paintings are on show, including a magnificent landscape of 1782 and a touching miniature of his wife, and among the memorabilia to be seen in the house are the artist's studio cabinet, his swordstick and his pocket watch. A changing

Lavenham Guildhall

programme of contemporary art exhibitions includes fine art, photography and sculpture, highlighting East Anglian artists in particular, and the print workshop hosts evening classes and summer courses in the techniques of etching, screenprinting, stone lithography and relief printing. A bronze statue of Gainsborough stands in the square.

About those churches: **All Saints** dates from the 15th century and has a glorious carved tracery pulpit and screens; 14th century **St Gregory's** is notable for a wonderful medieval font; and **St Peter's** has some marvellous painted screen panels and a piece of 15th century embroidered velvet.

Other buildings of interest are the Victorian **Corn Exchange**, now a library; **Salter's Hall**, a 15th century timbered house; and the **Quay Theatre**, a thriving centre for the arts.

Unlike Lavenham, Sudbury kept its weaving industry longer because it was a port, and the result is a much more varied architectural picture. The surrounding countryside is some of the loveliest in Suffolk, and the River Stour is a further plus, with launch trips and fishing available.

The decline of the cloth trade in East Anglia had several causes. Fierce competition came from the northern and western weaving industries, which generally had easier access to water supplies for fulling; the wars on the continent of Europe led to the closure of some trading routes and markets; and East Anglia had no supplies of the coal that was used to drive the new steam-powered machinery. In some cases, as at Sudbury, weaving or silk took over as smaller industries.

CONSTABLE COUNTRY

England's greatest landscape painter was born at East Bergholt in 1776 and remained at heart a Suffolk man throughout his life. His father, Golding Constable, was a wealthy man who owned both Flatford Mill and Dedham Mill, the latter on the Essex side of the Stour. The river was a major source of inspiration to the young John Constable, and his constant involvement in country matters gave him an expert knowledge of the elements and a keen eye for the details of nature. He was later to declare: *'I associate my careless boyhood with all that lies on the banks of the Stour. Those scenes made me a painter and I am grateful.'*

Salter's Hall, Sudbury

His interest in painting developed early and was fostered by his friendship with John Dunthorne, a local plumber and amateur artist. Constable became a probationer at the Royal Academy Schools in 1799, and over the following years developed the technical skills to match his powers of observation. He painted the occasional portrait and even attempted a couple of religious works, but he concentrated almost entirely on the scenes that he knew and loved as a boy. Two quotations from Constable himself reveal much about his aims and philosophy:

'In a landscape I want to give one brief moment caught from fleeting time a lasting and sober existence.'

'I never saw any ugly thing in my life; in fact, whatever may be the shape of an object, light, shade or perspective can always make it beautiful.'

The most significant works of the earlier years were the numerous sketches in oil which were forerunners of the major paintings of Constable's mature years. He had exhibited at the Royal Academy every year since 1802, but it was not until 1817 that the first of his important canvases, *Flatford Mill on the River Stour*, was hung. This was succeeded by the six large paintings which became his best-known works. These were all set on a short stretch of the Stour, and all except *The Hay Wain* show barges at work. These broad, flat-bottomed craft were displayed in scenes remarkable for the realism of the colours, the effects of light and water and, above all, the beautiful depiction of clouds. His fellow-artist Fuseli declared that whenever he saw a Constable painting he felt the need to reach for his coat and umbrella. Though more realistic than anything that preceded them, Constable's paintings were never lacking soul, and his work was much admired by the painters of the French Romantic School.

At the time of his death in 1837, Constable's reputation at home was relatively modest, though he had many followers and admirers in France. Awareness and understanding of his unique talent grew only in the ensuing years, so that, today, his place as England's foremost landscape painter is rarely disputed.

The Suffolk tradition of painting continues to this day, with many artists drawn to this part of the county. While nowadays crowds congregate throughout the Stour valley at summer weekends, at other times the tranquillity and loveliness are just as unmatched as they were in Constable's day.

BRANTHAM
8 miles SW of Ipswich on the A137

Also known as 'Burnt Village' – possibly because it was sacked during a Danish invasion 1,000 years ago – Brantham's **Church of St Michael** owns one of the only two known religious paintings by Constable, *Christ Blessing the Children*, which he executed in the style of the American painter Benjamin West. It is kept in safety in Ipswich Museum. The church

Suffolk has produced many other painters of distinction. Thomas Gainsborough, born in Sudbury in 1727, was an artist of great versatility, innovative and instinctive, and equally at home with portraits and landscapes. He earned his living for a while from portrait painting in Ipswich before making a real name for himself in Bath. His relations with the Royal Academy were often stormy, however, culminating in 1784 in a major dispute over the height at which a painting should be hung. He withdrew his intended hangings from the exhibition and never again showed at the Royal Academy. Mary Beale, born at Barrow in 1633, was a noted portrait painter and copyist; some of her work has been attributed to Lely and Kneller, and it was rumoured that Lely was in love with her. Philip Wilson Steer (1860-1942) was among the most distinguished of the many painters who were attracted to Walberswick. He studied in Paris and acquired the reputation of being the best of the English impressionist painters.

113

also has a large and interestingly curved lychgate by architect Edward Schroeder Prior.

EAST BERGHOLT

8 miles SW of Ipswich on the B1070

Narrow lanes lead to this picturesque and much-visited little village. The **Constable Country Trail** starts here, where the painter was born, and passes through Flatford Mill and on to Dedham in Essex. The actual house where he was born no longer stands, but the site is marked by a plaque on the fence of its successor, a private house called Constables. A little further along Church Street is Moss Cottage, which Constable once used as his studio.

St Mary's Church is one of the many grand churches built with the wealth brought by the wool trade. This one should have been even grander, with a tower to rival that of Dedham across the river. The story goes that Cardinal Wolsey pledged the money to build the tower, but fell from grace before the funds were forthcoming. The tower got no further than did his college in Ipswich, and a bellcage constructed in the churchyard as a temporary house for the bells became their permanent home, which it remains to this day. In this unique timber-framed structure the massive bells hang upside down and are rung by hand by pulling on the wooden shoulder stocks - an arduous task, as the five bells are among the heaviest in England.

The church is naturally something of a shrine to Constable,

his family and his friends. There are memorial windows to the artist and to his beloved wife Maria Bicknell, who bore him seven children and whose early death was an enormous blow to him. His parents, to whom he was clearly devoted, and his old friend Willy Lott, whose cottage is featured famously in The Hay Wain, are buried in the churchyard.

East Bergholt has an interesting mix of houses, some dating back as far as the 14th century. One of the grandest is **Stour House**, once the home of Randolph Churchill. Its gardens are open to the public, as is **East Bergholt Place Garden** on the B1070.

A leafy lane leads south from the village to the Stour, where two of Constable's favourite subjects, **Flatford Mill** and **Willy Lott's Cottage**, both looking much as they did when he painted them, are to be found. Neither is open to the public, and the brick watermill is run as a residential field study centre.

STRATFORD ST MARY

10 miles SW of Ipswich off the A12

Another of Constable's favourite locations, Stratford St Mary is the most southerly village in Suffolk. *The Young Waltonians* and *A House in Water Lane* (the house still stands today) are the best known of his works set in this picturesque spot. The village church is typically large and imposing, with parts dating back to 1200. At the top of the village are two splendid half-timbered cottages called the Ancient House and the Priest's House. Stratford was once on the main coaching route to London, and the largest of the four pubs had stabling for 200 horses. It is claimed that Henry Williamson, author of *Tarka the Otter*, saw his first otter here.

NAYLAND

14 miles SW of Ipswich on the B1087

On a particularly beautiful stretch of the Stour in Dedham Vale, Nayland has charming colour-washed cottages in narrow, winding streets, as well as two very fine 15th century buildings in Alston Court and the Guildhall. **Abels Bridge**, originally built of wood in the 15th century by wealthy merchant John Abel, divides Suffolk from Essex. In the 16th century a hump bridge replaced it, allowing barges to pass beneath. The current bridge carries the original keystone, bearing the initial A. In the **Church of St James** stands an altarpiece by Constable entitled *Christ Blessing the Bread and Wine*.

STOKE BY NAYLAND

12 miles SW of Ipswich on the B1087

The drive from Nayland reveals quite stunning views, and the village itself has a large number of listed buildings. The magnificent **Church of St Mary**, with its 120-feet tower, dominates the scene from its hilltop position. This church also dominates more than one Constable painting, the most famous showing the church lit up by a rainbow. William Dowsing destroyed 100 'superstitious pictures' here in his Puritan purges, but plenty of fine work is still to be seen, including several monumental brasses.

POLSTEAD

11 miles SW of Ipswich off the B1068

Polstead is a very pretty village set in wooded, hilly countryside, with thatched, colour-washed cottages around the green and a wide duck pond at the bottom of the hill. Standing on a rise above the pond are **Polstead Hall**, a handsome Georgian mansion, and the 12th century **Church of St Mary**. The church has two features not found elsewhere in Suffolk – a stone spire and the very early bricks used in its construction. The builders used not only these bricks, but also tiles and tufa, a soft, porous stone much used in Italy. In the grounds of the hall stand the remains of a 'Gospel Oak' said to have been 1,300 years old when it collapsed in 1953. Legend has it that Saxon missionaries preached beneath it in the 7th century; an open-air service is still held here annually.

Polstead has two unique claims to fame. One is for Polstead Blacks, a particularly tasty variety of cherry which was cultivated in orchards around the village and which used to be honoured with an annual fair. The other is much less agreeable, for it was here that the notorious Red Barn murder hit the headlines in 1827. A young girl called Maria Marten, daughter of the local molecatcher, disappeared with William Corder, a farmer's son who was the girl's lover and father of her child. It was at first thought that they had eloped, but Maria's stepmother dreamt three times that she had been murdered and buried

One mile west of Nayland, at the end of a track off the Bures road, stands the Norman Church of St Mary at Wissington. The church has a number of remarkable features, including several 13th century wall paintings, a finely carved 12th century doorway and a tiebeam and crown post roof.

•
There are accounts from 1405 which tell of a dragon being seen in Bures, eating many sheep (and shepherds), and terrorising the community – the neighboring village of Wormingford claim to have slayed it. Amusing as this tale is – it is thought that this was indeed an escaped crocodile, given to Richard I as a gift, rather than a mythical creature.
•

in a red barn. A search of the barn soon revealed this to be true. Corder was tracked down to Middlesex, tried and found guilty of Maria's murder and hanged. Until August 2004 his skeleton was kept at the Royal College of Surgeons of England's Hunterian Museum in London, where it was taken in 1949. After a long campaign by a descendant of Corder, the skeleton was released and was cremated at London's Streatham crematorium.) The murder aroused a great deal of interest at the time, and today's visitors to the village will still find reminders of the ghastly deed: the thatched cottage where Maria lived stands, in what is now called Marten's Lane, and the farm where the murderer lived, now called Corder's Farm. Maria is buried in St Mary's Church in Polstead.

BOXFORD

12 miles W of Ipswich on the A1071

A gloriously unspoilt weaving village, downhill from anywhere, surrounded by the peaceful water meadows of the River Box, Boxford's **St Mary's Church** dates back to the 14th century. Its wooden north porch is one of the oldest of its kind in the country. In the church is a touching brass in memory of David Byrde, son of the rector, who died a baby in 1606. At the other end of the continuum is Elizabeth Hyam, four times a widow, who died in her 113th year.

BURES

17 miles W of Ipswich on the B1508

At this point the River Stour turns

sharply to the east, creating a natural boundary between Suffolk and Essex. The little village of Bures straddles the river, lying partly in each county. Bures St Mary in Suffolk is where the church is, overlooked by houses of brick and half-timbering.

Bures wrote itself very early into the history books when on Christmas Day AD 855 it is thought that our old friend Edmund the Martyr, the Saxon king, was crowned at the age of 15 in the Chapel of St Stephen. For some time after that momentous occasion, Bures was the capital seat of the East Anglian kings.

EDWARDSTONE

14 miles W of Ipswich off the A1071

Just to the north of Boxford and close to Edwardstone Hall and the Temple Bar Gate House, Edwardstone is now a 700-acre estate originally home to the Winthrop family. Winthrop was born in Edwardstone and emigrated to the New World, eventually becoming Governor of Massachusetts.

BURY ST EDMUNDS

'A handsome little town, of thriving and cleanly appearance'. Thus Charles Dickens described Bury in his *Pickwick Papers.*

A gem among Suffolk towns, rich in archaeological treasures and places of religious and historical interest, Bury St Edmunds takes its name from St Edmund, who was born in Nuremberg in AD 841 and came here as a teenager to become the last King of East Anglia. He was a staunch Christian, and his refusal to deny his faith caused him to be tortured and killed by the Danes in AD 870. Legend has it that although his body was recovered, his head (cut off by the Danes) could not be found. His men searched for it for 40 days, then heard his voice directing them to it from the depths of a wood, where they discovered it lying protected between the paws of a wolf. The head and the body were seamlessly united and, to commemorate the wolf's deed, the crest of the town's armorial bearings depicts a wolf with a man's head.

Edmund was possibly buried first at Hoxne, the site of his murder, but when he was canonised in about AD 910 his remains were moved to the monastery at Beodricsworth, which changed its name to St Edmundsbury. A shrine was built in his honour, later incorporated into the Norman Abbey Church after the monastery was granted abbey status by King Canute in 1032. The town soon became a place of pilgrimage, and for many years St Edmund was the patron saint of England, until replaced by St George. Growing rapidly around the great abbey, which became one of the largest and most influential in the land, Bury prospered as a centre of trade and commerce, thanks notably to the cloth industry.

The next historical landmark was reached in 1214, when on St Edmund's Feast Day the then Archbishop of Canterbury, Simon Langton, met with the Barons of England at the high altar of the Abbey and swore that they would force King John to honour the proposals of the Magna Carta. The twin elements of Edmund's canonisation and the resolution of the Barons explain the motto on the town's crest: '*sacrarium regis, cunabula legis*' – '*shrine of a king, cradle of the law*'.

Rebuilt in the 15th century, the Abbey was largely dismantled after its Dissolution by Henry VIII, but imposing ruins remain in the colourful Abbey Gardens beyond the splendid **Abbey Gate** and Norman Tower.

St Edmundsbury Cathedral was originally the Church of St James, built in the 15th/16th

Norman Abbey Gatehouse, Bury St Edmunds

One of Bury's oldest residents and a major attraction is the Greene King Brewery Visitor Centre. Greene King has been brewed here in Bury since 1799; the museum's informative storyboards, artefacts, illustrations and audio displays bring the history and art of brewing to life. Brewery tours include a look round the museum and beer-tasting (and the best view of Bury from the brewhouse roof). The shop sells a variety of memorabilia, souvenirs, gifts and clothing – as well, of course, as bottles and cans of the frothy stuff. Tel: 01284 714297/ 714382

•

Steeped though it is in history, Bury also moves with the times, and its sporting, entertainment and leisure facilities are impressive. A mile and a half outside town on the A14 (just off the East Exit) is Nowton Park, 172 acres of countryside landscaped in Victorian style and supporting a wealth of flora and fauna; the avenue of limes, carpeted with daffodils in the spring, is a particular delight. There's also a play area and a ranger centre. Hardwick Heath, its sister park, features a tree gallery and 200-year-old Cedars of Lebanon.

117

66 ST EDMUNDSBURY CATHEDRAL

Bury St Edmunds

A magnificent Cathedral with outstanding features including a magnificent hammerbeam roof and a monumental bishop's throne.

 see page 263

century and accorded cathedral status (alone in Suffolk) in 1914. The original building has been much extended over the years (notably when being adapted for its role as a cathedral) and outstanding features include a magnificent hammerbeam roof, whose 38 beams are decorated with angels bearing the emblems of St James, St Edmund and St George. The monumental Bishop's throne depicts wolves guarding the crowned head of St Edmund, and there's a fascinating collection of 1,000 embroidered kneelers. Work was recently completed to crown the Cathedral with a 140feet Gothic-style tower.

St Mary's Church, in the same complex, is also well worth a visit: an equally impressive hammerbeam roof, the detached tower standing much as Abbot Anselm built it in the 12th century, and several interesting monuments, the most important commemorating Mary Tudor, sister of Henry VIII, Queen of France and Duchess of Suffolk. Her remains were moved here when the Abbey was suppressed; a window in the Lady Chapel recording this fact was the gift of Queen Victoria.

The **Abbey Gardens**, laid out in 1831, have as their central feature a great circle of flower beds following the pattern of the Royal Botanical Gardens in Brussels. Some of the original ornamental trees can still be seen, and other - later - features include an Old English rose garden, a water garden and a garden for the blind where fragrance counts for all. Ducks and geese live by the little River Lark, and there are tennis courts, putting and bowls greens and children's play equipment.

Bury is full of fine non-ecclesiastical buildings, many with Georgian frontages concealing medieval interiors. Among the most interesting are the Victorian **Corn Exchange** with its imposing colonnade; the **Athenaeum**, hub of social life since Regency times and scene of Charles Dickens's public readings; **Cupola House**, where Daniel Defoe once stayed; the **Angel Hotel**, where Dickens and his marvellous creation Mr Pickwick stayed; and the marvellous **Theatre Royal**, built in 1819 by William Wilkins (also responsible for the National Gallery in London), recently superbly renovated and one of the

Theatre Royal, Bury St Edmunds

oldest working theatres in Europe. It once staged the first performance of *Charley's Aunt*. Also there is the **Nutshell**, owned by Greene King Brewery, which lays claim to the title of smallest pub in the country. Whether or not this is so is under debate – but at 15ft by 7ft floor space, with a full capacity at 15 patrons, it certainly isn't spacious! In 1984, a record number of 102 people and a dog squeezed into the pub, and all fortunately survived.

A new development in Bury St Edmunds is the **Arc** – a huge shopping centre, named after the impressive arched front over the Debenhams department store, and cost a reported £100 million to complete as part of a regeneration scheme for central Bury St Edmunds. It houses all of the major high street shops, and it is hoped will support the economy in the town, while providing some 300 long term jobs for residents.

The **Bury St Edmunds Art Gallery** is housed in one of Bury's noblest buildings, built to a Robert Adam design in 1774. It has filled many roles down the years, and was rescued from decline in the 1960s to be restored to Adam's original plans. It is now one of the county's premier art galleries, with eight exhibitions each year and a thriving craft shop.

Outside the Spread Eagle pub on the western edge of town is a horse trough erected to the memory of the Victorian romantic novelist 'Ouida' (Maria Louisa Ramee, 1839-1908).

AROUND BURY ST EDMUNDS

HENGRAVE

3 miles NW of Bury St Edmunds on the A1101

A captivating old-world village of flint and thatch, excavations and aerial photography indicate that there has been a settlement at Hengrave since Neolithic times.

Those parts of the village that are of archaeological interest are now protected. Hengrave Hall is a rambling Tudor mansion built partly of Northamptonshire limestone and partly of yellow brick by Sir Thomas Kytson, a wool merchant. A notable visitor in the early days was Elizabeth I, who brought her court here in 1578. Several generations of the Gage family were later the owners of Hengrave Hall - one of them, with a particular interest in horticulture, imported various kinds of plum trees from France. Most of the bundles were properly labelled with their names, but one had lost its label. When it produced its first crop of luscious green fruit, someone had the bright idea of calling it the Green Gage. The name stuck, and the descendants of these trees, planted in 1724, are still at the Hall, which is not open to the public.

FLEMPTON

4 miles NW of Bury St Edmunds on the A1101

An interesting walk from this village just north of the A1101 follows the **Lark Valley Park**

Arriving in Bury in 1698, Celia Fiennes, the inveterate traveller and stern architecture critic, was uncharacteristically favourable in her remarks about Cupola House, which had just been completed at the time of her visit. William Cobbett (1763-1835), a visitor when chronicling his Rural Rides, did not disagree with the view that Bury St Edmunds was 'the nicest town in the world' - a view which would be endorsed by many of today's inhabitants and by many of the millions of visitors who have been charmed by this jewel in Suffolk's crown.

119

through Culford Park, providing a good view of Culford Hall, which has been a school since 1935. A handsome cast-iron bridge dating from the early 19th century - and recently brought to light from among the reeds - crosses a lake in the park.

WEST STOW

6 miles NW of Bury St Edmunds off the A1101

An Anglo-Saxon cemetery was discovered in the village in 1849; subsequent years have revealed traces of Roman settlements and the actual layout of the original **Anglo-Saxon Village**. A trust was established to investigate further the Anglo-Saxon way of life and their building and farming techniques. Several buildings were constructed using, as accurately as could be achieved, the tools and methods of the 5th century. The undertaking has become a major tourist attraction, with assistance from guides both human (in Anglo-Saxon costume) and in the form of taped cassettes. There are pigs and hens, growing crops, craft courses, a Saxon market at Easter, a festival in August and special events all year round. This fascinating village, which is entered through the Visitor Centre, is part of the 125-acre **West Stow Country Park**, a large part of which is designated a Site of Special Scientific Interest (SSSI). Over 120 species of birds and 25 species of animals have been sighted in this Breckland setting, and a well-marked 5-mile nature trail links this nature reserve with the woods, a large lake

and the River Lark. The Park is open daily all year.

ICKLINGHAM

8 miles NW of Bury St Edmunds on the A1101

The village of Icklingham boasts not one but two churches - the parish **Church of St James** (mentioned in the *Domesday Book*) and the deconsecrated thatched-roofed **Church of All Saints**, with medieval tiles on the chancels and beautiful east windows in the south aisle. The church of All Saints is presently looking particularly grand having recently been rethatched. Amazingly there are original hassocks (large 19th century kneelers made from sage) which have survived all this time; they were removed from All Saints church and placed in St James, where they can still be seen.

At the point where the Icknield Way crosses the River Lark, Icklingham has a long history, brought to light in frequent archaeological finds, from pagan bronzes to Roman coins. The place abounds in tales of the supernatural, notably of the white rabbit who is seen at dusk in the company of a witch, causing – it is said - horses to bolt and men to die.

GREAT WELNETHAM

2 miles S of Bury St Edmunds off the A134

One of the many surviving Suffolk windmills is to be found here, just south of the village. The sails were lost in a gale 80 years ago, but the tower and a neighbouring old barn make an attractive sight.

THE BRADFIELDS

7 miles SE of Bury St Edmunds off the A134

The Bradfields - St George, St Clare and Combust - and also the village of Cockfield (see below) thread their way through a delightful part of the countryside and are well worth a little exploration, not only to see the picturesque villages themselves but for a stroll in the historic **Bradfield Woods**. These woods stand on the eastern edge of the parish of Bradfield St George and have been turned into an outstanding nature reserve, tended and coppiced in the same way for more than 700 years, and home to a wide variety of flora and fauna. They once belonged to the Abbey of St Edmundsbury, and one area is still today called Monk's Park Wood.

Coppicing involves cutting a tree back down to the ground every ten years or so. Woodlands were managed in this way to provide an annual crop of timber for local use and fast regrowth. After coppicing, as the root is already strongly established, regrowth is quick. Willow and hazel are the trees most commonly coppiced. Willow is often also pollarded, a less drastic form of coppicing where the trees are cut far enough from the ground to stop grazing animals having a free lunch.

Bradfield St Clare, the central of the three Bradfields, has a rival claim to that of Hoxne as the site of the martyrdom of St Edmund. The St Clare family arrived with the Normans and added their name to the village, and to the church, which was originally All Saints but was then rededicated to St Clare; it is the only church in England dedicated to her. Bradfield Combust, where the pretty River Lark rises, probably takes it's curious name from the fact that the local hall was burnt to the ground during the 14th century riots against the Abbot of St Edmundsbury's crippling tax demands.

COCKFIELD

8 miles SE of Bury St Edmunds off the A1141

Cockfield is perhaps the most widely spread village in all Suffolk, its little thatched cottages scattered around and between no fewer than nine greens. Great Green is the largest, with two football pitches and other recreation areas, while Parsonage Green has a literary connection: the **Old Rectory** was once home to a Dr Babbington, whose nephew Robert Louis Stephenson was a frequent visitor and who is said to have written Treasure Island while staying there. Cockfield also shelters one of the last windmills to have been built in Suffolk (1891). Its working life was very short but the tower still stands, now in use as a private residence.

THORPE MORIEUX

9 miles SE of Bury St Edmunds off the B1071

St Mary's Church in Thorpe Morieux is situated in as pleasant a setting as anyone could wish to find. With water meadows, ponds, a

121

67 BRIGHTHOUSE FARM

Lawshall

A great spot in the Suffolk countryside offering B & B, self catering and camping accommodation.

 see page 264

68 THE OLD PEAR TREE

Whepstead

Homely B & B set in a great location amongst the beautiful Suffolk countryside.

see page 263

stream and a fine Tudor farmhouse to set it off, this 14th century church presents a memorable picture of old England. Look at the church, then take the time to wander round the peaceful churchyard with its profusion of springtime aconites, followed by the colourful flowering of limes and chestnuts in summer.

LAWSHALL

8 miles S of Bury St Edmunds off the A134

A spread-out village first documented in AD 972 but regularly giving up evidence of earlier occupation, Lawshall was the site where a Bronze Age sword dated at around 600 BC was found (the sword is now in Bury Museum). The **Church of All Saints**, Perpendicular with some Early English features, stands on one of the highest points in Suffolk. Next to it is **Lawshall Hall**, whose owners once entertained Queen Elizabeth I. An interesting site in Lawshall is the **Wishing Well**, a well-cover on the green put up in memory of Charles Tyrwhitt Drake, who worked for the Royal Geographic Society and was killed in Jerusalem.

ALPHETON

10 miles S of Bury St Edmunds on the A134

There are several points of interest in this little village straddling the main road. It was first settled in AD 991 and its name means 'the farm of Aefflaed'. That lady was the wife of Ealdorman Beorhtnoth of Essex, who was killed resisting the Danes at the Battle of Maldon

and is buried in Ely Minster.

The hall, the farm and the church stand in a quiet location away from the main road and about a mile from the village. This remoteness is not unusual: some attribute it to the villagers moving during times of plague, but the more likely explanation is simply that the scattered cottages, originally in several tiny hamlets, centred on a more convenient site than that of the church. Equally possible is that the church was located here to suit the local landed family (who desired to have the church next door to their home). The main features at the **Church of St Peter and St Paul** are the flintwork around the parapet (the exterior is otherwise fairly undistinguished), the carefully restored 15th century porch and some traces of an ancient wall painting of St Christopher with the Christ Child. All in all, it's a typical country church of unpretentious dignity and well worth a short detour from the busy main roads.

HARTEST

9 miles S of Bury St Edmunds on the B1066

Hartest, which has a history as long as Alpheton's, celebrated its millennium in 1990 with the erection of a village sign (the hart, or stag). It's an agreeable spot in the valley, with colour-washed houses and chestnut trees on the green. Also on the green are All Saints Church (mentioned in the Domesday Book) and a large glacial stone, the **Hartest Stone**, which was dragged by a team of 45 horses from where it was found in a field in neighbouring Somerton. Just outside the village is **Gifford's Hall**, a smallholding which includes 14 acres of nearly 12,000 grapevines, as well as a winery producing white and rosé wines and fruit liqueurs. There are also organic vegetable gardens, wildflower meadows, black St Kilda sheep, black Berkshire pigs, goats and free-range fowl, together with a trailer ride ('The Grape Express') and children's play area. The Hall is particularly famous for its sweet peas and roses, and an annual festival is held on the last weekend in June. Open from Easter to the end of October. From 1789 until the 1930s, Hartest staged a St George's Day Fair, an annual event celebrating King George III's recovery from one of his spells of illness.

SHIMPLING

9 miles S of Bury St Edmunds off the B1066

Shimpling is a peaceful farming community whose church, **St George's**, is approached by a lime avenue. It is notable for Victorian stained glass and a Norman font, and in the churchyard is the **Faint House**, a small stone building where ladies overcome by the tightness of their stays could decently retreat from the service. The banker Thomas Hallifax built many of Shimpling's cottages, as well as the village school and Chadacre Hall, which Lord Iveagh later turned into an agricultural college (a role it ceased to hold in 1989 - the Hall is today again in private hands).

GLEMSFORD

12 miles S of Bury St Edmunds off the B1066

Driving in from the north on the B1066, the old Church of St Mary makes an impressive sight on what, for Suffolk, is quite a considerable hill. Textiles and weaving have long played a prominent part in Glemsford's history, and thread from the silk factory, which opened in 1824 and is still going strong, has been woven into dresses and robes for various members of the royal family, including Princess Diana's wedding dress.

LONG MELFORD

13 miles S of Bury St Edmunds off the A134

The heart of this atmospheric wool town is its very long and, in stretches, fairly broad main street, set on an ancient Roman site in a particularly beautiful part of south Suffolk. In Roman times the Stour was a navigable river, and trade flourished. Various Roman finds have been unearthed, notably a blue glass vase which is now on display in the British Museum in

Long Melford Hall Gateway

123

Long Melford is a great place for leisurely strolls, and for the slightly more energetic there's a scenic 3-mile walk along a disused railway track and farm tracks that leads straight into Lavenham.

London. The street is filled with antique shops, book shops and art galleries, and is a favourite place for collectors and browsers. Some of the houses are washed in the characteristic Suffolk pink, which might originally have been achieved by mixing ox blood or sloe juice into the plaster.

Holy Trinity Church, on a 14-acre green at the north end of Hall Street, is a typically exuberant manifestation of the wealth of the wool and textile trade. It's big enough to be a cathedral, but served (and still serves) comparatively few parishioners. John Clopton, grown rich in the woollen business, was largely responsible for this magnificent Perpendicular-style edifice of Holy Trinity, which has a 180-feet nave and chancel and half timbers, flint 'flushwork' (stonework) of the highest quality, and 100 large windows to give a marvellous sense of light and space. Medieval glass in the north aisle depicts religious scenes and the womenfolk of the Clopton family. There are many interesting monuments and brasses, and in the chantry entrance is a bas relief of the Three Wise Men, the Virgin and Child, and St Joseph. In the Lady Chapel, reached by way of the churchyard, a children's multiplication table written on one wall is a reminder that the chapel served as the village school for a long period after the Reformation.

The tower was struck by lightning in the early 18th century; the present brick construction dates from around 1900. The detail of this great church is of endless fascination, but it's the overall impression that stays in the memory, and the sight of the building floodlit at night is truly spectacular. The distinguished 20th century poet Edmund Blunden spent his last years at Hall Mill in Long Melford and is buried in the churchyard. The inscription on his gravestone reads *'I live still to love still things quiet and unconcerned.'*

Melford Hall, east of town beyond an imposing 16th century gateway, was built around 1570 by Sir William Cordell on the site of an earlier hall that served as a country retreat, before the Dissolution of the Monasteries, for the monks of St Edmundsbury Abbey. There exists an account of Cordell entertaining Queen Elizabeth I at the Hall in 1578, when she was welcomed by '200 young gentlemen in white velvet, 300 in black and 1,500 serving men'. Much of the fine work of Sir William (whose body lies in Holy Trinity Church) has been altered in restoration, but the pepperpot chimneys are original, as is the panelled banqueting hall. The rooms are in various styles, some with ornate walnut furniture, and there's a notable collection of Chinese porcelain on show.

Most delightful of all the rooms at Melford Hall is the Beatrix Potter room, with some of her watercolours, first editions of her books and, among the toys, the original of Jemima Puddleduck. She was a frequent visitor here (her cousins, the Hyde Parkers, were then the owners), bringing small

124

animals to draw. The Jeremy Fisher illustrations were mostly drawn at Melford Hall's fishponds, and the book is dedicated to Stephanie Hyde Parker. The Hall, which is a National Trust property, stands in a lovely garden with some distinguished clipped box hedges. On the green near the hall is a vast brick conduit built to supply water to the hall and the village. William Cordell was also responsible for the red-brick almshouses, built in 1593 for '12 poor men', which stand near Holy Trinity.

Kentwell Hall is a red-brick Tudor moated mansion approached by a long avenue of limes. Its grounds include a unique Tudor rose maze, and are set out to illustrate and re-create Tudor times, with a walled garden, a bakery, a dairy and several varieties of rare-breed farm animals. The buildings include a handsome 14th century aisle barn. The Hall was the setting for a film version of *Toad of Toad Hall*.

CAVENDISH

3 miles W of Long Melford on the A1092

A most attractive village, where the Romans stayed awhile - the odd remains have been unearthed - and the Saxons settled, Cavendish is splendidly traditional, with its church, thatched cottages, almshouses, Nether Hall and the **Sue Ryder Foundation Museum** spread around the green. The latter, in a 16th century rectory by the pond, illustrates the work of the Sue Ryder Foundation, and was formally opened by Queen

Elizabeth II in 1979. Once a refuge for concentration camp victims, it houses abundant war photographs and memorabilia. It is open year round 10am-5.30pm. **Nether Hall** is a well-restored 16th century building and the headquarters of Cavendish Vineyards.

In the **Church of St Mary**, whose tower has a pointed bellcote and a room inside complete with fireplace and shuttered windows, look for the two handsome lecterns, one with a brass eagle (15th century), the other with two chained books; and for the Flemish and Italian statues.

CLARE

6 miles W of Long Melford on the A1092

'A little town with a lot of history'.

A medieval wool town of great importance, Clare repays a visit today with its fine old buildings and some distinguished old ruins. Perhaps the most renowned tourist attraction is **Ancient House**, a timber-framed building dating from 1473 and remarkable for its pargeting. This is the decorative treatment of external plasterwork, usually by dividing the surface into rectangles and decorating each panel. It was very much a Suffolk speciality, particularly in the 16th and 17th centuries, with some examples also being found in Cambridgeshire and Essex. The decoration could be simple brushes of a comb, scrolls or squiggles, or more elaborate, with religious motifs, guild signs or family crests. Some pargeting is incised, but the

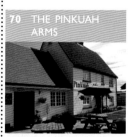

69 SCHOOL BARN FARM

Pentlow

Environmentally conscious accommodation in the beautiful Stour Valley.

🛏 *see page 265*

70 THE PINKUAH ARMS

Pentlow

This pink pub provides wonderful food in a warm and charming setting.

🍴 *see page 265*

71 THE COCK INN AT
    CLARE

Clare

A thriving family business
dedicated to creating a
welcoming atmosphere to all
in the rural town of Clare.

see page 266

best is in relief – pressing moulds
into wet plaster or shaping it by
hand. Ancient House sports some
splendid entwined flowers and
branches, and a representation of
two figures holding a shield. The
best-known workers in the unique
skill of pargeting had their own
distinctive styles, and the expert eye
could spot the particular
'trademarks' of each man (the same
is the case with the master
thatchers). Ancient House is now a
museum, open during the summer

months and housing an exhibition
on local history.

Another place of historical
significance is **Nethergate House**,
once the workplace of dyers,
weavers and spinners. The Swan
Inn, in the High Street, has a sign
which lays claim to being the oldest
in the land. Ten feet in length and
carved from a solid piece of wood,
it portrays the arms of England and
France.

Clare Castle was a motte-and-
bailey fortress that sheltered a
household of 250. Clare Castle
Country Park, with a visitor centre
in the goods shed of a disused
railway line, contains the remains
of the castle and the moat, the
latter now a series of ponds and
home to varied wild life. At the
Prior's House, the original cellar
and infirmary are still in use.
Established in 1248 by Augustine
friars and used by them until the
Dissolution of 1538, the priory was
handed back to that order in 1953
and remains their property.

A mile or so west of Clare on
the A1092 lies **Stoke-by-Clare**, a
pretty village on one of the region's
most picturesque routes. It once
housed a Benedictine priory, whose
remains are now in the grounds of
a school. There's a fine 15th
century church and a vineyard:
Boyton Vineyards at Hill Farm,
Boyton End, is open early April to
the end of October for a tour, a
talk and a taste.

PENTLOW

3 miles East of Clare

The scattered village of Pentlow is

Priest's House and Ancient Church, Clare

126

pleasantly situated on the south side of the Stour Valley, opposite Cavendish, in Suffolk. **Pentlow Hall**, a fine ancient mansion, which has recently been repaired and enlarged, is encompassed by well wooded grounds, near the river. It was successively held by the Baynard, Fitzwalter, Ratcliff, Fitz-Humphrey, Norman, Cavendish, Felton, Kemp, and other families, some of whom were long seated here. A great part of the parish belongs to Earl Howe, the Rev. Edward Pemberton, J. Sperling, Esq., and several smaller owners, mostly freeholders.

St. Gregory Church is an interesting structure of great antiquity, having a semicircular east end, and a round tower, containing five bells. The architecture is a mixture of the pure Norman and pointed styles, and the large stone font has a wooden covering, ornamented in the florid style of the time of Henry Vll. The walls of the tower are of flint, 4 feet thick. On the north side of the chancel is Kemp's Chapel, in which is a very fine tomb, on which are recumbent effigies of Judge Kemp, his lady, and his son John, who died in the early part of the 17th century. Round the tomb are 14 kneeling figures of children. The Chapel window is filled with stained glass, and the roof is divided into compartments, with Gothic quartrefoils, etc. In the chancel is a curious old tomb of the Feltons, who were connected by marriage with the noble family of Hervey.

HORRINGER

3 miles SW of Bury St Edmunds on the A143

Rejoining the A143 by Chedburgh, the motorist will soon arrive at Horringer, whose village green is dominated by the flintstone Church of St Leonard. Beside the church are the gates of one of the country's most extraordinary and fascinating houses, now run by the National Trust. **Ickworth House** was the brainchild of the eccentric 4th Earl of Bristol and Bishop of Derry, a collector of art treasures and an inveterate traveller (witness the many Bristol Hotels scattered around Europe). His inspiration was Belle Isle, a house built on an island in Lake Windermere, and the massive structure is a central rotunda linking two semi-circular wings. It was designed as a treasure house for his art collection, and work started in 1795. Sadly, the first collection of the Earl's treasures was seized by Napoleon in 1798, so never reached England.

Derry died in 1803 and his son, after some hesitation, saw the work through to completion in 1829. Its chief glories are some marvellous paintings by Titian, Gainsborough, Hogarth, Velasquez, Reynolds and Kauffman, but there's a great deal more to enthral the visitor: late Regency and 18th century French furniture, a notable collection of Georgian silver, friezes and sculptures by John Flaxman, frescoes copied from wall paintings discovered at the Villa Negroni in Rome in 1777.

Arable land surrounds Horringer, with a large annual crop of sugar beet grown for processing at the factory in Bury, the largest of its kind in Europe.

127

Haverhill Local History Centre, in the Town Hall, has an interesting collection of memorabilia, over 6,000 photographs, the earliest dating from 1860, and 3,000 publications, research papers and maps. It is open Thurday and Friday 2pm-4pm, Saturday 10.30am-3.30pm and every first Tuesday of the month 7pm-9pm (no admission after 8pm), admission is free.

HAVERHILL

18 miles SW of Bury St Edmunds on the A604

Notable for its fine Victorian architecture, Haverhill also boasts one fine Tudor gem. Although many of Haverhill's buildings were destroyed by fire in 1665, **Anne of Cleves House** was restored and is well worth a visit. Anne was the fourth wife of Henry VIII and, after a brief political marriage, she was given an allowance and spent the remainder of her days at Haverhill and Richmond.

East Town Park is an attractive country park on the east side of Haverhill.

KEDINGTON

2 miles N of Haverhill on the B1061

Haverhill intrudes somewhat, but the heart of the old village of Kedington gains it's appeal through the presence of the River Stour. Known to many as the 'Cathedral of West Suffolk', the **Church of St Peter and St Paul** is the village's chief attraction. Almost 150 feet in length, it stands on a ridge overlooking the Stour Valley. It has several interesting features, including a 15th century font, a Saxon cross in the chancel window, a triple-decker pulpit (with a clerk's desk and a reading desk) and a sermon-timer, looking rather like a grand egg-timer. The foundations of a Roman building have been found beneath the floorboards.

The Bardiston family, one of the oldest in Suffolk, had strong links with the village and many of the family tombs are in the church. In the church grounds is a row of ten elm trees, each, the legend says, with a knight buried beneath its roots.

GREAT AND LITTLE THURLOW

3 miles N of Haverhill on the B1061

Great and Little Thurlow form a continuous village on the west bank of the River Stour a few miles north of Haverhill. Largely undamaged thanks to being in a conservation area, together they boast many 17th century cottages and a Georgian manor house. In the main street is a schoolhouse built in 1614 by Sir Stephen Soame, one-time Lord Mayor of London, whose family are commemorated in the village church.

A short distance further up the B1061 stands the village of **Great Bradley**, divided in two by the River Stour, which rises just outside the village boundary. Chief points of note in the tranquil parish church are a fine Norman doorway sheltering a Tudor brick porch and some beautiful stained glass poignantly depicting a soldier in the trenches during the First World War. The three bells in the tower include one cast in the 14th century, among the oldest in Suffolk.

DENSTON

6 miles NE of Haverhill just off the A143

Denston lies just east of the A143 on the River Glem, and is notable chiefly for its magnificent

Perpendicular church, one of 18 dedicated to St Nicholas, patron saint of sailors. Stop and admire the fan vaulting in the roof (a comparative rarity in Suffolk), the outstanding brasses and the wide variety of carved animals.

HAWKEDON
7 miles NE of Haverhill off the A143

Hawkedon is designated a place of outstanding natural beauty. Here the **Church of St Mary** is located atypically in the middle of the village green. The pews and intricately carved bench-ends take the eye here, along with a canopied stoup (a recess for holding holy water) and a Norman font. There is a wide variety of carved animals, many on the bench-ends but some also on the roof cornice. One of the stalls is decorated with the carving of a crane holding a stone in its claw: legend has it that if the crane were on watch and should fall asleep, the stone would drop and the noise would wake it.

WICKHAMBROOK
8 miles NE of Haverhill on the B1063

Wickhambrook is a series of tiny hamlets with no fewer than 11 greens and three manor houses. The greens have unusual names - Genesis, Nunnery, Meeting, Coltsfoot - whose origins keep local historians busy. One of the two pubs has the distinction of being officially half in Wickhambrook and half in Denston.

NEWMARKET

On the western edge of Suffolk, Newmarket is home to some 17,000 human and 4,000 equine inhabitants. The historic centre of British racing lives and breathes horses, with 73 training establishments, 70 stud farms, the top annual thoroughbred sales and two racecourses (the only two in Suffolk). Thousands of the population are involved in the trade, and racing art and artefacts fill the shops, galleries and museums; one of the oldest established saddlers even has a preserved horse on display - 'Robert the Devil', runner-up in the Derby in 1880.

History records that Queen Boudica of the Iceni, to whom the six-mile Devil's Dyke stands as a memorial, thundered around these parts in her lethal chariot behind her shaggy-haired horses. She is said to have established the first stud here. In medieval times the chalk heathland was a popular arena for riders to display their skills. In 1605, James I paused on a journey northwards to enjoy a spot of hare coursing. He enjoyed the place and said he would be back. By moving the royal court to his Newmarket headquarters, he began the royal patronage which has remained strong throughout the years. James' son, Charles I, maintained the royal connection, but it was Charles II who really put the place on the map when he, too, moved the Royal court here in the

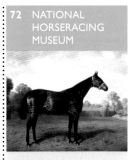

72 NATIONAL HORSERACING MUSEUM

Newmarket

"The Newmarket Experience" comprises two separate attractions: The National Horseracing Museum and The National Stud.

 see page 266

129

One of Newmarket's two racecourses, the Rowley Mile, takes its name from Old Rowley, a favourite horse of the Merry Monarch. Here the first two classics of the season, the 1,000 and 2,000 Guineas, are run, together with important autumn events including the Cambridgeshire and the Cesarewich. There are some 18 race days at this track, while on the leafy July Course, with its delightful garden-party atmosphere, a similar number of race days take in all the important summer fixtures.

If you are new to Newmarket, you might wish to consider the service by "The Newmarket Experience", who conduct tailor-made guided tours around the town, which can include taking in a race at one of the two race tracks. They can also help you find suitable accommodation in any number of the lovely hotels and B&Bs in the town centre.

spring and autumn of each year. He initiated the Town Plate, a race which he himself won twice as a rider and which, in a modified form, still exists.

The visitor to Newmarket can learn almost all there is to know about flat racing and racehorses by making the grand tour of the several establishments open to the public (sometimes by appointment only). **The Jockey Club**, which was the first governing body of the sport and, until recently, its ultimate authority, was formed in the mid-18th century and occupied an imposing building which was restored and rebuilt in Georgian style in the 1930s. Originally a social club for rich gentlemen with an interest in the turf, it soon became the all-powerful regulator of British racing, owning all the racing and training land. When holding an enquiry the stewards sat round a horseshoe-shaped table while the jockey or trainer under scrutiny faces them on a strip of carpet by the door - hence the expression 'on the mat'.

A few steps away is **Palace House**, which contains the remains of Charles II's palace and which, as funds allow, has been restored over the years for use as a visitor centre and museum. In the same street is **Nell Gwynn's House**, which some say was connected by an underground passage beneath the street to the palace. The diarist John Evelyn spent a night in (or on?) the town during a royal visit, and declared the occasion to be 'more

resembling a luxurious and abandoned rout than a Christian court'.

Other must-sees on the racing enthusiast's tour are **Tattersalls**, where leading thoroughbred sales take place from February to December; the **British Racing School**, where budding jockeys are taught the ropes; the **National Stud**, open from February till the end of September (plus race days in October - booking essential); and the **Animal Health Trust** based at Lanwades Hall, where there's an informative Visitor Centre. The National Stud at one time housed no fewer than three Derby winners - Blakeney, Mill Reef, and Grundy.

Horses aren't all about racing, however. One type of horse you won't see in Newmarket is the wonderful Suffolk Punch, a massive yet elegant working horse which is part of the Hallowed Trinity of animals at the very centre of Suffolk's agricultural history; the others being the Suffolk Sheep and the Red Poll Cow. The Suffolk Punch can still be seen at work at Rede Hall Park Farm near Bury St Edmunds and at Kentwell Hall in Long Melford. Newmarket also has things to offer the tourist outside the equine world, including the churches of St Mary and All Saints, and St Agnes, and a landmark at each end of the High Street - a Memorial Fountain in honour of Sir Daniel Cooper and the Jubilee Clock Tower commemorating Queen Victoria's Golden Jubilee.

AROUND NEWMARKET

EXNING

2 miles NW of Newmarket on the A14

A pause is certainly in order at this ancient village, whether on your way from Newmarket or arriving from Cambridgeshire on the A14. Anglo-Saxons, Romans, the Iceni and the Normans were all here, and the *Domesday Book* records the village under the name of Esselinga. The village was stricken by plague during the Iceni occupation, so its market was moved to the next village along - thus Newmarket acquired its name.

KENTFORD

5 miles E of Newmarket by the A14

At the old junction of the Newmarket-to-Bury road stands the grave of a young boy who hanged himself after being accused of sheep-stealing. It was a well-established superstition that suicides should be buried at a crossroads to prevent their spirits from wandering. Flowers are still sometimes laid at the **Gypsy Boy's Grave**, sometimes by punters hoping for good luck at Newmarket races.

MOULTON

4 miles E of Newmarket on the B1085

This most delightful village lies in wonderful countryside on chalky downland in farming country; its proximity to Newmarket is apparent from the racehorses which are often to be seen on the large green. The River Kennett flows through the green before running north to the Lark, a tributary of the Ouse. Flint walls are a feature of many of the buildings, but the main point of interest is the 15th century Four-arch **Packhorse Bridge** on the way to the church.

DALHAM

5 miles E of Newmarket on the B1063

Eighty per cent of the buildings in Dalham are thatched (the highest proportion in Suffolk) and there are many other attractions in this pretty village. Above the village on one of the county's highest spots stands **St Mary's Church**, which dates from the 14th century. Its spire toppled over during the gales which swept the land on the night that Cromwell died, and was replaced by a tower in 1627. Sir Martin Stutteville was the leading light behind this reconstruction; an inscription at the back of the church notes that the cost was £400. That worthy's grandfather was Thomas Stutteville, whose memorial near the altar declares that 'he saw the New World with Francis Drake.' (Drake did not survive that journey - his third to South America.) Thomas' grandson died in the fullness of his years (62 wasn't bad for those times) while hosting a jolly evening at The Angel Hotel in Bury St Edmunds.

MILDENHALL

8 miles NE of Newmarket off the A11

On the edge of the Fens and Breckland, Mildenhall is a town

The parish of Mildenhall is the largest in Suffolk, so it is perhaps fitting that it should boast so magnificent a parish church as St Mary's, built of Barnack stone; it dominates the heart of the town and indeed its west tower commands the flat surrounding countryside. Above the splendid north porch are the arms of Edward the Confessor and of St Edmund. The chancel, dating back to the 13th century, is a marvellous work of architecture, but pride of place goes to the east window, divided into seven vertical lights. Off the south aisle is the Chapel of St Margaret, whose altar, itself modern, contains a medieval altar stone. At the west end, the font, dating from the 15th century, bears the arms of Sir Henry Barton, who was twice Lord Mayor of London and whose tomb is located on the south side of the tower. Above the nave is a particularly fine hammerbeam roof whose outstanding feature is the carved angels. Efforts of the Puritans to destroy the angels failed, though traces of buckshot and arrowheads remain and have been found embedded in the woodwork.

73 THE CROWN

Brandon

A warm and friendly pub, close to Centre Parks, offering great food and service all week long.

 see page 267

74 BRANDON COUNTRY PARK

Brandon

At Brandon, you can stroll and picnic in the charming walled garden. You can also head further afield, following the invigorating walks and cycle trails that guide you through the arboretum, commercial forest and restored heathland.

 see page 267

which has many links with the past. It was once a port for the hinterlands of West Suffolk, though the River Lark has long ceased to be a trade route. Most of the town's heritage is recorded in the excellent **Mildenhall & District Museum** (Tel: 01638 716970) in King Street. Here will be found exhibits of local history (including the distinguished RAF and USAAF base), crafts and domestic skills, the natural history of the Fens and Breckland and, perhaps most famously, the chronicle of the 'Mildenhall Treasure'. This was a cache of 34 pieces of 4th century Roman silverware - dishes, goblets and spoons - found by a ploughman in 1946 at Thistley Green and now on display in the British Museum in London, while a replica makes its home here where it was found. There is evidence of much earlier occupation than the Roman era, with flint tools and other artefacts being unearthed in 1988 on the site of an ancient lake.

The other focal point in Mildenhall is the Market Place, with its 16th century timbered cross.

BARTON MILLS

1 mile S of Mildenhall off the A11

Known as Barton Parva (Little Barton) in Saxon times, this village changed its name during the 18th century. St Mary's Church can trace its origins back to at least 1150, and one of its early rectors had the Pope as his patron. Sir Alexander Fleming had a country house in the village of Barton Mills, and it is

possible that he worked on the invention of penicillin in a shed in the garden.

BRANDON

9 miles NE of Mildenhall on the A1065

On the edge of **Thetford Forest** by the Little Ouse, Brandon was long ago a thriving port, but flint is what really put it on the map. The town itself is built mainly of flint, and flint was mined from early Neolithic times to make arrowheads and other implements and weapons of war. The gun flint industry brought with it substantial wealth, and a good flint-knapper could produce up to 300 gun flints in an hour. The invention of the percussion cap killed off much of the need for this type of work, however, so they turned to shaping flints for church buildings and ornamental purposes. **Brandon Heritage Centre** (Tel: 07882 891022), in a former fire station in George Street, provides visitors with a splendid insight into this industry, while for an even more tangible feel, a visit to **Grime's Graves**, just over the Norfolk border, reveals an amazing site covering 35 acres and 300 pits (one of the shafts is open to visitors). With the close proximity of numerous warrens and their rabbit population, the fur trade also flourished here, and that, too, along with forestry, is brought to life in the Heritage Centre (see also under Thetford in the Norfolk chapter).

The whole of this

northwestern corner of Suffolk, know as Breckland, offers almost unlimited opportunities for touring by car, cycling or walking. A mile south of town on the B1106 is **Brandon Country Park**, a 30-acre landscaped site with a tree trail, forest walks, a walled garden and a visitor centre. There's also an orienteering route leading on into Thetford Forest, Britain's largest lowland pine forest. Three miles west of Brandon on the county border lies the Norfolk Wildlife Trust's **Weeting Heath**, famous for its extraordinary-looking stone curlews.

The High Lodge Forest Centre, near **Santon Downham** (off the B1107), also attracts with walks, cycle trails and adventure facilities.

ELVEDEN

5 miles S of Brandon on the A11

The road from Brandon leads south through the forest to a historic estate village with some unusual architectural features. Where the three parishes of Elveden, Eriswell and Icklingham meet, a tall war memorial in the form of a Corinthian column is a landmark.

133

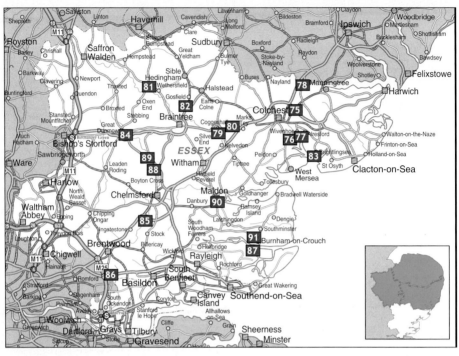

Essex

Northeast Essex has the essence of true East Anglia, particularly around the outstanding villages of the Stour Valley - which has come to be known as Constable Country (along with its near neighbour southern Suffolk.) The inland villages and small towns here are notably historic and picturesque, offering very good touring and walking opportunities.

A plethora of half-timbered medieval buildings, farms and churches mark this region out as of particular historical interest. Monuments to engineering feats past and present include Hedingham Castle, Chappel Viaduct and the postmill at Bocking Church Street. Truly lovely villages such as Finchingfield abound, rewarding any journey to this part of the county. There are also many lovely gardens to visit, and this region's principal town, Colchester, is a mine of interesting sights and experiences.

The North Essex coast has a distinguished history and a strong maritime heritage, as exemplified in towns like Harwich, Manningtree and Mistley. Further examples are the fine Martello Towers - circular brick edifices built to provide a coastal defence against Napoleon's armies - along the Tendring coast at Walton and Clacton. Dating from 1808 to 1812, each is mounted with a gun on the roof.

The Tendring Peninsula has a rich and varied heritage ranging from prehistoric remains to medieval churches and elegant Victorian villas. The Tendring Coast contains an interesting mix of extensive tidal inlets, sandy beaches and low cliffs. Place names include the Danish ending 'by', meaning a settlement, and the Old English 'ea' and 'ey' for an island. Among the many attractive villages in the district are Thorpe-le-Soken, Kirby-le-Soken and Great Bentley - the last reputed to have the largest village green in England. The Stour Estuary, Hamford Water and the Colne Estuary are all renowned for seabirds and other wildlife, and many areas are protected nature reserves. The Manningtree-Ramsey road passes through some of the best coastal scenery in Essex, with some outstanding views of the Suffolk shore.

This is, of course, also the part of the county known as 'the sunshine holiday coast', where the resorts of Clacton, Frinton and Walton-on-the-Naze are to be found; with all the attractions and long sandy beaches you could wish from a seaside resort.

The small northwest Essex towns of Saffron Walden, Thaxted, Great Dumnow and Stansted Mountfichet are among the loveliest and most interesting in the land. This area is also home to a wealth of picturesque villages boasting weatherboarded houses and pargeting. The quiet country lanes are perfect for walking, cycling or exploring. Here can be seen three historic windmills, at Stansted Mountfichet, Aythorpe Roding and Thaxted. Visitors to southwest Essex and Epping Forest will find a treasure-trove of woodland, nature reserves, superb gardens and other rural delights. Epping Forest dominates much of the far western corner, but all this part of the county is rich in countryside, forests and parks, including the magnificent Lee Valley regional Park, Thorndon Country Park at Brentwood and Weald Country Park at South Weald. Bordering the north bank of the Thames, the borough of Thurrock has long been a gateway to London but also affords easy access to southwest Essex and Kent. Along the 18 miles of Thames frontage there are many important marshland wildlife habitats. History, too, abounds in this part of the county. Henry VIII built riverside block houses at East and West Tilbury, and it was at West Tilbury that Elizabeth I gave her famous speech to her troops, gathered to meet the threat of the Spanish Armada. At the extreme southeast of the county, Southend is a popular seaside resort with a wealth of sights and amenities. The area surrounding the Rivers Blackwater and Crouch contains a wealth of ancient woodland and other natural beauty, particularly along the estuaries of the Chelmer & Blackwater Canal. This part of Essex affords some marvellous sailing, walking, cycling, birdwatching and other outdoor activities.

COLCHESTER

This ancient market town and garrison stands in the midst of rolling East Anglian countryside. England's oldest recorded town, it has over 2,000 years of history, there to be discovered by visitors. First established during the 7th century BC, west of town there are the remains of the massive earthworks built to protect Colchester in pre-Roman times. During the 1st century, Colchester's prime location made it an obvious target for invading Romans. The Roman Emperor Claudius accepted the surrender of 11 British Kings in Colchester. In AD 60, Queen Boudica helped to establish her place in history by taking revenge on the Romans and burning the town to the ground, before going on to destroy London and St Albans. Here in this town that was once capital of Roman Britain, Roman walls - the oldest in Britain - still surround the oldest part of town. **Balkerne Gate**, west gate of the original Roman town, is the largest surviving Roman gateway in the country, and remains magnificent to this day.

The town affords plenty to see and explore. There are many guided town walks available, as well as bus tours. The local Visitor Information Centre on Queen Street has details of the many places to visit. Market days in this thriving town are Friday and Saturday. Today, Colchester is presided over by its lofty town hall and enormous **Victorian Water Tower**, nicknamed 'Jumbo' after London Zoo's first African elephant, an animal sold to P T Barnum (causing some controversy) in 1882. The tower has four massive pillars made up of one-and-a-quarter million bricks, 369 tons of stone and 142 tons of iron, all working to support the 230,000-gallon tank.

A good place to start any exploration of the town is **Colchester Castle** and its museum. When the Normans arrived, Colchester (a name given the town by the Saxons) was an important borough. The Normans built their castle on the foundations of the Roman temple of Claudius. Having used many of the Roman bricks in its construction, it boasts the largest Norman keep ever built in Europe - the only part still left standing. The keep houses the **Castle Museum**, one of the most exciting hands-on historical attractions in the country. Its fascinating collection of Iron Age, Roman and medieval relics is one

Colchester Castle

of the most important in the country. Among the numerous attractions are a Roman bronze statue of Mercury; the original charter granted to Colchester in 1413; the Colchester Vase, one of the most important examples of Roman pottery found in Britain; the Colchester Sphinx, once part of a Roman tomb; gold coins of King Cunobelin; and a new interactive gallery affording a walk through virtual Colchester. Visitors can try on a toga and medieval hats and shoes, feel the weight of Roman armour and experience the town's murkier past by visiting the Castle prisons, where witches were interrogated by the notorious Witchfinder General Matthew Hopkins.

The castle and museum are set in the glorious **Castle Park and Gardens**, which has lovely lake-side walks, a Victorian bandstand, modern children's play area and boating lake, crazy golf and putting green and a traditional café.

Also on the edge of the park is the free entry **Hollytrees Museum** (Tel: 01206 282940), in a fine Georgian home dating back to 1718. This award-winning museum houses a wonderful collection of toys, costumes, curios and antiquities from the last two centuries. Purchased for the town by Viscount Cowdray it first opened as a museum in 1920. Across the road you will find the **Natural History Museum**, housed in the former All Saints' Church, with many hands-on displays illustrating the natural

history of Essex from the Ice Age right up to the present day. Recent additions to the museum include a garden, and stag beetle exhibition. Tel: 01206 282941.

At the top of the High Street in central Colchester, beside the Tourist Information Centre, is the innovative £24million **First Site Visual Art Gallery** (due to be opened in Spring 2011). A stunning building designed by Rafael Vinoly Architects, which will contain inspiring exhibitions, innovative learning for all ages, a resource centre, shop selling work by local artists and a café – a new attraction to look out for!

Further along just off the High Street, an arch in Trinity Street leads to **Tymperleys Clock Museum**, the 15th century timber-framed home of William Gilberd, who entertained Elizabeth I with experiments in electricity. Today this fine example of architectural splendour houses a magnificent collection of 18th and 19th century Colchester-made clocks. Tymperleys now houses part of the famous Bernard Mason Collection, one of the largest collections of clocks in Britain. All were made in Colchester between 1640 and 1840 and give a fascinating insight into this specialist trade. The museum is open Tuesday - Saturday 10am - 1pm and 2pm - 5pm, it is closed from November to March. Tel: 01206 282939.

At the end of the High Street, not far from Balkerne Gate, and beside the impressive Jumbo Water Tower is **Colchester Arts Centre**,

• *Colchester Zoo, just off the A12 outside the town, stands in the 40-acre park of Stanway Hall, with its 16th century mansion and church dating from the 14th century. Founded in 1963, the Zoo has a wide and exciting variety of attractions. The Zoo has gained a well-deserved reputation as one of the best in Europe. Its award-winning enclosures allow visitors closer to the animals and provides naturalistic environments for upwards of 200 species. The daily displays include the chance to help feed elephants and giraffes, and watch the free-flying birds of prey. Other attractions include the African Zone, the Penguin Parade, the Tiger Taiga enclosure and the sea lion pool with a viewing tunnel. The zoo is open 9:30am-6:30pm during Summer holidays, 9:30am-6:00pm from Easter to September, and through June & July until the start of the summer holidays, and 9:30am-dusk (or 5pm if later) October to March.* •

137

75 LA CASCADA

Colchester

An authentic Spanish restaurant offering fine food, excellent service and a delightful dining experience.

¶ *see page 268*

76 THE WHALEBONE INN

Fingringhoe

With views over some of the best scenery in Essex, this Grade II listed building is the ideal place for that special occasion.

¶ *see page 268*

which features a regular programme of visual arts, drama, music, poetry and dance; also here is the **Mercury Theatre** which is the town's premier site for stage dramas, comedies and musical theatre.

Just north of the centre of town, **High Woods Country Park** offers 330 acres of woodland, grassland, scrub and farmland. A central lake is fed by a small tributary of the River Colne. The land originated as three ancient farms, and forms part of a Royal hunting forest. Large numbers of musket balls dating from the Civil War period have been unearthed, indicating that the woods served as a base for the Roundheads. On Bourne Road, south of the town centre just off the B1025, there's a striking stepped-and-curved gabled building known as **Bourne Mill**, now owned by the National Trust. Built in 1591 from stone taken from the nearby St John's Abbeygate, this delightful restored building near a lovely millpond was originally a fishing lodge, later

converted (in the 19th century) into a mill - and still in working order.

AROUND COLCHESTER

WIVENHOE

4 miles SE of Colchester off the A133

This riverside town on the banks of the River Colne was once renowned as a smugglers' haunt, and there is a very pretty quayside that is steeped in maritime history. There are still strong connections with the sea, with boat-building having replaced fishing as the main industry. The pretty church, with its distinctive cupola atop a sturdy tower, stands on the site of the former Saxon church and retains some impressive 16th century brasses.

The small streets lead into each other and end at the picturesque waterfront, where fishing boats and small sailing craft bob at their moorings. On the Quay visitors will find the **Nottage Institute**, the River Colne's nautical academy; classes here teach students about knots, skippering and even how to build a boat! It is open to visitors on Sunday afternoons in summer (or during the week by appointment. Tel: 01206 824142). The **Wivenhoe Trail**, by the river, is an interesting walking and cycle track starting at the railway station and continuing along the river to Colchester Hythe. Wivenhoe Woods is dotted with grassy glades set with tables, the perfect place for a picnic.

East of Wivenhoe quay, the public footpath takes visitors to the

Bourne Mill, Colchester

Tidal Surge Barrier, one of only two in the country. Volunteers run a ferry service operating across the River Colne between the Quay at Wivenhoe, Fingringhoe and Rowhedge. Nearby **Wivenhoe Park** has been the site of the campus for the University of Essex since 1962. Visitors are welcome to stroll around the grounds.

ABBERTON

3 miles S of Colchester off the B1026

Abberton Reservoir Nature Reserve is a 1,200-acre reservoir and wildlife centre, ideal for birdwatching. Designated a Site of Special Scientific Interest, it is home to hundreds of goldeneye, wigeon, gadwall and shovellers, as well as a resting colony of cormorants; the site has a conservation room, shop, toilets and hides.

GREAT WIGBOROUGH

6 miles S of Colchester off the B1026 or B1025

This area had a number of experiences with Zeppelins during the First World War. In September 1916 Zeppelin L33, which had been hit over Bromley, crashed near here. The event is commemorated in an account in St Stephen's Church, framed by metal from the wreck. Another part of L33 can be seen in the Church of St Nicholas in neighbouring Little Wigborough.

LAYER BRETON

5½ miles SW of Colchester off the B1026

On the right side of Layer Breton Heath there's **Stamps and Crows**, a must for gardening enthusiasts. Two and a half acres of moated garden surrounding a 15th century farmhouse boast herbaceous borders, mixed shrubs, old roses and good ground cover. There is also a bog garden and dovecote.

LAYER MARNEY

6 miles SW of Colchester off the B1022

The mansion, which was planned to rival Hampton Court, was never completed, but its massive 8-storey Tudor gatehouse, known as **Layer Marney Tower**, is very impressive. Built between 1515 and 1525, it is

77 THE BAKE HOUSE

Wivenhoe

A fine restaurant which serves classic English food with a French twist.

🍴 *see page 269*

Layer Marney Tower

one of the most striking examples of 16th century architecture in Britain. Its magnificent four red brick towers, covered in 16th century Italianate design, were built by Lord Marney, Henry VIII's Lord Privy Seal. As well as spectacular views from the top of the towers, they are surrounded by formal gardens designed at the turn of the century, with lovely roses, yew hedges and herbaceous borders. There is also on site a rare breeds farm, farm shop and tea room.

TIPTREE

7 miles SW of Colchester on the B1023

As all true jam-lovers will know, Tiptree is famed as the home of the **Wilkin and Son Ltd** jam factory, a Victorian establishment which now boasts a fascinating visitors' centre in the grounds of the original factory, as well as a museum, shop and very popular tearoom. There are some great events held here all year round, including tasting sessions. Tel: 01621 814524 for more information.

CHAPPEL

5 miles W of Colchester off the A604

Here, on an open-air site with beautiful valley views beside Chappel and Wakes Colne Station, is the **East Anglian Railway Museum**, a comprehensive collection spanning 150 years of railway history, with period railway architecture, engineering and memorabilia in beautifully restored station buildings. For every railway buff, young or old, this is the place to try your hand at being a signalman and admire the handsome restored engines and carriages. They also run special railway experience courses in driving and firing a steam locomotive, as well as special events all year round including the popular beer and cider festivals and Christmas rides with Santa. Easy to find on the A1124 (off the A12), the Museum is open daily from 10am to 4.30pm.

Chappel Galleries (free entry) is a commercial gallery with a programme of changing exhibits of fine art.

EARLS COLNE

7 miles W of Colchester off the A604

The de Veres, Earls of Oxford, and the River Colne bestowed this village with its name. Aubery de Vere founded a Benedictine priory here in the 12th century, and both he and his wife, sister of William the Conqueror, were buried there. Today the site is marked by a redbrick Gothic mansion. Though the commuter culture has spread modern housing around the village, the cluster of timbered cottages hearkens back to this village's distinguished past. At **Pound Green**, on the Coggeshall road, stands a pump erected in 1853 by benefactor Mary Gee in thanks for the absence of cholera in the village.

ELMSTEAD MARKET

4 miles E of Colchester off the A133

Just up the road from the pretty village of Elmstead Market is **Beth**

Chatto Gardens; which started life as an overgrown wasteland in 1960 with gravelly soil and boggy hollows, and has been transformed into 6 acres of beautiful gardenscapes, harmonising with the surrounding countryside. The flowers, trees and plants specially selected for their suitability in the conditions here, have flourished. With a gravel garden, wet pond area and woodland garden, there is also a nursery where you can chose the perfect greenery for your own garden from over 2000 plant varieties on the advice of professionals. The modern tearoom overlooks the picturesque gravel garden and serves a delicious range of food, mostly locally sourced including Tiptree jams and award winning ice cream from the Manor Farm Creamery in Bury St Edmunds. Open year round Mon-Sat 9am to 4pm and Sundays 10am to 4pm.

DEDHAM

6 miles NE of Colchester off the A14

This is true Constable country, along the border with Suffolk, the county's prettiest area. The village has several fine old buildings, especially the 15th century flint church, its pinnacled tower familiar from so many Constable paintings. There's also the school Constable went to, and good walks through the protected riverside meadows of Dedham Vale to **Flatford**, where Bridge Cottage is a restored thatched 16th century building housing a display about Constable, who featured this cottage in several

of his paintings (his father's mill is across the river lock in Dedham).

The **Art & Craft Centre** on Dedham's High Street is well worth a visit. Marlborough Head, a wool merchant's house dating back to 1475, is now a pub.

BRAINTREE

This town and its close neighbour Bocking are sited at the crossing of two Roman roads and were brought together by the cloth industry in the 16th century. Flemish weavers settled here, followed by many Huguenots. One, Samuel Courtauld, set up a silk mill in 1816 and, by 1866, employed over 3,000 Essex inhabitants.

The magnificent former **Town Hall** is one of the many Courtauld legacies in the town. It was built in 1928 with panelled walls, murals by Grieffenhagen showing stirring scenes of local history, and a grand central tower with a five-belled striking clock. A smaller but no less fascinating reminder of Courtauld's generosity is the 1930s bronze fountain, with bay, shell and fish, near St Michael's Church.

The **Braintree District Museum**, housed in a converted Victorian school in the historic market square tells the story of Braintree's diverse industrial heritage and traditions; exhibits include a re-created Victorian classroom, the wool and silk industries and various country crafts. The **Town Hall Centre** is a Grade II listed building housing the Tourist Information Centre and the

Dedham Vale Family Farm on Mill Street in Dedham is a nicely undeveloped 16-acre farm boasting a comprehensive collection of British farm animals, including many different breeds of livestock such as pigs, sheep, cattle, Suffolk horses, goats and poultry. Children may enter certain of the paddocks to stroke and feed the animals (bags of feed provided). Open March-Sept 10.30am-5.30pm.

78 MARLBOROUGH HEAD INN

Dedham

A character-filled listed public house with luxurious accommodation, home cooked food, ale and sun trap terrace to enjoy.

see page 270

79 THE CLOCKHOUSE

Coggeshall

A truly unique building full of quirks to accompany the spectacular cakes and treats on offer.

see page 271

80 THE KINGS ARMS

Broad Green

A lively country pub with family accommodation serving fine home cooked pub favourites all year round.

see page 270

Art Gallery, which boasts a continuous changing programme of exhibitions and works.

Much of the town centre has been pedestrianised, and many of the pubs and cafés offer continental-style outdoor seating where you can sit and watch the world go by. Market days are Wednesdays and Saturdays, but all week there is a wealth of small independent shops for visitors to explore.

AROUND BRAINTREE

COGGESHALL

5 miles E of Braintree on the A120

This medieval hamlet, a pleasant old cloth and lace town, has some very fine timbered buildings.

Located in Stoneham Street beside the village hall, in a building which once housed a brewery, **Coggeshall Heritage Centre** displays items of local interest and features changing exhibitions on themes relating to the past of this historic wool town.

The National Trust also owns the restored **Coggeshall Grange Barn**, which dates from around 1140 and is the oldest surviving timber-framed barn in Europe. Built for the monks of the nearby Cistercian Abbey, it is a magnificent example of this type of architecture.

Paycocke's House on West Street in Coggeshall is a delightful timber-framed medieval merchant's home dating from about 1500, boasts unusually rich panelling and wood carvings, and is owned by the National Trust. Inside there's a superb carved ceiling and a display of Coggeshall lace. Outdoors there's a lovely garden. The village also has some good antique shops and a working pottery.

Marks Hall is a historic estate and arboretum that began life in Saxon times, and is mentioned in the *Domesday Book*. In the 15th century, then-owner Sir Thomas Honywood was a leading Parliamentarian who commanded the Essex Regiment during the Civil War. Local legend has it that the two artificial lakes on the grounds were dug by Parliamentary troops during the siege of Colchester in 1648. One of his successors, General Philip Honywood, in 1758 forbade (under the terms of his will) any of his successors to fell timber - thus his lasting legacy of avenues of mature oaks, limes and horse chestnuts, surrounded by one of the largest continuous areas of ancient woodland in the county.

Paycocke's House, Coggeshall

CRESSING

4 miles E of Braintree off the B1018

Cressing Temple Barns, set in the centre of an ancient farmstead, are two splendid medieval timber barns commissioned in the 12th century by the Knights Templar. They contain the timber of over 1,000 oak trees; an interpretive exhibition explains to visitors how the barns were made, as a special viewing platform brings visitors up into the roof of the magnificent Wheat Barn for a closer look. There's also a beautiful walled garden re-creating the Tudor style, with an arbour, fount, physic garden, and shop. Special events are held throughout the year. All facilities are open April until September Sun-Fri 10am to 5pm and March until October Sun-Fri 10am-4pm; between November and February visitors can see the gardens and grounds 10am-3pm.

FEERING

6 miles E of Braintree off the A12

Feeringbury Manor near Feering has a fine, extensive riverside garden with ponds, streams, a little waterwheel, old-fashioned plants and bog gardens, and fascinating sculpture by artist Ben Coode-Adams.

KELVEDON

6 miles SE of Braintree off the A12

This village alongside the River Blackwater houses the **Feering and Kelvedon Museum**, which is dedicated to manorial history and houses artefacts from the Roman settlement of Canonium, agricultural tools through the ages and other interesting exhibits. It is open Monday 2pm-5pm and Saturday 9.30am-12.30pm from April until September.

FAIRSTEAD

4 miles S of Braintree off the A131

Fairstead (or Fairsted) is an undulating parish about three miles east of the A131. The **Church of St Mary and St Peter** is an ancient building of flint, in the Norman style, consisting of chancel, nave, north porch and a western tower with a lofty shingled spire with four bells, one of which dates back to before the Reformation. During restoration in the late 1800s various handsome mural paintings were discovered, including, over the chancel arch, those entitled Our Lord's Triumphal Entry into Jerusalem, The Last Supper, The Betrayal, Our Lord being Crowned with Thorns, and Incidents on the way to Calvary.

BLAKE END

3 miles W of Braintree off the A120

The **Great Maze** at Blake End is one of the most challenging in the world. Set in over 10 acres of lovely North Essex farmland, it is grown every year from over half a million individual maize and sunflower seeds, and is open every summer. Continuing innovations bring with them extra twists and turns, making this wonderful maze, with more than five miles of pathways, even more of a brain teaser. A viewing platform makes it

Finchingfield

A popular B&B and restaurant offering the very best in comfort and cuisine.

see page 272

easy to help anyone hopelessly lost! Ten per cent of all profits go to the Essex Air Ambulance service. It is open from 10am and last admission is at 4.30pm.

GREAT SALING

4 miles NW of Braintree off the A120

Saling Hall Garden is a 12-acre garden including a walled garden dating from 1698. The small park boasts a collection of fine trees, and there are ponds, a water garden, a working kitchen garden, and an extensive collection of unusual plants with an emphasis on rare trees.

WETHERSFIELD

5 miles NW of Braintree on the B1053

Boydells Dairy Farm is a working farm where visitors are welcome to join in with tasks such as milking, feeding and more. A popular guided tour mixes fun with education, and all questions are most welcome. From bees to llamas, just about every kind of farm animal can be found here. Their guest book is brimming with thanks from happy visitors. It is open 2pm-5pm on weekends all summer. Tel: 01371 850481.

GREAT BARDFIELD

6 miles NW of Braintree off the B1053

Here in one of the prettiest villages in all of Essex, Great Bardfield Museum occupies a 16th century charity cottage and 19th century village lockup (the Cage), and features exhibits of mainly 19th and 20th century domestic and agricultural artefacts and some fine examples of rural crafts such as corn dollies and straw-plaiting. The Museum is open on Saturday, Sunday and Bank Holiday afternoons from 2.00 – 5.30 pm between Easter and the last Sunday in September.

This old market town on a hill above the River Pant is a pleasant mixture of cottages and shops, nicely complemented by the 14th century **Church of St Mary the Virgin**. Perhaps Great Bardfield's most notable feature is, however, a restored windmill that goes by the strange name of Gibraltar.

Just outside of Great Bardfield, along Braintree road, is another rustic treat in **The Blue Egg**. This pretty shop has an amazing range of locally sourced produce including award winning smoked fish from Pinney's of Orford, Tiptree preserves, locally brewed beers, wines and liquors, and delicious biscuits and moist cakes. Also here you can buy some unique gifts and homeware, fresh flowers and garden herbs, and coal, logs and kindling.

FINCHINGFIELD

6 miles NW of Braintree off the B1053

This charming village is graced with thatched cottages spread generously around a sloping village green that dips to a stream and duck pond at the centre of the village. Nearby stands an attractive small 18th century **Post Mill** with one pair of stones and tailpole winding. Extensively restored, today's visitors can climb up the first two floors.

Just up the hill, visitors will find the Norman **Church of St John the Baptist** and the **Guildhall** (mentioned in the *Domesday Book*), which has a small museum open Sundays and also houses a local heritage centre with displays of artwork, paintings, pottery, sewing and weaving.

Finchingfield is easily one of the most picturesque and most photographed villages in Essex, featured in many television programmes and the home of the series Lovejoy. Here visitors will also find the privately owned Tudor stately home, **Spains Hall**, which has a lovely flower garden containing a huge Cedar of Lebanon planted in 1670 and an Adams sundial. Rose bushes surround the kitchen garden, which contains an ancient Paulonia tree and a bougainvillea in the greenhouse. This is one Essex's premiere wedding locations.

Dodie Smith, author of *101 Dalmatians*, lived for many years in a 17th century cottage in the village.

GOSFIELD

4 miles N of Braintree off the A1017

Gosfield Lake Leisure Resort, the county's largest freshwater lake, lies in the grounds of Gosfield Hall. This Tudor mansion was remodelled in the 19th century by its owner Samuel Courtauld. He also built the attractive mock-Tudor houses in the village. The privately family-run resort offers a whole host of activities ranging from fishing to waterskiing, as well as camping and some picturesque

Spains Hall, Finchingfield

picnic spots beside the 36 acre lake. Tel: 01787 475043.

HALSTEAD

The name Halstead comes from the Old English words hald (refuge, shelter) and stede (site, place), meaning 'safe place' or 'place of refuge'. Like Braintree and Coggeshall, Halstead was an important weaving centre. **Townsford Mill** is certainly the most picturesque reminder of Halstead's industrial heritage. Built in the 1700s, it remains one of the most handsome buildings in a town with a number of historic buildings. This white, weather-boarded three-storey mill across the River Colne at the Causeway was once a landmark site for the Courtauld empire, producing both the famous funerary silk crepe– including that used in Queen Victoria's mourning gowns - and rayon. Today the Mill is an antiques centre, one of the largest in Essex, with thousands of items of

82 GOSFIELD
SHOPPING VILLAGE

Gosfield

A great shopping complex with a wide range of independent shops featuring arts and crafts.

🏛 ⅋ see page 273

145

There are several historic buildings in the shopping centre of Halstead, which is part of a designated conservation area. Markets are held every Friday and Saturday.

furniture, porcelain, collectibles, stamps, coins, books, dolls, postcards, costume, paintings, glass and ceramics, old lace and clocks.

Halstead's most famous product was once mechanical elephants. Life-sized and weighing half a ton, they were built by W Hunwicks. Each one consisted of 9,000 parts and could carry a load of eight adults and four children at speeds of up to an impressive 12 miles per hour. It is rumored that the famous actor Peter Sellers, an avid antiques collector, had a

mechanical elephant such as this in his collection – though it is not certain that it was sourced from Halstead. Indeed there was a period where these fascinating creations were very popular and Britain was the leading producers of them in the world; the 1950's saw one trundling up and down the promenade at Margate.

AROUND HALSTEAD

CASTLE HEDINGHAM
3 miles NW of Halstead off the B1058

This town takes its name from its **Norman Castle**, which dominates the landscape. One of England's strongest fortresses in the 11th century, even now it is impossible not to sense its power and strength. The impressive stone keep is one of the tallest in Europe, with four floors and rising over 100 feet, with 12-feet thick walls. The banqueting hall and minstrels' gallery can still be seen. It was owned by the Earls of Oxford, the powerful de Vere family, one of whom was among the barons who forced King John to accept the Magna Carta. Among those entertained at the castle were Henry VII and Elizabeth I.

The village itself is a maze of narrow streets radiating from Falcon Square, named after the half-timbered Falcon Inn. Attractive buildings include many Georgian and 15th century houses comfortably vying for space, and the **Church of St Nicholas**, built by the de Veres, which avoided Victorian 'restoration' and is

Castle Hedingham

146

virtually completely Norman, with grand masonry and interestingly carved choir seats. There is a working pottery in St James' Street.

SIBLE HEDINGHAM
3 miles NW of Halstead off the A1017

Mentioned in the *Domesday Book* as the largest parish in England, Sible Hedingham was the birthplace of Sir John Hawkwood, one of the 14th century's most famous soldiers of fortune. He led a band of mercenaries to Italy, where he was paid to defend Florence and where he married the daughter of the Duke of Milan. He died in Italy and was buried in Florence Cathedral, where a commemorative fresco was painted by Uccello. His body was returned to Essex and was reputedly buried in the south aisle of Sible Hedingham's **Church of St Peter**. A monument to him in the church is decorated with hawks and various other beasts.

GESTINGTHORPE
5 miles N of Halstead off the A131

The **Church of St Mary the Virgin** in Gestingthorpe is distinctive in many respects. Witness to centuries of Christian worship, the *Domesday Book* of 1086 tells that 'Ghestingetorp' was held by Ledmer the priest before 1066. The oldest part extant of the existing building is the blocked-up lancet window in the north wall of the chancel, which dates back to the 1200s. Apart from this, most of the chancel, nave and south aisle dates from the 14th century. The tower, constructed in about 1500, is

66 feet high. Of the six bells hung in the tower, four were cast in 1658-9 by Miles Gray, a Colchester bellfounder. The 16th century fifth and sixth bells were cast in Bury St Edmunds, and recast in 1901. The west door, set in a stepped brick arch, is the original. The unusual tracery in the East window consists of arches placed atop the apexes of the arches beneath them. The late 15th century/early 16th century nave roof is of the double hammer-beam type, and one of the finest in Essex. The font is late 14th century. One of the handsome memorials in Gestinthorpe's church commemorates Captain L E G Oates, who died in an attempt to save the lives of his companions on an ill-fated expedition to the Antarctic in 1912.

LITTLE MAPLESTEAD
3 miles NE of Halstead off the A131

Little Maplestead has an unusual **Round Church**, dedicated to St John the Baptist, modelled on the Holy Sepulchre in Jerusalem, and used as a stopping-point for pilgrims on their way there. Built more than 600 years ago by the military order of the Knights Hospitallers, their 'Perceptory' at Little Maplestead was suppressed more than 400 years ago by Henry VIII.

THE NORTH ESSEX COAST

CLACTON-ON-SEA
16 miles SE of Colchester on the A133

Clacton is a traditional sun-and-

69 SCHOOL BARN FARM

Pentlow

Environmentally conscious accommodation in the beautiful Stour Valley.

⊨ *see page 265*

70 THE PINKUAH ARMS

Pentlow

This pink pub provides wonderful food in a warm and charming setting.

❙ *see page 265*

sand family resort with a south-facing, long sandy beach, lovely gardens on the seafront and a wide variety of shops and places to explore. It also boasts a wide variety of special events and entertainment taking place throughout the year.

Settled by hunters during the Stone Age - which is borne witness to by the wealth of flint implements and the fossilised bones of the cave lion, straight-tusked elephant and wild ox unearthed on the Clacton foreshore and at Lion Point - the town grew over the centuries from a small village into a prosperous seaside resort in the 1800s, when the craze for the health benefits of coastal air and bathing was at its peak. The **Pier** was constructed in 1871; at first paddle steamers provided the only mode of transport to the resort, the railway arriving in 1882. The Pier was widened from 30 to over 300 feet in the 1930s. On the pier, apart from the marvellous traditional sideshows, big wheel, restaurants and fairground rides,

there is the fascinating **Seaquarium and Reptile Safari**.

Amusement centres include the arcades and Clacton Pavilion. The two theatres, Princes Theatre and West Cliff, are open all year. Clacton Pavilion boasts a range of attractions, including crazy golf and dodgems. The Clifftop Public Gardens also repay a visit. In August there is an annual Air Show, with breath-taking aerial displays and events held through the town.

Great Clacton is the oldest part of town, comprising an attractive grouping of shops, pubs and restaurants within the shadow of the 12th century parish church.

HOLLAND-ON-SEA
1½ miles NE of Clacton off the B1032

This attractive community, sandwiched between the bustling seaside resorts of Frinton and Clacton, is home to the tranquil **Holland Haven Country Park**, 100 acres of unspoilt open space near the seashore, ideal for watching the marine birds and other wildlife of the region. Throughout the area there are a number of attractive walks which take full advantage of the varied coastal scenery – the park is a perfect place to come and get away from it all.

FRINTON-ON-SEA
3 miles NE of Clacton off the B1032

Once a quiet fishing village, this town was developed as a select resort by Sir Richard Cooper, and expanded in the 1880s to the genteel family resort it is today. Situated on

Clacton Pier

148

a long stretch of sandy beach, Frinton remains peaceful and unspoilt. The tree-lined residential avenues sweep elegantly down to the Esplanade and extensive clifftop greensward. The **Church of Old St Mary** in Frinton contains some panels of stained glass in the East window designed by the Pre-Raphaelite artist Burne-Jones. A good example of 20th century English vernacular architecture is **The Homestead** at the corner of Second Avenue and Holland Road, built in 1905 by C F Voysey.

The area south of Frinton Gates has a unique local character, being laid out with detached houses set along broad tree-lined avenues.

WEELEY

5 miles NW of Clacton off the A133

St Andrew's Church is the handsome parish church just south of the centre of this picturesque village. There is a lovely tree-lined path that passes Weeleyhall Wood and Weeley Lodge, with its beautifully kept gardens. Here visitors will also pass a navigational beacon that forms part of Aircraft Flight Operations for both civil and military flights.

A mile south, off the B1411, **Weeley Heath** is a small and attractive community boasting a lovely village green and stunning surrounding countryside.

LITTLE CLACTON

3 miles NW of Clacton off the A133

Though it shares its name with its near neighbour, this is a village apart. Quiet and secluded, multiple-

winner of the Best Kept Village award, Little Clacton features a lovely Jubilee Oak, planted to celebrate Victoria's 50th year on the throne.

The fine **Church of St James** has been described as one of the most beautiful medieval churches in Essex, and sits at the heart of the village.

TENDRING

7 miles NW of Clacton off the A133

This village that gives its name to both the peninsula and the district council contains the handsome **Church of St Edmund**, whose elegant spire can be seen for miles around. The church is dedicated to the last King of independent East Anglia, martyred by the Danes in the 9th century.

WALTON-ON-THE-NAZE

8 miles NE of Clacton on the B1034

Walton is all the fun of the fair. It is a traditional, singular and cheerful resort which focuses on the pier and all its attractions, including a ten-pin bowling alley. The gardens at the seafront are colourful and the beach has good sand. The Backwaters to the rear of Walton are made up of a series of small harbours and saltings, which lead into Harwich harbour.

Walton has an outstanding sandy beach. The town's seafront was developed in 1825 and provides a fine insight into the character of an early Victorian seaside resort. The charming narrow streets of the town contain numerous shops, restaurants and

•

Along Frinton's main shopping street in Connaught Avenue, the 'Bond Street' of the East Coast, shopkeepers maintain a tradition of friendly and courteous service. Summer theatre and other open-air events take place throughout the season, and there are also some excellent tennis and golf clubs in the town. The grace and elegance of this sophisticated resort is evidenced at every turn, as are hints of its distinguished past: Victorian beach huts still dot the extensive beach. The long and clean cliff-top greensward gives this part of the seafront a real sense of space, and makes a lovely place to enjoy a leisurely picnic.

•

149

pubs overlooking the second longest pier in the country. **Marine Parade**, originally called The Crescent, was built in 1832. The **Pier**, first built in 1830, was originally constructed of wood and measured 330 feet long. It was extended to its present length of 2,610 feet in 1898, at the same time as the electric train service began. The **Old Lifeboat House Museum** at East Terrace, in a building over 100 years old, houses an interpretive museum of local history and development, rural and maritime, covering Walton, Frinton and the Sokens

The wind-blown expanse of **The Naze** just north of Walton is an extensive coastal recreation and picnic area, pleasant for walking, especially out of season when the visitor is likely to have all 150 acres

virtually to him or herself, with great views out over the water. The shape of the Naze is constantly changing, eroded by wind, water and tide.

The year 1796 saw the demise of the medieval church, and somewhere beyond the 800-feet pier lies medieval Walton. The sandstone cliffs are internationally important for their shell fossil deposits. Inhabitants have been enjoying the bracing sea air at Walton since before Neolithic times: flint-shaping instruments have been found here, and the fossil teeth and the ears of sharks and whales have been discovered in the Naze's red crag cliffs. The **Naze Tower** is brick built and octagonal in shape, originally built as a beacon in 1720 to warn seamen of the West Rocks off shore. It is now an art gallery, which exhibits some amazing work of local artists, and a café which is open 1st April to 31st October everyday 10am to 5pm. A nature trail has been created nearby, and the Essex Skipper butterfly and Emperor moth can be seen here.

A market is held in Market Millennium Square every Thursday (and Monday's during the summer), and Wednesdays remain an early closing day for many shops in the town.

BRIGHTLINGSEA

7 miles W of Clacton on the B1029

Brightlingsea enjoys a long tradition of shipbuilding and seafaring. In 1347, 51 men and five ships were sent to the siege of

The Marina, Walton-on-the-Naze

Calais. Among the crew members of Sir Francis Drake's fleet which vanquished the Spanish Armada was one 'William of Brightlingsea'. Brightlingsea has the distinction of being the only limb of the Cinque Ports outside Kent and Sussex.

All Saints Church, which occupies the highest point of the town on a hill about a mile from the centre, is mainly 13th century. Here are to be found some Roman brickwork and a frieze of ceramic tiles commemorating local residents whose lives were lost at sea. Its 97-feet tower can be seen from 17 miles out to sea. A light was once placed in the tower to guide the town's fishermen home

The **Town Hard** is where you can see all the waterfront comings and goings, including the activities of the Colne Smack Preservation Society, which maintains a seagoing link with the past. The 13th century **Jacobes Hall** in the centre of Brightlingsea is one of the oldest occupied buildings in Essex. It is timber-framed with an undulating tile roof and an external staircase. Used as a meeting hall during the reign of Henry III, its name originates from its first owner, Edmund, Vicar of Brightlingsea, who was known locally as Jacob le Clerk. **Brightlingsea Museum** in Duke Street offers an insight into the lives, customs and traditions of the area, housing a collection of exhibits relating to the town's maritime connections and the oyster industry.

The award-winning "Brightlingsea In Bloom" organisation has since 1997 planted some amazing displays, both near the waterfront and through the town, and continue to do so in on-going projects which have bonded the whole community. In the summer a free four day music festival is held in the town.

For those wanting to get out on the water, there is a luxurious charter boat which can be hired for fishing trips (which include hot drinks and a packed lunch). Tel: 07774 492856.

ELMSTEAD MARKET
6 miles N of Brightlingsea off the A120

The **Church of St Anne and St Lawrence** to the north of this village has a rare carved oak recumbent effigy of a knight in armour. Also at Elmstead Market is the **Beth Chatto Gardens** (previously mentioned in the Suffolk chapter). Close by is the **Rolts Nursery Butterfly Farm**.

THORRINGTON
3 miles NW of Brightlingsea off the B1027

Thorrington Tide Mill, built in the early 19th century, is the only remaining Tide Mill in Essex, and one of very few left in East Anglia. It has been fully restored, and although no longer in use, the Wheel can be run for guided groups. A public footpath runs along the creek here.

POINT CLEAR
2 miles SE of Brightlingsea off the B1027

The **East Essex Aviation Society & Museum**, located in the Martello Tower at Point Clear, not

83 MOOCH @ NO 9

Brightlingsea

A smart and chic cafe in the town centre providing great snacks and meals.

see page 274

151

only retains its original flooring and roof, but today contains interesting displays of wartime aviation, military and naval photographs, uniforms and other memorabilia with local and US Air Force connections. There are artefacts on show from the crash sites of wartime aircraft in the Tendring area, including the engine and fuselage section of a recovered P51D Mustang fighter. The museum also explores civil and military history from both World Wars. There are very good views from the tower over the Colne Estuary and Brightlingsea. Open 7pm-9pm Mondays all year round, and Wednesdays and Sundays 10am-2pm in summer. Tel: 07899 917144. Free parking is available at the Ferryboat Inn next door, where you can get a drink and some good food.

ST OSYTH

3 miles SE of Brightlingsea off the B1027

This pretty little village has a fascinating history – the parish contains 112 buildings listed as being of historical or special architectural interest. The most impressive of these is the Norman **Church of St Peter and St Paul** and the ancient ruins of **St Osyth Priory**, founded in the 12th century, both Grade I listed buildings. The village and Priory were named by Augustinian Canons after St Osytha, martyred daughter of Frithenwald, first Christian King of the East Angles, who was beheaded by Diceian pirates AD 653. Little of the original Priory remains, except for the magnificent late-15th century flint gatehouse, complete with battlements. The **Church of St Peter and St Paul** in the village centre has unusual internal red brick piers and arches. The nearby creek has a small boatyard.

MERSEA ISLAND

2 miles SW of Brightlingsea off the B1025

Much of this island is a National Nature Reserve, home to its teeming shorelife. The island is linked to the mainland by a narrow causeway which is covered over at high tide – so trips need to be appropriately timed. The towns of both East and West Mersea have excellent facilities for sailing enthusiasts, and East Mersea is also a haven for birdwatchers. **Mersea Island Museum** contains exhibits on Mersea's social and natural history, archaeology and the fishing industry, including a fisherman's cottage. The traditional local activities of fishing, oystering, wild fowling and boat building are also represented in informative displays. It is open through the summer

St Osyth Priory

2pm-5pm Wednesday-Sunday (and Bank Holiday Mondays). Visitors to **Mersea Island Vineyard** can sample the fine wines made here (white and usually dry to medium-dry) with some delectable meals at the Courtyard Café and Shop (Open Wed-Sun 10.30am-4pm). Tours of the 10 acre vineyard are available through the summer months, with free tasting included, private tours for groups by prior arrangement. Tel: 01206 385900.

West Mersea

HARWICH

Harwich's name probably originates from the time of King Alfred, when 'hare' meant army, and 'wic' a camp. This attractive old town was built in the 13th century by the Earls of Norfolk to exploit its strategic position on the Stour and Orwell estuary; the town has an important and fascinating maritime history, the legacy of which continues into the present.

During the 14th and 15th century French campaigns, Harwich was an important naval base. The famous Elizabethan seafarers Hawkins, Frobisher and Drake sailed from Harwich on various expeditions; in 1561 Queen Elizabeth I visited the town, describing it *'a pretty place and want[ing] for nothing'*. Christopher Newport, leader of the Goodspeed expedition which founded Jamestown, Virginia, in 1607, and Christopher Jones, master of the Pilgrim ship *The Mayflower*, lived in Harwich (the latter just off the quay in King's Head Street), as did Jones' kinsman John Alden, who sailed to America in 1620. The famous diarist Samuel Pepys was MP for the town in the 1660s, thus it was also during this time headquarters for the King's Navy. Charles II took the first pleasure cruise from Harwich's shores. Other notable visitors included Lord Nelson and Lady Hamilton, who are reputed to have stayed at The Three Cups in Church Street.

The Harwich Society owns and runs four fascinating museums throughout Harwich; all of them are open to the public between 10am and 5pm from the start of March until the end of August. The first, a **Lifeboat Museum** off Wellington Road, contains the last Clacton offshore 34-feet lifeboat and a history of the lifeboat service in Harwich. Harwich is a very busy lifeboat station with around 100 call-outs a year; the all-weather lifeboat often goes far out into the North Sea, while the inshore boat attends the rivers and coal areas.

153

The Treadwheel Crane now stands on Harwich Green, but for over 250 years it was sited in the Naval Shipyard. It is worked by two people walking in two 16-feet diameter wheels, and is the only known British example of its kind. Amazingly, it was operational up until the 1920s.

The **Ha'penny Pier Visitor Centre** is also on the Quay. This wonderfully refurbished Victorian pier ticket office contains a small exhibition of local history and offers a free information service on what to see, where to eat and where to stay in Harwich. The Ha'penny Pier now boasts a Mayflower exhibition, which is a must for anyone interested in history.

The importance of Harwich's port during the 19th century is confirmed by **The Redoubt**, a huge grey fort built between 1808 and 1810. Its design is an enlarged version of the Martello towers which dotted the English coast, awaiting a Napoleonic invasion that never came (some of these towers, of course, still exist). Today the Harwich Society has largely restored it as a voluntary project, and opened it as a small museum – the only one of its kind open to the public.

Lastly is the **Harwich Maritime Museum,** housed in a decommissioned lighthouse with excellent views over the harbour.

The lighthouse that previously occupied this site was painted by John Constable, possibly around 1800, a painting now owned by the Tate Gallery. The present lighthouse was built, along with the high lighthouse a few hundred yards away, in 1818. The museum contains some superb nautical displays.

Harwich Society also runs free guided tours around Harwich, starting from the Ha'penny Pier Visitors Centre. They start at 2pm every Saturday between the start of May and end of Sept.

The old town also contains many ancient buildings, including the **Guildhall**, which was rebuilt in 1769 and is located in Church Street. The Council Chamber, Mayor's Parlour and other rooms may be viewed. The former gaol contains unique graffiti of ships, probably carved by prisoners, and is well worth putting aside a morning to explore (by appointment only). Documents on show include those detailing the connection of Harwich with Pepys, the Pilgrim Fathers, and the Virginia settlement.

A fascinating piece of Harwich's history is the **Electric Palace Cinema**, built in 1911 and now the oldest unaltered purpose-built cinema in Britain. It was restored by a trust and re-opened in 1981.

AROUND HARWICH

DOVERCOURT
1 mile S of Harwich off the A120

This residential and holiday suburb of Harwich has Market Day on

Treadwheel Crane, Harwich

Fridays. With its attractive cliffs and beach (which has been awarded the Blue Flag for cleanliness), it also boasts the Iron Lighthouse or 'Leading Lights' located just off lower Marine Parade. It has a small but busy shopping area, a village green, and the oldest church in the area, the sturdy All Saints' founded in the 11th century. There is much for a visitor to do during their visit here, including a boating lake, model yacht pond, roller-skating rink, tennis courts, putting green, crazy golf course, croquet lawn, petanque terrain and amusement arcade. If there weather is less than ideal a trip to the **Indoor Pool**, with fitness centre, never fails to deliver. Events here include weekly water aerobics classes and junior fun days where a large inflatable raft is put in the pool for young ones to play on. Tel: 01255 508266.

Mistley Towers

The town has been settled from prehistoric times, as attested to by the late-Bronze Age axe-heads found here (now in Colchester Museum). The Romans found the town a useful source of the stone 'Septaria', taken from the cliffs and used in building. The town that visitors see today developed primarily in Victorian times as a fashionable resort.

MISTLEY

7 miles W of Harwich off the B1352

Here at the gateway to Constable Country, local 18th century landowner and MP Richard Rigby had grand designs to develop Mistley into a fashionable spa to rival Harrogate and Bath, adopting

the swan as its symbol. Sadly, all that remains of Rigby's ambitious scheme is the Swan Fountain, a small number of attractive Georgian houses and **Mistley Towers** (English Heritage), the remains of a church (otherwise demolished in 1870) designed by the flamboyant architect Robert Adams. Pictures of the church which once stood with these two unusual towers can be seen inside the east tower. From the waterfront, noted for its colony of swans, there are very pleasant views across the estuary to Suffolk.

Mistley Quay Workshops in the High Street feature a pottery workshop, lute/cello maker, harpsichord maker, wood worker, bookbinder, and stained-glass window maker and restorer. There

Manningtree has been a market town since 1238, and is still a busy shopping centre. It proudly holds the title of smallest town in Britain; though a stroll through the streets reveals the rich diversity of its past, and it suddenly doesn't seem so small! There are still traditional (and mainly Georgian) restaurants, pubs and shops, as well as handcraft and specialist outlets.

Back in Tudor times, Manningtree was the centre of the cloth trade, and later a port filled with barges carrying their various cargoes along the coast to London. Water still dominates today and the town is a centre of leisure sailing.

is also a café here, which serves delicious breakfast, lunches and cakes, and has panoramic views over the estuary. It is open 10am-5pm year round (closed Mondays, except Bank Holidays).

MANNINGTREE

9 miles W of Harwich off the B1352

In 1848, William White's Gazetteer of Essex described Manningtree as "...an improving market town, and forms with Mistley, a port.... pleasantly situated on the south side of the Stour..." – and this is still true of Manningtree today.

The Walls, on the approach to Manningtree along the B1352, offer unrivalled views of the Stour estuary and the Suffolk coast, and the swans for which the area is famous. Lying on the River Stour amid beautiful rolling countryside, the scene has often been depicted by artists over the centuries.

The views over the river are well known to birdspotters, sailors and ramblers. The town has an intriguing past - as a river crossing, market, smugglers' haven and home of Matthew Hopkins, the reviled and self-styled Witchfinder General who struck terror into the local community during the 17th century. Some of his victims were hanged on Manningtree's small village green.

It is believed that the reference in Shakespeare's Henry IV to Falstaff as 'that roasted Manningtree ox' relates to the practice of roasting an entire ox, which at that time was a highlight of the town's annual fair.

Manningtree Museum (Tel:

01206 395548) in the High Street opened in the late 1980s and mounts two exhibitions a year, together with permanent photographs and pieces relating to the heritage of Manningtree, Lawford, Mistley and the local area. Manningtree railway station is an alternative to Dedham as a start point of a walk to Constable Country, taking in Cattawade Marshes (SSSI), Willy Lot's Cottage and Flatford Mill. In the station itself is a buffet serving a range of excellent traditional English dishes.

ARDLEIGH

10 miles W of Harwich off the A137

Tendring's westernmost village comprises an attractive group of 16th and 17th century cottages grouped around the fine 15th century **St Mary the Virgin Church**, which was renovated in a Gothic style by William Butterfield in 1882. **Spring Valley Mill**, a now privately owned 18th century timber-framed and weather-boarded edifice, was once a working watermill, later adapted to steam. This mostly residential area has avoided being seen as a tourist spot, despite its location on the edge of the beautiful Stour Valley beside the reservoir, and so is a great place to relax and avoid the crowds in high season.

Day and half-day canoeing and sailing lessons can be taken at the **Ardleigh Outdoor Education Centre**. Nearby is **Ardleigh Reservoir**, offering many opportunities for water sports and trout fishing.

SOUTH AND WEST ESSEX

SAFFRON WALDEN

Named after the Saffron crocus - grown in the area to make dyestuffs and fulfil a variety of other uses in the Middle Ages - Saffron Walden has retained much of its original street plan, as well as hundreds of fine old buildings, many of which are timbered and have overhanging upper floors and decorative plastering (also known as pargeting). Gog and Magog (or, in some versions, folk-hero Tom Hickathrift and the Wisbech Giant) battle forever in plaster on the gable of the **Old Sun Inn**, where, legend has it, Oliver Cromwell and General Fairfax both lodged during the Civil War.

A typical market town, Saffron Walden's centrepiece is its magnificent church. Market days, which have been held here since 1141, are now on Tuesdays and Saturdays and provide an amazing array of food, crafts and art. An additional country market is held on Friday mornings at the back of the town hall.

At the **Saffron Walden Museum**, which is set beside the historic 12th century ruins of **Walden Castle**, a glove reputedly worn by Mary Queen of Scots on the day she died can be seen. The museum first opened to the public at its present location in 1835 (now it is one of the oldest museums in England) and was founded 'to

gratify the inclination of all who value natural history'. It remains faithful to this credo, while widening the museum's scope in the ensuing years. The museum has won numerous awards, including joint winner of the Museum of the Year Award for best museum of Industrial or Social History in 1997. Over the two floors of this friendly, family-sized museum visitors can try their hand at corn grinding with a Romano-British quern, see how a medieval timber house would have been built, admire the displays of Native American and West African embroidery, and come face to face with Wallace the Lion, the museum's faithful guardian; as well as see exhibits on town and country, with furniture and woodwork, costumes, ancient Egyptian artifacts, geology exhibits, and ceramics and glass. The museum is open 363 days a year, and has an enclosed grass meadow which is ideal for picnics if the

•

On the local Common in Saffron Walden, once known as Castle Green, is the largest surviving Turf Maze in England. Only eight ancient turf mazes survive in England – there were many more in the Middle Ages, but if they are not looked after they soon become overgrown and are lost. This one is believed to be some 800 years old, a circular labyrinth of medieval Christian design.

•

Turf Maze, Saffron Walden

To the north of Saffron Walden are the Bridge End Gardens, a wonderfully restored example of early Victorian gardens, complete with the wonderful Hedge Maze, which was planted in 1840 in the Italian Renaissance style and has 610 metres of paths. Close to Bridge End is the Anglo-American War Memorial dedicated by Field Marshal the Viscount Montgomery of Alamein in 1953 to the memory of all the American flyers of the 65th Fighter Wing who lost their lives in the Second World War.

weather is fine. There is good disabled access.

Next to Bridge End Gardens is the **Fry Public Art Gallery**, with a unique collection of work by 20th century artists and designers such as Edward Bawden, Michael Rothenstein, Eric Ravilious, John Aldridge and Sheila Robinson. It also exhibits work by contemporary artists working in Essex today, demonstrating the area's continuing artistic tradition. The gallery was purpose-designed and opened in 1856 to house the collection of Francis Gibson. The gallery also houses the Lewis George Fry RBA, RWA (1860-1933) Collection, which is exhibited each summer, along with works by Robert Fry (1866-1934) and Anthony Fry.

Audley End House was built by the first Earl of Suffolk, and was at one time owned by Charles II. The original early 17th century house, with its two large courtyards, had a magnificence claimed to match that of Hampton Court. Remodelled in the 18th century by Robert Adam, unfortunately the subsequent earls lacked their forebears' financial resources, and much of the house was demolished as it fell into disrepair. Nevertheless it remains today one of England's most impressive Jacobean mansions; its distinguished stone façade set off perfectly by Capability Brown's lake. Fascinating introductory talks help visitors get the most from any visit to this, one of the most magnificent houses in England. This jewel also has a kitchen garden

and grounds landscaped by Capability Brown, including the 'Temple of Concord' dedicated to George III. There is a lovely parterre, lake and Pond Garden. Circular walks help visitors make the most of all there is to see. The organic kitchen garden was recently opened to the public for the first time in 250 years.

AROUND SAFFRON WALDEN

RADWINTER

4 miles E of Saffron Walden off the B1053

Radwinter boasts a fine church, **St Marys**, which was largely renovated and rebuilt in the 19th century by architect William Eden Nesfield and has a fine Tudor porch with a room above. The village also has cottages and almshouses designed by Nesfield.

HEMPSTEAD

5 miles E of Saffron Walden off the B1054

This delightful little village has won, or been runner up, in the "Best kept village" competition for four consecutive years now.

The highwayman, Dick Turpin, was born here in 1705 in what was then the Bell Inn, which was kept by his parents at the time. Dick Turpin trained as a butcher before turning to cattle and deer stealing, smuggling and robbery. Narrowly avoiding capture, he fled to Yorkshire and carried on his nefarious ways as John Palmer. He was captured while horse-stealing and was hanged in York in 1739.

Inside the 14th/15th century Hempstead village church, **St Andrews**, an impressively life-like bust carved by Edward Marshall recalls the town's rather worthier son, William Harvey (1578-1657), who is buried in a white marble sarcophagus in the crypt. Harvey was chief physician to Charles I and the discoverer of the circulation of blood around the human body. Like many other villages, Hempstead once boasted a village cockpit (used for cock fighting); its faint outline can still be traced, though the steep banks are now crowned with trees.

THAXTED

7 miles SE of Saffron Walden on the B184

This small country town has a recorded history that dates back to before the *Domesday Book*. Originally a Saxon settlement, it developed around a Roman road. The town's many beautiful old buildings contribute to its unique character and charm. To its credit Thaxted has no need of artificial tourist attractions, and is today what it has been for the last ten centuries: a thriving and beautiful town.

The town's famous Grade II listed **Tower Windmill** was built in 1804 by John Webb. In working order until 1907, it had fallen into disuse and disrepair but has recently been restored and contains a rural life museum, well worth a visit. Open to the public 2:00 pm to 6:00 pm Saturdays, Sundays and Bank Holidays, from Easter to end of September, and there is a picnic area surrounding it. Close to the windmill are the town's Almshouses, which continued to provide homes for the elderly even 250 years after they were built for that purpose.

Thaxted's **Church of St John** stands on a hill and soars cathedral-like over the town's streets. It has been described as the finest parish church in the country and, though many towns may protest long and loud at this claim, it certainly is magnificent. Gustav Holst, composer of, among other pieces, the renowned 'Planets' Suite', lived in Thaxted from 1914 to 1925, and often played the church organ. To celebrate his connection with the town there is a music festival in late June/early July which attracts performers of international repute.

There is a bustling market held in the town of Thaxted 7am – 2pm every Friday. For a really special sight however you should visit at the end of May, when the town is overrun with the colours and music of Morris dancers. Far from being

•

Thaxted has numerous attractively pargeted and timber-framed houses, and a magnificent Guildhall, built as a meeting-place for cutlers around 1390. The demise of the cutlery industry in this part of Essex in the 1500s led it to becoming the administrative centre of the town. Restored in Georgian times, it became the town's Grammar School, as well as remaining a centre of administration. Once more restored in 1975, the Parish council still holds its meetings here.

•

Thaxted Moot Hall & Church

159

84 THE STARR RESTAURANT WITH ROOMS

Great Dunmow

A great traditional inn providing sumptuous food with comfortable and individual accommodation.

🍴 🛏 see page 275

a doomed pastime, as has been speculated, numbers have doubled for the ring meeting in recent years (last year an amazing 400 dancers and musicians visited the town). There is also an annual town festival held June-July, with many events and entertainment for visitors and residents to enjoy.

GREAT EASTON

10 miles SE of Saffron Walden off the B184

Great Easton boasts a wealth of cottages and farmhouses with ornamental plasterwork, clustered Tudor chimneys and half-timbering. Great Easton's well-known and very popular Green Man pub occupies a handsome building dating back to the 15th century.

LITTLE EASTON

10 miles SE of Saffron Walden off the B184

The charming 12th century **Church of St Mary** is rich in historic features. Its Maynard Chapel features some outstanding marble monuments of the family that gives the chapel its name, as well as some famous brasses. The church's oldest treasures are, however, a well-preserved and priceless 12th century wall painting and several 15th century frescoes. Two more recent additions, a pair of stained glass windows, were unveiled in 1990. The 'Window of the Crusaders' and the 'Window of Friendship and Peace' are a lasting memorial to the American 386th Bomb Group. Known as 'The Crusaders', they were stationed nearby for 13 months and lost over 200 of their number in battle

overseas during that short time. They flew from an airstrip created in the park of **Easton Lodge**, the favourite home of Frances, Countess of Warwick – Edward VII's 'Darling Daisy'. Harold Peto designed the gardens for her in 1902. The house was demolished in 1950 but the pavilions were restored in 1996 and much other restoration has taken place in the garden, including the sunken Italian garden; the Glade, formerly Peto's Japanese garden; and the living sundial with a border featuring every plant mentioned in Shakespeare's plays and sonnets. The 17th century dovecote houses an exhibition of photography, prints and writings on the history of the Lodge since 1950.

BROXTED

10 miles SE of Saffron Walden off the B1051

The parish **Church of St Mary** the Virgin here in the handsome village of Broxted has two remarkably lovely stained glass windows commemorating the captivity and release of John McCarthy and the other Beirut hostages, dedicated in January 1993. Though just a few minutes drive from Stansted Airport off the M11, it is a welcoming haven of rural tranquillity.

GREAT DUNMOW

13 miles SE of Saffron Walden on the A120

The town is famous for the 'Flitch of Bacon', an ancient ceremony which dates back as far as the early 12th century. A prize of a flitch, or side, of bacon was awarded to the local man who *'does not repent of his marriage nor quarrel, differ or dispute with his wife within a year and a day after the marriage'.*

Amidst great ceremony, the winning couple would be seated and presented with their prize. The custom, which lapsed on the Dissolution of the Monasteries, was briefly revived in the 18th century, and became established again after 1885. 'Trials' to test the truth are all in good fun, and carried out every leap year. The successful couple are carried through the streets on chairs and then presented with the Flitch. The original 'bacon chair' can be seen in Little Dunmow parish church.

Other places of historical interest include the **Parish Church of St Mary** at Church End, Great Dunmow, dating back to 1322. The Clock House, a private residence built in 1589, was the home of St Anne Line, martyred for sheltering a Jesuit priest. Clock House was subsequently occupied by Sir George Beaumont. He used it to store and display his extensive art collection, which he bequeathed to the nation and which forms the nucleus of the National Gallery collection in London. H G Wells lived at Brick House in Great Dunmow, overlooking the Doctor's Pond, where in 1784 Lionel Lukin is reputed to have tested the first unsinkable lifeboat.

The **Flitch Way** is a 15-mile country walk along the former Bishop's Stortford-to-Braintree railway, taking in Victorian stations, impressive views, and a wealth of woodland wildlife.

PLESHEY

18 miles SE of Saffron Walden off the A130

Pleshey, midway between Chelmsford and Great Dunmow, is surrounded by a mile-long earthen rampart, protecting its castle, of which only the motte with its moat and two baileys survive. There are good views from the mound, which although only 60 feet high, is nonetheless one of the highest points in Essex. The village is truly delightful, with a number of thatched cottages, and the area is excellent for walkers and ramblers.

WIDDINGTON

4 miles S of Saffron Walden off the B1383

Covering over 25 acres, **Mole Hall Wildlife Park** has a focus on rare breed farm animals and natural wildlife; in the past more exotic zoo type animals were housed here, but it has been decided that a more educational route applicable to our own environment is going to be taken by the park. Animals include Black Welsh Mountain sheep, Alpacas, rare French Maran Hens, and "Monty" a Chinese Water Deer. The Butterfly Pavilion remains here as a lovely attraction which offers a tropical experience where brilliantly coloured butterflies flit about freely. Within the tropical pavilion you can also find lovebirds and small monkeys, along with a variety of snakes, spiders and insects (safe behind glass). From 2009 the park has been temporarily closed to undertake major work, but it should be open in 2010. Tel: 01799 540400.

•

The Great Dunmow Maltings, opened to the public in 2000 after a sympathetic restoration costing £750,000, is the most complete example of a medieval timber-framed building of its type in the United Kingdom, and a focal point for local history in the shape of Great Dunmow Museum, with changing displays illustrating the history of the town from Roman times to the present day. Open to the public on Saturdays and Sundays 11.00am - 4.00pm, it has an easy access lift.

•

Widdington is also home to Priors Hall Barn, one of the finest surviving medieval 'aisled' barns in all of southeast England, and owned by English Heritage.

TAKELEY

13 miles S of Saffron Walden off the A120

The village is built on the line of the old Roman Stane Street. There are plenty of pretty 17th century timbered houses and barns to be seen in the village, and the church, **The Holy Trinity**, still has many of its original Norman features along with some Roman masonry. Rather unusually, it has a modern font that is surmounted by a six-feet-high medieval cover.

HATFIELD BROAD OAK

15 miles S of Saffron Walden off the B184

This very pretty village has many notable buildings for visitors to enjoy, including a church dating from Norman times, some delightful 18th century almshouses and several distinctive Georgian houses.

AYTHORPE RODING

15 miles S of Saffron Walden off the B184

Aythorpe Roding Windmill is the largest remaining post mill in Essex. Four storeys high, it was built around 1760 and remained in use up until 1935. It was fitted in the 1800s with a fantail which kept the sails pointing into the wind. Volunteers open the mill up to the public from April to September, on the last Sunday of each month, and give a very informative tour answering any questions you might

have about this fascinating building and its history.

STANSTED MOUNTFICHET

8 miles SW of Saffron Walden off the B1383

Pilots approaching the airport may be surprised at the sight of a Norman Village, complete with domestic animals, and the reconstructed motte-and-bailey **Mountfichet Castle**, standing just two miles from the runway. The original castle was built after 1066 by the Duke of Boulogne, a cousin of the Conqueror. Siege weapons on show include two giant catapults. The Castle was voted Essex attraction of the year in 2002 by the Good Britain Guide, and visitors can take a trip to the top of the siege tower and tiptoe into the baron's bed chamber while he sleeps!

Next door to the castle is the **House on the Hill Museum Adventure**, where there are three museums for the price of one. The **Toy Museum** is the largest of its kind in the world, with over 70,000 items on show, and here children of every age are treated to a unique and nostalgic trip back to their childhood. There is every toy imaginable here (many of them now highly prized collectors' items); including barbies, annuals, charming tinplate amusements from as far back as the 1860's, and a huge range of space and robot toys which will delight boys young and old. There is a shop selling new toys and a collectors' shop with many old toys and books to choose from. The **Rock 'n' Roll, Film and Theatre Experience** and the **End-of-the-pier Amusement Machine** displays also contribute to a grand day out here in Stansted Mountfichet.

HADSTOCK

6 miles N of Saffron Walden off the B1052

As well as claiming to have the oldest church door in England, at the parish **Church of St Botolph**, Hadstock also has a macabre tale to tell. The church's north door was once covered with a piece of skin, now to be seen in Saffron Walden Museum. Local legend says it is a 'Daneskin', from a Viking flayed alive, but recent DNA analysis has disproved this legend. Lining doors with animal leather was common in the Middle Ages, and many so-called 'Daneskins' are just that. The door itself is Saxon, as are the 11th century carvings, windows and arches, rare survivors that predate the Norman Conquest.

BARTLOW

5 miles NE of Saffron Walden off the B1052

Bartlow Hills are reputed to be the largest burial mounds in Europe dating from Roman times, one 15 metres high. They date back to the 2nd century.

WALTHAM ABBEY

The town of Waltham began as a small Roman settlement on the site of the present-day Market Square. The early Saxon kings maintained a hunting lodge here; a town formed round this, and the first church was built in the 6th century. By the 8th century, during the reign of Cnut, the town had a stone minster church with a great stone crucifix that had been brought from Somerset, where it had been found buried in land owned by Tovi, a trusted servant of the king. This cross became the focus of pilgrims seeking healing. One of those cured of a serious illness, Harold Godwinsson, built a new church, the third on the site, which was dedicated in 1060 - and it was this self-same Harold who became king and was killed in the battle of Hastings six years later. Harold's body was brought back to Waltham to be buried in his church. The church that exists today was built in the first quarter of the 12th century. It was once three times its present length, and incorporated an Augustinian Abbey, built in 1177 by Henry II. The town became known for the Abbey, which was one of the largest in the country and the last to be the victim of Henry VIII's Dissolution of the Monasteries, in 1540.

The **Abbey's Church Centre**

•

Linton Zoo near Hadstock village has a wealth of rare and exotic creatures to see including Tigers, Lions, Tapirs, Lemurs, Binturongs, Owls, Parrots, Giant Tortoises, and Tarantula Spiders. Set in 18 acres of beautiful gardens with plenty of picnic areas and a children's play area. There is also a café and gift shop (with restricted winter opening times) and free parking. Open everyday from 10.30am to 4.00pm, with the last admission at 3.00pm.

•

Waltham Abbey

163

Gunpowder production became established in Waltham as early as the 1660s, and in 1787 the Royal Gunpowder Mills were acquired by the Crown. They became the pre-eminent powder works in Britain, employing up to 500 workers; production did not cease until 1943, after which time the factory became a research facility. In the spring of 2000, however, all this changed and much of the site is open to the public; some of the rest is a Site of Scientific Interest and the largest heronry in Essex. The parts open to the public now include, along with the historical buildings, informative exhibitions, many activities for children, re-enactment events, and tours of the mill grounds on a land train. Also there is a café, gift shop and picnic areas. Open on weekends during the summer.

houses an interesting exhibition explaining the history of both the Abbey and the town, highlighting the religious significance of the site. Some visible remains of the Augustinian Abbey include the chapter house and precinct walls, cloister entry and gateway in the surrounding Abbey Gardens. The Abbey Gardens are also host to a Sensory Trail exploring the highlights of hundreds of years of the site's history; there's also a delightful Rose Garden. Along the Cornhill Stream, crossed by the impressive stone bridge, Waltham Abbey's Dragonfly Sanctuary is home to over half the native British species of dragonflies and damselflies. It is noted as the best single site for seeing these species in Greater London, Essex and Hertfordshire.

Sun Street is Waltham Abbey's main thoroughfare, and it is pedestrianised. It contains many buildings from the 16th century onwards. The Greenwich Meridian (0 degrees longitude) runs through the street, marked out on the pavement and through the Abbey Gardens.

In spite of its proximity to London and more recent development, the town retains a peaceful, traditional character, with its timber-framed buildings and small traditional market which has been held here since the early 12th century (now every Tuesday and Saturday). The whole of the town centre has been designated a conservation area. The **Market Square** boasts many fine and

interesting buildings such as the lych-gate and The Welsh Harp, dating from the 17th and 16th centuries respectively.

The **Town Hall** offers a fine example of Art Nouveau style design, and houses the Waltham Abbey Town Council Offices and Epping Forest District Council Information Desk. The Tourist Information Centre is in Highbridge Street, opposite the entrance to the Abbey Church.

Lee Valley Park Farms, along Stubbins Hall Lane, boasts two farms on site: Hayes Hill and Holyfield Hall. At Hayes Hill Farm, visitors can interact with the animals and enjoy a picnic or the children's adventure playground. This traditional farm also boasts old-fashioned tools and equipment, an exhibition in the medieval barn and occasional craft demonstrations. At Holyfield Hall Farm, a working farm and dairy, visitors can see milking and learn about modern farming methods. Seasonal events such as sheep-shearing and harvesting are held, and there's an attractive farm tea room and a toy shop. Tractor rides are available on weekends and during school holidays. A farm trail is another of the site's attractions, offering wonderful views of the Lee Valley, an expanse of open countryside dotted with lakes and wildflower meadows attracting a wide range of wildlife including otters, bats, dragonfly, kingfisher, great-crested grebe and little-ringed plover. The area is ideal for walking or fishing, and the bird hides are open to all at weekends; permits available for daily access. Guided tours by arrangement. To the west of town, the **Lee Navigation Canal** offers opportunities for anglers, walkers, birdwatching and pleasure craft. Once used for transporting corn and other commercial goods to the growing City of London, and having associations with the towns important gunpowder industry for centuries, the canal remains a vital part of town life.

Also in **Abbey Walton** is the **EppingForest District Museum**, which offers some interesting artefacts and insight into the forest's history (Tel: 01992 716882). And the **Firehouse Play Centre** – a fire-service themed indoor play centre for toddlers and children. (Tel: 01992 788119)

AROUND WALTHAM ABBEY

LOUGHTON

5 miles SE of Waltham Abbey off the A121

Corbett Theatre in Rectory Lane in Loughton is a beautiful Grade I listed converted medieval tithe barn, where classical, modern and musical theatre productions are performed. The theatre is set in a five-acre site with lovely gardens.

The main employer in Loughton is the Bank of England Printing Works, where all English paper money is made.

Loughton borders **Epping Forest**, a former Royal hunting forest stretching for over 12 miles from east London into southwest Essex. There are miles of leafy

walks and rides (horses can be hired locally), with some rough grazing and occasional distant views. Just off the A104 running through the forest, in the middle of a field called The Warren, stands an obelisk that is a memorial to the horse of General Thomas Grosvenor, who lived here and died at the Battle of Waterloo in 1815.

ABRIDGE

7 miles SE of Waltham Abbey off the A113

The village of Abridge lies on the historically important coaching route between London and Chipping Ongar and has been an important crossing point of the River Roding for many centuries. There are several prominent listed buildings in the **Market Place** the oldest of which is the "hall house" (known as the Coach House), which dates from the 14th century and is listed Grade II. Other interesting buildings include 18th century Maltsters Arms, and Roding House which dates back to late medieval era.

The **BBC Essex Garden** at Crowther Nurseries, Ongar Road, is a working garden consisting of a vegetable plot, two small greenhouses, lawns and herbaceous and shrub borders. The garden is also home to a range of farmyard animals which visitors are welcome to see and interact with, and there's a delightful tea shop filled with homemade cakes.

CHIGWELL

8 miles SE of Waltham Abbey off the A113

Hainault Forest Country Park is

●

Lee Valley Regional Park is a leisure area stretching for 26 miles along the River Lea (sometimes also spelled Lee) from East India Dock Basin, on the north bank of the River Thames in East London, to Hertfordshire. There's a range of facilities ideal for anglers, walkers, horse riders, cyclists and birdwatchers – as well as an ice rink, golf course and athletics centre. The Lee Valley is an important area of high biodiversity, sustaining a large range of wildlife and birds. Two hundred species of birds, including internationally important populations of Gadwall and Shoveler ducks, can be seen each year on the wetlands and water bodies along the Lea. Of national importance for over-wintering waterbirds including rare species of bittern and smew, this fine park makes an ideal place for a picnic. Guided tours by appointment.

●

165

For entertainment in Harlow there is The Square, a dynamic live music venue, or The Harlow Playhouse and the small 100 seat Victoria Hall Theatre, both of which show a whole range of plays year round.

an ancient woodland covering 600 acres, with a lake and rare breeds farm, managed by the London Borough of Redbridge and the Woodland Trust for Essex County Council. There have been some interesting permanent art sculptures placed through the park, sympathetic to the environment, one of which is "woodhenge" – a wooden version of Stone Henge, with each part inscribed with something about the forest or the environment. This, along with the year-round peace which can be found here, makes for some delightful walks.

CHINGFORD

6 miles S of Waltham Abbey off the A11

Queen Elizabeth's Hunting Lodge is a timber-framed building covered in brightly coloured heraldic banners and standing on a hill above the plains and trees of Epping Forest. Originally called the Great Standing, it was built in 1543 on the orders of Henry VIII for the staging of royal deer hunts and entertainments in the forest. Displays include the handiwork of Tudor carpenters and food made from authentic recipes; also Tudor dressing-up clothes for children, and brass rubbing of Henry VIII and Elizabeth, are available. From the upper of the three floors has a spectacular view over the forest and surroundings – well worth a look! (Tel: 020 85296681)

HODDESDON

6 miles NW of Waltham Abbey off the A10

Rye House Gatehouse in Rye

Road was built by Sir Andre Ogard, a Danish nobleman, in 1443. It is a moated building and a fine example of early English brickwork. Now restored, visitors can climb up to the battlements. A permanent exhibition covers the architecture and history of the Rye House Plot to assassinate Charles II in 1683. Guided tours by prior arrangement. The building lies adjacent to a Royal Society for the Protection of Birds reserve. Other features include an information centre, shop, and circular walks around the site.

HARLOW

The 'New Town' (now 60 years old) of Harlow sometimes gets short shrift, but it is in fact a lively and vibrant place with a great deal more than excellent shopping facilities. There are some very good museums and several sites of historic interest. The **Gibberd Collection** in Harlow Town Hall offers a delightful collection of British watercolours featuring works by Blackadder, Sutherland, Frink, Nash and Sir Frederick Gibberd, Harlow's master planner and the founder of the collection.

Gibberd Gardens, on the eastern outskirts of Harlow in Marsh Lane, Gilden Way, is well worth a visit, reflecting as it does the taste of Sir Frederick. This 7-acre garden was designed by Sir Frederick on the side of a small valley, with terraces, wild garden, landscaped vistas, large ceramic pots, a gazebo, a moated castle, pools & streams, and some 80 sculptures. It really is the most unusual and wonderful garden which is a must for anyone visiting Harlow, as is **Gibberd's House** at the same location which has select public openings in season. At the entrance to the gardens is a gift shop and café serving delicious cakes. If the sculptures here interest you, then you will love Harlow town. Through a project undertaken by the Harlow Arts Trust – the sculptures of well and lesser known artists have been placed permanently throughout the town, three of which are Grade II listed pieces.

AROUND HARLOW

ROYDON
3 miles W of Harlow off the A414

Preserved in this handsome village are the old parish cage, stocks and a whipping post. Just about 1 mile southwest of Roydon are the ruins of Tudor **Nether Hall**, a manor house that once belonged to the Coates family. Here Thomas More came to woo and win the elder daughter of John Coates.

CHIPPING ONGAR
8 miles SE of Harlow on the A414

Today firmly gripped in the commuter belt of London, Chipping Ongar began as a Saxon market town protected beneath the walls of a Norman castle. The motte and bailey were built by Richard de Lucy in 1155. Only the mound and moat of the castle remain, but the contemporary **Church of St Martin of Tours**

Harlow Mill

still stands. Built in 1080, it has fine Norman flint walls and an anchorite's recess. The White House and Castle House are the largest houses in the town which date from the 16th century. The only other building from this period which still stands within the town enclosure is the Old Market House - No. 171 High Street - which housed the market in the 1840's. The town was given its market charter in the 12th century, indeed the town's name comes from 'cheaping', meaning market; and the weekly market is still held here on Wednesdays.

The explorer David Livingstone was a pupil pastor at Chipping Ongar's United Reform Church, and lived in what are now called Livingstone Cottages before his missionary work in Africa began.

167

BOBBINGWORTH

2 miles NW of Chipping Ongar off the A414

A short drive to the north of Bobbingworth is the village of **High Laver**, where the philosopher John Locke (1632-1704) is buried in the churchyard of All Saints.

WILLINGALE

3 miles NE of Chipping Ongar off the B184

St Christopher's and **St Andrew's**, churches of the respective parishes of Willingale Doe and Willingale Spain, stand side by side in the same churchyard in the heart of this lovely village. St Andrew's is the older, dating back to the 12th century.

FYFIELD

2 miles N of Chipping Ongar off the B184

The name 'Fyfield' means five river meadows. Originally a Saxon enclave, the village Church of St Nicholas is Norman. There's a beautiful mill house with flood gates in the village. Fyfield Hall, opposite the church, is said to be the oldest inhabited timber frame building in England (it dates from AD 870).

BEAUCHAMP RODING

3 miles NE of Chipping Ongar off the B184

One of the eight Rodings, it was at Beauchamp Roding that a local farm labourer, Isaac Mead, worked and saved enough to become a farmer himself in 1882. To show his gratitude to the land that made him his fortune, he had a corner of the field consecrated as an eternal resting place for himself and his family. Their graves can still be seen in the undergrowth. Beauchamp's **Church of St Botolph** stands alone in the fields, marked by a tall 15th century tower and reached by a track off the B184. Inside, the raised pews at the west end have clever space-saving wooden steps, pulled out of slots by means of iron rings.

GOOD EASTER AND HIGH EASTER

5 miles NE of Chipping Ongar off the B184

A quiet farming village, now in the commuter belt for London, Good Easter's claim to fame is the making of a world-record daisy chain (6,980 feet 7 inches) in 1985. The village's interesting name is probably derived from 'Easter', the Old English for 'sheepfolds' and 'Good' from a Saxon lady named Godiva.

Close to Good Easter, and thus named because it stands on higher ground than its neighbour, High Easter is a quiet and very picturesque village not far from the impressive **Aythorpe Post Mill**. In High Easter is the **Punch Bowl**; a Restaurant housed in a listed Tudor building which was formerly a Coaching Inn, constructed in the early 15th century. Today the Punch Bowl retains its original character with exposed beams in the dining room, and in the bar is the only solid willow floor in Essex.

BLACKMORE

3 miles E of Chipping Ongar off the A414

The plague almost totally destroyed the village of Blackmore. Red Rose

Lane was so-named because a red rose had to be given at the toll to indicate clear health from the dreaded disease. Henry VIII's mistress Bessie Blount lived in Jericho Priory in the village. Her son by Henry, the Earl of Rochford, also made his home here.

INGATESTONE

6 miles E of Chipping Ongar off the B1002

Ingatestone Hall on Hall Lane is a 16th century mansion set in 10 acres of grounds that include a fine walled garden and extensive lawns with specimen trees. It was built by Sir William Petre, Secretary of State to four monarchs, whose family continue to reside here. The Hall contains family portraits, furniture and memorabilia accumulated over the centuries. The Church of St Edmund and St Mary is notable for its magnificent redbrick tower and the many monuments to Sir William, who rebuilt the south chapel, and other members of the Petre family. The house and grounds are open to the public from noon to 5 p.m. (last entry 4 p.m.) on Wednesday (except Wednesdays in June), Sunday & Bank Holiday Monday afternoons from Easter until the end of September. While the house is open, so is the Summer Parlour – which serves a delicious range of light lunches and teas, as well as a shop. Unfortunately dogs are not allowed in the house or grounds.

MARGARETTING TYE

6 miles E of Chipping Ongar off the A12

The nickname of this town is 'Tigers Island'. Legend has it that in bygone days, bare-knuckle fights known as 'Tigers' would take place on Fridays, and the 'island' part of its soubriquet derives from the fact that in ancient times the area was subject to flooding all round the village.

MOUNTNESSING

6 miles SE of Chipping Ongar off the A12

This village has a beautifully restored early-19th century windmill as its main landmark, though the isolated church also has a massive beamed belfry. **Mountnessing Post Mill** in Roman Road is open to the public. This traditional weather-boarded post mill was built in 1807 and restored to working order in 1983. Visitors can see the huge wooden and iron gears; one pair of stones have been opened up for viewing.

There is a superb circular walk which can be taken around Mountnessing (roughly 6 miles in length), which takes you from the post mill, past St John's Church to Mountnessing Hall and St Giles Church, over the village green, to Westland's farm and then Bacons Farm, beside the banks of the River Wid to the nearby Ingatestone Hall and back to the post mill.

KELVEDON HATCH

4 miles S of Chipping Ongar off the A128

A nondescript bungalow in the rural Essex village of Kelvedon Hatch is the deceptively simple exterior for the **Kelvedon Secret Nuclear Bunker** (which isn't so secret now – though it is enough

Just north of Ingatestone, at Fryerning, the 16th century Church of St Mary contains a memorial to the MP Airey Neave, a native of the parish who was killed by the IRA in 1979. The window was designed by his cousin Penelope and shows St Michael and St Christopher, with roundels depicting Colditz, where he was a prisoner of war, and the Houses of Parliament.

Margaretting Tye
Renowned for its outstanding ales and food, now the White Hart provides comfortable accommodation as well.

🍴 🛏 see page 276

The village of Greensted has associations with the Tolpuddle Martyrs - six Dorset farm labourers who were taken to court on a legal technicality because they agitated for better conditions and wages, and formed a Trades Union. After their conviction in 1834 they were condemned to transportation to Australia for seven years. There was a public outcry for their release, and their sentences were commuted in 1837. Unable to return to Dorset, they were granted tenancies in Greensted and High Laver. One of the martyrs, James Brine, of New House Farm (now Tudor Cottage, on Greensted Green), married Elizabeth Standfield, daughter of one of his fellow victims - the record of their marriage in 1839 can be seen in the parish register.

out of the way to avoid huge crowds). In 1952, 40,000 tons of concrete were used to create a base some 80 feet underground for up to 600 top Government and civilian personnel, possibly including the Prime Minister, in the event of nuclear war. Visitors can explore room after room to see communications equipment, a BBC studio, a sick bay and surgery, massive kitchens and dormitories, military supplies stores, power and filtration plants, a government administration room and the scientists' room, where nuclear fall-out patterns would have been measured. Admission includes personal handsets which give you a guided tour around the bunker. It is open everyday through the summer, and Thursday to Sunday 10am – 4pm in winter. Tel: 01277 364883.

GREENSTED

1½ miles SW of Chipping Ongar off the A414

St Andrew's Church in Greensted is almost certainly the world's oldest wooden church, dating from the 9th to 11th centuries, with a later Tudor chancel. It is famous as the only surviving example of a Saxon log church extant in the world, built from split oak logs from Epping Forest, held together with dowells. It is amazing to think the wooden logs used to build this church are now between 900 and 1000 years old. Over the centuries the church has been enlarged and restored; later additions include the simple weather-boarded tower, Norman flint walls, the Tudor tiled

roof, Victorian stone coping, porch and stained glass windows. The body of King Edmund (later canonised a saint) is believed to have rested here in 1013.

NORTH WEALD

3 miles W of Chipping Ongar off the A414

North Weald Airfield Museum and Memorial at Ad Astra House, Hurricane Way, North Weald Bassett is a small, meticulously detailed 'House of Memories' displaying the history of the famous airfield and all who served at RAF North Weald from 1916 to the present. There is a large collection of fascinating, and quite moving, photographs and artefacts such as uniforms on display, plotting the amazing history of the base. Guided tours of the airfield can be arranged for large groups. It is open to the public every Sunday (and some Saturdays) from early April till the end of October - 12noon till 5pm, last entry 4pm.

BRENTWOOD

Brentwood is a busy shopping and entertainment centre, with quite a distinguished past. The town was on the old pilgrim and coaching routes to and from London. Mainly post-war in character, the town is the setting for the UK headquarters of Ford Motors.

There have been breweries in Brentwood for 100 years, and although nothing now remains of the original brewers, the Brentwood Brewery Company is continuing the tradition of honest robust beers and ales which can be bought in many places throughout Essex.

Brentwood Centre on Doddinghurst Road is one of the top entertainment venues in the UK, with an extensive programme of concerts, shows, bands and top comedy names, and extensive sports and fitness facilities.

Brentwood Museum at Cemetery Lode in Lorne Road, in the Warley Hill area of Brentwood, is a small and picturesque cottage museum concentrating on local and social history during the late 19th and early 20th centuries.

The leisure centre in the town has a large pool, excellent modern fitness suite, squash courts and a health & beauty section which offers sports massages and alternative therapies.

AROUND BRENTWOOD

BILLERICAY

6 miles E of Brentwood off the A129

There was a settlement here as far back as the Bronze Age, though there is to date no conclusive explanation of Billericay's name. There is no question about the attraction of the High Street, though, with its timber weather-boarding and Georgian brick. The **Chantry House**, built in 1510, was the home of Christopher Martin, treasurer to the Pilgrim Fathers.

Barleylands Craft Village & Farm Centre, next to Billericay on the A12 and A127, has a whole range of activities and things to see for all the family. In the farm

centre you can try your hands at milking a cow, have close up encounters with cute animals in the Bunny Barn, the children can run amok in the adventure play area, and there are plenty of machines used in agriculture to see. The craft village has probably the biggest collection of working crafts in East Anglia, with around 60 individual workshops with a huge variety of crafts (including glass blowing); there is much to see, buy and do with lots of hands-on craft sessions (having a go on the potters wheel is a favourite!). A farmers market is held in the park regularly throughout the year, there is also the Essex Country Show which is held here annually in early September and is quite an event. A small train circuit which takes visitors all around the grounds runs all year round (weather permitting), it is normally one of a few miniature steam trains, though they are being repaired through 2009 so it is 'Derek' the diesel engine train who you will find on the tracks presently. The whole centre is open every day, all year round, including Bank Holidays between 10.00am and 5.00pm (March to October) and 10.00am and 4.00pm (November to February).

GREAT WARLEY

1 mile S of Brentwood on the B186

Warley Place was formerly home to one of the most famous female gardeners, Ellen Willmott, who died in 1934. She introduced to Warley - and to Britain - many exotic plants. A trail takes visitors

•
Brentwood Cathedral on Ingrave Road was built in 1991. This classically-styled church incorporates the original Victorian church that stood on this spot. It was designed by the much-admired architect Quinlan Terry, with roundels by Raphael Maklouf (who also created the relief of the Queen's head used on current coins).
•

86 THE KILNS HOTEL

Great Warley

A luxurious boutique hotel at an affordable price offering world class dining and events just far enough away from London to breath in country air.

⊨ ‖ *see page 277*

171

through what is now **Warley Place Nature Reserve**, with 16 acres of what was once domesticated garden but has now reverted to woodland. A fascinating selection of trees, shrubs and wildlife makes this well worth a visit.

SOUTH WEALD

2 miles W of Brentwood off the A12

This very attractive village has, at its outskirts, **Weald Country Park**, a former estate with medieval deer park, partially landscaped in the 1700s. Featuring lake and woodland, visitors' centre, landscapes exhibition and gift shop, with facilities for fishing and horse-riding, there are guided events and activities programmes held throughout the year.

Another good day out in the open air can be had at **Old Macdonald's Farm Park**, where visitors can see the largest selection of pure-bred British farm animals and poultry in the southeast of England; as well as alpacas, otters, and wallabies. The park has an indoor soft play area with café, and a heap of outdoor adventure parks and amusements. The park is open all week April – Sept 10am-5pm, and all week Oct – March 10am-4pm (except January when it is only open on weekends).

THE NORTH THAMES CORRIDOR

Bordering the north bank of the Thames, the borough of **Thurrock** has long been a gateway to London but also affords easy access to southwest Essex and to Kent. This thriving borough encompasses huge swathes of green belt country, and along its 18 miles of Thames frontage there are many important marshland wildlife habitats. This stretch of Essex affords some marvellous walking, cycling, birdwatching and other nature pursuits. The area has many bridleways, footpaths and country parks, including Davy Down within the Mardyke Valley. The river's flood plain is a broad tract of grassland which is an important feature of the landscape of the area.

GRAYS

4 miles S of Brentwood off the M25

Thurrock Museum is in the Thamesside Complex in Grays. It

Weald Country Park, South Weald

collects, conserves and displays items of archaeology and local history from prehistoric times to the end of the 20th century. The archaeological items include flint and metal tools of people who lived in prehistoric Thurrock and pottery, jewellery and coins from the Roman and Saxon period. It is open all week, until 7pm on certain nights of the week. Tel: 01375 413965.

WEST THURROCK

1½ miles SW of Grays off the A13

Immortalised by the film Four Weddings and a Funeral, little **St Clement's Church** occupies a striking location and is one of a number of picturesque ancient churches in the borough. Although this 12th century church is now deconsecrated, it was in its day a stopping point for pilgrims; visitors can see the remains of its original round tower. There is also a mass grave to the boys of the reformatory ship Cornwall who were drowned in an accident off Purfleet.

PURFLEET

3 miles W of Grays off the M25/A13

Fans of Bram Stoker's novel *Dracula* will know that in this book the famous vampire buys a house called 'Carfax' in Purfleet. The town's esteemed Royal Hotel, by the Thames, is said to have played host to Edward VII, while still Prince of Wales in the 1880s and 1890s, at which time the hotel was called Wingrove's.

AVELEY

3 miles NW of Grays off the A13

Mardyke Valley is an important wildlife corridor running from Ship Lane in Aveley to Orsett Fen. Many pleasant views can be had along the seven-mile stretch of footpaths and bridleways. Davy Down within Mardyke Valley consists of riverside meadows, ponds and wetland. The **Visitors' Centre** is in the well-preserved water pumping station on the B186 near South Ockendon.

Aveley's 12th century **St Michael's Church** features many Flemish brasses and other items of historical interest.

SOUTH OCKENDON

3 miles N of Grays off the A13/A1306

South Ockenden's **Church of St Nicholas** has one of only six round church towers in Essex. This one was built in the 13th century and used to have a spire, which was sadly destroyed by lightning in the 17th century.

Belhus Woods Country Park covers approximately 250 acres and contains an interesting variety of habitats, including woodland, two lakes and the remains of a pond designed by 'Capability' Brown. The Visitors' Centre to this superb park can be found at the main entrance off Romford Road. Belhus Park Golf Course is a well-established 18-hole course set within this beautiful parkland.

HORNDON-ON-THE HILL

6 miles NE of Grays off the B1007/A13

Listed in the *Domesday Book* as

•

The graveyard of St Margaret's Church in Stanford-le-Hope has an unusual half-barrelled tomb, for one James Adams (d. 1765), that is decorated with a gruesome stone-carved symbol of death.

•

Horninduna, a name which also appears on a Saxon coin of Edward the Confessor (1042-1066), it is said to have once been the site of a Royal Anglo-Saxon mint. The town's 16th century **Woolmarket** indicates the importance of the wool trade to the region, and is one of the area's historical treasures. The upper room served as Horndon's manor courtroom, while the lower, open area was used for trading in woollen cloth.

The main entrance and Visitors' Centre for **Langdon Hills Conservation Centre and Nature Reserve** are located off the Lower Dunton Road north of Horndon-on-the-Hill. A bridleway and footpaths lead visitors to meadows, a pond and outstanding ancient woods. Also within the reserve is the **Plotlands Museum**, housed in an original 1930s plotland bungalow known as the Haven.

LINFORD

3 miles NE of Grays off the A13/A1013

Walton Hall Museum on Walton Hall Road has a large collection of historic farm machinery in a 17th century barn. It affords visitors the opportunity to watch traditional craftsmen, such as a blacksmith, saddlemaker, printer and wheelwright, together with a printing shop, dairy and nursery. The bakery at the museum is very popular as well; you can mould the dough into any shape you wish and they can cook it for you. Open Thurs – Sun 10am-5pm from April until November.

STANFORD-LE-HOPE

4 miles NE of Grays off the A1014

Stanford Marshes is an area to the south of Stanford-le-Hope, next to the Thames. The Marshes are home to a variety of wildlife and are an ideal location for birdwatching. **Grove House Wood** in Stanford-le-Hope is a nature reserve managed by Essex Wildlife Trust and the local Girl Guides. A footpath here leads to reed beds, a pond and a brook as well as an area of woodland.

CANVEY ISLAND

10 miles NE of Grays off the A130

Canvey Island is a picturesque stretch of land overlooking the Thames estuary with views to neighbouring Kent.

The island boasts an unusual museum: **Dutch Cottage Museum**, which is an early 17th century eight-sided cottage, built by Dutch workmen for Dutch workmen and boasts many traditional Flemish features. The museum contains a variety of displays including models of the types of sailing craft which would have sailed by the island from Roman times onward, and an interesting collection of corn dollies. Tel: 01268 753587.

WEST TILBURY

3 miles E of Grays off the A1089

West Tilbury was the site chosen for the Camp Royal in 1588, to prepare for the threatened Spanish invasion. Queen Elizabeth I visited the army here, and made her famous speech,

'I know I have the body but of a weak and feeble woman: but I have the heart and stomach of a king, and a king of England too.'

Hidden away in rural tranquillity over-looking the Thames estuary, West Tilbury remains unspoilt in spite of its proximity to busy, industrial Tilbury. The former local church (now a private dwelling) in West Tilbury is a nautical landmark used for navigation. The list of Rectors of the church, dating from 1279-1978, when the church was disestablished, can be seen in The Kings Head Pub.

EAST TILBURY

5 miles E of Grays off the A13

Coalhouse Fort is considered to be one of the best surviving examples of a Victorian Casement fortress in the country. As such it is a protected Scheduled Ancient Monument. Built between 1861 and 1874 as a first line of defence to protect the Thames area against invasion, it stands on the site of other defensive works and fortifications dating back to around 1400. Even before the Middle Ages, this was an important site.

Part of the construction work on the Fort was overseen by Gordon of Khartoum. It was constructed to be a dedicated Artillery casement fortress, which meant that the guns were housed in large vaulted rooms with armour-plated frontages. Beneath these rooms lies an extensive magazine tunnel system to service the artillery.

Over the years many alterations were made to the Fort to accommodate new artillery. The Fort was manned during both World Wars, and is now owned by Thurrock Borough Council and administered by The Coalhouse Fort Project, a registered charity manned entirely by volunteers. Open to the public, it contains reconstructions of period guns and other displays, and also houses the Thamesside Aviation Museum, with a large collection of local finds and other aviation material. In the two parade grounds visitors will find various artillery pieces and military vehicles. One recent addition to the many pieces of historical military equipment is a Bofor Anti-Aircraft Gun of the Second World War. The site also offers visitors the chance to handle period equipment or to try on a period uniform.

The Bata Estate at East Tilbury is a conservation area of architectural and historical interest. Established in 1933, the British Bata Shoe Company was the creation of Czech-born Thomas Bata, who also developed a housing estate for his workforce. The uniform flat-roofed houses can still be seen on the site.

TILBURY

3 miles SE of Grays off the A1089

Tilbury Fort (English Heritage) is a well-preserved and unusual 17th century structure with double moat. The largest and best example of military engineering in England at that time, the fort also affords tremendous views of the Thames

During the year the Coalhouse Fort hosts a range of shows, including an historic artillery rally when various big guns are fired by crews in the uniforms of the period, including a Second World War crew firing a 1940 25-pounder field gun. A guided tour (included in the price of admission) allows visitors to see the magazine tunnels beneath the gun casements and offers a feel for the work and conditions of a Victorian gunner. The tour also takes in the roof of the Fort, from which you will be able to judge for yourself the value of a fortification at this point along the Thames. The view from here is outstanding, taking in the two sister forts in Kent and, on a clear day, Southend.

Tilbury Festival is held every year in July in the field near the fort, and features arena events, craft and food stalls, and living history re-enactments.

Sir John Betjeman once said, "The Pier is Southend, Southend is the Pier" and indeed it is the pier which first catches your attention on any visit to Southend. Southend Pier and Museum brings to life the fascinating past of this, the longest Pleasure Pier in the world. The Pier itself is well over a mile in length and visitors can either enjoy a leisurely walk along to the end or take advantage of the regular diesel railway service that plies up and down the pier alongside the walkway.

estuary. The most violent episode in the fort's history occurred in 1776, during a particularly vociferous cricket match which left three people dead. For a small fee visitors to the fort can fire a 1943 3.7mm anti-aircraft gun - a prospect most children and many adults find irresistible! Owned by English Heritage, the site was used for a military Block House during the reign of Henry VIII and was rebuilt in the 17th century. It remains one of Britain's finest examples of a star-shaped bastion fortress. Extensions were made in the 18th and 19th centuries, and the Fort was still being used in the Second World War. For those with an interest in military history there are new displays of guns and gunpowder barrels, and information on advances in military engineering. The recently revised audio tour includes Elizabeth I's Armada speech, and a description of life at the fort by Nathan Makepiece, the fort's Master Gunner. Open year round, there are restricted areas where dogs are allowed on leads.

Tilbury Energy and Environment Centre at Tilbury Power Station provides a nature reserve and study centre for schools and community education. There is a flat two-mile nature trail leading to and from the Centre.

SOUTHEND-ON-SEA

Beside the seaside in Southend-on-Sea there is always plenty to do and see, and many events are held throughout the year to ensure its continuing interest and popularity. The town is one of the best loved and most friendly resorts in Britain, featuring the very best ingredients for a break at the seaside. With seven miles of beaches, this treasure trove boasts Adventure Island theme park, Priory Park Bandstand, Cliffs Pavilion, a distinguished art gallery and several interesting museums.

Prittlewell Priory Museum, slightly north of Southend town centre in Priory Park, is a well-preserved 12th century Cluniac Priory set in lovely grounds and housing collections of the Priory's history, natural history and the Caten collection of radios and communications equipment. The **Southchurch Hall Museum** in Park Lane is a delightful 13th to 14th century timber-framed manor house with various displays and landscaped gardens. Period room settings are among this museum's many delights.

Central Museum, Planetarium and Discovery Centre on Victoria Avenue features local history exhibits, archaeology and wildlife exhibits, while **Beecroft Art Gallery** boasts the work of four centuries of artistic endeavour, with some 2,000 works on display.

A floral trail guided tour around the parks and gardens will reveal why Southend has won the Britain in Bloom Awards so often, as well as winning medals at the Chelsea Flower Show.

The **Kursaal** on the Eastern Esplanade is an indoor

entertainment complex, one of the largest in the country, with indoor bowling, a fun casino, children's play area, snooker and pool. Boat trips in summer include occasional outings on a vintage paddle steamer. Ferry trips to Felixstowe are also available from Southend.

AROUND SOUTHEND

OLD LEIGH

½ mile W of Southend off the A13

The unspoilt fishing village of Old Leigh has a long and distinguished history. It is picturesque, with seafront houses and narrow winding alleys. It has also earned its place in history: The pilgrim ship *The Mayflower* restocked here en route to the New World of America back in the mid-17th century, and the Dunkirk rescue embarked from here, as commemorated in a framed poem on the wall of the local pub, The Crooked Billet.

LEIGH-ON-SEA

2 miles W of Southend off the A13

Leigh-on-Sea has a character quite different from Southend, being more intimate and serene, with wood-clad buildings and shrimp boats in the working harbour. The shellfish stall on the harbourside is justly famous. The **Leigh Heritage Centre**, housed in a former ancient blacksmith's in the waterside High Street of the Old Town, now houses historical artefacts including a photographic display of the history of Leigh-on-Sea.

Leigh-on-Sea

HADLEIGH

5 miles NW of Southend off the A13

Hadleigh Castle, built originally for Edward III, is owned by English Heritage and once belonged to Anne of Cleves, Catherine of Aragon and Katherine Parr. The ruins were also immortalised in a spectacular painting by Constable, which depicts the ruins, and Thames in the distance, the morning after a turbulent storm. The remains of this once impressive castle can still

Hadleigh Castle

177

Wallasea Island

A friendly and contemporary bar that serves good food and drink all week long.

🍴 see page 278

be seen. The curtain walls towers, which survive almost to their full height, overlook the Essex marshes and the Thames estuary. **Hadleigh Castle Country Park** offers a variety of woodland and coastal walks in grounds overlooking the Thames estuary, and it is open daily 8am-dusk. A Guided Events programme runs throughout the year.

HULLBRIDGE
8 miles NW of Southend off the A132

Jakapeni Rare Breed Farm at Burlington Gardens in Hullbridge is a pleasant smallholding set in 30 acres of rolling countryside. Specialising in sheep and pigs, with other pets and wildlife, there's also a fishing lake, country walk and pets corner. Snacks and light refreshments are available from the café, and there's an attractive shop. Tel: 01702 232394.

HOCKLEY
6 miles NW of Southend off the A129

Hockley Woods is a 280-acre ancient woodland, managed for the benefit of wildlife and for the public. Traditional coppice management encourages a diverse array of flora and fauna, including the nationally rare Heath Fritillary butterfly.

RAYLEIGH
6 miles NW of Southend off the A1016

Dutch Cottage at Crown Hill in Rayleigh is a tiny traditional Flemish eight-sided cottage based on a 17th century design created by Dutch settlers.

Rayleigh Mount is a prominent landmark in this part of the county. Once a motte-and-bailey castle built in the 11th century, it was abandoned some 200 years later. **Rayleigh Windmill**, in Bellingham Lane close to Rayleigh Mount, was built around 1809 and has had a £340,000 restoration to transform it into a major tourist and educational attraction. The four stories of modern displays include a fascinating collection of bygones mostly used in and around Rayleigh. The mill will be reopened to the public in April 2010. Refreshments are available from the coffee shop adjacent to the mill, also worth visiting for the sensory garden.

ROCHFORD
3 miles N of Southend off the B1013

The **Old House**, at 17 South Street, is an elegant, lovingly restored house originally built in 1270. The twisting corridors and handsome rooms of this fine structure offer a glimpse into the past; the building now houses some District Council offices, and is said to be haunted.

CHELMSFORD

Roman workmen cutting their great road linking London with Colchester built a fort at what is today called Chelmsford. Then called Caesaromagus, it stands at the confluence of the Rivers Chelmer and Can. The town has always been an important market centre and is now the bustling county town of Essex. It is also directly descended from a new town planned by the Bishop of London in 1199. At its centre are the principal inn, the Royal Saracen's Head, and the elegant **Shire Hall** of 1791. Three plaques situated high up on the eastern face of the Hall overlooking the High Street represent Wisdom, Justice and Mercy. The building now houses the town magistrates court.

Christianity came to Essex with the Romans and again, later, with St Cedd (AD 654); in 1914 the diocese of Chelmsford was created. **Chelmsford Cathedral** in New Street dates from the 15th century and is built on the site of a church constructed 800 years ago. The cathedral is noted for the harmony and unity of its perpendicular architecture. It was John Johnson, the distinguished local architect who designed both the Shire Hall and the 18th century Stone Bridge over the River Can, who also rebuilt the Parish Church of St Mary when most of its 15th century tower fell down. The church became a cathedral when the new diocese of Chelmsford was created. Since then it has been enlarged and re-organised inside. The cathedral boasts memorial windows dedicated to the USAAF airmen who were based in Essex from 1942 to 1945.

Three modern technologies - electrical engineering, radio, and ball and roller bearings - began in Chelmsford. At the **Engine House Project** at Sandford Mill

Waterworks, museum collections from the town's unique industrial story provide a fun and fascinating insight into the science of everyday things. **Moulsham Mill Business & Craft Centre**, set in a renovated early 18th century water mill at Parkway, houses a variety of craft workshops and businesses. Crafts featured include jewellery, pottery, flowers, lace-making, dolls houses and bears, and decoupage work. There is a charming picnic area nearby, and a good café.

Other Chelmsford attractions

Chelmsford Cathedral

179

There are many beautiful parks and gardens in Chelmsford. The manicured Admirals Park and Tower Gardens; 30 hectares of peaceful parkland on the banks of the River Can, with an ancient wooded track covered in wild violets in Spring. Boleyn Gardens, built in 2001, is an established landscaped garden which includes ponds and wild flower areas to encourage wildlife, a children's play area and award winning Elements Garden crammed full of herbaceous plants. Galleywood Common Local Nature Reserve is popular with dog walkers, nature enthusiasts and local residents; mostly heathland and woodland, this sprawling 47 hectare ground is bustling with wildlife.

include the **Riverside Ice and Leisure Centre**, which has several swimming pools for all abilities and an ice rink which also has shows on ice. There are also two theatres (the Civic and the Cramphorn), and a pedestrianised high street with many shops.

AROUND CHELMSFORD

GREAT BADDOW

1 mile S of Chelmsford off the A12/A130

Baddow Antiques Centre at The Bringy, Church Street, is one of the leading antiques centres in Essex. Here, 20 dealers offer a wide selection of silver, porcelain, glass, furniture, paintings and collectibles.

SANDON

2 miles SE of Chelmsford off the A414

The village green here in Sandon has produced a notable Spanish oak tree, the biggest in the country, planted in the centre of the village green. This oak tree is remarkable not so much for its height as for the tremendous horizontal spread of its branches. Around the green are a fine church and a number of attractive old houses, some dating back to the 16th century when Henry VIII's Lord Chancellor, Cardinal Wolsey, was Lord of the Manor of Sandon.

SOUTH HANNINGFIELD

6 miles S of Chelmsford off the A130

The placid waters of nearby **Hanningfield Reservoir** were created by damming Sandford

Brook, and transformed the scattered rural settlement of Hanningfield into a lakeside village. Now on the shores of the lake, **St Peter's** belfry has been a local landmark in the flat Essex countryside for centuries. Some of the timbers in the belfry are said to have come from Spanish galleons, wrecked in the aftermath of Sir Francis Drake's defeat of the Armada.

The **Visitor Centre** at the Reservoir overlooks the 870-acre reservoir and the gateway to the 100-acre woodland beyond. The Centre also offers refreshments, a gift shop and toilet, it is open daily 9am-5pm.

STOCK

6 miles S of Chelmsford along the B1007

This brilliant little hidden village between Chelmsford and Billericay, which used to be named "Stock Harvard", has some endearing features. **All Saints Church**, one of the three churches here, has its first written recording in 1232 and it is thought a church was erected here in the early Norman period; the church which stands now has a weatherboarded belfry and 12th century stone face.

The beautiful windmill in Stock, which has been restored to working order, is open to the public on various weekends throughout the year. The woodland just outside the village is managed by the Woodland Trust and provides some lovely walks – particularly around Easter time when it is carpeted with bluebells.

WRITTLE

2 miles W of Chelmsford off the A414

Hylands House was built in 1728; this beautiful neo-Classical Grade II listed villa is set in over 500 acres of parkland landscaped by Repton. Rooms that are open to the public include the Blue Room, Entrance Hall, Library, Saloon, Boudoir and Drawing Room. Host to many outdoor events, including the annual 'V' concerts and the Chelmsford Spectacular, Hylands Park features lawns, rhododendron bushes, woodland paths, ornamental ponds and Pleasure Gardens adjacent to the House.

Writtle's parish **Church of St John** features a cross of charred timbers, a reminder of the fire which gutted the chancel in 1974. Ducks swim on the pond of the larger and quite idyllic main village green, which is surrounded by lovely Tudor and Georgian houses. From a tucked-away corner of St John's Green came Britain's first regular broadcasting service, an experimental 15-minute programme beamed out nightly by Marconi's engineers.

WITHAM

6 miles NE of Chelmsford off the A12/B1018

The River Brain flows through this delightful town; a continuous walk has been created along its length for a distance of about three miles. The settlement dates back to at least the 10th century; remains of a Roman temple have been found at Ivy Chimneys, off Hatfield Road. Blackwater Lane leads to

Whetmead, a nature reserve of 25 acres between the rivers Blackwater and Brain.

The **Dorothy L Sayers Centre** in Newland Street houses a collection of books by and about Sayers, the theologian, Dante scholar and novelist/creator of the Lord Peter Wimsey mysteries (and the first female graduate from the University of Oxford), who lived in Witham from 1929 when she moved there with her husband until her death in 1957. Tel: 01376 519625.

LITTLE BRAXTED

6 miles NE of Chelmsford off the A12/B1018

Little Braxted has been voted the best-kept village on a regular basis since 1973. The privately owned St Mary's chapel was built in 1888, and can accommodate only 12 people at a time. The village **Church of St Nicholas**, mentioned in the *Domesday Book*, is famous for its murals.

LITTLE BADDOW

5 miles E of Chelmsford off the A414

Blakes Wood is a designated Site of Special Scientific Interest, an ancient woodland of hornbeam and sweet chestnut renowned for its bluebells. There is a good circular way-marked one-and-a-half mile walk.

DANBURY

5 miles E of Chelmsford off the A414

This village is said to take its name from the Danes who invaded this part of the country in the Dark

88 THE ROSE & CROWN

Great Waltham

The place for ale enthusiasts, several local favourites on offer at all times!

see page 278

89 COMPASSES INN

Littley Green

A night in the slow lane with real fires, real ale, great food and great conversation is promised at Compasses, perfect for family unwinding.

see page 279

90 THE HOT PLATE CAFÉ

Maldon

The perfect place to sit awhile and enjoy a home made snack or meal.

🍴 *see page 279*

Ages. In the fine **Parish Church of St John the Baptist**, under a rare 13th century carved effigy, a crusader knight was found when the tomb was opened in 1779, perfectly preserved in the pickle which filled his coffin. Fine carving is also a feature of the bench ends; the oldest among them have inspired modern craftsmen to continue the same style of carving on all the pews. In 1402, 'the devil appeared in the likeness of Firor Minor, who entered the church, raged insolently to the great terror of the parishioners ... the top of the steeple was broken down and half the chancel scattered abroad.' And, in 1941, another harbinger of disaster, a 500-lb German bomb, reduced the east end to ruins.

At **Danbury Common**, ther are acres of gorse flower in a blaze of golden colour for much of the year. Along with Lingwood Common, Danbury Common is at the highest point of the gravel ridge between Maldon and Chelmsford. There is evidence here of Napoleonic defences and old reservoirs. Circular nature trails make exploring the area easily accessible. To the west, **Danbury Country Park** offers another pleasant stretch of open country, boasting woodland, a lake and ornamental gardens.

WOODHAM WALTER

6 miles E of Chelmsford off the B1010

Woodham Walter is a small village which lies two and a half miles west of the ancient market town and coastal port of Maldon. It is

rumoured that Henry VIII hunted in Woodham Walter during his reign. During the troubled times after Henry's death, Mary Tudor was concealed in Woodham Walter Hall, from where she was planning to escape from England in 1550. The **Church of St Michael the Archangel** is the only Elizabethan church in Essex, and one of only six built in England in the reign of Elizabeth I.

MALDON

10 miles E of Chelmsford on the A414

Maldon's High Street has existed since medieval times, and the alleys and mews leading from it are full of intriguing shops, welcoming old inns and good places to eat. One of the most distinctive features of the High Street is the **Moot Hall**. Built in the 15th century for the D'Arcy family, this building passed into the hands of the town corporation and was the seat of power in Maldon for over 400 years. The original brick spiral staircase (the best-preserved of its kind in England) and the 18th century courtroom are of particular interest. Guided tours are available on Saturdays in summer and by appointment with the Hall Manager Tel: 07711985540.

A colourful appliquéd 42ft embroidery made to commemorate the 1,000th anniversary of the crucial Battle of Maldon in AD991 (see Northey Island, below) is on display at the **Maeldune Heritage Centre** (Maeldune being the Saxon name for Maldon). The Centre is housed in the Grade I listed St

Peter's Building, erected in the 17th century by a local benefactor when the nave of the church that had once stood on this site collapsed. It can be found at the junction of the High Street and the steep and architecturally interesting Market Hill. The benefactor, one Thomas Plume, erected the building to house his collection of 6,000 books and a school; the **Plume Library** in St Peter's Building is open to the public.

A few minutes' walk down one of the small roads leading from the High Street brings you to the waterfront, where the old wharfs and quays are still active. Moored at **Hythe Quay** are several Thames Sailing Barges, all over 100 years old and still boasting their traditional rigging and distinctive tan sails. The barges and Quay are overlooked by two pubs, the Queen's Head and the Jolly Sailor. Maldon, famous for its sea salt, is the only place in England still making salt from sea water. Salt production in Maldon dates from Roman times, and from its current premises on the waterfront has continued uninterrupted since 1882.

Housed in what was originally the park-keeper's lodge, by the park gates, **Maldon District Museum** looks back on the colourful history of the town through permanent and changing displays of exhibits and objects associated with the area and the people of Maldon. Another attraction is the **Combined Military Services Museum** in Station Road, where the displays

St Giles Leper Hospital, Maldon

include armour and ancient weaponry, uniforms, a spy collection and many items brought home from the Gulf Wars. A Chieftain tank is among the external exhibits.

Ruins are all that remain of the **St Giles the Leper Hospital**, founded by King Henry II in the 12th century. As with all monastic buildings, it fell into disuse after Henry VIII's Dissolution of the Monasteries, though it retained its roof and was used as a barn until the late 19th century. Many other buildings in Maldon, almost as old, fortunately remain - including two fine churches.

LANGFORD

2 miles NW of Maldon on the B1019

The **Museum of Power**, Hatfield Road, covers all aspects of power, from domestic batteries to the massive machines that powered British industry. It includes the steam-powered pumping-station machinery of the redundant waterworks in which the museum is

183

housed. Additions to the museum include a miniature steam railway and model village. The grounds outside have been left mostly untouched for wildlife to flourish.

NORTHEY ISLAND

1 mile SE of Maldon off the B1018

This small island, comprising mainly salt-marsh, is owned by the National Trust. Access to this nature reserve is on foot via a causeway passable at low tide with prior arrangement with the warden. It is a Site of Special Scientific Interest, important to over-wintering birds.

TOLLESBURY

9 miles NE of Maldon on the B1023

Located at the mouth of the River Blackwater is the marshland village of Tollesbury. **Tollesbury Marina** has been designed as a family leisure centre for the crews and passengers of visiting yachts. The Marina, with its tennis courts, heated covered swimming pool, bar and restaurant is ideally located for exploring the Blackwater and the neighbouring estuaries of the Crouch, Colne, Stour and Orwell. **Tollesbury Wick** is a 600-acre nature reserve owned and run by Essex Wildlife Trust; it lies at one end of the North Blackwater Trail, which runs for 12 miles along the estuary to Heybridge Basin.

MUNDON

3 miles S of Maldon off the B1018

Mundon and the surrounding area boasts some excellent walking. **St Peter's Way**, a long-distance path

from Ongar to St Peter's Chapel, Bradwell-on-Sea, leads through the village and past the disused Church of St Mary. This 14th century church is no longer open to the public as the building is unsafe following a fall of masonry. Tolstoy is known to have visited the village.

ALTHORNE

6 miles SE of Maldon on the B1012

The **Church of St Andrew**, some 600 years old, has a fine flint and stone tower, built in the perpendicular style. Inside the church there's a 15th century font which retains its original carvings of saints and angels. A brass plaque dated 1508 records that William Hyklott 'Paide for the werkemanship of the wall'; an inscription over the west door remembers John Wylson and John Hyll, who probably paid for the tower.

To the south, where Station Road meets Burnham Road, stands the villagers' own **War Memorial**. This solid structure of beams and tiles lends dignity and honour to the tragic roll-call of names listed on it.

To the north of the village is the golden-thatched and white-walled Huntsman and Hounds, an alehouse since around 1700.

STEEPLE AND ST LAWRENCE

8 miles SE of Maldon off the B1018

Public footpaths lead down to the water from the village of Steeple; the houses of St Lawrence stand close to the water. Several sailing clubs and some waterside caravan and camping parks ensure that there is plenty of activity on the adjacent stretch of the River Blackwater. **St Lawrence Rural Discovery Church**, on high ground further inland, overlooks the villages and the River Blackwater to the north; it also offers views over the River Crouch to the south. Exhibitions with local themes are held in the church during the summer months.

BURNHAM-ON-CROUCH

12 miles SE of Maldon on the B1012

Burnham-on-Crouch is attractively old-fashioned, and probably best known as a yachting venue. It is lively in summer, especially at the end of August when the town hosts one of England's premier regattas, Burnham Week. This week of racing and shore events attracts many visiting craft and landlubbers alike. In winter many yachts are left to ride at anchor offshore, and the sound of the wind in their rigging is ever-present.

Behind the gaily-coloured cottages along the Quay lie the High Street and the rest of the town, its streets lined with a delightful assortment of old cottages and Victorian and Georgian houses and shops.

In past times, working boats thronged the estuary where yachts now ply to and fro. Seafarers still come ashore to buy provisions, following a tradition that goes back to medieval times when Burnham was the market centre for the isolated inhabitants of Wallasea and Foulness Islands in the estuary.

Burnham-on-Crouch & District Museum on The Quay features agricultural, maritime and social history exhibits relating to the Dengie Hundred Peninsula. There is also a small archaeological collection. Special exhibitions are mounted periodically.

St Mary's Church is constructed of Kentish ragstone that was transported to Burnham by sea. Construction was begun in the 12th century and was completed in the 14th century, but since that time the nucleus of the town has moved closer to the waterfront. The arches and pillars are particularly fine examples of medieval craftsmanship, hence the church being known as 'The Cathedral of the Dengie'.

SOUTHMINSTER

3 miles N of Burnham on the B1021

The old market town of Southminster was important as the economic centre for the isolated marshland communities of the Dengie Peninsula.

BRADWELL-ON-SEA/ BRADWELL WATERSIDE

12 miles NE of Burnham off the B1021

A visit to Bradwell-on-Sea (the name derives from the Saxon words brad pall, meaning 'broad wall') is well worth the long drive for its sense of being right out on the edge of things – the timeless emptiness is, if anything, exaggerated by the distant views of buildings across the water on Mersea Island and the bulk of the nearby (now decommissioned)

91 OYSTER SMACK

Burnham on Crouch

The benefits of being run by an experienced chef shine through here with quality food, drink and accommodation.

see page 280

•

Mangapps Railway Museum on the edge of Burnham-on-Crouch town offers an extensive collection of railway relics of all kinds, including steam and diesel engines, carriages and wagons, relocated railway buildings, one of the largest collections of signalling equipment open to the public, a complete country station and items of East Anglian railway history.

•

185

Marsh Farm Country Park in Marsh Farm Road, South Woodham Ferrers, is a working farm and country park adjoining the River Crouch. Sheep, pigs, cattle and hens roam; visitors can also partake of the adventure play area, farm trail, Visitors' Centre, gift shop and tea rooms. Guided tours are available by prior arrangement. Special events are held throughout the year.

nuclear power station. A walk eastwards along the old Roman road across the marshes takes you to the site of their fort, 'Othona', on which the visitors of today will find the **Chapel of St Peter's on the Wall**, built by St Cedd and his followers in AD 654 using rubble from the ruined fort. In the 14th century the chapel was abandoned as a place of worship, and over the following centuries used at various times as a barn and a shipping beacon. Restored and re-consecrated in 1920, it is well worth the half-mile walk from the car park to reach it. It is the site of a pilgrimage each July. It has claims to be the oldest church in the land, with St Martin's in Canterbury and St Paul's in Jarrow as other contenders. St Cedd did not survive all that long after founding this chapel, dying of a fever in Yorkshire in AD 664. **Bradwell Lodge**, in the village centre, is a part-Tudor former rectory that has known some famous visitors. Gainsborough, the Suffolk artist, used rooms as a studio, while the Irish writer Erskine Childers, who was shot by the Irish Free State in 1920 because he fought for the IRA, wrote *The Riddle of the Sands* here.

An unusual war memorial marks the site of the **Bradwell Bay Secret Airfield**, used during the Second World War for aircraft unable to return to their original base. At **Bradwell Waterside**, a large marina has berths for 300 boats.

PURLEIGH

5 miles SW of Maldon on the B1010

The first recorded vineyard in Purleigh was planted in the early 12th century, only 400 yards from the site of **New Hall Vineyards** in Chelmsford Road. It covered three acres of land next to **Purleigh Church**, where first US president George Washington's great-great-grandfather was the rector - until the time he was removed from this office for sampling too much of the local brew! Purleigh Vineyard became Crown property in 1163; subsequently the wines produced were taken each year to London to be presented to the monarch.

SOUTH WOODHAM FERRERS

5 miles SW of Maldon off the B1012

The empty marshland of the Crouch estuary, a yachtsman's paradise, was chosen by Essex County Council as the site for one of its most attractive new towns schemes. At its centre, this successful 20th century new town boasts a traditional market square surrounded by pleasant arcades and terraces built in the old Essex style with brick, tile and weather-board.

RETTENDON

6 miles SW of Maldon off the A130

The **Royal Horticultural Society Garden** at Hyde Hall comprises 28 acres of year-round hillside colour, with a woodland garden, large rose garden, ornamental ponds with lilies and fish, herbaceous borders, shrubs, trees, and a National Collection of viburnums. 3,000 trees have recently been planted, and a dry garden features huge boulders from Scotland. There is also the Ronbinson Garden dedicated to the original owners of Hyde Hall, themed vegetable plots, and a wonderful gift shop – the proceeds of which support the RHS.

BATTLESBRIDGE

7 miles SW of Maldon off the A132

Battlesbridge Antiques Centre at Hawk Hill in Battlesbridge is the largest in Essex. Housed in five period buildings, more than 70 dealers display and sell their wares. The heart of the Centre is Cromwell House, its ground floor dedicated to specialist dealers with individual units. They will advise, value and give an expert opinion free of charge. They offer a wide variety of old and interesting pieces and collectibles.

The Centre's Haybarn Cottages were constructed as dwellings, while, alongside, The Bridgebarn began life as a barn with thatched roof and dates from the 19th century, at which time there were lime kilns nearby. It was converted to its present tiled roof in the 1930s. The building retains some fine oak beam work, and houses a small 'penny arcade' with working model roundabout, fortune teller, and 'What the Butler Saw' as well as a large collection of antiques for sale. From the top floor there are superb views of the River Crouch and the surrounding area.

This location is also the site of a **Classic Motorcycle Museum**, with displays evoking the history of motorcycling through the ages and some interesting memorabilia. Three classic vehicle events are held annually. Open most Sundays between 11am-4pm, or by appointment. Tel: 01268 561700.

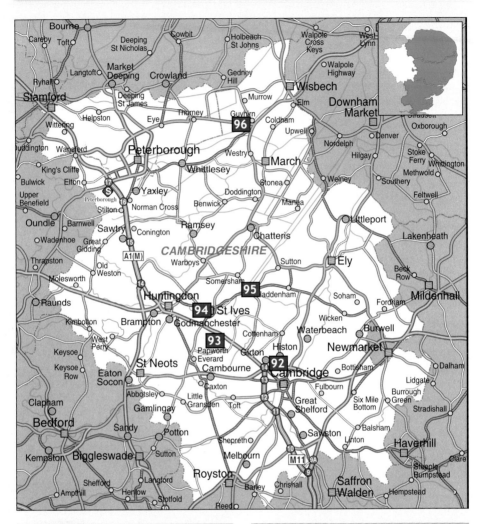

Cambridgeshire

Cambridgeshire is a county with a rich rural heritage, with attractive villages strung along the banks of the Great Ouse and the flat land of the Fens. Far removed from the hustle and bustle of modern life, the Fens are like a breath of fresh air. Extending over much of Cambridgeshire from the Wash, these flat, fenland fields contain some of the richest soil in England. Villages such as Fordham and small towns like Ely rise out of the landscape on low hills.

Before the Fens were drained, this was a land of mist, marshes and bogs, of small islands inhabited by independent folk, their livelihood the fish and waterfowl of this eerie, watery place. The region is full of legends of web-footed people, ghosts and witchcraft.

Today's landscape is the result of human ingenuity, with its constant desire to tame the wilderness and create farmland. This fascinating story spans the centuries from the earliest Roman and Anglo-Saxon times, when the first embankments and drains were constructed to lessen the frequency of flooding. Throughout the Middle Ages large areas were reclaimed, with much of the work being undertaken by the monasteries. The first straight cut bypassed the Great Ouse, allowing the water to run out to sea more quickly. After the Civil War, the New Bedford River was cut parallel to the first. These two still provide the basic drainage for much of Fenland.

The significant influence of the Dutch lives on in some of the architecture and place names of the Fens. Over the years it became necessary to pump rainwater from the fields up into the rivers and, as in the Netherlands, windmills took on this task. They could not always cope with the height of the lift required, but fortunately the steam engine came along, to be replaced eventually by the electric pumps that can raise thousands of gallons of water a second to protect the land from the ever-present threat of rain and tide.

The Fens today offer unlimited opportunities for exploring on foot, by car, bicycle or by boat. Anglers are well catered for, and visitors with an interest in wildlife will be in their element. The jewel in the crown of the Fens is Ely, with its magnificent cathedral. A few miles to the south, Wicken Fen is the oldest nature reserve in the country – 600 acres of undrained fenland that is famous for its varied plant, insect and bird life.

Southeastern Cambridgeshire covers the area around the city of Cambridge and is rich in history, with a host of archaeological sites and monuments to visit, as well as many important museums. The area is fairly flat, so it makes for great walking and cycling tours, and offers a surprising variety of landscapes. The Romans planted vines here, and to this day the region is among the main producers of British wines.

At the heart of it all is Cambridge itself, one of the leading academic centres in the world and a city which deserves plenty of time to explore - on foot, by bicycle or by the gentler, more romantic option of a punt.

The old county of Huntingdonshire is the heartland of the rural heritage of Cambridgeshire. Here, the home of Oliver Cromwell beckons with a wealth of history and pleasing landscapes. Many motorists follow the Cromwell Trail, which guides tourists around the legacy of buildings and places in the area associated with the man. The natural start of the Trail is Huntingdon itself, where he was born the son of a country gentleman.

The Ouse Valley Way (26 miles long) follows the course of the Great Ouse through pretty villages and a variety of natural attractions. A gentle cruise along this area can perfectly fill a lazy day, but for those who prefer something more energetic on the water there are excellent, versatile facilities at Grafham Water.

The Nene-Ouse Navigation Link, part of the Fenland Waterway, provides the opportunity for a relaxed look at a lovely part of the region. It travels from Stanground Lock near Peterborough to a lock at the small village of Salters Lode in the east, and the 28-mile journey passes through several Fenland towns and a rich variety of wildlife habitats.

ELY

Ely is the jewel in the crown of the Fens, and the fen's influence is apparent even in the name: Ely was once known as Elge or Elig ('eel island') because of the large number of eels which lived in the surrounding fenland. Ely owes its existence to St Etheldreda, wife of King Egfrid and Queen of Northumbria, who in AD 673 founded a monastery on the 'Isle of Ely', where she remained as abbess until her death in AD 679.

It was not until 1081 that work started on the present majestic **Cathedral**, and in 1189 this remarkable example of Romanesque architecture was completed. The most outstanding feature in terms of both scale and beauty is the Octagon, built to replace the original Norman tower, which collapsed in 1322. Alan of Walsingham was the inspired architect of this massive work, which took 30 years to complete and whose framework weighs an estimated 400 tons. Many other notable components include the 14th century Lady Chapel, the largest in England, the Prior's Door, the painted nave ceiling and St Ovin's cross, the only piece of Saxon stonework in the building.

The Cathedral, sometimes known as the 'Ship of the Fens', is set within the walls of the monastery, and many of the ancient buildings still stand as a tribute to the incredible skill and craftsmanship of their designers and builders. Particularly worth visiting among these are the monastic buildings in the College, the Great Hall and Queens Hall.

There are different tours available of the Cathedral, all of which are run by knowledgeable guides and offer a different perspective of the fascinating building. Tours of the ground floor of the Cathedral are free of charge, and give a view into the worship which has been conducted here for hundreds of years, as well as the amazing architecture and art. There are two interesting tower tours; the West Tower is the tallest at 215ft, and dates from the 13th and 14th centuries, and provides breathtaking views over miles of fenscapes; and the pre-mentioned Octagon, with its Lantern Tower in wood, lead and glass is rightly considered the jewel in the Cathedral crown. Both tours run daily from the start of April until the end of October, and a reasonable level of fitness is required to make the hundreds of

Bishop's Old Palace, Ely

steps to the top – spaces are limited so it is advised that you pre-book to avoid disappointment (Tel: 01353 667735).

Just beside the Cathedral is the Almonry, in whose 12th century vaulted undercroft visitors can take coffee, lunch or tea - outside in the garden if the weather permits. The **Stained Glass Museum**, housed in the south Triforium of the Cathedral, is the only museum of stained glass in the country and contains over 100 original panels from every period, tracing the complete history of stained glass. (Tel:01353 660347). The cannon on Palace Green opposite the Cathedral was captured from the Russians in Sebastopol and was given to the citizens of Ely by Queen Victoria after the Crimean War. The gift was made in recognition of the formation of the Ely Rifle Volunteers.

Ely's **Tourist Information Centre** is itself a tourist attraction, since it is housed in a pretty black-and-white timbered building that was once the home of Oliver Cromwell. It is the only remaining house, apart from Hampton Court, where Oliver Cromwell and his family are known to have lived; parts of it trace back to the 13th century, and its varied history includes periods when it was used as a public house and, more recently, a vicarage. There are eight period rooms, exhibitions and videos to enjoy.

The Old Gaol, in Market Street, houses **Ely Museum**, with

The Marina, Ely

nine galleries telling the Ely story from the Ice Age to modern times. The tableaux of the condemned and debtors' cells are particularly fascinating and poignant.

The **Riverside Trail** takes in the **Babylon Gallery** in a converted 18th century brewery warehouse, where visitors will find an exciting collection of contemporary arts and crafts, in a programme of changing local and international exhibitions; the Jubilee Gardens; Ely Park; and the Quai d'Orsay, named after the twinning of East Cambridgeshire with the town of Orsay in France in 1981.

AROUND ELY

PRICKWILLOW

4 miles NE of Ely on the B1382

On the village's main street is the **Prickwillow Drainage Engine Museum**, which houses a unique collection of large engines associated with the drainage of the Fens. The site had been in

•
Ely is not just the past, and its fine architecture and sense of history blend well with the bustle of the streets and shops and the riverside. That bustle is at its most fervent on Thursdays, when the largest general market in the area is held. Every Saturday there's a craft and collectibles market, and on the second and fourth Saturdays of the month Ely hosts a Farmers' Market from 8am-4pm (it is advised to arrive early as the fresh bread usually sells out by 11am, and is not to be missed). In addition to this there are many annual events held in the town – including the brilliant Folk Festival in early July, and some magical events around Christmas.
•

191

A mile further west of Sutton, there's a great family attraction in the Mepal Outdoor Centre; on the shore of a 20 acre lake, this outdoor leisure centre has a children's play park, an adventure play area, boat hire, canoe and kayaking, and a paintball course. Tel: 01354 692251

continuous use as a pumping station since 1831, and apart from the engines there are displays charting the history of Fens drainage, the effects on land levels and the workings of the modern drainage system. Tel: 01353 688360.

LITTLEPORT
6 miles N of Ely on the A10

St George's Church, with its very tall 15th century tower, is a notable landmark here in Littleport. Of particular interest are two stained-glass windows depicting St George slaying the dragon. Littleport was the scene of riots in 1861, when labourers from Ely and Littleport, faced with unemployment or low wages, and soaring food prices, attacked houses and people in this area, causing several deaths. Five of the rioters were hanged and buried in a common grave at St Mary's church. A plaque commemorating the event is attached to a wall at the back of the church.

LITTLE DOWNHAM
3 miles N of Ely off the A10

Little Downham's **Church of St Leonard** shows the change from Norman to Gothic in church building at the turn of the 13th century. The oldest parts are the Norman tower and the elaborately carved south door. Interior treasures include what is probably the largest royal coat of arms in the country. At the other end of the village are the remains (mainly the gatehouse and kitchen) of a 15th century palace built by a Bishop of Ely.

COVENEY
3 miles W of Ely off the A10/A142

A Fenland hamlet on the Bedford Level just above West Fen, Coveney's **Church of St Peter-ad-Vincula** has several interesting features, including a colourful German screen dating from around 1500 and a painted Danish pulpit. Unusual figures on the bench ends and a fine brass chandelier add to the opulent feel of this atmospheric little church.

SUTTON
6 miles W of Ely off the A142/B1381

A very splendid 'pepperpot' tower with octagons, pinnacles and spire tops marks out Sutton's grand **Church of St Andrew**. Inside, take time to look at the 15th century font and a fine modern stained-glass window. The reconstruction of the church was largely the work of two Bishops of Ely, whose arms appear on the roof bosses. One of the Bishops was Thomas Arundel, appointed at the age of 21.

The shopping centre of Sutton is now fully padestrianised, has two shopping centres, and has adopted a slight cosmopolitan air with many outdoor seating areas at cafes and restaurants.

HADDENHAM
5 miles SW of Ely on the A1123

More industrial splendour: **Haddenham Great Mill**, built in 1803 for a certain Daniel Cockle, is a glorious sight, and one definitely not to be missed. It has four sails and three sets of grinding stones, one of which is working. The mill last worked commercially in 1946 and was restored between 1992 and 1998.

STRETHAM

5 miles S of Ely off A10/A1123

The **Stretham Old Engine**, a fine example of a land-drainage steam engine, is housed in a restored, tall-chimneyed brick engine house. Dating from 1831, it is one of 90 steam pumping engines installed throughout the Fens to replace some 800 windmills. It is the last to survive, having worked until 1925 and is still under restoration. During the great floods of 1919 it really earned its keep by working non-stop for 47 days and nights.

This unique insight into Fenland history and industrial archaeology is open to the public on some days through the summer season, and on certain dates the engine and its wooden scoop-wheel are rotated (by electricity, alas!). The adjacent stoker's cottage contains period furniture and photographs of fen drainage down the years. Tel: 01353 648578.

WICKEN

9 miles S of Ely off the A1123

Wicken Fen is the oldest nature reserve in the country, and the very first nature reserve to be owned by the National Trust. 600 acres of undrained fenland famous for its rich plant, insect and bird life and a delight for both naturalists and ramblers ever since it opened in 1899. Features include boardwalk and nature trails, hides and watchtowers, a workman's cottage with 1930s furnishings, a working wind pump (the oldest in the country), a visitor centre and a shop. It is also home to Highland cattle and wild Konik ponies. Open daily, dawn to dusk. **Wicken Windmill** is a fine and impressive smock windmill restored back to working order. One of only four smock windmills making flour by windmill in the UK, it is open the first weekend of every month 10am-5.30pm and every Bank Holiday (except Christmas and Good Friday) from 11am-5pm, and also over the National Mills Weekend, the second week in May.

SOHAM

6 miles SE of Ely off the A142

Downfield Windmill was built in 1726 as a smock mill, destroyed by gales and rebuilt in 1890 as an octagonal tower mill.

Unfortunately, another storm a few years ago once again caused extensive damage to this beautiful and unique building, and the future of the mill is now unsure. It is hoped the funding for repairs (an estimated £100,000!) can be found, and English Heritage has acknowledged the need for desperate restoration in their annual "Buildings at Risk" register.

St Andrew's Church is a fine example of the Perpendicular style of English Gothic architecture. Very grand and elaborate, it was built on the site of a 7th century cathedral founded by St Felix of Burgundy. The 15th century west tower has an ornate parapet and

St Lawrence's Church in Wicken is well worth a visit, small and secluded among trees. In the churchyard are buried several members of Oliver Cromwell's family, including his fourth son Henry. One of Cromwell's many nicknames was 'Lord of the Fens': he defended the rights of the Fenmen against those who wanted to drain the land without providing adequate compensation.

A plaque in Soham commemorates engine driver Ben Gimbert and fireman James Nightall, who were taking an ammunition train through the town when a wagon caught fire. They uncoupled it and began to haul it into open country. The wagon exploded, killing the fireman and a signalman.

two medieval porches. Note, too, the chancel with its panelling and stained glass.

ISLEHAM

10 miles SE of Ely off the B1104

The remains of **Isleham Priory Church**, a Benedictine priory, with a lovely Norman chapel under the care of English Heritage, are a great draw here in Isleham. Also well worth a visit is the Church of St Andrew, a 14th century cruciform building entered by a very fine

lychgate. The 17th century eagle lectern is the original of a similar lectern in Ely Cathedral.

FORDHAM

10 miles SE of Ely off the A142

A small village on the Newmarket Cycle Way. The poet James Withers spent most of his life in Fordham and is buried in the churchyard; a stained-glass window in the church is inscribed in his memory.

During witch craft trials in 1590 two couples in Fordham were executed for suspected dealings in witchcraft – as well as one man in neighboring Aldham in 1598.

SNAILWELL

12 miles SE of Ely off the A142

Snailwell's pretty, mainly 14th century church of **St Peter** on the banks of the River Snail boasts a 13th century chancel, a hammerbeam and tie beam nave roof, a 600-year-old font, pews with poppy heads and two medieval oak screens. The Norman round tower is unusual for Cambridgeshire.

CAMBRIDGE

Cambridge was an important town many centuries before the scholars arrived, standing at the point where forest met fen, at the lowest fording point of the river. The Romans took over a site previously settled by an Iron Age Belgic tribe, to be followed in turn by the Saxons and the Normans. Soon after the Norman Conquest, William I built a wooden motte-and-bailey castle; Edward I built a

King's College, Cambridge

stone replacement: a mound still marks the spot. The town flourished as a market and river trading centre, and in 1209 a group of students fleeing the Oxford riots arrived. These students made their own arrangements for accommodation, and it was not until 1284 that the first residential college was opened. This was **Peterhouse**, founded by the Bishop of Ely, and in the next century Clare, Pembroke, Gonville & Caius, Trinity Hall and Corpus Christi followed. One of the modern Colleges is Robinson College, the gift of self-made millionaire David Robinson. The Colleges represent various architectural styles, the grandest and most beautiful being King's. Robinson has the look of a fortress; its concrete structure covered with a 'skin' of a million and a quarter hand-made red Dorset bricks.

Mathematical Bridge, Cambridge

The Colleges are all well worth a visit, but places that simply must not be missed include **King's College Chapel** with its breathtaking fan vaulting, glorious stained glass and Peter Paul Rubens' *Adoration of the Magi*; **Pepys Library**, including his diaries, in Magdalene College; and Trinity's wonderful **Great Court**. A trip by punt along the 'Backs' of the Cam brings a unique view of many of the Colleges and passes under six bridges, including the **Bridge of Sighs** (St John's) and the extraordinary wooden **Mathematical Bridge** at Queens'. It is not only the bricks and mortar

and the treasures within that bring visitors to the colleges, as many have gardens of particular interest, some of them open to the public at various times. Notable among these is **Christ's College**, where the trees include an ancient mulberry and a cypress grown from seed from the tree on Shelley's grave in Rome. Oliver Cromwell's final resting place is an unmarked grave near the chapel in Sidney Sussex College. The **University Botanic Garden** in the south of the city covers 40 acres and has a triple role of research, education and amenity.

The Colleges apart, Cambridge is packed with interest for the visitor, with a wealth of grand buildings both religious and secular, and some of the country's leading museums, many of them run by the University. The **Fitzwilliam**

•

On the corner of the Corpus' Taylor Library is a rather unusual, and terrifying, clock named the "Grasshopper Clock". Unveiled by Professor Stephen Hawking in 2008, the clock depicts the "eating" of time as the huge grasshopper rocks open jawed atop the golden dial. There are no hands, rather LED lights which run around the dial and stop on the appropriate time. Although seemingly modern the mechanism running this clock is deeply rooted in traditional clock making, and it is predicted to run for two centuries.

•

195

One of the best ways to see Cambridge, particularly of the College, is from the water on a traditional Cambridge Punt. You can hire a chauffeured punt, the driver of which also serves as an amusing guide, or self-hire all through the week. There are special ghostly tours which have a 45min punt ride and a 45min creepy Cambridge tour on foot. They run all through the summer, and weather permitting through the winter. Tel: 01223 457574 to book.

Museum is renowned for its art collection, which includes works by Titian, Rembrandt, Gainsborough, Hogarth, Turner, Renoir, Picasso and Cezanne, and for its antiquities from Egypt, Greece and Rome. **Kettle's Yard** has a permanent display of 20th century art in a house maintained just as it was when the Ede family donated it, with the collection, to the University in 1967. The **Museum of Classical Archaeology** has 500 plaster casts of Greek and Roman statues, and the **University Museum of Archaeology and Anthropology** covers worldwide prehistoric archaeology with special displays relating to Oceania and to the Cambridge area. The **Museum of Technology**, housed in a Victorian sewage pumping station, features an impressive collection of steam, gas and electric pumping engines and examples, great and small, of local industrial technology. Anyone with an interest in fossils should make tracks for the **Sedgwick Museum of Earth Sciences**, while in the same street (Downing) the **Museum of Zoology** offers

a comprehensive and spectacular survey of the animal kingdom. The **Whipple Museum of the History of Science** tells about science through instruments; and the **Scott Polar Research** Institute has fascinating, often poignant exhibits relating to Arctic and Antarctic exploration.

The work and life of the people of Cambridge and the surrounding area are the subject of the **Cambridge and County Folk Museum**, housed in a 15th century building that for 300 years was the White Horse Inn. Topics include Crafts & Trades, Town & Gown, and Skating & Eels, and throughout the year themed talks and exhibitions take place. One of the city's greatest treasures is the **University Library**, one of the world's great research libraries with 6 million books, a million maps and 350,000 manuscripts. The Library was built between 1930 and 1934 to a design of Giles Gilbert Scott.

Cambridge also has many fine churches, some of them used by the Colleges before they built their own chapels. Among the most notable are **St Andrew the Great** (note the memorial to Captain Cook); **St Andrew the Less**; **St Benet's** (its 11th century tower is the oldest in the county); **St Mary the Great**, a marvellous example of Late Perpendicular Gothic; and **St Peter Castle Hill**. This last is one of the smallest churches in the country, with a nave measuring just 25 feet by 16 feet. Originally much larger, the church was largely demolished in 1781 and rebuilt in

St Bennet's Church, Cambridge

its present diminished state using the old materials, including flint rubble and Roman bricks. The **Church of the Holy Sepulchre**, always known as the Round Church, is one of only four surviving circular churches in England.

AROUND CAMBRIDGE

BOTTISHAM

5 miles E of Cambridge on the A1303

John Betjeman ventured that Bottisham's **Holy Trinity Church** was 'perhaps the best in the county', so time should certainly be made for a visit. Among the many interesting features are the 13th century porch, an 18th century monument to Sir Roger Jenyns and some exceptionally fine modern woodwork in Georgian style.

SWAFFHAM PRIOR

8 miles NE of Cambridge on the B1102.

Swaffham Prior gives double value to the visitor, with two churches in the same churchyard and two fine old windmills. The **Churches of St Mary and St Cyriac** stand side by side, a remarkable and dramatic sight in the steeply rising churchyard. One of the mills, a restored 1850s tower mill, still produces flour and can be visited by appointment.

LODE

6 miles NE of Cambridge on the B1102

Anglesey Abbey (National Trust) dates from 1600 and was built on the site of an Augustinian priory, but the house and the 100-acre garden came together as a unit thanks to the vision of the 1st Lord Fairhaven. The garden, created in its present form from the 1930s, is a wonderful place for a stroll, with 98 acres of landscaped gardens including wide grassy walks, open lawns, a riverside walk, a working water mill and one of the finest collections of garden statuary in the country. There's also a plant centre, shop and restaurant. In the house itself is Lord Fairhaven's magnificent collection of paintings, sumptuous furnishings, tapestries and clocks. The garden is open 10.30am-4.30pm Wed-Sun all year round, particularly lovely in late Jan/early Feb during snowdrop season. The restaurant,

At Swaffham Bulbeck, a little way to the south of Swaffham Prior, stands another Church of St Mary, with a 13th century tower and 14th century arcades and chancel. Look for the fascinating carvings on the wooden benches and a 15th century cedarwood chest decorated with biblical scenes.

Anglesey Abbey, Lode

shop and plant centre have the same opening times, the house is open to the public 11am-5pm April until November. Tel: 01223 810080.

BURWELL

10 miles NE of Cambridge on the B1102

Burwell is a village of many attractions with a history going back to Saxon times. **Burwell Museum** reflects many aspects of a village on the edge of the Fens up to the middle of the 20th century. A general store, model farm, local industries and children's toys are among the displays. Next to the museum is the famous **Stephens Windmill**, built in 1820 and extensively restored, with more restorations expected to be undertaken through 2010. The museum and windmill are open 2 - 5pm on Thursdays, Sundays & Bank Holiday Mondays from Easter Sunday to the last Sunday in October.

The **Devil's Dyke** runs through Burwell on its path from Reach to Woodditton. This amazing dyke, 30 yards wide, was built, it is thought, to halt Danish invaders.

REACH

8 miles NE of Cambridge off the A4280

The charming village of Reach is home to the oldest fair in England, which celebrated its 800th anniversary on 1st May, 2000.

WATERBEACH

5 miles N of Cambridge off the A10

Denny Abbey, easily accessible on the A10, is an English Heritage Grade I listed Abbey with ancient earthworks. On the same site, and run as a joint attraction, is the **Farmland Museum**. The history of Denny Abbey runs from the 12th century, when it was a Benedictine monastery. It was later home to the Knights Templar, Franciscan nuns and the Countess of Pembroke, and from the 16th century was a farmhouse. The old farm buildings have been splendidly renovated and converted to tell the story of village life and Cambridgeshire farming up to modern times. The museum is ideal for family outings, with plenty of hands-on activities for children and a play area, gift shop and weekend tearoom. Among the top displays are a village shop, agricultural machinery, a magnificent 17th century stone barn, a traditional farmworker's cottage and the workshops where various crafts are practised. The museum is open daily 12noon-

Devils Dyke, Burwell

198

5pm from the start of April until the end of October.

MILTON

3 miles N of Cambridge off the A10

Milton Country Park offers fine walking and exploring among acres of parkland, lakes and woods – with the main sections of the two miles of paths being accessible for wheelchairs and buggies. There's a visitor centre, a picnic area, children's play park, and a place serving light refreshments. Dogs are welcome and can be walked off the lead at the northern end of the park.

COTTENHAM

5 miles NW of Cambridge on the B1049

All Saints Church has an unusual tower of yellow and pink Jacobean brick topped with four pinnacles that look like pineapples. The original tower fell down in a gale, and its replacement was partially funded by former US President Calvin Coolidge, one of whose ancestors had lived in the village at the time when the tower fell down.

RAMPTON

6 miles N of Cambridge off the B1050/B1049

A charming village in its own right, with a tree-fringed village green, Rampton is also the site of one of the many archaeological sites in the area. This is **Giant's Hill**, a motte castle with part of an earlier medieval settlement.

GIRTON

3 miles NW of Cambridge off the A14

The first Cambridge College for women was founded in 1869 in Hitchin, by Emily Davies. It moved here to Girton in 1873, to be 'near enough for male lecturers to visit but far enough away to discourage male students from doing the same'. The problem went away when Girton became a mixed College in 1983.

MADINGLEY

4 miles W of Cambridge on the A428

The American Cemetery is one of the loveliest, most peaceful and most moving places in the region, a place of pilgrimage for the families of the American servicemen who operated from the many wartime bases in the county. The cemetery commemorates service personnel who lost their lives in World War II serving as crew members of British-based American aircraft. The tablet of the missing records 5,126 missing in action, lost or buried at sea, and the graves area contains 3,812 headstones.

GREAT GRANSDEN

9 miles W of Cambridge on the B1046

Great Gransden is home to Britain's oldest surviving **Postmill**, which has been restored. A scheduled ancient monument, it dates from the early 17th century and was worked well into the early years of the 20th century.

BARTON

3 miles SW of Cambridge off the A603/B1046

Looking south from this pleasant village you can see the impressive

92   THE KING WILLIAM

Histon, nr Cambridge
A distinctive old coaching inn serving real ales and a fine selection of home-cooked food.

see page 281

array of radio telescopes that are part of Cambridge University's Mullard Radio Astronomy Observatory.

GRANTCHESTER

2 miles SW of Cambridge off the A603

A pleasant walk by the Cam through the woods and meadows of the **Paradise Nature Reserve** brings visitors from the bustle of Cambridge to the famous village of Grantchester, where Rupert Brooke lived and Byron swam.

The Orchard, with its Brooke connections, is known the world over. Brooke spent two happy years in Grantchester, and immortalised afternoon tea in The Orchard Tea Garden in a poem entitled "The Old Vicarage" he wrote while homesick in Berlin.

'Stands the church clock at ten to three
And is there honey still for tea?'

The wooden Tea Pavilion where Brooke enjoyed his tea still stands; the perfect place to enjoy the quiet and genteel English tradition of afternoon tea, including the scones.

Brooke also wrote the memorable lines

'If I should die, think only this of me,
That there's some corner of a foreign field
That is forever England'

Brooke died aged 28 on service to his country in 1915 in the Dardanelles.

Time should also be allowed for a look at the **Church of St Andrew and St Mary**, in which the remains of a Norman church have been incorporated into the 1870s main structure.

ARRINGTON

8 miles SW of Cambridge off the A603/A1198

Arrington's 18th century **Wimpole Hall**, owned by the National Trust, is probably the most spectacular country mansion in the whole county, and certainly the largest country house in Cambridgeshire. The lovely interiors are the work of several celebrated architects, and there's a fine collection of furniture and pictures. The mansion's state and private rooms show how the last owner Mrs Elsie Bambridge, a daughter of Rudyard Kipling, lived at Wimpole trying to restore the house and estate to its former glory. The magnificent formally laid-out grounds include a Victorian parterre (with some surprising modern sculptures), a rose garden and a walled garden. The park provides miles of wonderful walking and is perfect

Church of St Andrew and St Mary, Grantchester

for anything from a gentle stroll to a strenuous hike. On the grounds there is also a bookshop, gift shop, restaurant and working farm where visitors can experience all the delights of farming, including milking demonstrations. Dogs are welcome in the surrounding park. Tel: 01223 206000

SHEPRETH

8 miles S of Cambridge off A10

A paradise for lovers of nature and gardens and a great starting point for country walks, **Shepreth L-Moor Nature Reserve** is an L-shaped area of wet meadowland - now a rarity - that is home to birds and many rare plants. The nearby **Shepreth Wildlife Park** started life as a refuge for injured and orphaned British birds and mammals. It now houses a collection of wild and domestic animals including wolves, monkeys, birds and reptiles. In the Water World and Bug City visitors can see fish and insects, including the amazing leaf cutter ants. The park is open 10am-6pm through summer and autumn, and 10am-dusk in winter and spring.

DUXFORD

8 miles S of Cambridge off A505 by J10 of M11

Part of the Imperial War Museum, **Duxford Aviation Museum** is probably the leader in its field in Europe, with an outstanding collection of over 150 historic aircraft from biplanes through Spitfires, Concorde and Gulf War fighters. The American Air

Museum, where aircraft are suspended as if in flight, is part of this terrific place, which was built on a former RAF and USAAF fighter base. Major air shows take place several times a year, and among the permanent features are a reconstructed wartime operations room, a hands-on exhibition for children and a dramatic land warfare hall with tanks, military vehicles and artillery. Everyone should take time to see this marvellous show - and it should be much more than a flying visit! A free bus service operates from Cambridge City Centre.

LINTON

10 miles SE of Cambridge on the B1052

The village is best known for its zoo, but visitors will also find many handsome old buildings and the **Church of St Mary the Virgin**, built mainly in Early English style.

A world of wildlife set in 16 acres of spectacular gardens, **Linton Zoo** is a major wildlife breeding centre and part of the inter-zoo breeding programme for endangered species. Among the rare and exotic creatures to be seen are Grevy's zebra, snow leopards, tigers, lions, tapirs, lemurs, binturongs, owls, parrots, giant tortoises and tarantulas. The gardens also include picnic areas, a children's play area and, in summer, pony rides and a bouncy castle.

Chilford Hall Vineyard, on the B1052 between Linton and Balsham, comprises 18 acres of vines, with tours and wine-tastings available.

Surrounding 18th century Docwra's Manor at Shepreth is a series of enclosed gardens with multifarious plants that are open for visits Wednesday and Friday all year and the first Sunday afternoons from April to October. Fowlmere, on the other side of the A10, is an 86-acre nature reserve designed as a Site of Special Scientific Interest, with hides and trails for bird-watching.

River Ouse, Huntingdon

Some two miles further off the A1307, **Bartlow Hills** are the site of the largest Roman burial site to be unearthed in Europe.

HUNTINGDON

The former county town of Huntingdonshire is an ancient place first settled by the Romans. It boasts many grand Georgian buildings, including the handsome three-storeyed **Town Hall**.

Oliver Cromwell was born in Huntingdon in 1599 and attended Huntingdon Grammar School. The schoolhouse was originally part of the Hospital of St John the Baptist, founded during the reign of Henry II by David, Earl of Huntingdon. Samuel Pepys was also a pupil here.

Cromwell was MP for Huntingdon in the Parliament of 1629, was made a JP in 1630 and moved to St Ives in the following year. Rising to power as an extremely able military commander in the Civil War, he raised troops from the region and made his headquarters in the Falcon Inn.

Appointed Lord Protector in 1653, Cromwell was ruler of the country until his death in 1658. The school he attended is now the **Cromwell Museum**, located on Huntingdon High Street, housing the only public collection relating specifically to him, with exhibits that reflect many aspects of his political, social and religious life. The museum's exhibits include an extensive collection of Cromwell family portraits and personal objects, among them a hat and seal, contemporary coins and medals, an impressive Florentine cabinet - the gift of the Grand Duke of Tuscany - and a surgeon's chest made by Kolb of Augsburg. This fine collection helps visitors interpret the life and legacy of Cromwell and the Republican movement. Tel: 01480 375830

All Saints Church, opposite the Cromwell Museum, displays many architectural styles, from medieval to Victorian. One of the two surviving parish churches of Huntingdon (there were once 16), All Saints was considered to be the church of the Hinchingbrooke part of the Cromwell family, though no memorials survive to attest to this. The Cromwell family burial vault is contained within the church, however, and it is here that Oliver's father Robert and his grandfather Sir Henry are buried. The church has a fine chancel roof, a very lovely organ chamber, a truly impressive stained glass window and the font in which Cromwell was baptised, as it's the old font from the destroyed St John's church, discovered in a local garden in 1927!

Huntingdon's other important church, **St Mary's**, dates from Norman times but was almost completely rebuilt in the 13th century. It boasts a fine Perpendicular west tower, which partially collapsed in 1607. The damage was extensive, and the tower was not completely repaired until 1621. Oliver Cromwell's father Robert was one of two bailiffs who contributed to the cost of the repairs, as recorded on the stone plaque fixed to the east wall on the nave, north of the chancel arch. **Cowper House** (No 29 High Street) has an impressive early 18th century frontage. A plaque commemorates the fact that the poet William Cowper (pronounced 'Cooper') lived here between 1765 and 1767. "Huntingdon is one of the neatest towns in England" wrote Cowper, so it's not surprising that he made it his home. Among Huntingdon's many fine former coaching inns is the **George Hotel**. Although badly damaged by fire in 1865, the north and west wings of the 17th century courtyard remain intact, as does its very rare wooden gallery. The inn was one of the most famous of all the posting houses on the old Great North Run. It is reputed that Dick Turpin used one of the rooms here. The medieval courtyard, gallery and open staircase are the scene of annual productions of Shakespeare.

Along the south side of the Market Square, the **Falcon Inn** dates back in parts to the 1500s. Oliver Cromwell is said to have used this as his headquarters during the Civil War. Chartered markets are held in the Market Place every Wednesday and Saturday 8am-4pm.

Huntingdon is twinned with Salon de Provence in France, Wertheim am Main in Germany and Szentendre in Hungary.
Hinchingbrooke Country Park covers 170 acres of grassy meadows, mature woodland, ponds and lakes. There is a wide variety of wildlife including woodpeckers, herons, kestrels, butterflies and foxes. The network of paths makes exploring the park easy, and battery-powered wheelchairs are provided for less able visitors. Dogs are welcome. The Visitor Centre serves refreshments and hot food at peak times. Half a mile north of Hinchingbrooke, **Spring Common** offers another chance to enjoy some marvellous Cambridgeshire countryside. Covering 13 acres, its name comes from the natural spring that runs constantly and has long been a gathering place. The town developed around, rather than within, this area of rural tranquillity, which boasts a range of diverse habitats including marsh, grassland, scrub and streams. Plant life abounds, providing food and shelter for a variety of animals, amphibians, birds and invertebrates. There are

The Church of St Thomas à Becket of Canterbury forms an impressive vista at the end of the Ramsey High Street. Dating back to about 1180, it is thought to have been built as a hospital or guesthouse for the Abbey. It was converted, perhaps a century later, to a church to accommodate the many pilgrims who flocked to Ramsey. The church has what is reputed to be the finest nave in Huntingdonshire, dating back to the 12th century and consisting of seven bays. The church's other treasure is a 15th century carved oak lectern, thought to have come from the Abbey. Oliver Cromwell's uncle Sir Oliver is buried in the church.

several other parks and commons within Huntingdon; Town Park with its colourful flower beds, interesting maze and bandstand, where local organisations stage music and drama events in the Summer; Castle Hill with a brick built residence of 1786 which was the wartime HQ of the RAF's Pathfinder Force; the Riverside Park; and Mill Common.

AROUND HUNTINGDON

UPWOOD

8 miles NE of Huntingdon off the B1040

Upwood is a pleasant, scattered village in a very tranquil and picturesque setting. **Woodwalton Fen Nature Reserve**, home to an impressive list of many rare plants, insect, birds and mammals, is a couple of minutes' drive to the west.

RAMSEY

9 miles NE of Huntingdon on the B1040

A pleasant market town with a broad main street down which a river once ran, Ramsey is home to the medieval **Ramsey Abbey**, founded in AD 969 by Earl Ailwyn as a Benedictine monastery. The Abbey became one of the most important in England in the 12th and 13th centuries, and as it prospered, so did Ramsey, so that by the 13th century it had become a town with a weekly market and an annual three-day festival at the time of the feast of St Benedict. After the Dissolution of the Monasteries in 1539, the Abbey and its lands

were sold to Sir Richard Williams, great-grandfather of Oliver Cromwell. Most of the buildings were then demolished, the stones being used to build Caius, Kings and Trinity Colleges at Cambridge, the towers of Ramsey, Godmanchester and Holywell churches, the gate at Hinchingbrooke House and several local properties. In 1938 the house was converted for use as a school, which it remains to this day. To the northwest are the ruins of the once magnificent stone gatehouse dating from the late 15th century - only the porter's lodge remains, but inside can be seen an unusual large carved effigy made of Purbeck marble and dating back to the 14th century. It is said to represent Earl Ailwyn, founder of the Abbey. The gatehouse, now in the care of the National Trust, can be visited daily from April to October.

The unusual **Ramsey War Memorial**, standing almost at the end of Church Green, is a listed Grade II memorial consisting of a fine bronze statue of St George slaying the dragon atop a tall, octagonal pillar crafted in Portland stone.

ALCONBURY

3 miles NW of Huntingdon off the A1

Fenland walks can be interspersed with pauses at the local inns and a look at the **Church of St Peter and St Paul**, whose steeple and chancel are particularly noteworthy. This long village has a large green, an ancient village pump and a 15th century bridge crossing the brook that runs through Alconbury.

SAWTRY

8 miles NW of Huntingdon on the A1

The main point of interest here has no point! **All Saints Church**, built in 1880, lacks both tower and steeple, and is topped instead by a bellcote. Inside the church are marvellous brasses and pieces from ancient Sawtry Abbey.

Just south of Sawtry, **Aversley Wood** is a conservation area with abundant birdlife and plants.

HAMERTON

9 miles NW of Huntingdon off the A1

Aversley Wood, Sawtry

Hamerton Zoological Park has hundreds of animals from tortoises to tigers. Specially designed enclosures make for unrivalled views of the animals, and the park features meerkats, marmosets and mongooses, lemurs, gibbons, possums and sloths, snakes and even creepy-crawlies such as cockroaches! Also there are adorable Pygmy Goats, which visitors are allowed to get into the pen with and give a little feed. New additions include two play areas, one for toddlers and one for older children, a covered picnic area and garden, coffee shop and gift shop. It is conveniently open everyday of the year (except Christmas) at 10.30am-6pm in the summer and 10.30am-4pm in the winter.

GREAT GIDDING

10 miles NW of Huntingdon off the B660

Stained-glass windows are a notable feature of **St Michael's Church** in this, the largest of the three Giddings. A fire ravaged the village in the 1860s and the church was one of the few buildings to survive. Today the church is the atmospheric setting for concerts and plays.

STILTON

12 miles NW of Huntingdon off the A1

Stilton has an interesting main street with many fine buildings, and is a good choice for the hungry or thirsty visitor, as it has been since the heyday of horse-drawn travel. Journeys were a little more dangerous then, and Dick Turpin is said to have hidden at the Bell Inn. The tradition of Stilton's famous cheese (originating in the 18th century) is alive and well, still produced and sold here; and so is the bizarre annual event of cheese rolling which is held on May Day on the village high street, and celebrated its 50th year in 2009.

ELLINGTON

4 miles W of Huntingdon off the A14

Ellington is a quiet village just south of the A14 and about a mile

205

north of Grafham Water. Both Cromwell and Pepys visited, having relatives living in the village, and it was in Ellington that Pepys' sister Paulina found a husband, much to the relief of the diarist, who had written: 'We must find her one, for she grows old and ugly.' **All Saints Church** at Ellington is magnificent, like so many in the area, and among its many fine features are the 15th century oak roof and the rich carvings in the nave and the aisles. The church and its tower were built independently.

BARHAM

6 miles W of Huntingdon off the A1/A14

This delightful hamlet boasts 12 houses and an ancient church with box pews, surrounded by undulating farmland. Nearby attractions include angling and sailing on Grafham Water, go-karting at Kimbolton and National Hunt racing at Huntingdon.

SPALDWICK

6 miles W of Huntingdon off the A14

A sizable village that was once the site of the Bishop of Lincoln's manor house, Spaldwick boasts the grand **Church of St James**, which dates from the 12th century and has seen restoration in most centuries, including the 20th, when the spire had to be partly rebuilt after being struck by lightning.

Two miles further west, **Catworth** is another charming village, regularly voted Best Kept Village in Cambridgeshire and well worth exploring.

KEYSTON

12 miles W of Huntingdon off the A14

A delightful village with a pedigree that can be traced back to the days of the Vikings, Keyston has major attractions both sacred and secular: the **Church of St John the Baptist** is impressive in its almost cathedral-like proportions, with one of the most magnificent spires in the whole county.

BRAMPTON

2 miles SW of Huntingdon off the A1

Brampton is where **Huntingdon Racecourse** is situated. An average of 18 meetings (all jumping) are scheduled every year, including Bank Holiday fixtures (extra-special deals for families). In November, the Grade II Peterborough Chase is the feature race.

Brampton's less speculative attractions include the 13th century church of St Mary, and **Pepys House**, the home of Samuel's uncle, who was a cousin of Lord Sandwich and who got Samuel his job at the Admiralty.

BUCKDEN

4 miles SW of Huntingdon on the A1

This historic village was an important coaching stop on the old Great North Road. It is known particularly as the site of **Buckden Towers**, the great palace built for the Bishops of Lincoln. In the splendid grounds are the 15th century gatehouse and the tower where Henry VIII imprisoned his first wife, Catherine of Aragon, in 1533 (open only on certain days of the year).

GRAFHAM

5 miles SW of Huntingdon on the B661

Created in the mid-1960s as a reservoir, **Grafham Water** offers a wide range of outdoor activities for visitors of all ages, with 1,500 acres of beautiful countryside, including the lake itself. The ten-mile perimeter track is great for jogging or cycling, and there's excellent sailing, windsurfing and fly-fishing. They also offer great courses in a whole variety of activities, including powerboating, archery, and canoeing – some of which the whole family can enjoy together. The area is a Site of Special Scientific Interest, and an ample nature reserve at the western edge is run jointly by Anglian Water and the Wildlife Trust. There are nature trails, information boards, a wildlife garden and a dragonfly pond. Bird-watchers have the use of six hides, three of them accessible to wheelchairs. An exhibition centre has displays and video presentations of the reservoir's history, a gift shop and a café. Tel: 0845 6346022.

KIMBOLTON

8 miles SW of Huntingdon on the B645

History aplenty here, and a lengthy pause is in order to look at all the interesting buildings. **St Andrew's Church**, a 14th and 15th century building with a fine selection of table tombs in the churchyard, would head the list were it not for **Kimbolton Castle**, which, along with its gatehouse, dominates the village. Parts of the original Tudor building are still to be seen, but the appearance of the castle today owes much to the major remodelling carried out by Vanbrugh and Nicholas Hawksmoor in the first decade of the 18th century. It is open to the public, though only on certain days through the year so it is always best to check before your visit. Tel: 01480 860505

BUSHMEAD

10 miles SW of Huntingdon off the B660

The remains of **Bushmead Abbey**, once a thriving Augustinian community, are well worth a detour. The garden setting is delightful, and the surviving artefacts include some interesting stained glass. Open weekends in July and August.

LITTLE PAXTON

8 miles SW of Huntingdon off the A1/A428

Fewer than three miles north of St Neots at Little Paxton is **Paxton Pits Nature Reserve**. Created alongside gravel workings, the Reserve attracts thousands of water birds for visitors to observe from hides. The wealth of wildlife means that the area is an SSSI (Site of Special Scientific Interest) and ensures a plethora of colour and activity all year round. The site also features nature trails and a visitors' centre. It has thousands of visiting waterfowl, including one of the largest colonies of cormorants, and is particularly noted for its wintering wildfowl, nightingales in late spring and kingfishers. Other animals you could get a glimpse of

The magnificent parish Church of St Mary the Virgin in St Neots is a very fine edifice, known locally as the Cathedral of Huntingdonshire. It is an outstanding example of Late Medieval architecture. The gracious interior complements the 130-feet Somerset-style tower, with a finely carved oak altar, excellent Victorian stained glass and a Holdich organ, built in 1855. St Neots Museum – opened in 1995 – tells the story of the town and the surrounding area. Housed in the former magistrates' court and police station, it still has the original cells. Eye-catching displays trace local history from prehistoric times to the present day. Open Tuesday to Saturday 11am-4pm.

during a visit are Muntjac Deer, Smooth or Great Crested Newts in the shallows, or even otters though they are rarely seen. There are about four miles of walks, some suitable for wheelchairs. Spring and summer also bring a feast of wildflowers, butterflies and dragonflies. The visitors centre here has a sightings board – which is constantly updated – interactive displays about the wildlife for children, and refreshments (with ice cream in summer).

ST NEOTS

10 miles SW of Huntingdon off the A1

St Neots dates back to the founding of a Saxon Priory, built on the outskirts of Eynesbury in AD 974. Partially destroyed by the Danes in 1010, it was re-established as a Benedictine Priory in about 1081 by St Anselm, Abbot of Bec and later Archbishop of Canterbury. For the next two centuries the Priory flourished. Charters were granted by Henry I to hold fairs and markets. The first bridge over the Great Ouse, comprising 73 timber arches, was built in 1180. The name of the town comes from the Cornish saint whose remains were interred in the Priory some time before the Norman Conquest. With the Dissolution of the Monasteries, the Priory was demolished. In the early 17th century the old bridge was replaced by a stone one. This was then the site of a battle between the Royalists and Roundheads in 1648 - an event sometimes re-enacted by Sealed Knot societies.

St Neots repays a visit on foot, since there are many interesting sites and old buildings tucked away. The famous Market Square is one of the largest and most ancient in the country. A market has been held here every Thursday since the 12th century.

EYNESBURY

11 miles SW of Huntingdon on the A428

Eynesbury is actually part of St Neots, with only a little stream separating the two. Note the 12th century **Church of St Mary** with its Norman tower. Rebuilt in the Early English period, it retains some well-preserved locally sculpted 14th century oak benches.

History has touched the quiet lovely village of Eynesbury from time to time: it was the home of the famous giant James Toller, who died in 1818 and is buried in the middle aisle of the church. Only 21 when he died, he measured 8 feet and six inches tall - it is said he was buried here to escape the attention of body-snatchers, whose activities were widespread at the time. Eynesbury was also the birthplace of the Miles Quads, the first-ever surviving quadruplets in Britain.

GODMANCHESTER

2 miles SE of Huntingdon off the A1

Godmanchester is linked to Huntingdon by a 14th century bridge across the River Ouse. It was a Roman settlement and one that continued in importance down the years, as the number of handsome buildings testifies. One such is **Island Hall**, a mid-18th century mansion built for John Jackson, the Receiver General for Huntingdon; it contains many interesting pieces. This family home has lovely Georgian rooms, with fine period detail and fascinating possessions relating to the owners' ancestors since their first occupation of the house in 1800. The tranquil riverside setting and formal gardens add to the peace and splendour - the house takes its name from the ornamental island that forms part of the grounds. Octavia Hill was sometimes a guest, and wrote effusively to her sister that Island Hall was 'the loveliest, dearest old house, I never was in such a one before.' Open only to pre-booked groups. The **Queen Elizabeth School**, founded in 1559 with its gabled porch and interesting sundial clock, was closed after the Second World War for being "unsuitable for its purpose by modern standards"; the students were moved to a new school in Huntingdon. It is now for community use.

PAPWORTH EVERARD

6 miles SE of Huntingdon on the A1198

One of the most recent of the region's churches, St Peter's dates mainly from the mid-19th century. Neighbouring **Papworth St Agnes** has an older church in St John's, though parts of that, too, are Victorian. Just up the road at Hilton is the famous **Hilton Turf Maze**, cut in 1660 to a popular medieval design with a pillar in the centre.

BOXWORTH

7 miles SE of Huntingdon off the A14

A village almost equidistant from Huntingdon and Cambridge, and a pleasant base for touring the area, Boxworth's **Church of St Peter** is unusual in being constructed of pebble rubble.

A mile south of Boxworth is **Overhall Grove**, one of the largest elm woods in the country – which also contains 35 oaks with wide spreading crowns, up to 300 years old - and home to a variety of wildlife. The remains of a mediaeval manor surrounded by a moat can still be seen in the northern end of the wood, which is now home to a family of badgers. Their digging has unearthed shards of pottery, which date the manor back to the 11th to 15th centuries.

THE GREAT OUSE VALLEY

HEMINGFORD ABBOTS

3 miles SE of Huntingdon off the A14

Once part of the Ramsey Abbey Estate, Hemingford Abbots is set around the 13th century church of St Margaret, along the banks of the Great Ouse. Opportunities for angling and boating facilities, including rowing boats for hire, as well as swimming, country walks, golf and a recreation centre are all within a couple of miles. The village hosts a flower festival every two years.

Just to the east of Hemingford Abbots is Hemingford Grey, with its

In Godmanchester, a footpath leads from the famous Chinese Bridge (1827) to Port Holme Meadow, at 225 acres one of the largest in England and the site of Roman remains. It is a Site of Special Scientific Interest, with a huge diversity of botanical and bird species. Huntingdon racecourse was once situated here, and it was a training airfield during the First World War. Another site of considerable natural activity is Godmanchester Pits, accessed along the Ouse Valley Way and home to a great diversity of flora and fauna.

93 THE WHITE SWAN

Conington

A friendly and convivial pub that serves excellent food and drink all week long.

see page 283

church on the banks of the Ouse.

Hemingford Grey Manor is reputedly the oldest continuously inhabited house in England, built around 1130, much of the original house remains virtually intact. One of the owners was the author Lucy Boston, who used it as the house of Green Knowe in her children's books. She used the upstairs hall during World War II to give gramophone record recitals twice a week to the RAF. The 1929 EMG gramophone is still in use in this room. This remarkable lady made a collection of exquisite patchworks, most of which are on display, and she also designed the garden, including topiary in the form of chess pieces in the garden. The garden is open daily 11am-5pm, the house by appointment. Tel: 01480 463134.

FENSTANTON

7 miles SE of Huntingdon off the A14 bypass

Capability Brown was Lord of the Manor from 1768, and he, his wife and his son are buried in the medieval church. Lancelot Brown (1716-1783) acquired his nickname from assuring innumerable clients that he could see the capabilities in their lands. He became head gardener and clerk of works at Stowe in 1741, where he helped in executing the designs of William Kent. He branched out on his own as an 'improver of gardens' in 1751, creating more than 140 splendid parks: Blenheim, Burghley and Badminton are among his many masterpieces –

and that's just a few of the Bs! Any visit here should also take in the red-brick **Clock Tower**, which was originally a 17th century lock-up. There are several pleasant footpaths around the village.

WYTON

2 miles E of Huntington off the A1123

Wyton is mentioned in the *Domesday Book* and is thought to have been founded in the 8th century. It is a popular tourist destination thanks to its proximity to **Houghton Mill** (National Trust) and opportunities for riverside walks, as well as its charming thatched buildings and shops. The large, impressive, timber-built water mill dates from the 17th century – and is now the only working watermill on the Great Ouse. Potto Brown, a Quaker merchant and non-conformist, was one of its famous millers. It has a beautiful river-side location, which provides some lovely walks. There are hands-on exhibits for all the family to enjoy here, a tea room and bookshop, as well as stone-ground flour to buy. Tel: 01480 301494 for opening times, and milling days (subject to river levels).

HOUGHTON

5 miles E of Huntingdon on the A1123

Houghton Meadows is a Site of Special Scientific Interest with an abundance of hay meadow species. One of the most popular walks in the whole area links Houghton with St Ives.

ST IVES

6 miles E of Huntingdon off the A1123

'As I was going to St Ives
I met a man with seven wives.

Each wife had seven sacks,
each sack had seven cats,
each cat had seven kits.

Kits, cats, sacks and wives,
how many were there going to St Ives?'

Just the story teller, of course, but today's visitors are certain to have a good time while they are here.

This is an ancient town on the banks of the Great Ouse which once held a huge annual fair; it is named after St Ivo, said to be a Persian bishop who came here in the Dark Ages to spread a little light. In the Middle Ages, kings bought cloth for their households at the village's great wool fairs and markets, and a market is still held every Monday and Friday. The Bank Holiday Monday markets are particularly lively affairs, and the Michaelmas fair fills the town centre for three days.

Seagoing barges once navigated up to the famous six-arched **River Bridge**, which was built in the 15th century and has a most unusual chapel in its middle: the two-storey Chapel of St Leger is one of only four surviving bridge chapels in the country. Oliver Cromwell lived in St Ives in the 1630s; his statue on Market Hill, with its splendid hat, is one of the village's most familiar landmarks. It was made in bronze, with a Portland stone base, and was erected in 1901. It was originally designed for Huntingdon, but they wouldn't accept it!

The beautiful **All Saints Church** in its yard beside the river is well worth a visit. The quayside provides a tranquil mooring for holidaymakers and there are wonderful walks by the riverside.

Clive Sinclair developed his tiny TVs and pocket calculators in the

•

In early July the two day St Ives carnival and music festival fills the town with music, rides and colour. On the first day an impressive convoy of carnival floats travel across the town and are judged by the Mayor of St Ives, starting the festivities.

•

94   SLEPE HALL

St Ives

A former Victorian girls' boarding school is now a splendidly appointed hotel with all the modern amenities.

see page 282

Medieval Chapter, River Ouse, St Ives

95 THE OLD RIVERVIEW INN

Earith

A friendly and convivial inn providing quality food, comfortable accommodation and excellent service.

see page 284

town, and another famous son of St Ives was the great Victorian rower John Goldie, whose name is remembered each year by the second Cambridge boat in the Boat Race.

The **Norris Museum**, founded in 1933 by the St Ives historian Herbert Norris in a delightful setting by the river, tells the story of Huntingdonshire from the age of the dinosaurs to flint tools, Roman artefacts and Civil War armour, lace-making and ice-skating displays, and contemporary works of art. Exhibitions include a life-size replica of a 160-million-year-old ichthyosaur. Special, changing exhibitions are held at various months through the year – showcasing some of the photos, objects and art from the museums extensive otherwise unseen collection. The real hidden gem of this museum is its garden, a peaceful haven of herbs and flowers by the river, particularly lovely in May when the wisteria is in full bloom and giving off its

gorgeous fragrance. There are some interesting stone Roman coffins in the garden, which were found near Water Newton during the building of a dual carriageway. The museum is open May-Sept Monday to Saturday 10am-5pm and Sunday 2pm-5pm, and Oct-April Monday to Friday 10am-4pm and Saturday 10am-1pm.

EARITH
4 miles E of St Ives on the A1123

The **Ouse Washes**, a special protection area, run northeast from the village to Earith Pits, a well-known habitat for birds and crawling creatures; some of the pits are used for fishing. The Washes are a wetland of major international importance supporting such birds as ruffs, Bewick and Whooper swans, and hen harriers. The average bird population is around 20,000. Some of the meadows flood in winter, and ice-skating is popular when the temperature really drops. There's a great tradition of ice-skating in the Fens, and Fenmen were the national champions until the 1930s.

WOODHURST
2 miles NE of St Ives off the B1040

The **Raptor Foundation** is a bird of prey rescue centre set in 20 acres of woodland and home to 300 birds of prey, mostly injured, orphaned or unwanted. There are flying demonstrations where you can witness some of these glorious birds in action, held daily at 12pm, 2pm and 4pm (there is an indoor flying area if the weather is bad).

River Great Ouse, Earith

Attractions include regular falconry displays, a flower garden, tea room, art gallery, craft village and picnic area. It is open to the public everyday from 10am-5pm (dusk in winter). Nearby **Somersham** once had a palace for the Bishops of Ely, and its splendid Church of St John the Baptist would have done them proud.

PETERBOROUGH

The second city of Cambridgeshire has a long and interesting history that can be traced back to the Bronze Age, as can be seen in the archaeological site at Flag Fen. Although a cathedral city, it is also a New Town (designated in 1967), so modern development and expansion have vastly increased its facilities while retaining the quality of its historic heart.

Peterborough's crowning glory is, of course, the Norman **Cathedral**, built in the 12th and 13th centuries on a site that had seen Christian worship since AD 655. Henry VIII made the church a cathedral, and his first queen, Catherine of Aragon, is buried here, as for a while was Mary Queen of Scots after her execution at Fotheringay. Features to note are the huge (85-feet) arches of the West Front, the unique painted wooden nave ceiling, some exquisite late 15th century fan vaulting, and the tomb of Catherine, who died at Kimbolton Castle.

Though the best-known of the city's landmarks, the Cathedral is by no means the only one. The

Peterborough Cathedral

Peterborough Museum and Art Gallery covers all aspects of the history of Peterborough from the Jurassic period to Victorian times.

There are twin attractions for railway enthusiasts in Peterborough in the shape of **Railworld**, a hands-on exhibition dealing with modern rail travel, and the wonderful **Nene Valley Railway**, which operates 15-mile steam-hauled trips between Peterborough and its HQ and museum at Wansford. A feature on the main railway line at Peterborough is the historic Iron Bridge, part of the old Great Northern Railway and still virtually as built by Lewis Cubitt in 1852.

A farmers market is held every 2nd and 4th Thursday of the month 9am-4pm in front of the guildhall in Cathedral Square – which is a vibrant place any time of the week with gorgeous flower displays, and alfresco cafes. There are also many shops and modern shopping centres through

Peterborough, as well as a static covered market.

Just outside the city, by the river Nene, is **Thorpe Meadows Sculpture Park**, one of several open spaces in and around the city with absorbing collections of modern sculpture.

AROUND PETERBOROUGH

LONGTHORPE

2 miles W of Peterborough off the A47

Longthorpe Tower, part of a fortified manor house, is graced by some of the very finest 14th century domestic wall paintings in Europe, featuring scenes both sacred and secular: the Nativity, the Wheel of Life, King David, the Labours of the Months. The paintings were discovered during renovations after the Second World War.

WATER NEWTON

7 miles W of Peterborough on the A605

The church in this pretty village, unusually dedicated to St Remigius, has some nice features including, a very ancient stone effigy of a man praying in a long gown which is said to date from the time of Edward III, a fine example of a Roman coffin in the churchyard, and the original apex (complete with cross) set in the churchyard wall.

NASSINGTON

11 miles W of Peterborough on the A47

The Grade I listed **Prebendal Manor House** is the earliest

surviving dwelling in Northamptonshire. It includes a 16th century dovecote, a large 18th century tithe barn and a 15th century lodgings building. The present stone house dating from the early 13th century stands on a historic site, which includes two medieval fishponds, and archaeological and historical evidence of one of King Cnut's royal timber halls. The gardens here, described by Alan Titchmarsh as a "stunning example of a recreated medieval garden", were planted to represent both the practical and decorative features that could be found in a high status garden between the 13th and 15th centuries. There is an informative museum here in the tithe barn, which also serves home-made teas and cakes. It is open on bank holiday Mondays, and Sunday to Wednesday through the summer. Tel: 01780 782575.

ELTON

6 miles SW of Peterborough on the B671

Elton is a lovely village on the river Nene, with stone-built houses and thatched roofs. **Elton Hall** is a mixture of styles, with a 15th century tower and chapel, and a major Gothic influence. The grandeur is slightly deceptive, as some of the battlements and turrets were built of wood to save money. The hall's sumptuous rooms are filled with art treasures (Gainsborough, Reynolds, Constable) and the library has a wonderful collection of antique tomes.

THORNHAUGH

8 miles NW of Peterborough off the A1/A47

Hidden away in a quiet valley is **Sacrewell Farm and Country Centre**, whose centrepiece is a working watermill. All kinds of farming equipment are on display, and there's a collection of farm animals, along with gardens, nature trails and general interest trails, play areas, a gift shop and a restaurant serving light refreshments and hot meals. There is also a campsite here. It is open year round, with reduced admission prices out of season. Tel: 01780 782254.

PEAKIRK

7 miles N of Peterborough off the A15

Peakirk boasts a village church of Norman origin that is the only one in the country dedicated to **St Pega**, the remains of whose hermit cell can still be seen.

CROWLAND

10 miles NE of Peterborough off the A1073

It is hard to imagine that this whole area was once entirely wetland and marshland, dotted with inhospitable islands. Crowland was one such island, then known as Croyland, and on it was established a small church and hermitage back in the 7th century, which was later to become one of the nation's most important monasteries. The town's impressive parish church was just part of the great edifice which once stood on the site. A wonderful exhibition can be found in the **Abbey** at Crowland, open all year round. The remains cover a third of the Abbey's original extent.

THORNEY

8 miles E of Peterborough on the A47

The **Abbey Church of St Mary and St Botolph** is the dominating presence in this village even though what now stands is but a small part of what was once one of the greatest of the Benedictine abbeys. Gravestones in the churchyard are evidence of a Huguenot colony that settled here after fleeing France in the wake of the St Bartholomew's Day massacre of 1572. The **Thorney Heritage Museum** is a small, independently-run museum of great fascination, describing the development of the village from a Saxon monastery, via Benedictine Abbey to a model village built in the 19th century by the Dukes of Bedford. The main innovation was a 10,000-gallon water tank that supplied the whole village; other villages had to use unfiltered river water. The Museum is open Sunday in the afternoons from 2pm-5pm Easter Sunday to the last Sunday in September, as well as August Bank Holiday from 11am-2pm.

WHITTLESEY

5 miles E of Peterborough off the A605

The market town of Whittlesey lies close to the western edge of the Fens and is part of one of the last tracts to be drained. Brick-making was a local speciality, and 180-feet brick chimneys stand as a reminder of that once-flourishing industry.

Crowland's second gem is the unique Trinity Bridge - set in the centre of town on dry land! Built in the 14th century, it has three arches built over one over-arching structure. Before the draining of the Fens, this bridge crossed the point where the River Welland divided into two streams. A small market is held in the main street every Friday – there is also an endearingly old fashioned Teashop in the town, well worth a visit for a rest and a slice of cake.

A highlight of Whittlesey's year is the Straw Bear Procession, which is part of a four-day January festival. A man clad in a suit of straw dances and prances through the streets, calling at houses and pubs to entertain the townspeople. The origins are obscure: perhaps it stems from pagan times when corn gods were invoked to produce a good harvest; perhaps it is linked with the wicker idols used by the Druids; perhaps it derives from the performing bears which toured the villages until the 17th century. What is certain is that at the end of the jollities the straw suit is ceremoniously burned.

96 CHILL OUT

Guyhirn

A family run restaurant that offers fine dining with great service.

🍴 *see page 283*

The **Church of St Andrew** is mainly 14th century, with a 16th century tower; the chancel, chancel chapels and naves still have their original roofs.

A walk round this charming town reveals an interesting variety of buildings: brick, of course, and also some stone, thatch on timber frames, and rare thatched mud boundary walls.

Whittlesey Museum, housed in the grand 19th century Town Hall in Market Street, features an archive of displays on local archaeology, agriculture, geology, brick-making and more. Reconstructions include a 1950s corner shop and post office, blacksmith's forge and wheelwright's bench. It is open Friday and Sunday afternoons 2.30pm-4.30pm and Saturdays 10am-12noon.

FLAG FEN

6 miles E of Peterborough signposted from the A47 and A1139

Flag Fen Bronze Age Centre comprises massive 3,000-year-old timbers that were part of a major settlement and have been preserved in peaty mud. The site includes a Roman road with its original surface, the oldest wheel in England, re-creations of a Bronze Age settlement, a museum of artefacts, rare breed animals, and a visitor centre with a shop and restaurant. Ongoing excavations, open to the public, make this one of the most important and exciting sites of its kind. Tel: 01733 313414.

MARCH

14 miles E of Peterborough off the A141

March once occupied the second-largest 'island' in the great level of Fens. As the land was drained the town grew as a trading and religious centre, and in more recent times as a market town and major railway hub. **March and District Museum**, in the High Street, tells the story of the people and the history of March and the surrounding area, and includes a working forge and a reconstruction of a turn-of-the-century home. Open Wednesdays and Saturdays 10.30am-3.30pm.

The uniquely dedicated **Church of St Wendreda**, at Town End, is notable for its magnificent timber roof, a double hammerbeam with 120 carved angels, a fine font and some impressive gargoyles. John Betjeman declared the church to be 'worth cycling 40 miles into a headwind to see'.

The **Nene-Ouse Navigation Link** runs through the town, affording many attractive riverside walks and, just outside the town off the B1099, **Dunhams Wood** comprises four acres of woodland set among the fens. The site contains an enormous variety of trees, along with sculptures and a miniature railway.

CHATTERIS

8 miles S of March off the A141

A friendly little market town, where the **Chatteris Museum and Council Chamber** features a series of interesting displays on Fenland life and the development of the town. Themes include education, agriculture, transport and local trades, along with temporary exhibitions and local photographs, all housed in five galleries. Admission is free. Tel: 01354 696319.

The **Church of St Peter and St Paul** has some 14th century features but is mostly more modern in appearance, having been substantially restored in 1909.

STONEA

3 miles SE of March off the B1098

Stonea Camp is the lowest 'hill'-fort in Britain. Built in the Iron Age, it proved unsuccessful against the Romans. A listed ancient monument whose banks and ditches were restored after excavations in 1991, the site is also an increasingly important habitat for wildlife.

WELNEY

4 miles SE of March off the A1101

The **Wildfowl & Wetlands Trust** in Welney is a nature reserve that attracts large numbers of swans and ducks in winter. Special floodlit 'swan evenings' are held, and there is also a wide range of wild plants and butterflies to be enjoyed.

WISBECH

One of the largest of the Fenland towns, a port in medieval times and still enjoying shipping trade with Europe, Wisbech is at the centre of a thriving agricultural region. The 18th century in

Peckover House & Gardens, Wisbech

particular saw the building of rows of handsome houses, notably in North Brink and South Brink, which face each other across the river. The finest of all the properties is undoubtedly **Peckover House**, built in 1722 and bought at the end of the 18th century by Jonathan Peckover, a member of the Quaker banking family. The family gave the building to the National Trust in 1948. Behind its elegant brick façade are splendid panelled rooms, Georgian fireplaces with richly carved overmantels, and ornate plaster decorations. At the back of the house is a beautiful walled garden with summerhouses, pond and rose garden and an

Wisbech's Lilian Ream Photographic Collection is named after a daughter of Wisbech born in the late 19th century who at the time of her death in 1961 had amassed a collection of over 200,000 photographs of Wisbech people, places and events, making for a unique and fascinating insight into the history and culture of the town. The collection is housed in the Tourist Information Centre in Bridge Street.

*On the B1101 between
March and Wisbech in
the village of Friday
Bridge is a new family
attraction: Woodhouse
Farm Park is a genuine
working farm where
visitors can meet a wide
variety of animals,
including rabbits, guinea
pigs, sheep, pigs, goats,
horses, donkeys,
peacocks, chickens and
turkeys.*

orangery with 300-year-old orange trees.

8 South Brink is the birthplace of Octavia Hill (1838-1912), co-founder of the National Trust, campaigner for open spaces and a tireless worker for the cause of the poor, particularly in the sphere of housing. The house is now the **Octavia Hill's Birthplace House** with displays and exhibits commemorating her work.

More Georgian splendour is evident in the area where the Norman castle once stood. The castle was replaced by a bishop's palace in 1478, and in the 17th century by a mansion built for Cromwell's Secretary of State, John Thurloe. Local builder Joseph Medworth built the present Regency villa in 1816; of the Thurloe mansion, only the gate piers remain.

The **Wisbech and Fenland Museum** is one of the oldest purpose-built museums in the country, and in charming Victorian surroundings, visitors can view displays of porcelain, coins, rare geological specimens, Egyptian tomb treasures and several items of national importance, including the manuscript of Charles Dickens' *Great Expectations*, Napoleon's Sèvres breakfast set captured at Waterloo, and an ivory chess set that belonged to Louis XIV.

Another Wisbech attraction is the impressive 68-feet limestone memorial to Thomas Clarkson, one of the earliest leaders of the abolitionist movement. The **Clarkson Memorial** was designed by Sir George Gilbert Scott in Gothic style.

Still a lively commercial port, Wisbech boasts a yacht harbour with facilities for small craft that include floating pontoons with berths for 128 yachts. There is also a new boat lift here and a wetdock.

The **Angles Theatre** – one of the oldest working theatres in Britain – is a vibrant centre for the arts located in a Georgian building with a history stretching back over 200 years. Some of the best talent in the nation, from poets and musicians to dance, comedy and

Bulb Fields near Wisbech

theatrical troupes – come to perform in the intimate 112-seat auditorium.

AROUND WISBECH

WEST WALTON AND WALTON HIGHWAY

3 miles NE of Wisbech off the A47/B198

Several attractions can be found here, notably the **Church of St Mary the Virgin** in West Walton with its magnificent 13th century detached tower that dominates the landscape. Walton Highway is home to the Fenland and West Norfolk Aviation Museum, whose exhibits include Rolls-Royce Merlin engines, a Lightning jet, a Vampire and a Jumbo jet cockpit simulator. The museum is open weekends and Bank Holidays 9.30am to 5.00pm, from Good Friday to the end of September.

LEVERINGTON

1 mile NW of Wisbech off the A1101

The tower and spire of the **Church of St Leonard** date from the 13th and 14th centuries. The most exceptional feature of an exceptionally interesting church is the 15th century stained-glass Jesse window in the north aisle. There are many fine memorials in the churchyard. Oliver Goldsmith wrote *She Stoops to Conquer* while staying in Leverington.

PARSON DROVE

6 miles W of Wisbech on the B1187

Parson Drove is a Fenland village which Samuel Pepys visited in 1663. He stayed at the village's Swan Inn and mentions it in his diaries, though he was not complimentary. The village was a centre of the woad industry until 1914, when the last remaining woad mill was demolished. Parson Drove is most certainly not the 'heathen place' once described by Pepys! **Parson Drove Visitor Centre** is set in the old Victorian lock-up on the village green, a building with an unusual 170-year history. Photographs and documents trace the story of this lovely Fenland village.

Quite amusingly, Parson Drove has most recently been the host of the World Championship Pillow Fight Tournament, as part of the village show each summer.

Accommodation, Food & Drink and Places of Interest

The establishments featured in this section includes hotels, inns, guest houses, bed & breakfasts, restaurants, cafes, tea and coffee shops, tourist attractions and places to visit. Each establishment has an entry number which can be used to identify its location at the beginning of the relevant chapter or its position in this section. In addition full details of all these establishments and many others can be found on the Travel Publishing website - www.findsomewhere.co.uk. This website has a comprehensive database covering the whole of Britain and Ireland.

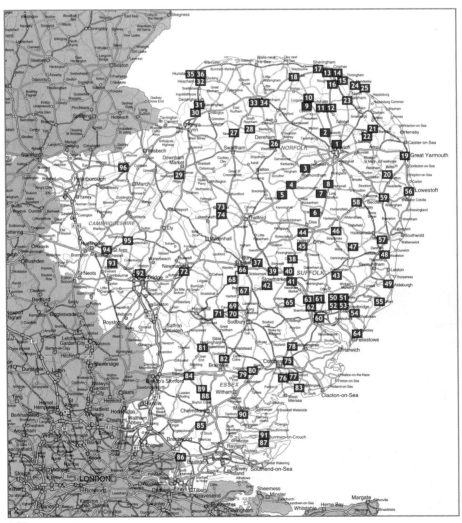

🛏 ACCOMMODATION

1 Catton Old Hall, Old Catton, nr Norwich
2 Becklands Guest House, Horsford, nr Norwich
4 Sherbourne Country House and Holly's Restaurant, Attleborough
5 White Lodge Traditional Coaching Inn, Attleborough
7 Wilderness House, Wacton, nr Long Stratton
8 Barn Lodge, Tasburgh, nr Norwich
11 The Old Pump House, Aylsham
13 Bon Vista Guesthouse, Cromer
23 Bradfield House, North Walsham
24 Breakaway Holidays, Mundesley
25 Castaways Holiday Park, Bacton
26 Hill House Hotel, Dereham
27 Lodge Farm, Castle Acre, nr Kings Lynn
28 Bull Inn, Litcham, nr Kings Lynn
33 The Bull, Fakenham
37 The Grange Country House Hotel, Thurston, nr Bury St Edmunds
39 Kiln Farm Guesthouse, Elmswell, nr Bury St Edmunds
40 Red House Farm, Haughley, nr Stowmarket
43 The Cretingham Bell, Cretingham
44 Rookery Farm B&B, Wortham, nr Diss
45 Thornham Hall, Eye
46 Gables Farm B&B, Wingfield, nr Diss
47 The Kings Head (The Low House), Laxfield
48 The White Horse Inn, Westleton, nr Saxmundham
49 The Railway Inn, Aldeburgh
51 Robert Blake Holidays, Woodbridge
52 The Cherry Tree, Woodbridge
54 The Plough Inn, Sutton, nr Woodbridge
55 The Jolly Sailor, Orford
61 Damerons Farm Holidays, Henley, nr Ipswich
63 The Sorrel Horse Inn, Barham, nr Ipswich
64 Fishermans Hall, Felixstowe
65 Riverside Cottage and Hornes B&B, Great Bricett, nr Ipswich
67 Brighthouse Farm, Lawshall, nr Bury St Edmunds
68 The Old Pear Tree, Whepstead
69 School Barn Farm, Pentlow, nr Sudbury
78 Marlborough Head Inn, Dedham, nr Colchester
80 The Kings Arms, Coggeshall, nr Colchester
84 The Starr Restaurant with Rooms, Great Dunmow

85 The White Hart Inn, Margaretting Tye
86 The Kilns Hotel, Great Warley, nr Brentwood
91 Oyster Smack, Burnham on Crouch
94 Slepe Hall, St Ives

🍴 FOOD & DRINK

3 The Heart of Wymondham, Wymondham
4 Sherbourne Country House and Holly's Restaurant, Attleborough
5 White Lodge Traditional Coaching Inn, Attleborough
6 Gissing Crown, Gissing, nr Diss
9 The Earle Arms, Hetdon, nr Norwich
10 The Duke's Head, Corpusty, nr Norwich
14 Rumbletums Restaurant, Cromer
15 The Foundry Arms, Northrepps
16 New Inn & Seremban Restaurant, Roughton, nr Norwich
21 The Kings Arms, Ludham
26 Hill House Hotel, Dereham
28 Bull Inn, Litcham, nr Kings Lynn
32 Frans Pantry Fayre, Heacham, nr Kings Lynn
33 The Bull, Fakenham
34 Cafe Coffeeholics, Fakenham
36 Fishers of Hunstanton, Hunstanton
37 The Grange Country House Hotel, Thurston, nr Bury St Edmunds
42 The Six Bells, Felsham
43 The Cretingham Bell, Cretingham
47 The Kings Head (The Low House), Laxfield
48 The White Horse Inn, Westleton, nr Saxmundham
49 The Railway Inn, Aldeburgh
50 The Anchor Inn, Woodbridge
52 The Cherry Tree, Woodbridge
54 The Plough Inn, Sutton, nr Woodbridge
55 The Jolly Sailor, Orford
57 The Star Inn, Wenhaston
58 The Chequers Inn, Bungay
59 The Swan House, Beccles
60 The Royal Oak , Ipswich
62 The Greyhound Public House, Claydon, nr Ipswich
63 The Sorrel Horse Inn, Barham, nr Ipswich
70 The Pinkuah Arms, Pentlow, nr Sudbury
71 The Cock Inn at Clare, Clare
73 The Crown, Brandon
75 La Cascada, Ardleigh, nr Colchester
76 The Whalebone Inn, Fingringhoe, nr Colchester
77 The Bake House, Wivenhoe,

nr Colchester
78 Marlborough Head Inn, Dedham, nr Colchester
79 The Clockhouse, Coggeshall, nr Colchester
80 The Kings Arms, Coggeshall, nr Colchester
81 The Three Tuns, Finchingfield, nr Braintree
82 Gosfield Shopping Village, Gosfield
83 Mooch @ No 9, Brightlingsea
84 The Starr Restaurant with Rooms, Great Dunmow
85 The White Hart Inn, Margaretting Tye
86 The Kilns Hotel, Great Warley, nr Brentwood
87 Essex Marina Bar, Wallasea Island, nr Rochford
88 The Rose & Crown, Great Waltham, nr Chelmsford
89 Compasses Inn, Littley Green, nr Chelmsford
90 The Hot Plate Cafe, Maldon
91 Oyster Smack, Burnham on Crouch
92 The King William, Histon, nr Cambridge
93 The White Swan, Connington
94 Slepe Hall, St Ives
96 Chill Out, Guyhirn, nr Wisbech

🏛 PLACES OF INTEREST

12 Bure Valley Railway, Aylsham
17 North Norfolk Railway, Sheringham
18 Letheringsett Windmill, Letheringsett, nr Holt
19 Great Yarmouth Row Houses, Great Yarmouth
20 Fritton Lake Countryworld, Fritton
22 Fairhaven Woodland and Water Garden, South Walsham
29 Denver Windmill, Denver, nr Downham Market
30 Castle Rising Castle, Castle Rising
31 Sandringham House, Sandringham
35 Hunstanton Sealife Sanctuary, Hunstanton
38 Mechanical Music Museum and Bygones, Cotton, nr Stowmarket
41 Museum of East Anglian Life, Stowmarket
53 Sutton Hoo , Sutton Hoo, nr Woodbridge
56 Lowestoft Maritime Museum, Lowestoft
66 St Edmundsbury Cathedral, Bury St Edmunds
72 National Horseracing Museum, Newmarket
74 Brandon Country Park, Brandon
82 Gosfield Shopping Village, Gosfield

I CATTON OLD HALL

**Lodge Lane, Old Catton, Norwich,
Norfolk NR6 7HG
Tel: 01603 419379**

Tucked away from the hustle and bustle of city life, **Old Catton Hall** is a small, family run private boutique bed and breakfast. Always greeted by a friendly welcome, travellers to this character-filled guest house return time and time again to enjoy a warm and comfortable stay. Built as a Gentleman's House in 1632 from reclaimed Caen stone, local flint and fine oak timbers with mullioned windows, wide inglenook hearths with log fires and generously proportioned rooms this old mayor's home has entertained guests for centuries. The character of the house has been carefully preserved to retain the best features and each room meets the exacting needs of the modern traveller.

The bedrooms are individually decorated and the beds are

made up with Egyptian cotton sheets to make visitors' stay that much better. Full English breakfasts are served in the morning. There are plenty of things to do in the area, including, sailing, bird watching, walking, fishing and golf. Located in the ideal position for those wanting to explore the Norfolk countryside and the Norfolk Broads, there are some great sites to be seen. Norwich Cathedral, The Forum, the Norman Castle and Norwich Market are just some of the sites popular with visitors.

3 THE HEART OF WYMONDHAM

**29 Market Street, Wymondham,
Norfolk NR18 0AJ
Tel: 01953 423083**

The Heart of Wymondham is a family run establishment offering the very best in fresh pub cuisine. The family friendly inn is located in the popular market town of Wymondham and the entrance is particularly inviting, decorated with beautiful hanging baskets of flowers. The establishment, which retains original features, beams and fireplaces, has recently been lovingly restored and offers varied menus for lunches. There is a wide range of food on offer, with plenty of filled sandwiches and baguettes, grilled paninis and jacket potatoes on the light lunch menu. Full English breakfasts are extremely popular and the finest cuts of beef and pork are cooked to order with a mouth-watering selection of

steaks and burgers to choose from. Main meals include Thai red king prawn curry, fresh mussels and homemade chunky chilli con carne.

There is a fantastic beer garden for customers to enjoy on brighter days and there is ample parking in the area. Just a two minute walk from Wymondham Abbey the building was once badly damaged in a fire in 1615. The inn is open 11am-11pm from Monday-Thursday, 11-12pm on Friday and Saturdays and between 12pm and 10.30pm on a Sunday, when a traditional Sunday lunch can be enjoyed.

2 BECKLANDS GUEST HOUSE

105 Holt Road, Horsford, nr Norwich,
Norfolk NR10 3AB
Tel: 01603 898582 Fax: 01603 754223
e-mail: becklands@aol.com
website: www.visitnorwicharea.co.uk

Set in a handsome village off the B1149 not far
from Norwich airport, **Becklands Guest
House** has been offering hospitality and great
accommodation to visitors for many years.
Conveniently located for access to Aylsham, the
Horse Sanctuary at Caldicott, the National
Trust properties of Blickling Hall and Felbrigg
Hall, the coast and other sights and attractions
of the area, this modern establishment has 9
gracious and attractive guests bedrooms, all with
en suite facilities.

Tastefully and comfortably decorated and
furnished, all rooms are welcoming, warm, quiet
and lovely. All boast every amenity and in
addition there's a comfortable, spacious guests'
lounge. The delicious and hearty breakfast is
served in the elegant dining room. Owner
Angela Magnus offers all her guests a warm
welcome and a high standard of quality and
attentive service. Becklands enjoys a 4-
Diamonds Recommended status from the
English Tourism Council.

4 SHERBOURNE COUNTRY HOUSE AND HOLLY'S RESTAURANT

8 Norwich Road, Attleborough,
Norfolk NR17 2JX
Tel: 01953 454363
e-mail: stay@sherbourne-house.co.uk
website: www.sherbourne-house.co.uk

If it is a relaxing stay and quality food you are after then **Sherbourne House** is highly recommended. Located in the historic market town of Attleborough the Country House Hotel has an AA rosette for its food under the supervision of head chef, Phil Woodcock. The seasonal menu incorporates a large amount of local produce, with the meat sourced by a local farmer and butcher. All of the tasty dishes are freshly prepared and reasonably priced making Holly's at Sherbourne House a popular choice to dine out in the area.

Built around 1740 the house is privately run and located just 20 miles from Norwich. It is ideally placed for those wanting to visit Snetterton motor racing circuit, Thetford Forest, Old Buckenham airfield, Bressingham and Wymondham. The family-run Sherbourne House

boasts eight exquisite bedrooms, individually styled to a high standard. Lovingly furnished, the owners have added personal touches to the spacious rooms, which all have en-suite facilities (six of the rooms have a bath too). There is ample car parking within the grounds of the house and dogs are welcomed.

Holly's is open Wednesdays to Saturdays from 6.30pm. Last orders are at 8.45 pm. From Sunday to Tuesday the menu is available to residents only.

findSOMEWHERE.co.uk

For people who want to explore Britain and Ireland

Places to Stay

Our easy-to use website contains details and locations of places to stay, places to eat and drink, specialist shops and places of interest throughout England, Wales, Scotland and Ireland.

Places to Stay:	Places to Eat and Drink:	Places of Interest:	Specialist Shops:	Gardens:
Hotels, guest accommodation, bed & breakfast, inns, self-catering accommodation	Restaurants, pubs, inns, cafes, tea rooms	Historic buildings, gardens, art galleries, museums, nature parks, wildlife parks, indoor and outdoor activities	Fashion shops, art and craft shops, gift shops, food and drink shops, antique shops, jewellery shops	Garden centres and retail nurseries

London Road, Attleborough,
Norfolk NR17 1AY
Tel: 01953 452474
e-mail: tc.whitlodge@yahoo.co.uk
website: www.whitelodge-
attleborough.co.uk

Located at the edge of Attleborough between Thetford and Norwich, just off the main A11 Attleborough roundabout sits the **White Lodge**. This magnificent 14th century thatched building simply oozes character and quality service acting as a function room, campsite and play area but is best known for being one of the area's best pubs.

Carol Stokes and Terry Martin have much experience in the trade and offer fantastic service to all that come here. They welcome families and children, individuals, couples, tourists, walkers, cyclists, sporting groups and societies from all walks of life, making it an ideal stop off for any break in the beautiful countryside of Norfolk. The inn also hosts 'biker meet nights' on a Wednesday evening with special deals for all sorts of motor bike rides. They are just minutes from many local attractions including Wymondham Abbey, Thetford Forest, Banham Zoo and Snetterton Racetrack.

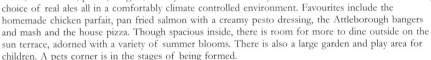

The pub itself gives a mature feel yet relaxed feel, retaining many original features including oak beams and real wood fireplaces. It serves a great selection of light snacks and bar meals, main meals, pizzas, burgers, Sunday lunches and a healthy choice of real ales all in a comfortably climate controlled environment. Favourites include the homemade chicken parfait, pan fried salmon with a creamy pesto dressing, the Attleborough bangers and mash and the house pizza. Though spacious inside, there is room for more to dine outside on the sun terrace, adorned with a variety of summer blooms. There is also a large garden and play area for children. A pets corner is in the stages of being formed.

Separate from the pub bistro is a function room that is available to hire for any occasion and has proved a popular place for weddings, christenings, birthdays and engagement parties.

For those visitors who love the area or need a convenient spot to pitch for the night before heading off to watch the racing the White Lodge also has three quarters of an acre in which you can pitch your tents and park your camper vans for the night with easy access to all pub facilities, perfect for those looking for a gentler camping experience. The White Lodge is open from 11am-11pm seven days a week and serves food from 11am-9pm daily and 12 - 8pm on Sunday.

Lower Street, Gissing, Diss,
Norfolk IP22 5UJ
Tel: 01379 677718
e-mail: juliegissingcrown@googlemail.com
website: www.gissingcrown.co.uk

Situated in the beautiful rural village of Gissing and just five miles from the historic market town of Diss, the **Gissing Crown** is well worth the drive through the tight country lanes. The Gissing Crown lies in the heart of the village, opposite the striking Saxon round tower church which is one of just 124 in Norfolk.

The exterior of this 18th century pub exudes a welcoming feel; the stone build, sash windows with hanging baskets and planters decorating the walls all collude to entice you through the front door. Inside, the beamed ceilings, horse brasses and inglenook fireplace remind you of the pub's long history, whilst the decor brings the place into the 21st century in style. The lounge bar is comfortable and cosy, whilst the 40 cover dining area is functional and well laid out.

With a large selection of well kept real ales and fine wines, the bar is very well stocked; the real ales varying between regular favourites and guests from local breweries. Attracting customers from all over Norfolk is the excellent food; home cooked traditional pub classics using only the finest of locally sourced produce, examples include a variety of cuts of steaks, homemade pies and fresh fish dishes. The menu is extensive and offers something for every taste and diet, altering with the seasons to make the most of the in season ingredients. A popular evening at the Gissing Crown is the curry night, held on the first Wednesday of every month; sample a well cooked curry in great surroundings. Every Friday evening the speciality is fresh fish and homemade chips; cooked to order there and then, your meal can be eaten as a takeaway. Special occasions can be catered for; outside bars, events and even Christmas Day; enjoy succulent turkey at a great price. Wednesday evenings sees an influx of locals for the ever popular pub quiz and 'play your cards right' games night.

Other facilities at this very child friendly pub include a huge children's play area in the beer garden, a games room, complete with a pool table, dart board, cribbage and dominoes and a heated smokers' shelter. The pub is also a registered motor home stop area, with mention on www.motorhomestopover.co.uk. The Gissing Crown is always keen to welcome new patrons, advertising "New customers always required. No experience necessary!"

7 WILDERNESS HOUSE

Church Road, Wacton, nr Long Stratton,
Norfolk NR15 2UG
Tel: 01508 531006
website: www.south-norfolk.net/
wilderness

Nestled in acres of rolling countryside, **Wilderness House** is the ideal get-away for those wanting to explore Norfolk. Built in 1590 the house is magnificent both inside and out and offers two comfortable double bedrooms and one single bedroom, each with either an en-suite or private bathroom and guests also have a large private sittingroom. Guests can look forward to a full English quality breakfast, which is more than enough to set them up for a day exploring the area.

The Broads, north Norfolk coast and Sandringham are all within easy reach of the 16th century, timber framed farmhouse, which is located on the edge of a small village 12 miles south of the historic city of Norwich. The child-friendly B&B is a delightful retreat and owner, Juliet Pettitt, is happy for guests to bring their dogs. Hidden from view, at the end of a long tree lined drive, Wilderness Farm House really is the perfect oasis to stay for those wanting to take in the peace and tranquility of the surrounding countryside. There are some excellent walks to be had and many places of interest to visit, including Bressingham Gardens, Wymondham Abbey and several museums.

Long-term lets available for a single professional person or couple. There is a private well-equipped kitchen/diner for self catering. Beloved Labradors featured in this article are Willow Lark and Sofia Balerina. Male Labrador, Yogi Ranger appears with the entire Farmhouse.

8 BARN LODGE

1 Church Road, Tasburgh,
Norwich NR15 1ND
Tel: 01508 471508
e-mail: sarah.barnlodge@googlemail.com
website: www.barnlodge.co.uk

Barn Lodge is an attractive Victorian barn conversion located just eight miles from the city of Norwich. The B&B, with its exposed beams and character features, is welcoming and relaxing and there are plenty of pubs in the area to enjoy an evening meal or lunch. Offering three comfortable rooms (one en-suite), they are all located on the ground floor, with easy disabled access, and there is plenty of off-road parking for guests.

The breakfasts are superb and local produce is used. There is a large garden and delightful patio area for guests to use on brighter days and on colder days they can sit by the cosy log burning stove in the downstairs sitting areas.

Barn Lodge is located in the large historic village of Tasburgh, which has a round-towered church at its heart, dating back to the 11th century. It is in the ideal location to explore the medieval streets of Norwich and the many National Trust properties in the area and is just 30 minutes from the beach and Broads. Open all year except for Christmas. Cheque and cash only. Well-behaved dogs over 1 year old are welcome, and are allowed to stay in their owner's room.

227

9 THE EARLE ARMS

Heydon, Norwich, Norfolk NR11 6AD
Tel: 01263 587376

The Earle Arms is a 16th century, former coaching house nestled in the pretty, privately owned, village of Heydon in the beautiful rural heartland of Norfolk. The village is situated only five miles west of the market town of Aylsham and only one mile from the B1149. Yet, as you follow the finger-post signs, it is an absolute delight when you enter what can only be described as a veritable time-warp. The pub is surrounded by Grade 2 listed cottages and houses seemingly untouched since they were built as a model village in the late 18th century. Oliver Cromwell is reputed to have stayed in the pub and would that he could have enjoyed all that The Earle Arms has to offer in the 21st century.

The food is locally sourced and seasonal, the meats are outdoor reared only a few miles away and fish is delivered every day from the coast. The menu, which also caters for vegetarians and special needs (please arrange at time of booking), has been described in the Norwich Evening news as "adventurous, locally produced, reasonably priced, and does not disappoint" There is always a good selection of real ales and ciders and a fine collection of wines is available. "H" is the horse-racing mad landlord and chef who is not only responsible for preparing your meal, but also for the "sport of kings" memorabilia that adorns every available space. He parts owns a racehorse and will gladly give you a tip....but we wouldn't suggest you put your shirt on it!

The unique venue, which has featured in the *Sunday Times* article *"Of All The Gin Joints In All The World"* together with a special feature in the *Sunday Supplement* of the *Eastern Daily Press* entitled *"The real cat's whiskers"*, is perfect for parties, weddings or that special event. For all enquiries please telephone 01263 587376. Open 12 noon – 3pm and 6pm – 11pm every day, except Monday, and all day on Sunday (kitchen closed Sunday evening).

findSOMEWHERE.co.uk

For people who want to explore Britain and Ireland

Places to Eat and Drink

Our easy-to use website contains details and locations of places to stay, places to eat and drink, specialist shops and places of interest throughout England, Wales, Scotland and Ireland.

Places to Stay:	**Places to Eat and Drink:**	**Places of Interest:**	**Specialist Shops:**	**Gardens:**
Hotels, guest accommodation, bed & breakfast, inns, self-catering accommodation	Restaurants, pubs, inns, cafes, tea rooms	Historic buildings, gardens, art galleries, museums, nature parks, wildlife parks, indoor and outdoor activities	Fashion shops, art and craft shops, gift shops, food and drink shops, antique shops, jewellery shops	Garden centres and retail nurseries

The Street, Corpusty, Norwich,
Norfolk NR11 6QG
Tel: 01263 587529
e-mail: emma.owen9@btinternet.com

Overlooking the pleasant country village green, **The Duke's Head** is now the last pub left in Corpusty and the recent refurbishment has created a wonderful place to enjoy a meal, a drink or a friendly chat. Parts of the building date back 300 years and some great features still remain; on the ground floor there are terrific bay windows which provide a brilliant spot to sit, enjoy a pint and watch the world drift by. The cream exterior is interrupted by splashes of bright colours from the hanging baskets, resplendent in the spring and summer months; the door is always open and a friendly welcome sign visible to entice you in.

Once inside there will be a warm hello from the staff as you contemplate the large range of ales and beers on tap at the well stocked bar and chat with the sociable locals. The refurbishment has created a light and airy feel throughout the restaurant and bar with a fresh and clean décor, yet some original features remain; for example there is an exposed brick chimney breast complete with wood burning stove. Little touches such as this give you something to look at and admire whilst waiting for the sumptuous food to admire.

The well constructed menu is extensive and there really is something for everyone, no matter how hungry they are. The main menu features snacks, such as burgers and ploughman's lunches, jacket potatoes with a variety of fillings, sandwiches and baguettes and a whole host of extras to add. The main meals are made up of pub classics, cooked fresh to order and each more delicious than the last. As well as the standard main menu, you can choose from the steaks, curries or the specials. Examples of the tempting specials are; the minted lamb shank, spinach and ricotta ravioli and the haddock and spring onion fishcakes. The specials are changed daily and feature the best of the in season produce available. Food is served daily between 12 pm – 3 pm and 6 pm – 9pm except for Mondays, when they are closed. The pub is open from 12 – 12 every day and the beer garden has to be one of the finest places in the Norwich area to enjoy a nice pint of a summer's day. Well tended and tidy, the garden is huge and is stocked with colourful flowers, shrubs and ancient trees.

11 THE OLD PUMP HOUSE

Holman Road, Aylsham,
Norfolk NR11 6BY
Tel: 01263 733789   Fax: 01263 734513
email:theoldpumphouse@btconnect.com
website: www.theoldpumphouse.com

A warm, welcoming Georgian House that is full of character, **The Old Pump House** is ideally situated close to Norwich, the Norfolk Broads, the coast, nature reserves and stately homes (just one mile from Blickling Hall which is famed for its long gallery, fine tapestries, paintings and rare books). Built around 1750, the Old Pump house has had a rich and interesting past due to its history as a farm, boarding school and rectory. These days it is run by Marc James, an antiques dealer and Charles Kirkman, an ex banker, who make for perfect hosts and your stay an extremely enjoyable one.

There are five twin or doubles all en-suite including one four-poster room and two family rooms. All rooms have wireless Internet connection, central heating, LCD, Freeview TVs, CD, radio alarm clocks and hairdryers. The rooms were totally refurbished in 2007 by the owners who have only recently taken over the establishment and this could now be straight out of a House & Gardens magazine. Each room is themed and tastefully decorated, such as the 'Oak Room', which as its name suggests is furnished predominately in oak. Hospitality trays with fresh milk, teas, coffee, hot chocolate, biscuits and even a bottle of water are provided.

Delicious English breakfasts (with local bacon, sausages and free range eggs) are cooked to order and served in the elegant, pine shuttered Georgian Room where you can watch the birds feeding by

the pond in the pretty, tranquil garden. Vegetarian and Continental breakfasts are served on request. Pre booked evening meals are available outside high season, and freshly prepared sandwiches and picnic lunches are always available to order.

The unspoilt surrounding countryside with its wealth of attractive villages and historic town is perfect for walking, bird watching and cycling (local bicycle hire is available) and there are several steam railways within easy reach.

12 BURE VALLEY RAILWAY

Aylsham Station, Norwich Road,
Aylsham, Norfolk NR11 6BW
Tel: 01263 7338585 Fax: 01263 733814
e-mail: info@bvr.co.uk
website: www.bvrw.co.uk

Norfolk's longest narrow gauge heritage railway is a 15" gauge line operating between the old market town of Aylsham and Wroxham, a distance of nine miles. The **Bure Valley Narrow Gauge Railway** was opened in July 1990 with new station buildings and workshops at Aylsham and a new station adjacent to Hoveton and Wroxham station. The railway is operated primarily by steam locomotives, of which there are four. Passengers are carried in 22 fully enclosed and luxuriously upholstered coaches. Two wheelchair accessible coaches can each carry four wheelchairs with their carers. The journey time is 45 minutes.

At Aylsham the workshops are usually open to visitors; on site are a small museum and model railway, a well-stocked gift shop and the Whistlestop Restaurant open for full English breakfasts, lunch and high tea. A shop selling confectionery and drinks is located at Wroxham station. There is ample free car and coach parking at both stations, with fully equipped facilities for disabled visitors.

The Bure Valley Railway specialises in joint operations with other attractions. There is a regular boat train facility from Aylsham connecting with cruises on the Broads from Wroxham. In off-peak periods the railway operates Steam Locomotive Driving Courses for beginners and the more experienced. The Bure Valley Railway operates regular services from April to October, Santa Specials towards Christmas and Day out with Thomas the Tank Engine events in May and September. The Railway is paralleled along its whole length by the scenic Bure Valley Walk and cycle path.

13 BON VISTA GUESTHOUSE

12 Alfred Road, Cromer,
Norfolk NR27 9AN
Tel: 01263 511818
e-mail: jim@bonvista-cromer.co.uk
website: www.bonvista-cromer.co.uk

Bon Vista Guest House is a comfortable Victorian building close to the seafront at the West Cliff end of Cromer. Tastefully renovated to retain many of the best original features, the house has five guest bedrooms – three doubles, a family room and a superior room with one superking or two twin beds; all have en-suite facilities, television and beverage tray. Cromer has a wide variety of attractions for the visitor, including golden sands, the delightful pier, golf, cycling, fossil collecting, birdwatching and amazing sea views; within a short drive the area has many more places of interest, among them the National Trust properties of Felbrigg Hall, Blickling Hall and Sheringham Park. Bon Vista, which is open all year round, is a comfortable, quiet and civilised base for discovering all that this lovely part of Norfolk has to offer.

14 RUMBLETUMS RESTAURANT

**7 Hamilton Road, Cromer,
Norfolk NR27 9HL
Tel: 01263 514894
e-mail: carol_pitt@hotmail.co.uk**

The lovely seaside town of Cromer has a lot going for it; the long sandy beach and the famous pier among many. Just two minutes walk from these is **Rumbletums Restaurant**, a friendly and homely place almost adjacent to the church of St. Peter & St.

Paul. This busy and bustling street ensures Rumbletums is well frequented by locals and tourists alike, the sumptuous smells emanating from the open door acting as a magnet to hungry patrons. Inside the décor is light and breezy, the wall to wall window at the front allowing the light to flood in and create a lovely airy atmosphere. The walls are adorned with well made prints depicting local scenes which give guests something to admire whilst waiting for their meals.

All of the food is created using locally sourced produce

where possible and the large menu guarantees a choice for even the most eclectic of tastes. The menu is spit into a variety of headings, visitors can choose from all day breakfasts, breakfast butties, burgers, jacket potatoes, lunch meals, salads, fish dishes and the list goes on! As well as all these, fresh sandwiches are made on site with a seemingly endless range of fillings.

15 THE FOUNDRY ARMS

**Church Street, Northrepps,
Norfolk NR27 0AA
Tel: 01263 579256
website: www.northnorfolkpub.co.uk**

Located in the country village of Northrepps **The Foundry Arms** is a fantastic traditional pub that welcomes everyone. Attracting plenty of walkers and cyclists, great home-cooked food is served throughout the week. Just three miles from the seaside town of Cromer it has an extremely positive reputation in the area. The child-friendly pub was built in 1861 and it still retains magnificent beamed ceilings and fireplaces, which add to the character of the place. The Foundry Arms provides the ideal resting place for visitors to the area and there is a large parking area for customers to use.

17 NORTH NORFOLK RAILWAY

**Sheringham Station, Sheringham,
Norfolk NR26 8RA
Tel: 01263 820800
e-mail: enquiries@nnrailway.com
website: ww.nnr.co.uk**

When the Midland & Great Northern Joint Railway was extended from Holt to Sheringham and Cromer in 1887, it gave birth to the tourist industry in North Norfolk. Over a hundred years later, much remains the same. The views of coast and country are as breathtaking as ever. Poppies still flaunt their scarlet beauty every summer. The **Poppy Line**, successor to the M&GN, carries thousands of visitors each year on one of the most scenic steam heritage railways in Britain – a 5.5 mile trip from Sheringham along the coast to Weybourne and up through the heathland to Holt.

16 NEW INN AND SEREMBAN RESTAURANT

Norwich Road, Roughton, Norwich,
Norfolk NR11 8SJ
Tel: 01263 761389
e-mail: newinnroughton@aol.com
website: www.thenewinnroughton.com

Located in the countryside village of Roughton the **New Inn and Seremban Restaurant** really does have something for everyone. Whether it is a simple drink, snack or three course meal you are looking for, the owners welcome you whole heartedly.

The extensive and imaginative oriental and English menus have a lot to offer and all of the dishes are freshly prepared and cooked to order. On the oriental (Malaysian and Chinese) menu

the mouth-watering dishes offered are everything you would expect from a good quality oriental restaurant and choices include shredded char sui chow mein and malaka style chicken with mango. All of the dishes are superbly presented and the service is hard to fault.

Alternatively if it is good British cooking you are after then the British menu is sure to have something to suit your taste. Steaks, burgers, chicken and fish dishes are all available as well as some traditional homemade pies. There is separate lunch and evening menus, set or a la carte. If it is more of a bar meal or snack you are after The New Inn has a fine selection of filled baguettes, jacket potatoes, omelettes, salads and burgers that can be consumed in the bar area and there is a delightful beer garden for people to enjoy on sunnier days, with a small play area where younger guests will be aptly occupied.

Just three miles from the seaside town of Cromer the restaurant and inn are located in the ideal location for visitors to the area. The small village of Roughton, steeped in history, is a few miles inland on the main road to Norwich and has a church with a 1000 year old tower. In September 1933 Albert Einstein famously stopped off in a hut on Roughton Heath en route to America, while fleeing Nazi persecution.

The New Inn is an impressive building and well presented. Outside, the entrance is extremely inviting, with plenty of floral pots and hanging baskets and the interior of the building is clean and tastefully decorated throughout. Built in 1878 the impressive establishment retains original features, including fireplaces and is traditionally furnished throughout, giving it a wonderful and warm atmosphere. The premise is open Monday to Friday between 12-3pm and 5pm-12am. On Saturdays and Sundays opening hours are between 12pm-12am.Traditional roast dinners are served and there is also an extensive choice on the daily specials board. There is disabled access.

18 LETHERINGSETT WATERMILL

Riverside Road, Letheringsett, Holt,
Norfolk NR25 7YD
Tel: 01263 713153

In the attractive village of Letheringsett is a fully functional water powered **Flour Mill** generally accepted to be the only producing one in Norfolk. You are invited to visit this outstanding part of working Norfolk history.

The Norfolk red brick Mill was built in 1802 on a Doomsday site. Until 1982 when restoration work was started, the Mill was slowly falling into disrepair The miller and his staff would like to welcome you to see their skills of making flour using this traditional method on their demonstration days when the miller will give a running commentary. If however you would prefer to visit the mill when standing idle you are more than welcome.

Staff are always on hand and ready to answer any of your questions - they are proud to share their interest and knowledge. Before you leave perhaps you would like to purchase some of the flour you have seen being made during your visit or browse in the Gift Shop.

**The Ducks outside
are always hungry!**

19 GREAT YARMOUTH ROW HOUSES

Great Yarmouth, Norfolk NR30 2RQ
Tel: 01493 857900
website: www.english-heritage.org.uk

Experience the sights and sounds of yesterday's Great Yarmouth. Visit these unique and vividly-presented houses, one set in c.1870 and the other in 1942, just before incendiary bombing. Find out how Yarmouth's 'Herring Girls' lived, hear an original BBC wartime broadcast and 'Mr Rope's sea shanties'. See the amazing collection of artefacts rescued from Row houses after World War II bombing, and contrast tenement conditions with 'respectable' merchant's interiors.

Open daily April to September

HIDDEN PLACES GUIDES

Explore Britain and Ireland with *Hidden Places* guides - a fascinating series of national and local travel guides.

Packed with easy to read information on hundreds of places of interest as well as places to stay, eat and drink.

Available from both high street and internet booksellers

For more information on the full range of *Hidden Places* guides and other titles published by Travel Publishing visit our website on

www.travelpublishing.co.uk
or ask for our leaflet by phoning
**01752 697280   or emailing
info@travelpublishing.co.uk**

20 FRITTON LAKE COUNTRYWORLD

Beccles Road, Fritton, Great Yarmouth,
Norfolk NR31 9AB
Tel: 01493 488288 Fax: 01493 488355
website: www.somerleyton.co.uk

For an enjoyable day out in the country, **Fritton Lake Countryworld** has few rivals. The beautiful grounds of Somerleyton House offer a splendid contrast between natural woodland and formal Victorian gardens, and Fritton Lake, with fishing and boating both available, is one

of the loveliest stretches of water in East Anglia.

A miniature railway runs by the lake, and among the many attractions are a family cycle trail, an orienteering course and giant outdoor board games. Also on site are a 9 hole par 3 golf course and an18-hole putting green, displays of falconry and basket-making, a growing collection of waterfowl, a children's farm and a heavy horse centre with working Suffolk Punches and Shires.

21 THE KINGS ARMS

High Street, Ludham,
Norfolk NR29 5QQ
Tel: 01692 678386
e-mail: kingsarmsludham@hotmail.com
website: www.kingsarmsludham.co.uk

Feted as 'the best kept secret on the broads', **The Kings Arms** will no longer be a secret should it carry on the way it has been! Situated on the beautiful Norfolk Broads in the sleepy town of Ludham, The Kings Arms provides excellent food and drink in a convivial and friendly manner. A recent refurbishment has transformed the bar area into a great place to sit and enjoy a refreshing pint of well kept ale whilst chatting with the sociable locals. Many visitors enjoy the wide screen television which shows many live sporting events, alternatively there is a pool table and a dart board to create your own live sports event!

The new restaurant is receiving rave reviews for its excellent home cooked food; the extensive menu offers a

sumptuous choice of classic pub fare, sizzling steaks, pastas and pizzas among others. There is certainly something for everyone! Sundays are a special occasion; the carvery is extremely popular as people arrive from miles around to help themselves to the various meats and mounds of vegetables on offer.

During the summer, the lovely beer garden is a very pleasant place to sit as the children make the most of the jungle gym.

235

19 Station Road, North Walsham,
Norfolk NR28 0DZ
Tel: 01692 404352
e-mail: info@bradfieldhouse.com
website: www.bradfieldhouse.com

Built in 1890, **Bradfield House** is packed full of stunning original features; high ceilings throughout, lovely wrought iron fireplaces and spacious rooms. The exterior is warm and inviting; the old red brick build is complemented by the ivy and wisteria growing up the walls and there is plenty of colour from the window boxes and hanging baskets. Around the back is a well kept garden; full of colours and smells which is open to be enjoyed by guests whatever the weather. Inside the décor creates a light and airy atmosphere, with the large windows letting the light flood in wherever you are in the house.

There are three rooms available, one king sized and two doubles. The king sized room has been recently renovated and is superb; the room boasts a walk in wardrobe, complete with a fridge, a wall mounted 17" television with Sky and Sky Sports and a view over the beautiful garden. The en suite bathroom has a bath with both an overhead Mira shower, plus a shower head on the taps. As well as the great king sized room, there are the two double rooms; which are equally well stocked with large, comfortable beds, en suite facilities and original fireplaces.

Chrissie and Mike are on hand to provide convivial welcomes and cater for your every need; they welcome all sorts, walkers, cyclists, tourists and people just looking to get away from it all. Just 30 minutes from Norwich, North Walsham is an historic market town with a fine selection of attractions, shops and restaurants all within easy reach of the guest house. Local attractions include golf, bird watching, fishing, boating and the nearby sandy beaches. There is also abundance of footpaths and quiet country lanes for cyclists and walkers to explore.

Breakfast is served between 7.30 and 9.30 in the morning and there is a huge range to choose from; the delicious English breakfasts are created using free range produce all sourced locally. The other option is a continental, and there is a large range of fruits, cereals, juices and conserves to prepare you for the hard day's exploring ahead. Evening meals can also be provided by appointment and all meals can be enjoyed in the lovely dining room, which offers great views out into the garden.

22 FAIRHAVEN WOODLAND AND WATER GARDEN

South Walsham, Norwich,
Norfolk NR13 6HY
Tel: 01603 270449
e-mail: fairhavengarden@btconnect.co.uk
website: www.fairhavengarden.co.uk

Set in the heart of the Norfolk Broads, **Fairhaven Woodland and Water Garden** is one of the county's best kept secrets. Boasting the UK's finest naturalised collection of Candelabra primulas, a 950 year old Oak Tree (home to a family of ducks), and 130 acres of natural woodland and water garden.

The garden was developed by the late 2nd Lord Fairhaven Major Henry Broughton, who bought South Walsham Estate in 1946. The estate had been used as a convalescence home for officers during the Second World War, and so the garden had become a jungle. The site was gradually cleared by hand and took 15 years to complete. Lord Fairhaven then set about planting the garden with shade and water loving plants including Camellias and Rhododendrons specially imported from the Himalayas.

Whether you choose to visit in the height of summer, or in the depths of winter there is always something to see.

25 CASTAWAYS HOLIDAY PARK

Paston Road, Bacton, Norfolk NR12 0JB
Tel: 01692 650436
e-mail: info@castawaysholidaypark.net
website: www.castawaysholidaypark.net

Castaways Holiday Park is a warm and welcoming family run business set in the quiet and peaceful village of Bacton on Sea. Just 25 miles from Great Yarmouth and a mere 10 miles from Cromer, Castaways is in a wonderful seafront location. Indeed, most of the accommodation offer spectacular sea views and steps down the cliff provide access to a beautiful sandy beach.

The accommodation is made up of lodges, caravans and flats, there are three pine lodges; Seagull, Puffin and Tern are all eight berth, three bedroomed, warm and comfortable lodges. There are six, eight and ten berth static caravans available, most with great sea views and all double glazed with central heating to ensure guest comfort, whatever the weather. For a relaxing home from home stay, there are also holiday apartments situated in the main house in a variety of sizes.

Whether it's a quiet pint and sandwich at lunchtime or enjoying evening entertainment with your dinner, the Jolly Roger Clubhouse provides a great atmosphere, friendly service and a sumptuous menu. Entertainment varies from live music and discos to Razz the Clown for the kids. There is also an amusement arcade, which includes a pinball machine and pool table.

11 Station Road, Mundesley,
Norfolk NR11 8JH
Tel: 01263 721172
e-mail: sue.hall@freeuk.com
website: www.break-away-holidays.co.uk

Mundesley is a charming seaside village situated on the North Norfolk coast close to Cromer. It's a relaxed, uncommercialised, place which is ideal for a peaceful beach holiday, or get away-from-it-all break. Without a doubt Mundesley's major attraction is its superb sandy beach. For several years now the beach has won Blue Flag recognition for its excellent water quality standards. It's also a very safe beach, with lifeguards during the summer, making it an ideal spot for toddlers & children to play in the fine sand.

For those not wishing to venture far from the beach the village centre has a varied selection of shops supplying everyday provisions including General Stores, Chemist, Green Grocers, Butchers, Florist, Tourist Information and it has a very pretty Post Office. You can also find cafes, tea-rooms, restaurants & pubs offering a wide range of eat-out food.

The cottages and chalets are all well equipped for self catering breaks. They are warm and cosy in the winter and each has a lovely garden and patio area allowing guests to enjoy the summer months. The chalets are of brick construction, many with uPVC sealed unit double glazing. The chalets also boast communal lawns allowing for childrens safe play. The cottages /chalets sleep 4-6 persons, and early booking is recommended.

26 HILL HOUSE HOTEL

26 Market Place, Dereham,
Norfolk NR19 2AP
Tel: 01362 699857
Fax: 01362 852970
e-mail: kevingrantham@btinternet.com
website: www.mjbhotels.com

The Hill House Hotel welcomes you to a luxurious stay in the heart of the historic Norfolk town of Dereham. It is located centrally with fantastic views across the town, just take the second exit off the A11 signposted Swaffham A47.

This handsome Queen Anne property was carefully and sympathetically renovated a few years back to open in 2006 as an independant hotel and since has struck up quite a following with visitors to the area. The house dates back to the 16th century and was previously the home of many Norfolk dignitaries including the 18th century scholar Sir John Fenn. Its impressive brick façade and modern styling create a contemporary yet refined feel for guests, who are guaranteed the finest service and comfort available. It is run by an efficient team of friendly staff who always have a smile on their faces and are always happy to do anything to make your stay as comfortable as possible.

There are a selection of spacious rooms to chose from ranging from a penthouse attic suite to galleried apartments with either double, small doubles or single rooms available. Each room retains some original features but have been fitted with the best facilities to ensure that 'luxury' will be the word on your lips. Each room is stylishly and uniquely decorated to maintain the room's original charm. Each room has its own shower or bath, tea and coffee making facilities, hair dryer, plasma TV with freeview and telephone. A full complimentary breakfast can be taken in the intimate dining room daily between 7:15-10:45am. Hill House also offers special extra services courtesy of Cooper's hairdressers at very reasonable rates.

Downstairs there is also a large 60 seater carvery restaurant with a glass roof, open every day for lunch and dinner for both residents and the public. Bookings are advised here as it's a popular choice most days, combining quality food and low prices. Drinks can also be enjoyed at Hill House in the log fired lounge. Parties or functions of all varieties can be catered for either in the dining room or the larger carvery available for hire all year round.

239

27 LODGE FARM

Castle Acre, Kings Lynn,
Norfolk PE32 2BS
Tel: 01760 755506
e-mail:
enquiries@countrysportsonline.com

This charming farmhouse in the depths of the
beautiful Norfolk countryside, nearby Castle
Acre, is owned and run by the Thompson
family. Built in the 1840's as a farm and hunting
lodge for the Earls of Leicester, this brick
farmhouse is simply stunning to look at. Many of the original features remain and the interior décor
manages to combine contemporary comforts with the traditional feel of the place.

There are three rooms available at **Lodge Farm**; a double, a twin and a family suite, camping sites
can also be provided with prior arrangement. The double and
the twin both have en suite facilities and the family suite has a
private bathroom. Breakfast at Lodge Farm is always a special
affair, locally sourced produce mean that the food is as fresh as
possible and any dietary requirements are happily catered for.

The location of the farmhouse is great, access to dozens of
footpaths and bridle ways mean the place is perfect for keen
ramblers, cyclists and horse riders. Just short drives away are the
beaches of the East coast, the markets of Swaffham and
Fakeham and the rest of Norfolk's great attractions.

29 DENVER WINDMILL

Denver, Downham Market,
Norfolk PE38 0EG
Tel: 01366 384009
e-mail: enquiries@denvermill.plus.com
website: www.denvermill.co.uk

Built in 1835, **Denver Windmill** produced flour
for over a hundred years until it was struck by
lightening in 1941. It is now fully restored and
milling flour by wind power once more.
Guided tours to the top of the mill and a
visitor's centre provide a fascinating insight into
this process. A bakery and tearoom selling
Denver Windmill flour and delicious products
in which it is an ingredient are
also on site as well as three
craft units. Stay in the miller's
house, now converted into
three charming holiday
cottages. School parties are
made welcome with special
activities. An education room
is available for use. Open 1st
April-31st Oct, Mon-Sat,
10am-5pm, Sun, 12pm-5pm.
1st Nov-31st March, Mon-Sat,
10am-4pm, Sun, 12pm-4pm.

30 CASTLE RISING CASTLE

Castle Rising, Norfolk PE31 6AH
Tel: 01553 631330
website: www.english-heritage.org.uk

Explore the imposing keep and vast earthworks
of this Norman castle. Set amid 12 acres of
mighty earthwork defences, this is one of the
largest and most ornate Norman buildings in all
England. Discover the stronghold's fascinating
history - including its links with 'Wicked Queen
Isabella' – in our audio tour.

1 Church Street, Litcham, Kings Lynn,
Norfolk PE32 2NS
Tel: 01328 701340
e-mail: bullinn1@yahoo.com
website: www.thebulllitcham.co.uk

The Bull Inn in Litcham is a traditional coaching inn dating back to the 1700's, however parts of the foundations were built in the mid 1300's, making the Bull the second oldest Inn in Norfolk. Its location meant that it was the first or last change of horses on the route between Kings Lynn and Great Yarmouth. Nowadays, though, the impressive main building has been modernised but maintains some traditional features through the contemporary décor. There has been recent refurbishment of the public bar and

the restaurant, but the work has kept the long established characteristics. Old oak beams are exposed and run the length of the ceilings and huge inglenook fireplaces provide warmth in the cold winter months. The bar features a bar top and four semi circular tables of thick welsh slate, which once were two cutting tables of the Royal Tailors, Gieves and Hawkes, No. 1 Saville Row London.

The stables and coach house have been converted into 3 double rooms, disabled friendly with large, en suite, shower rooms. There are four other twin or double rooms, two of which can sleep three people. Larger groups can be catered for in the family suite, capable of sleeping five people or the self contained cottage which can hold six. A function room is also available for hire, originally the local court room; it has now been restored to its former glory, with the old fireplace fully functional again. The three double rooms that used to be the stables and coach house are situated around a courtyard that provides secure parking over night for cars and bicycles.

A new venture for the family run Bull Inn is the restaurant, already receiving great reviews, the menu specialises in classic pub grub, cooked very well using the best of locally sourced produce. An example is the popular home made pies, choose from steak and kidney, chicken and mushroom or beef and onion. Served with healthy portions of chips, peas, mushrooms and onion rings, the pies are for the very hungry! As well as the main menu, there are daily specials featuring the best of the in season food from the area. The restaurant serves food between 12 pm and 2.30 pm and from 6 pm to 9 pm seven days a week.

31 SANDRINGHAM HOUSE

Sandringham, Norfolk PE35 6EN
Tel: 01553 772675 Fax: 01553 541571
e-mail: enquiries@sandringhamestate.co.uk

Sandringham House is the charming country retreat of Her Majesty The Queen hidden in the heart of sixty acres of beautiful wooded gardens. Still maintained in the style of Edward and

Alexandra, Prince and Princess of Wales (later King Edward VII and Queen Alexandra), all the main ground floor rooms used by The Royal Family, full of their treasured ornaments, portraits and furniture, are open to the public.

More family possessions are displayed in the Museum housed in the old stable and coach houses including vehicles ranging in date from the first car owned by a British monarch, a 1900 Daimler, to a half-scale Aston Martin used by Princes William and Harry. A display tells the mysterious tale of the Sandringham Company who fought and died at Gallipoli in 1915, which was made into a TV film "All the King's Men".

With so much to see and do, and a warm and friendly welcome whenever you visit, Sandringham is the epitome of English country house life – don't miss it!

32 FRANS PANTRY FAYRE

28 High St, Heacham, Kings Lynn,
Norfolk PE31 7EP
Tel: 01485 57220
website: www.pantryfood.webs.com

Frans Pantry Fayre is a quaint little tearoom set back amongst a row of cute cottages along the High Street of Heacham. While it may be small in size, Frans is jam packed full of character and a warm, friendly atmosphere.

Exposed brickwork walls are covered in photos, paintings and nik naks to study whilst waiting for your food.

The food is well worth waiting for, all home made and using recipes handed down to Fran from her mother and grandmother, she has also developed a menu suitable for diabetics, just ask for details.

HIDDEN PLACES GUIDES

Explore Britain and Ireland with *Hidden Places* guides - a fascinating series of national and local travel guides.

Packed with easy to read information on hundreds of places of interest as well as places to stay, eat and drink.

Available from both high street and internet booksellers

For more information on the full range of *Hidden Places* guides and other titles published by Travel Publishing visit our website on

www.travelpublishing.co.uk
or ask for our leaflet by phoning
01752 697280 or emailing
info@travelpublishing.co.uk

33 THE BULL

**Bridge Street, Fakenham,
Norfolk NR21 9AG
Tel: 01328 853410
website: www.thefakenhambull.co.uk**

The Bull is located in Fakenham, commonly known as the gateway to north Norfolk. The Bull is run by Ian and Vince who have a wealth of experience in catering and running bars in the area including the local racecourse bars. The Bull contains a beautifully light and modern, spacious bar serving a variety of draft and bottled beers, fine cask conditioned ales, wines, spirits, soft drinks and freshly ground coffee and offer a good choice of tasty lunches every day from 11:30am-3:00pm Mon-Sat and from 12-3pm on Sundays. You can choose from a large selection of sandwiches, baguettes, paninis, salads, jacket potatoes and hot lunches. Local favourites include beef stir fry, half pounder beef burger, local

butchers sausage and fried onion baguette and whole tail scampi. Every Wednesday the Bull holds a popular steak night from 6:30-9pm to make your mouth water! There is also a specials board sampling the best seasonal produce and a takeaway service for all their baguettes, sandwiches, paninis, jackets, salads and soups.

The Bull also sports 4 en suite spacious rooms complete with tea and coffee facilities and TV/DVD systems at a reasonable B&B rates for excellent quality.

34 CAFÉ COFFEEHOLICS

**Bridge Street, Fakenham,
Norfolk NR21 9AN
Tel: 01328 855015**

Café Coffeeholics is situated centrally in the ancient market town of Fakenham and it's the perfect spot for coffee lovers to sit, relax and chat. Run by Ian and Vince who also run many other service establishments in the area, their friendly welcome and wealth of experience will ensure you enjoy your visit.

They serve a range of coffees to suit every taste, with the option of de-caf, skinny low fat and extra espresso shots and are all made from organic, fair-trade and rainforest alliance certified coffee beans. Those with a sweet tooth can add a delicious syrup flavouring including vanilla, caramel and hazelnut or perhaps a shot of Brandy or Irish whiskey to get that kick! A variety of other alcoholic drinks is also available, along with a selection of teas, soft drinks, milkshakes and

freshly squeezed orange juice.

Tasty, freshly prepared light lunches are available, including sandwiches,

baguettes, salads, jacket potatoes, ploughmans, omelettes, snacks on toast and hot meals. Guests usually have the option of tailoring their meal to choice by opting for ham, cheddar, stilton or prawns with their ploughmans, or picking the filling for their omelettes ensuring satisfaction every time. Popular hot meals include mushroom stroganoff and chilli con carne and are finished off ideally with a scoop of Ronaldo's special ice creams. Open 10am-5pm Mon-Sat.

35 HUNSTANTON SEALIFE SANCTUARY

Southern Promenade, Hunstanton,
Norfolk PE36 5BH
Tel: 01485 533576
website: www.sealsanctuary.co.uk

Every year, many sick and abandoned seals are rescued and brought to the **Hunstanton Sea Life Sanctuary** to be nursed back to health. As well as seals, over 30 fascinating marine displays provide a haven for many other fascinating creatures, including otters, seahorses, penguins and sharks. There's fun for all the family with a full programme including talks, feeding displays and demonstrations.

The seals brought to the sanctuary are mostly young pups, ill or orphaned, and their plight is usually reported by concerned members of the public. Their rehabilitation begins in the Seal Hospital as soon as they arrive. In the capable hands of the animal care team, the pups gradually recover, and when they are able to feed, they are transferred to the convalescence pool. Here they build up their strength before returning to the wild. At the Seal Hospital you can learn how they care for a seal pup from rescue through to release.

HIDDEN PLACES GUIDES

Explore Britain and Ireland with *Hidden Places* guides - a fascinating series of national and local travel guides.

Packed with easy to read information on hundreds of places of interest as well as places to stay, eat and drink.

Available from both high street and internet booksellers

For more information on the full range of *Hidden Places* guides and other titles published by Travel Publishing visit our website on

www.travelpublishing.co.uk or ask for our leaflet by phoning **01752 697280** or emailing **info@travelpublishing.co.uk**

38 MECHANICAL MUSIC MUSEUM & BYGONES

Blacksmith Road, Cotton, nr Stowmarket,
Suffolk IP14 4QN
Tel: 01449 613876

Mechanical Music Museum & Bygones houses a unique collection of music boxes, polyphons, street pianos, pianolas and organs. Stars of the show include a Limonaire fairground organ dating from around 1850 and a mighty Wurlitzer theatre organ originally installed in the Stilwell Theatre, Brooklyn, in 1926. It was later shipped to England and for many years graced London's Luxury Theatre (later the Leicester Square Theatre), which was built by the great star Jack Buchanan. The Mechanical Museum acquired the Wurlitzer in the early 1980s. The Museum is open on Sunday afternoons from June to September, and for an annual fair organ enthusiasts day on the first Sunday in October.

2-4 Greengate, Hunstanton,
Norfolk PE36 6BJ
Tel: 01485 532487

This traditional Fish and Chip Shop and Restaurant was established in 1998 and since then has grown to be very popular. Ten welcoming friendly staff keep **Fishers of Hunstanton** running smoothly, and food is cooked in a traditional way. It is also a licensed bar, with a large selection of bottled beers (including Carling, Budweiser, Corona and Magners Cider), red wines and white wines.

There are children's play tables and books to keep them entertained while you finish your meal, and there is also some quality vegetarian options on the menu. Their take-away menu is of a high standard.

The good-looking roof garden (ten tables) has a magnificent view of the sea, especially when the sun is setting. The potatoes used to make their delicious chips are locally sourced, and the salads are locally produced too. They are an eco-friendly restaurant with hardly any wastage as everything is recycled.

The extensive menu includes a Kids Menu (with scampi, chicken nuggets, fishcake and more), Main Courses (massive range from pies to fried chicken, chicken burgers, pastys, savaloy, jacket potatoes, and fishcakes), and most importantly the Fish Menu (cod, haddock, plaice, scampi, eel, lobster tails and a magnificent seafood platter). The Fishers Challenge involves eating a whole giant prime cod with all the extras (including a drink), and those who complete the challenge receive a free dessert of their choice! There is also an impressive Side Orders section and of course Desserts.

Disabled access, child-friendly and ample parking. 100 yards from the lovely Princess Theatre with shows on all year round, and only one minute walk from the sea.

245

37 THE GRANGE COUNTRY HOUSE HOTEL

Barton Rd, Thurston, Bury St Edmunds,
Suffolk IP31 3PQ
Tel: 01359 231260 Fax: 01359 231387
e-mail: info@thegrangehotel.com
website: www.thegrangehotel.com

Situated just a few miles from Bury St Edmunds, **The Grange Country House Hotel** is a stunning mock Tudor style country house providing three star accommodation, with an in house restaurant and spa. Impressing from first sight, the building was constructed in 1895, just three miles from Bury St Edmunds in the quaint village of Thurston and just moments from the A14. Originally built for Colonel Henry Blagrave, The Grange was then known as Thurston House. It has had a varied history, starting as a gentlemen's club up until the Second World War where it was used as a makeshift hospital. After the war a Mr Berden converted it into bedsit flats and left it in a derelict state in 1971. Since then the owners have been committed to restoring The Grange to its former glory and current owners Mr and Mrs Khurana have managed to provide all the modern comforts amongst the traditional features.

Each of the 18 available rooms have been individually decorated to the highest standard, creating light and airy rooms with all displaying fantastic views over the wonderful landscaped gardens. All of the rooms have en suite facilities with either bath/shower or shower units. As well as the variety of sizes in the main house, there are also log cabins in the gardens which offer a lovely peaceful option. Beautifully decorated, the cabins boast verandas which provide the perfect place to enjoy those long summer evenings.

There are two restaurants on site at The Grange; the Garden restaurant and the slightly more formal Adam restaurant. Before your meal, the lounge bar has a splendid variety of real ales and wines to sample on the terrace and admire the magnificent gardens. The Executive Head Chef's style is influenced by cuisines from around the world and the menus reflect this in his highly original interpretations of some classical English dishes and the more elaborate French classics. A great deal of attention is made to the season and to the sourcing of the very best of local ingredients. Open for breakfast, lunch and dinner, the extensive menus will cater for every taste and diet.

The Grange is also the ideal venue for special occasions, weddings occur frequently here and in grand style. Other events can easily be organised, and in forthcoming months there is a murder mystery weekend and a wedding fayre, which is the perfect opportunity to see what the Grange can do for your wedding day.

39 KILN FARM GUESTHOUSE

Kiln Lane, Elmswell, nr Bury St Edmunds,
Suffolk IP30 9QR
Tel: 01359 240442
e-mail: davejankilnfarm@btinternet.com
website: www.kilnfarmguesthouse.com

The **Kiln Farm Guesthouse** is a beautiful Victorian farmhouse dating back to the late 19th century and set in a splendid rural setting. Dave and Jan Copeman are proud to welcome all kinds of visitors to this secluded place, situated amongst country roads just off the A14. The brick built main house has clearly been looked after over the years and during the spring and summer months the outside is adorned with hanging baskets and potted plants, creating a warm and relaxing environment.

The accommodation takes the form of six converted stables, all arranged around a lovely courtyard next to the main house. The six stables are comprised of five en suite twins or doubles and one family suite; one double room and one twin room sharing a private bathroom. The main house boasts a licensed bar, a conservatory with a TV and a restaurant where hearty award winning breakfasts are served. Evening meals can also be catered for by prior arrangement.

Also on the premises is a caravan site, with space for five pitches and is very popular with visitors touring the area. Elmswell and Woolpit are close by attractions and the farm is very well placed for exploring some of Suffolk's finest towns and villages.

40 RED HOUSE FARM

Haughley, Stowmarket, Suffolk IP14 3QP
Tel: 01449 673323 Fax: 01449 675413
e-mail:
mary@redhousefarmhaughley.co.uk
website:
www.redhousefarmhaughley.co.uk

Set in the picturesque mid Suffolk countryside is the **Red House Farm**, offering Bed & Breakfast, self catering and camping accommodation in fine style. The B & B rooms are provided in the main house, where Mary and Eric have lived since their marriage in 1966. The older part of the house is believed to date back 300 – 400 years and it is here that the one double room and two single rooms are located. There is also a twin room which boasts views of the front garden and the countryside beyond. All of the rooms have en suite facilities and are very comfortably furnished.

The caravan site has lovely views over the surrounding countryside, is a well sheltered, level site with hard standings and electric hook ups. The site is very well equipped with adequate water taps and chemical emptying and waste disposal points.

Self catering accommodation takes the form of converted farm buildings; the Garden cottage adjoins the farmhouse and will sleep two persons. The Stable has been transformed into a single storey cottage capable of sleeping four people. The en suite 'wet' room has been created with wheelchairs users in mind, with a drive in shower. Finally the Cob cottage has been created from a redundant piggery/cow shed and is suitable for two people.

41 MUSEUM OF EAST ANGLIAN LIFE

Stowmarket, Suffolk IP14 1DL
Tel: 01449 612229   Fax: 01449 672307
website: www.eastanglianlife.org.uk

The Museum of East Anglian Life occupies
a 75-acre site in the heart of Stowmarket. Its
rich collections of social, rural and industrial
history include a number of historic buildings
such as a working watermill, a smithy, a chapel
and a 13th century farmhouse.

There is something for the whole family to enjoy with
a variety of farm animals, adventure playground, picnic
sites, café and gift shop. Throughout the year the Museum
holds special events as well as demonstrations of crafts and
engines in steam. The Museum is open from April to
October.

42 THE SIX BELLS

Church Road, Felsham, Suffolk IP30 0PJ
Tel: 01449 736268

A charming 16th century building standing proud in
this picturesque Suffolk village, **The Six Bells** is a
popular pub providing locals and tourists alike with
fine food and drink. The exterior welcomes you in, the expert flint work and large sash windows
creating a traditional look that continues inside. Inside the smiling staff beckons you in further to enjoy
the wood burning stove and exposed oak beams that adorn the ceilings.

The Six Bells has been tastefully decorated in a contemporary style; exposed brick and chrome
detail make for a great atmosphere and ambience in which to enjoy the great food. Produced from
locally sourced ingredients, the menu
features snacks for the peckish and more
substantial fare for the hungry. Featuring
traditionally prepared home cooked meals;
the menu has been lovingly crafted by the
expert chefs and is enjoyed by visitors from
all over.

A bank of hand pumps mounted onto
the rear wall harks back to the pub's

heritage and well kept ales are still the bread and butter of
the inn. A good choice of ales available at the bar; the
owners of The Six Bells pride themselves on serving great
food and drink all week long. The Six Bells serves food all
week long with the exception of Monday afternoon when
they do not open.

The Street, Cretingham, Suffolk IP13 7BJ
Tel: 01728 685419
e-mail: cretinghambell@btconnect.com
website: www.cretinghambell.co.uk

Family run, **The Cretingham Bell** stands in the centre of a quiet Suffolk village called Cretingham; once the manor house originally built in 1545, the premises were converted into cottages and then into the village inn and one that the locals are extremely proud of. The ivy clad building is set amongst lovely Suffolk countryside and boasts a large and well kept beer garden which overlooks the village green and has an area outside for smokers. Inside, the traditional nature of the place comes through with beamed ceilings, wooden floors and exposed brick walls.

Under the watchful eyes of Charles, Sarah and Peter, The Cretingham Bell provides warm and comfortable accommodation, tasty and delicious food and sublime service that ensure visitors return week after week. There are three double en-suite letting rooms available for B&B.

A nice feature is that the rooms are all individually decorated with period fixtures and fittings. The rooms all have TV, tea & coffee making facilities and a WiFi hotspot to ensure that your visit is as pleasant as possible. Close by are several attractions, Otley Hall, Sutton Hoo, Framlingham Castle, the Suffolk showground, the coast and its beautiful towns of Aldeburgh and Southwold are all a short drive away and draw tourists from all over the country.

Peter has created a sumptuous menu and is very proud of the fact that all of the food is created fresh to order using some of the finest ingredients available locally. Customers can choose from a variety of wholesome home cooked dishes, including steak & ale pie, pork casserole in cider and a traditional roast dinner on Sunday's (booking advisable)

Well behaved children and pets are very welcome as Charles, Sarah and Peter encourage the whole family to have an enjoyable meal, walkers and cyclists are also warmly received. The two bars lend themselves to gatherings, there is the snug bar or lounge bar perfect for that pre dinner drink.

249

Farmhouse B & B, The Rookery, Wortham,
nr Diss, Norfolk IP22 1RB
Tel: 01379 783236
e-mail: maureen@therookeryfarm.co.uk
website: www.therookeryfarm.co.uk

Nestling amongst the beautiful East Anglia countryside, **Rookery Farm** is situated on the border between Norfolk and Suffolk and is ideally placed on key routes to both Bury St. Edmonds and Great Yarmouth. Set on a working dairy farm, the inn attracts all kinds of visitors, keen to escape the hustle and bustle of the city and explore all the surrounding countryside has to offer. With three rooms available for guests, Maureen has strived to decorate each individually and create accommodation with a homely touch and feel.

The house itself is a grade II listed farmhouse constructed during the Georgian era and sits amongst imposing trees at the end of a large driveway, oozing charm and character, creating a great first impression. The interior does not disappoint either, immaculately decorated and packed full of period favourites, a spectacular example is the kitchen with stone flooring and huge inglenook fireplace.

All three bedrooms have been named for farmyard plants; the Magnolia room is a twin bed en suite that looks out over the ancient walled garden. During the spring months, the glorious magnolia tree blooms beneath the window providing olfactory and visual delights. The Barley room has been decorated in traditional harvest colours and boasts a lovely Victorian feature fireplace along with a large double bed and half timbered en suite. Last but not least is the Hydrangea room, the large and spacious size a welcome characteristic, as is the magnificent four poster bed and half timbered en suite. Looking out of the huge period window you will see the herd from the nearby working dairy farm grazing on parkland.

Breakfast is a special occasion at Rookery Farm, Maureen ensures that the only produce served is sourced locally and of the highest quality. Included in the very reasonable tariff, from £26 per person per night, the breakfasts are not to be missed.

45 THORNHAM HALL

Thornham Magna, Eye, Suffolk IP23 8HA
Tel: 01379 783314
e-mail: thornhamhall@aol.com
website: www.thornhamhall.com

The magnificent 20th century **Thornham Hall** manages to hark back to bygone eras with influences from its Tudor, Georgian and Victorian predecessors. Standing at the heart of the Thornham Estate which features beautifully landscaped gardens and lovely parkland; a recently opened field centre provides information about 13 miles of walks and rides around the grounds. Also on the grounds are stables, which surround the house, a statuesque water tower and a charming roundhouse providing much to admire and look at during a stay.

Thornham Hall has been the country seat of the Barons of Hartismere and Henniker for three centuries and whilst the estate itself has been greatly reduced in size since the last century, it still maintains a large modern farming operation and many beautiful, ancient woods. The real gem though is the magnificent park, designed originally in Tudor times by the Killegrews, courtiers to Henry VIII. The Victorians altered many of the Tudor aspects, including the drive, and planted some wonderful Wellingtonias and cedars.

Inside is equally breathtaking; the influences of many periods are clear with lovely open fires, spacious rooms, fine porcelain and portraits and an elegant staircase which ascends from the huge drawing room. Spanning the width of the house, the drawing room is simply stunning, boasting huge French windows that offer splendid views across the croquet lawn to the landscaped gardens beyond. Just as impressive is the dining room, decorated in the green and pink style of Adams, diners are treated to a variety of Henniker portraits that adorn the walls.

Accommodation takes the form of three en suite rooms, all having views over the main park. Each is individually named and decorated, each having different selling points. The Blue room features a great four poster bath and a central view of the park. The Lake room boasts views over the main park as well as the lake and the Cedar Suite has a period four poster bed as well as stunning views. The tariffs are very reasonable and include a wonderful breakfast, full of choice. Seasonal and discounted rates ensure that anyone can enjoy the experience of staying at Thornham Hall.

Owner Lesley loves country food, but years abroad have introduced an eclectic style to the menu, introducing dishes that make the most of the local and seasonal foods but add a foreign flavour. Thornham Hall has always been famous for house parties and that reputation is well deserved, even now, Thornham Hall is the ideal place for weddings, dinner parties and all manner of special occasions.

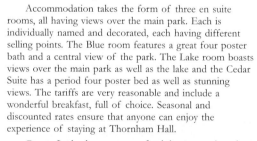

251

Gorams Mill Lane, Laxfield,
Suffolk IP13 8DW
Tel: 01986 798395
e-mail: lowhouse@kome.co.uk
website: www.laxfield-kingshead.co.uk

To say **The Kings Head** is unique is a great understatement; this 16th century pub has had a long and varied history and is currently thought to be the only pub in the UK without an actual bar! Originally known as The Low House, as it is sometimes called now, it was part of the Laxfield estate given to Edmund Beddingfield by Henry VIII, and has been run as an inn throughout the years. Approaching the premises, you really feel like you have travelled back through time; the well kept thatched roof, the dark sunken windows in the white washed walls and the occasional presence of a horse and cart. Moving inside, low beamed ceilings and the exposed wood create a cosy atmosphere that is enhanced by the smiling staff, friendly locals and crackling fire in the huge inglenook fireplace.

The unique feature that sets the Kings Head apart from other similar inns is the lack of a bar, instead ales and beers are poured straight from the casks in the tap room! Another popular attraction is the horse and carriage rides that are available at the weekends or can be arranged for any other time. Holiday accommodation is now on offer at the Kings Head; choose from a self-contained ground floor flat or two first floor double bedrooms complete with en suite facilities. Bob and Lynda have also just finished refurbishing a third letting unit in the old stable block to offer further choice. Eating at the Kings Head is a popular pastime in the local area, and after sampling the delicious menu, it is easy to see why. Changing periodically to make the most of the local in season produce, the menu is packed full of homemade pub classics, for example the steak and Adnams ale pie, Lowestoft undyed smoked kippers and salad or the local Lane Farm sausages and mash. Add to that the option of a truly scrumptious roast dinner on Sundays, the Kings Head is a must for any hungry visitors.

There is a quarterly newsletter, The Low Down, which outlines any and all special events occurring at the Kings Head; live music, themed dinner evenings and curry nights, to name just a few. This inn is truly the heart of Laxfield and must be visited to be truly appreciated!

46 GABLES FARM B&B

Wingfield, Diss, Norfolk IP21 5RH
Tel: 01379 586355
e-mail: enquiries@gablesfarm.co.uk
website: www.gablesfarm.co.uk

For truly unique accommodation, look no further than the moated **Gables Farm** in the beautiful Norfolk countryside near Diss. The lovely timbered 16th century farmhouse boasts three gorgeous bedrooms, two acres of landscaped gardens and oodles of charm and character. Inside the rooms are heavily timbered with exposed oak beams visible all over the house which is packed with features; including a huge inglenook fireplace that is perfect for those cold wintry nights.

All three rooms have individual decor and are identified by name; the Mullion room overlooks the moated gardens

and has been newly refurbished with pine furniture. The Hayloft room is situated in the oldest part of the house and has twin beds and comfortable chairs, finally the Gable End room also overlooks the moated front

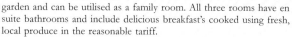

garden and can be utilised as a family room. All three rooms have en suite bathrooms and include delicious breakfast's cooked using fresh, local produce in the reasonable tariff.

The great location means that Gables Farm is perfect for walkers, ramblers, cyclists, fishermen and gardeners with many facilities in close proximity.

48 THE WHITE HORSE INN

Darsham Road, Westleton,
nr Saxmundham, Suffolk IP17 3AH
Tel: 01728 648222
e-mail: jennie@westleton-whitehorse.co.uk
website: www.westleton-whitehorse.co.uk

Rick and Jennie Powling offer a friendly greeting, Adnams real ales, home-cooked food and B&B accommodation at the **White Horse Inn**. The inn has three lovely guest rooms – an en suite double, a twin and a single available all year round. Behind the inn is a large beer garden with plenty of seating and room for children to romp in safety. Nestled between the A12 and the sea, Westleton is well placed for exploring Suffolk's Heritage

Coast: Minsmere bird sanctuary and the 'lost' town of Dunwich are just minutes away. Each August a Barrel Fair takes place on the village green, where the main barrel-pushing events are supported by side shows and morris dancing.

HIDDEN PLACES GUIDES

Explore Britain and Ireland with *Hidden Places* guides - a fascinating series of national and local travel guides.

Packed with easy to read information on hundreds of places of interest as well as places to stay, eat and drink.

Available from both high street and internet booksellers

For more information on the full range of *Hidden Places* guides and other titles published by Travel Publishing visit our website on

www.travelpublishing.co.uk
or ask for our leaflet by phoning
01752 697280 or emailing
info@travelpublishing.co.uk

1 Leiston Road, Aldeburgh,
Suffolk IP15 5PP
Tel: 01728 453864
e-mail: alderailway@fsmail.net
website: www.bandbaldeburgh.co.uk

There is a lot going for the 'Community Pub of the Year 2009/10', new licensees Karl and Shirl have come into **The Railway Inn** and put their stamp on this convivial and jolly pub. Named for the adjacent branch line 140 years ago, the Railway Inn provides quality food, drink and accommodation with warm and friendly service thrown in for good measure. The pretty inn stands on a roundabout overlooking Leiston Road in the historic town of Aldeburgh on the appealing Suffolk coastline. Brick and slate built, the exterior entices all who walk past with its colourful hanging baskets and well kept frontage. Inside

the decoration is clean and fresh; dotted around are various bits and bobs relating to the local lifeboat service courtesy of member Karl and railway memorabilia from down the years. Another separate room is decorated with some of Shirl's extensive collection of musically related artwork from the 60's.

In the spirit of local hospitality, of which there is no shortage, the Railway has installed three B & B ensuite guest rooms. Taking the form of a double, a twin and a single, they are all well appointed, comfortable and reasonably priced with a hearty full English breakfast to start the day. Facilities at this popular inn include a new decking area to the rear with benches and tables to make the most of those glorious summer days. The halogen heated canopy ensures guests can enjoy the outside air well into the evening and the regular Sunday barbeques throughout the summer season.

Breakfast is freshly prepared and provides a great way to start the day, for those special occasions Shirl is able to cater for private parties. There are plenty of places to eat just a short walk away. The bar is very well stocked; featuring Adnams' finest as well as a wide range of lagers, ciders, wines and spirits. Community spirit is rife at the Railway, sponsors of the local Aldeburgh Associates football team and the home to pool, crib and darts teams, Karl and Shirl make sure there is something to occupy everybody.

Saturday nights and Sunday afternoons are regular live music slots with Wednesday 'jammin' nights set aside for budding musicians. Monday nights are Quiz nights and Thursday sees the 'open the box' competitions with prizes amounting to as much as £300. Bingo is held alternate Thursdays.

50 THE ANCHOR INN

9 Quay Street, Woodbridge,
Suffolk IP12 1BX
Tel: 01394 382649

The Anchor Inn is a pretty little pub, set on the corner of Quay St in the ancient town of Woodbridge. Known for constructing Elizabethan era fighting ships, the nautically themed name comes as no surprise, considering the town's heritage. Dating back to mid 14th century, The Anchor was extended during Victorian times and is lucky to have retained a lot of original features and charm. Wooden floors throughout, exposed wooden beams in the ceiling and a spectacular inglenook fireplace create a warm and friendly atmosphere in which to enjoy a quiet pint or a full meal.

The restaurant's speciality is authentic Malaysian cuisine cooked using the finest of local produce, fresh to the door that day and home cooked to order. You can also choose from a menu featuring traditional pub classics, such as

fish and chips, sausage and mash with onion gravy and burger with fries and salad. Food is served between 12 pm and 2.30 pm and 6.30 – 9.00 pm every day of the week, with the pub open for drinks all day. A small and cosy seating area is situated out the front with a nice view of the river opposite, great for those balmy summer evenings.

51 ROBERT BLAKE HOLIDAYS

1A Moorfield Road, Woodbridge,
Suffolk IP12 4JN
Tel: 01394 382565
e-mail: robert@blake4110.fsbusiness.co.uk
website: www.robertblakeholidays.co.uk

Robert Blake Holidays is a family run business offering five stunning holiday homes in the Woodbridge area. The Robin's Nest complex can be found near the small village of Dallinghoo and it comprises three of the five holiday cottages on offer. The three properties can be rented individually or all together and are situated on four acres of pretty gardens and woodland, the beautiful rural location is perfect for those who are keen on flora and fauna. Guests can choose from The Thatched Cottage, a 16th cottage capable of sleeping up to 6 people, the Carpenter's Shop, a quality timber framed conversion which sleeps five and the Wheelwrights, a slightly smaller timber framed building for two/three people. All of the cottages have been modernised and refurbished to very high standards and are extremely comfortable.

Anvil Cottage is a grade II listed 16th century former artisan's cottage which has been extensively refurbished in recent years to create stylish and contemporary accommodation for up to four people. The other property available is The Old Forge; dating back to the 17th century, this tastefully renovated brick and flint built cottage is steeped in character and history. With space for up to four people, it is perfect for that small family getaway! Plus one luxury townhouse in Harrogate, Yorkshire.

52 THE CHERRY TREE

73 Cumberland Street, Woodbridge,
Suffolk IP12 4AG
Tel: 01934 384627
website: www.thecherrytreepub.co.uk

A landmark for visitors entering the town from Ipswich, the **Cherry Tree** is a flagship pub in the historic town of Woodbridge, equally popular as a place for locals to meet and chat and a refreshment stop or base for tourists.

The Grade II listed building, a blaze of colour in spring and summer with flower tubs and hanging baskets, is in the excellent acre of Sheila and Geoff Ford, who have been making friends ever since 2001 with their fine hospitality and the quality of the beer, food and accommodation. Cooking starts with breakfast, served from 7.30 to 10.30 (9 to 11 at the weekend), with the main menu coming on stream at midday and continuing right through to 9 in the evening. The choice of pub favourites runs from sandwiches, jacket potatoes and omelettes to scampi, cod, haddock and salmon, sausages & mash, lasagne, curry, beef & ale pie and

beef and gammon steaks. A range of Adnams with a minimum of eight real ales is served in the bar. The annual Beer Festival is held in May/June.

The guest bedrooms, in a converted Suffolk barn overlooking the garden, are named after Adnams brews: Broadside sleeps up to 4, Explorer is a double and Regatta is a twin with wheel chair access. All have TV with DVD and VCR and broadband access. The family-friendly Cherry Tree has a children's play area in the secluded garden.

53 SUTTON HOO

Tranmer House, Sutton Hoo, Woodbridge,
Suffolk IP12 3DJ
Tel: 01394 389700
website: www.suttonhoo.org.uk

In the early 7th century, about 200 years after Roman government was withdrawn from Britain, this place was chosen to make a great monument to a new kind of English power.

Over about 50 years an aristocratic was buried here under mounds near the terrace. This reached a climax in two outstanding burials with ships under high mounds, which declared to all, including visitors from the sea, that a power existed in this land. In about AD625, in a pagan consecration, the military, perhaps royal, master of a mighty household was buried here with goods reflecting his personal culture, public ceremonial and international contacts.

Sutton Hoo kept its secret for more than 1300 years, until, on the very brink of war in 1939, an incomparable buried treasure was discovered here. The sight of a huge buried ship, and the wealth of precious objects found within it, led to decades of further excavation and research, provoking questions that still await answers. The new exhibition which tells these stories has been made possible by a major grant from the Heritage Lottery Fund, and by the generous financial support of many other private and public bodies and individuals.

54 THE PLOUGH INN

Main Road, Sutton, Woodbridge,
Suffolk IP12 3DU
Tel: 01394 411785

New owners Paul and Diane Ward have come into **The Plough Inn** and set about enhancing its already considerable reputation. Providing bed and breakfast for weary travellers since Tudor times, this 500 year old pub is packed full of charm and character. From the quaint uneven tile roof, to the original exposed beams and tile floor, the Plough Inn is well worth an extended visit.

In keeping with the thoroughly hospitable nature of the Plough Inn, there are three warm and comfortable rooms available with the option of bed and breakfast or half board. As you would expect from such a traditional place, the menu is full of sumptuous pub classics, created using the finest of locally sourced ingredients. With space for 50 covers inside, it is recommended that reservations are made, busy all year round, the most popular form of dining during the summer is al fresco, with 20 spaces available outside.

The Plough Inn caters for everybody, there is a children's play area in the garden and during the summer months there is a pet corner, including pony rides! Inside there is a pool room and a games room, ensuring adults will not be easily bored as well!

56 LOWESTOFT MARITIME MUSEUM

Sparrows Nest Park, Whapload Road,
Lowestoft, Suffolk NR32 1XG
Tel: 01502 561963

Anyone with an interest in the sea and ships should steer a steady course for Britain's most easterly museum under the lighthouse on Whapload Road. Open daily from May to September, **Lowestoft Maritime Museum** specialises in the history of the Lowestoft fishing fleet, from early sail to steam and through to the modern diesel-powered vessels.

Methods of fishing are recorded, including trawling and the no longer practised driftnet fishing for herring, and other displays depict the evolution of lifeboats and the town's association with the Royal Navy. A replica of the aft cabin of a steam drifter and a fine picture gallery are other attractions of this fascinating museum, where the attendants are ex-seamen and others interested in the port of Lowestoft. They are all delighted to answer any questions visitors have about the Museum and its exhibits. School parties are particularly welcome, with takeaway educational packs available, and out-of-season parties can be catered for with notice.

The Museum, which is maintained by members of the Lowestoft and East Suffolk Maritime Society, was established in 1968 and extended in 1978, when the Duke of Edinburgh was guest of honour. The objects of the Society are to educate the public in shipping, old and modern, in Lowestoft and the County of Suffolk, and in trades and crafts associated with shipping lore in general and in particular to maintain the Museum.

55 THE JOLLY SAILOR

Quay Street, Orford, Suffolk IP12 2NU
Tel: 01394 450243
e-mail: hello@thejollysailor.net
website: www.thejollysailor.net

The Jolly Sailor has been providing high quality accommodation, food and drinks to smugglers, aristocracy, traders and locals for over 400 years. This 17th century inn is set amongst the historical and picturesque Suffolk heritage coast in the medieval town of Orford alongside the river Ore. Guests can while away an afternoon poking around the many nooks and crannies of this spacious building which takes up a large part of Quay Street which ends at the river. The building itself was allegedly built from the timbers of a wrecked ship and has a long standing reputation as a regular haunt for local smugglers.

Offering accommodation in the form of four beautifully renovated en suite rooms, The Jolly Sailor is well equipped to give guests a stay they won't forget in a hurry. Each of the rooms is individually decorated and boast views over the orchard, the river or the marshland surrounding the estuary, the Mural room even has a magnificent 17th century wall painting. For those who like the great outdoors, there is a camp site in the orchard which gives campers the enviable option of waking up to the sunrise and birds singing.

Making sure that everybody who visits has the best experience possible, licensee Gordon has placed books, board games and magazines dotted around the pub to keep even the most hyperactive occupied for an afternoon. Regulars John, Charlie and Keith have been frequenting the Jolly Sailor for over 80 years now and with a combined age of around 250 years are well placed to tell a tale or two! By far the most important aspect of the Jolly Sailor is the food; Gordon is your chef and learnt the French classics at a young age, creating a well thought out menu to tantalise any taste buds. The food is all freshly prepared to order using locally sourced ingredients in simple, sumptuous recipes. Fish is a mainstay of the menu, with the ever popular cod & chips and Gordon's signature dish; haddock Benedict.

Staying with the entertainment theme, the Jolly Sailor lays on live music on a regular basis; resident Nick Raison provides an eclectic mix of easy listening and jazz. While the Quay Street Whalers pop in every now and then to sing 19th and 20th century sea shanty's, getting somewhat ruder as the night progresses!

57 THE STAR INN

Hall Road, Wenhaston, Suffolk IP19 9HF
Tel: 01502 478240
e-mail: virginia@wenhastonstar.co.uk
website: www.wenhastonstar.co.uk

Set in the beautiful rolling Suffolk countryside, **The Star Inn** is a cosy village pub in Wenhaston, located four miles from the sea and the lost village of Dunwich it is also close to the historic church of Blythburgh .

The simple home cooking using local ingredients such as Suffolk Red Poll Beef that is reared in the village make The Star a popular choice with locals and visitors alike. The menu is constantly changing but there is always a tasty meal at a reasonable price.

There are open fires to warm the bones in the winter and a large garden with a boules pitch to enjoy in the summer. There is a range of traditional pub games to play and in the back room there is an old fashioned pianola which customers are welcome to use and explore the hundreds of music rolls.

The Star is on the bus route that connects Southwold, Halesworth and Lowestoft, so it's possible to take a tour of the countryside and coast, enjoy an interlude at The Star and not have to worry about driving. Wenhaston boasts the fantastic church of St. Peter's and its medieval doom and is walking distance from the acclaimed Woottens nursery.

The pub was built in 1839 and has traded continuously since 1841 and still retains the warm welcome that should be a part of any pub visit. This welcome extends to dogs, children and muddy boots, hence it's popular with walkers who are keen to enjoy the views from the five heaths of Wenhaston. For those visiting the area, camping is available at The Star by prior arrangement.

58 THE CHEQUERS INN

23 Bridge Street, Bungay,
Suffolk NR35 1HD
Tel: 01986 893579
e-mail:
belyndastarbuck.chequers@hotmail.co.uk

Located in the thriving country market town of Bungay, **The Chequers Inn** is a traditional pub with a great reputation in the area. Dating back to the 16th century, the former coach house has fantastic beamed ceilings and an open log fire giving the place a real homely feel to it.

Homemade food is the order of the day here and there is plenty to choose from on the menu, which has local produce at its heart. On sunnier days food and drink can be enjoyed in the superb large family beer garden and during the summer outdoor music and barbecues are had on a Sunday. Live music can be listened to every weekend and there are a range of real ales waiting to be sampled.

The Chequers Inn is in the ideal location for exploring Suffolk. The 11th century Bigod Castle is one of the many historical attractions in the area and is just a two minute walk from the pub. There are many activities going on in the vicinity, including water sports on the River Waveney, a local Thursday market and for those wanting to explore the Broads – they are just 10 minutes away.

The Chequers Inn is open from 10am-12am seven days a week.

259

59 THE SWAN HOUSE

By the tower, Beccles,
Suffolk NR34 9HE
Tel: 01502 713474
e-mail: info@swan-house.com
website: www.swan-house.com

Opened in 1993 to fill a niche for those with a taste for the unusual, **The Swan House** is cosy, slightly eccentric and highly popular. It has an eclectic mix of the owner's diverse influences from the Chelsea Arts Club to the Kampung Café, Bali. The Swan House specialises in modern Anglo and international cuisine and all of the food is of the highest standard and cooked to order.

Diners can enjoy a wide selection of dishes in the beautiful seating area, including confit of duck served with sauté potatoes and a honey and rosemary sauce. Highly recommended in the Broads region the award-winning upmarket restaurant is well known for its themed nights and has live entertainment on Mondays with a broad mix of talented musicians perfecting the unique ambiance. The establishment has recently been refurbished and it has a vibrant, contemporary new feel to it, carefully balanced with its existing inglenook fireplaces and ceiling beams.

The attention to detail is extremely important to owner, Roland Blunk, and it isn't surprising that diners return again and again. Freshly prepared cakes and pastries can be sampled during the morning and afternoon and each month a different artists' work is displayed on the walls.

60 THE ROYAL OAK

175, Felixstowe Rd, Ipswich,
Suffolk IP3 8EB
Tel: 0872 107 7077
website: www.theroyaloakipswich.com

Owners Andy and Kerry of The Six Bells in Felsham also possess another pub, **The Royal Oak** which is heralded as the place to be in Ipswich for live music. With live music on Friday and Saturday, and open mic jamming sessions on Thursday and Sunday evenings; this claim certainly looks to be confirmed on a weekly basis.

This brick built pub was constructed back in the 1700's and a refurbishment two years ago has brought the Royal Oak bang up to date. The contemporary and modern decor creates a warm and friendly greeting as you enter, enhanced by the background hum of regulars chatting away. Entertainment, if live music is not enough for you, is supplied in the form of a pool table and a dart board. Open from 4 pm till midnight from Monday to Thursday and from 12 till late from Friday to Sunday, this pub also has excellent disabled facilities.

62 THE GREYHOUND PUBLIC HOUSE

2 Ipswich Road, Claydon,
Suffolk IP6 0AR
Tel: 01473 830262

The Greyhound Public House is a grade II listed, 15th century building providing the people of and visitors to Claydon food and beverages all week long. The pink paint job means the Greyhound is quite difficult to miss and the well kept exterior sets the scene for this delightful pub. Inside, the place is superbly decorated; warm and welcoming, the atmosphere is amplified by the charm and character of the 15th century roots.

Eve and Sean Andesen have strived to create a menu that will suit everybody's palate, and using the best of locally sourced produce, they have managed. Serving food all day ensures guests will never go hungry whilst watching live sports on the two huge plasma televisions, playing pool or simply enjoying the sun in the garden. The well stocked bar boasts 2 well kept real ales, 4 lagers and a wide selection of wine.

Near to the beautiful East Anglia coastline and right next to Constable country, there is no shortage of attractions close by, making the Greyhound the perfect place to rest those weary legs and enjoy a spot of supper.

61 DAMERONS FARM HOLIDAYS

Damerons Farm, Henley, Ipswich,
Suffolk IP6 0RU
Tel: 01473 832454
website: www.dameronsfarmholidays.co.uk

Converted in 2005, the five cottages that comprise **Damerons Farm Holidays** offer cosy and comfortable countryside holiday accommodation at very reasonable rates. With sheep, horses, chickens and ducks strolling around, the old granaries and milking parlour make for a truly rural holiday with all of the modern comforts.

Sleeping a maximum total of 22, the cottages are all self catering and discounts can be had for hiring multiple cottages at a time. Facilities include a games room, complete with a pool table, table tennis and table football. A rare facility on offer is the option of stabling your horse to take full advantage of the local scenic bridleways.

64 FISHERMANS HALL

The Ferry, Felixstowe, Suffolk IP11 9RZ
Tel: 01394 670909
e-mail: brianblamp@aol.com
website: www.fishermanshall.co.uk

Fishermans Hall, nestling snugly in the delightful traditional fishing hamlet of Felixstowe Ferry, is an ideal

base for exploring the timeless charm of the Suffolk Heritage Coast. Surrounded by river, sea and open countryside, we are particularly attractive to those enjoying the peace, challenge and sheer joy of this largely unspoiled landscape. For the very active, facilities are available such as a drying room for wet gear and storage space for cycles and canoes, but many come simply to enjoy the gentle pace of the area. Comfortable rooms with beautiful views and a choice of delicious locally sourced breakfast will complete a most enjoyable experience.

261

Old Norwich Road, Barham, Ipswich,
Suffolk IP6 0PG
Tel: 01473 830327
e-mail: enquire@sorrelhorse.co.uk
website: www.sorrelhorse.co.uk

In a pleasant country setting, **The Sorrel Horse Inn** has been owned and run for many years by Bridget (Breda) Smith and her sons Matthew and Philip. The 17th century pink-washed, pantiled building first became an inn in about 1840, and the interior boasts original features such as wall and ceiling beams and open fireplaces. Hewn log-style tables and rustic chairs assist the traditional look, and the dining areas feature interesting collections of miniatures and foreign banknotes.

Among the inn's many assets is a large lawned garden with plenty of picnic benches and parasols, a summer barbecue, heated smoking area and a children's play area complete with slide.

Expertly kept real ales – Adnams Bitter and Shepherd Neame Spitfire – keep cask connoisseurs happy, and fresh-air appetites are satisfied with an excellent selection of home-cooked dishes served in the two dining areas. Lasagne, chicken curry, steaks and savoury pies are at the top of the all-time favourites, and there's always a good choice of vegetarian dishes. Lighter options are available at lunchtime, and the inn is also open for breakfast.

With many attractions nearby (the magnificent Shrubland Hall and its Victorian gardens are almost on the doorstep), the cheerful, friendly Sorrel Horse is an excellent base for touring the region, and the nearby A14 provides easy access to all parts.

Eight bedrooms in a splendidly converted barn provide quiet, comfortable accommodation; most of the rooms have en suite facilities, and all are equipped with televisions, telephones and drinks trays.

Ground-floor rooms are old-fashioned in style, with original beams, while those above have a more modern look, with smart pine furniture. One room has facilities for disabled guests.

65 RIVERSIDE COTTAGE & HORNES B&B

Great Bricett, nr Ipswich, Suffolk IP7 7DQ
Tel: 01473 658266
website: www.riversidecottagebandb.co.uk

Two Elizabethan thatched cottages make up the accommodation at the **Riverside Cottage & Hornes B&B**, which stands close to the 11th century church in the village of Great Bricett.

The main house has a double (£55 per night) and a twin bedroom (£60 per night), both with en suite facilities, and the day starts with a good choice for breakfast; evening meals are available by arrangement. Resident owners Charles and Jane Horne also offer self-catering accommodation in a self-contained one-bedroom studio adjoining the thatched house. The large garden provides gentle strolls, pleasant views, a tree house and a swimming pool. Riverside Cottage stands just off the B1078 Needham Market to Bildeston road.

66 ST EDMUNDSBURY CATHEDRAL

Angel Hill, Bury St Edmunds,
Suffolk IP33 1LS
Tel: 01284 754933 Fax: 01284 768655
website: www.stedscathedral.co.uk

The site of Suffolk's Cathedral has been one of pilgrimage and worship for almost 1,000 years. One church within the precinct of a Norman Abbey was built by Abbot Anselm in the 12th century and was dedicated to St James. The nave of today's church, started in 1503, is the

successor to that church, and though little remains of the abbey following the dissolution in 1539, St James' Church has continued to grow over the years and in 1914 it became the Cathedral Church of the Diocese of Saint Edmundsbury and Ipswich. Outstanding features of the Cathedral include a magnificent hammerbeam roof and a monumental bishop's throne.

68 THE OLD PEAR TREE

Whepstead, Suffolk IP29 4UD
Tel: 01284 850470
e-mail: jennyatpeartree@tiscali.co.uk
website: www.theoldpeartree.itgo.com

Less than six miles from Bury St Edmunds and the medieval towns of Lavenham and Long Melford, **The Old Pear Tree** offers homely bed and breakfast accommodation amongst the beautiful Suffolk countryside. This family run B&B has been in the capable hands of Jennifer Hobbs for four years now and in that time the place has built up a fine reputation and on approach it is easy to see how. The main house is spectacular; set in beautifully landscaped gardens, the 16th century red brick construction

fits in perfectly with the surrounding countryside. Indeed the location lends itself to walkers, cyclists and tourists as it is quite close to several attractions; sightseeing in Cambridge, watching the races at Newmarket or just strolling around Ickworth Country Park.

There are three rooms available, the family suite which has a King sized bed, a single bed and a cot, as well as an en suite, a double room with en suite and a twin room with a private bathroom. All of the rooms are named for different types of pear; the Conference, the Bartlett and the El Dorado.

67 BRIGHTHOUSE FARM

Melford Road, Lawshall,
nr Bury St Edmunds, Suffolk IP29 4PX
Tel: 01284 830385 Fax: 01284 830974
e-mail: brighthouse-farm@btconnect.com
website: www.brighthousefarm.co.uk

Guests are given a very warm welcome on arrival at **Brighthouse Farm** by John, Roberta and Odell Truin; who have lived and farmed in the area for five generations. The main house is certainly not easy to miss; painted a warm pink, this timber built, Georgian farmhouse is set in large landscaped gardens that are teeming with life. Free for everyone to enjoy and well stocked with trees, shrubs and flowers, you may also see owls, pheasants, or the odd deer!

The main house itself offers bed and breakfast in the form of three large, individually decorated rooms, two doubles and one twin, all with en suite facilities. Some even have their own sitting rooms for relaxing after a hard days sightseeing. In addition to the farmhouse, there are other forms of accommodation; The Terrace is a ground floor development which offers more B & B rooms, one double and one twin, both luxuriously appointed and feature patio doors which open onto a private terrace. The terrace has flower beds, a water feature and comfortable patio table, chairs and parasol from which to enjoy the morning sunshine.

There is also a self catering option; The Granary Suites have comfy double bedrooms with en suites, sitting rooms and fully equipped kitchens in recently a renovated grain loft. The suites are accessed by an exterior staircase, ensuring the suites full self sufficiency. Another option is the beautifully restored detached cottage; dating back to the period of Queen Anne (early 18th century), The Court sleeps up to five people in a double room with en suite and balcony, a twin room and a single room. Centrally heated, there is a well stocked kitchen, a dining area, a comfortable lounge with cottage furniture and log burning stove. For those who prefer to tow their home behind them, Brighthouse Farm boasts a quiet area of the farm with perfect views

over rolling countryside reserved for campers and caravans. The site has toilets, showers and electric hook-ups.

A magnificent full English breakfast cooked on the Aga in the farmhouse kitchen is served in the conservatory dining room, which overlooks the landscaped gardens. Brighthouse Farm is the perfect place from which to explore the surrounding countryside, made famous by East Anglian artists such as John Constable who captured the enormous blue skies and golden corn fields.

69 SCHOOL BARN FARM

Pentlow, Sudbury, Suffolk CO10 7JN
Tel: 01787 282556
e-mail: janesouthin@aol.com
website: www.schoolbarnfarm.co.uk

Set amongst the beautiful countryside of the Stour Valley, **School Barn Farm** offers country bed and breakfast and spa breaks in conjunction with nearby Atlantic Health & Spa. The handsome main house sits in twelve acres of land, all attractively landscaped and available for all of the guests. School Barn Farm takes the threat of the energy crisis very seriously and is committed to obtaining full sustainability and the reduction of their carbon footprint. Measures taken include the installation of solar energy panels, wood burners, the use of local or their own produce and links to other rural establishments.

The two bedrooms are individually decorated; the king size room is very homely and boasts a private bathroom, the twin room has ensuite facilities and has been furnished to a

high standard including flat screen tv and wi-fi. As a treat, both rooms feature indulgent, relaxing aromatherapy toiletries made locally and using the best natural products and ingredients.

Pentlow is ideally situated to explore the attractions of Cavendish, Clare, Long Melford and Lavenham. The Pinkuah Arms, a warm and friendly local pub, is within easy walking distance.

70 THE PINKUAH ARMS

Pinkuah Lane, Pentlow, Sudbury,
Suffolk CO10 7JW
Tel: 01787 280857
e-mail: mike_gate@live.co.uk
website: www.pinkuaharms.co.uk

Known locally as 'Pinkies', this 17th century pub is ably run by Mike and Laura, who between them boast many years of experience in the hospitality industry. **The Pinkuah Arms** has undergone an extensive restoration in recent years and the result is a bright and contemporary pub which embraces the traditional features such as exposed beams along the ceiling and the splendid inglenook fireplace. Brightly coloured pink on the outside sets the warm and friendly tone for your visit, inside the light and airy décor makes for a welcoming atmosphere, emphasised by the smiling staff behind the bar and serving the food.

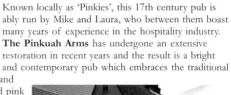

Laura provides all of the food, and the restaurant plays host to themed dining evenings once a month, for example, there is a Sicilian night, a Mexican night

and a feast of fish, all with food directly related to the name. As well as these, there is a regular pie and

pint night for just £8.00. Also a popular entertainment venue, the Pinkuah Arms regularly has live music on Saturday nights, for those who don't want to go home, a short walk away is the School Barn Farm (see above) in **Pentlow** which offers fine accommodation.

71 THE COCK INN AT CLARE

Caliss Street, Clare, Suffolk CO10 8PX
Tel: 01787 277391
e-mail: victoriasoutham@yahoo.co.uk

The Cock Inn at Clare is a thriving family business dedicated to the locals that keep the place alive. It is easily located in the heart of the charming town of Clare which sits on the banks of the River Stour.

Owners Simon and Victoria Eichorn have over 12 years of experience in the pub and restaurant trade and give a fantastic service to all those that come here. They have built up a strong following from locals and offer a hearty welcome to tourists, ramblers, cyclists, families, dogs, large groups and individuals all year round and have good disabled access.

The Inn itself dates back to the 1530's sporting a mature, warm atmosphere that makes you feel at home. There is good sized separate meeting room ideal for family parties or group meetings and a separate restaurant

which serves a fine selection of bar meals, sandwiches and main meals which are all beautifully home cooked and locally sourced available from 12-2pm and 6:30-9pm Mon-Sat and 12-4pm on Sundays. In the summer months there is a large secluded garden complete with a sheltered decking area where you can soak up the summer sunshine. Open daily from 12-3pm and 5pm-midnight Tues-Fri and noon until midnight on weekends.

72 NATIONAL HORSERACING MUSEUM

99 High Street, Newmarket, Suffolk CB8 0XE
Tel: 01638 667333 Fax: 01638 665600
website: www.nationalstud.co.uk

"The Newmarket Experience" comprises two separate attractions: **The National Horseracing Museum** and **The National Stud**. The story of racing throughout the ages is told through the Museum's permanent collections, featuring the horses, people, events and scandals that make the sport so colourful.

Highlights include the head of Persimmon, a great Royal Derby winner in 1896; a special display about Fred Archer, the Victorian jockey who committed suicide after losing the struggle to keep his weight down; the skeleton of Eclipse, ancestor of 90 per cent of modern thoroughbreds; items associated with Red Rum, Lester Piggott, Frankie Dettori and other heroes of the Turf. In the Practical Gallery, visitors can learn everything there is to know about the horse and jockey, and experience the thrill of riding on the horse simulator. The Gallery is

staffed by retired jockeys and trainers, who make the world of racing come alive. Special exhibitions have included "*Why* did you get that hat?", a display of Gertrude Shilling's outrageous Ascot outfits. Mrs Shilling (1910-1999) was one of the most colourful and eccentric personalities ever to grace the sport.

The National Stud extends a warm welcome to all its visitors. Breeding top-class thoroughbreds, the 500-acre site has 12 yards, 9 miles of roads and tracks, 60 miles of post and rail fencing, 21 houses, a feedmill and storage for 50 tons of hay and straw - all purpose built between 1963 and 1967.

73 THE CROWN

69 Crown Street, Brandon,
Suffolk IP27 0JU
Tel: 01842 810523
e-mail: thecrown.brandon@yahoo.co.uk

Back in the 50's, a flint built public house on Town Street in Brandon was demolished and replaced by the well loved inn standing there now. Still called **The Crown**, the replacement building has a lot of charm and character, bay windows and a unique shape create a welcoming feel as you approach the front door. The interior has been tastefully decorated with soft seating dotted around. Andy and Sharon encourage all kinds of visitors, walkers, cyclists and families from nearby Centre Parks to come and simply relax.

Utilising the space inside very well, there is a large restaurant area and a separate bar for those who just want to enjoy a quiet pint. The restaurant is very popular and with good reason, the menu made up of those classic pub favourites but created using local produce and fresh to order.

Monday to Thursday the pub is open between 12pm - 2pm and 4.30pm – midnight but is open all day Friday, Saturday and Sunday.

74 BRANDON COUNTRY PARK

Bury Road, Brandon, Suffolk IP27 0SU
Tel: 01842 810185

For thousands of years the area, where **Brandon Country Park** is now, was an open, sandy, windswept heath. Until 1942, when Lakenheath airbase was built, it was Europe's largest inland sand dune system.

Edward Bliss, a businessman, bought over a thousand hectares of the Brecks in 1820 to create a wooded park and arboretum. By the end of World War1, the park had fallen into neglect. As a result of the economic depression caused by the war, the Government was determined to become self-sufficient in timber. Thetford Forest, planted in 1927, is one of the lowland forests they created. At the end of the last century, English Nature leased land from the Forestry Commission to return some of the commercial forestry areas to the original heathland. Brandon Park Heath, only a mile from the Visitor Centre, is the result. In just under 200 years, we've come full-circle.

When you and your family want to enjoy nature, and learn about the environment and its history, visit Brandon Country Park. At Brandon, you can stroll and picnic in the charming walled garden. You can also head further afield, following the invigorating walks and cycle trails that guide you through the arboretum, commercial forest and restored heathland.

267

75 LA CASCADA

Fox Street, Ardleigh, Colchester,
Essex CO7 7PP
Tel: 01206 864030 Fax: 01206 868959
e-mail: r.lacascada@gmail.com

A truly authentic Spanish restaurant set in four lovely acres of Essex countryside, **La Casacada** is well known in the Colchester area for fine food, excellent service and a delightful dining experience. The exterior is modern and kept meticulous by managers Emma and David who are keen to ensure that every guest has a great visit. Inside the restaurant boasts a modern and contemporary decor that creates a welcoming and relaxed atmosphere enhanced by the sumptuous smells emanating from the kitchen.

Colchester has the distinction of being the oldest recorded town in the U.K. and being on the edge of Constable country; the area around La Cascada is certainly worth exploring. The

chefs make good use of the location by sourcing only the best local ingredients for the extensive Spanish menu. Dishes in this stunning menu include paella, tapas, suckling pig, lots of fresh fish and grilled steaks.

A selection of fine wines allow special wine tasting evenings and La Casacada is more than capable of hosting those special occasions, with room for large functions. An outside barbeque area is well used during the summer months and the large garden creates an excellent summer dining area.

76 THE WHALEBONE INN

Chapel Road, Fingringhoe,
Colchester CO5 7BG
Tel: 01206 729307
e-mail: vicki@thewhaleboneinn.co.uk
website: www.thewhaleboneinn.co.uk

Set at the top of the Roman river valley, and looking out over what is said to be some of the best scenery in Essex, **The Whalebone Inn** provides more than just an excellent meal. Just minutes from Colchester and Fingringhoe Nature Reserve, this grade II listed building also has a converted barn on the site which plays host to functions of all sizes and types. The building makes a good first impression as you arrive, clean and tidy, there are several flower pots and boxes dotted around the front and in the large beer garden. Looking out over the Roman river valley, the garden is a great place to set a marquee for a function or simply enjoy a quiet pint.

Inside the open fireplace, exposed beams and

wooden floors create a feeling of opulence and style as you recline in the leather sofas and admire the sculptures and artwork. The emphasis here is on quality food, created using the finest of locally sourced produce and cooked fresh to order, the menu packed full of delicious dishes. To accompany the food is a superb wine list, featuring great wines from Europe and the New World.

77 THE BAKE HOUSE

5 High Street, Wivenhoe,
Colchester CO7 9BJ
Tel: 01206 824369
e-mail:
info@thebakehouserestaurant.co.uk
website: www.wivenhoebakehouse.co.uk

Brimming with character and exuding period charm, this Grade-II listed building was the local bakery until 1957 before being brought back to life as **The Bake House** restaurant in 2003, complete with charred beams overhead signifying where the bakery ovens once lived.

Simon, who managed the restaurant since 2003, has now taken over the ownership along with his partner Sue from his parents Phil and Sue, continuing the reputation of good food, good wine and a warm welcome.

The menu here changes on a monthly basis, taking advantage of ingredients at their seasonal best and keeping things exciting for regular diners, as well as for creative-minded Chef, Derek Bryne. These fresh ingredients are sourced from the local area, reaping the rewards of East Anglia's fertility, and the resulting dishes are predominantly influenced by staples of British cuisine, but always feature an unmistakable soupcon of French flair.

Once seated in the intimate and elegant Bake House dining room, Simon is on hand to advise you of the comprehensive wine list and what wines best accompany the dishes whilst the waiters serve everyone with dedication and a smile and are always discreetly on hand for any requests.

This excellent restaurant is perfect for private parties and even small wedding receptions. Bespoke menus for up to 38 guests and buffets for a maximum of 45 diners can be created, with fabulous wine-tasting evenings, a dedicated team and amazing food – with everything from the fresh rolls to the chocolates handmade on site - there are surely awards aplenty waiting in the wings for this rising star.

Open: Weds-Sat 6.30 pm - 9.30pm; Sun noon 3pm
(other times by arrangement, for parties of ten or more)

269

78 MARLBOROUGH HEAD INN

Mill Lane, Dedham,
near Colchester, Essex CO7 6DH
Tel: 01206 323250
e-mail: jen.pearmain@tiscali.co.uk
website: www.marlborough-head.co.uk

In the heart of Constable Country in the charming village of Dedham just off the A12 sits the magnificent **Marlborough Head Inn**. Owner Jenny Pearmain offers great home cooked food, real ales, wines and coffees and fantastic accommodation all year round. Open from 11am-11pm daily this historic grade II* listed building retains its red roof and original oak beaming, and also sports a beautiful walled beer garden and sun trap terrace to enjoy.

The bar area is fresh and light yet holds that country feel, serving green King IPA, Adnams and Woodfordes Wherry before a real fire, with a pool table and flat screen TV nearby.

There are three en suite rooms to choose from; the luxurious Constable suite complete with an impressive four poster bed to sink into; the Munnings room another beautifully decorated double room and the Stour room with twin bed accommodation. Hospitality and relaxed atmosphere are combined here with the architectural character to guarantee an enjoyable stay.

80 THE KINGS ARMS

Broad Green near Coggeshall,
Colchester, Essex CO6 1RU
Tel: 01376 562006

Situated on the A120 between Marks Tey and Braintree, 6 miles from the historic walled town of Colchester is the Kings Arms, where John Murrey looks after the real ale and his partner Chris takes care of the country appetites.

The pub is open from 12-8pm Mon-Sat serving a variety of home cooked pub favourites including steak and ale pie; chicken, bacon and leek pie; steak and kidney pudding; fish pie, rabbit stew and other game dishes. There is a great children's menu and the option to dine outside in the large family beer garden in the warmer weather or the chance to sit in front of a roaring log fire in colder months.

John and Chris also now offer a large double/family room sleeping up to four if needed. It has great en suite facilities with its own shower, tv/freeview and tea and coffee making facilities. A great country pub the Kings Arms also provides entertainment with karaoke on the last Friday of every month and quiz night on Thursdays.

1 Stoneham Street, Coggeshall, Colchester,
Essex CO6 1TT
Tel: 01376 563242

Coggeshall is one of those ancient market towns that are just steeped in history, with old, pretty buildings lining the streets and monuments still standing from bygone ages, **The Clockhouse** is one such monument, standing proudly overlooking Coggeshall's market suare. Although the actual business is relatively new, the grade II building in which it is situated has a long and varied story. Originally built in the 14th century, this unique blue and white clock tower was rebuilt in 1887 to commemorate Queen Victoria's jubilee and was once used as a school for the poor children of the town. Approaching the cafe gives you time to admire the large bay window that floods the tea room with light and the quaintly wonky front door.

Inside is equally special; there isn't a straight wall in the place and the exposed beams with the wooden floors create a warm and cosy feeling as you are welcomed by the friendly and convivial staff. None of the furniture matches, all of the wooden tables and chairs have been chosen completely at random, as well as all of the tea cups and tea pots, but this only serves to enhance the charm. While it is a joy to sit inside, during the warmer months it is possible to sit outside, watch the world go by and enjoy a cup of Earl Grey.

Alongside the large range of teas and coffees, The Clockhouse has built up a fine reputation for good food and serves a huge selection of breakfasts, cakes, scones, and various hot meals. All of the food is cooked fresh to order using only the finest of locally sourced ingredients and in tried and tested recipes. Extremely popular is the extensive dessert menu, which features among many others; hot chocolate cake with ice cream, apple crumble and various cakes.

A new development at The Clockhouse is the recently created accommodation; comprising two en suite rooms, guests will be able to appreciate the fine antique and speciality shops in Coggeshall for longer by enjoying a comfortable night's sleep.

271

Wethersfield Road, Finchingfield, Braintree,
Essex CM7 4NR
Tel: 01371 810165
e-mail: enquiries@3tunspub.co.uk
website: www.3tunspub.co.uk

A well presented public house and restaurant, **The Three Tuns** is waiting to take your order. As well as a restaurant, The Three Tuns has two rooms available for bed and breakfast, both offered at reasonable prices. There is a large en-suite double bedroom, which boasts a luxury 42" Sky television. The second room is a comfortably sized medium double, which has the use of a luxury bathroom that includes a sumptuous roll top bath. Inside, the place is beautifully decorated, with all rooms finished to a high standard. There is a natural colour scheme throughout the building and there is plenty of charm and character oozing from the place.

The restaurant seats between 30 and 50 people and offers a tempting selection of freshly prepared food using, whenever possible, locally sourced produce. The Three Tuns is renowned for its scrumptious food. The menu is extensive, offering a wide choice of cuisine to please the fussiest of eaters. All of the dishes are reasonably priced, with home made soup of the day and

deep fried brie with home made chutney among the favourite starters. Moving on to the main courses, there are plenty of different meat options, as well as vegetarian alternatives. Calves' liver and bacon with Madeira onion gravy is a popular choice as well as pork fillet with a mushroom and cream sauce, and also the country vegetable bake. The dessert board is extremely tempting, even for those who aren't known for being sweet toothed. Dinner

reservations can be made over the telephone or online and this is advised to avoid disappointment at busy times. After sampling the delicious dishes on offer and the fine drinks from the bar, the comfortable lounge area, adjacent to the bar, is a great place to relax and unwind. It might be exactly what you need after a long day exploring the surrounding rolling countryside.

Owners, Maria and Mike Stone, are extremely friendly hosts and look forward to welcoming you for a meal or drink at the newly refurbished Three Tuns. The bar is extensively stocked with a selection of beers, lagers and wine by the glass or bottle. There is a fantastic lunch menu available offering a selection of new and traditional favourites and daily specials that take advantage of seasonal and local produce. The Sunday lunch menu, with choices of beef, chicken or lamb, is available each week between 12.30pm and 4pm.

Peterfield Lane, Gosfield, Essex CO9 1PU
Tel: 01787 479602
e-mail: jacquie@gosfieldshoppingvillage.co.uk
website: www.gosfieldshoppingvillage.com.uk

Stretching out over nine acres of Essex countryside between Halstead and Braintree, the **Gosfield Shopping Village** is former family farm that now hosts an array of independent shops under one cover and on one level. Open seven days a week, the complex also boasts a restaurant, a farm shop and an antiques and collectors barn. The independent shops are varied, from a Natural Twist; which is a company specialising in handmade bath and body products, to 'Bags of Class', a classy shop for classy ladies.

In addition to the shopping centre, there are eight acres of grassland that make an ideal space for horse and dog shows, caravan rallies, country fairs, the list is endless.

The restaurant and tea room in the courtyard serves a selection of sandwiches, jacket potatoes, Panini, salads and all sorts of snacks to restore the diminished energy levels from a hard days shop! Extremely popular are the monthly yard sales, they operate on the same principle as car boot sales just in the yard and are held on the first Sunday of each month. Open from 9 am till 5 pm each day although the shops are independent and so opening times may differ.

 findSOMEWHERE.CO.uk

For people who want to explore Britain and Ireland

Places to Visit

Our easy-to use website contains details and locations of places to stay, places to eat and drink, specialist shops and places of interest throughout England, Wales, Scotland and Ireland.

Places to Stay:	Places to Eat and Drink:	Places of Interest:	Specialist Shops:	Gardens:
Hotels, guest accommodation, bed & breakfast, inns, self-catering accommodation	Restaurants, pubs, inns, cafes, tea rooms	Historic buildings, gardens, art galleries, museums, nature parks, wildlife parks, indoor and outdoor activities	Fashion shops, art and craft shops, gift shops, food and drink shops, antique shops, jewellery shops	Garden centres and retail nurseries

9 Osbournes Court, Victoria Place,
Brightlingsea, Colchester, Essex CO7 0EB
Tel: 01206 305565
e-mail: mike@mooch-no9.co.uk

Peaceful and quiet, the quaint sea side town of Brightlingsea has a lot going for it, situated on the mouth of the river Colne, the area is well attended each year for various marine events. Visitors could do a lot worse than spend some time at **Mooch @ No 9**, a smart and cosmopolitan cafe which fits in well with the local European cafe culture. Set in the middle of the town centre, Mooch @ No 9 is frequented by a wide range of customers from a wide range of

backgrounds. The recently built property does not detract from the charm and character instilled by owner of five years Mike Palfrey, who has decorated in a modern and contemporary manner. Using bright colours such as burnt orange and white, Mike has created a light and airy interior, which is the perfect place to sit awhile, watch the world go past and enjoy a hot beverage.

Flagstone flooring throughout promotes a quality feel to the establishment as soon as you enter and the smiling staff couldn't be friendlier as they ensure you have a great dining experience. A nice touch is the quality crockery and cutlery used; they're modern, white and wavy and more than adequate for presenting a Panini on! The food is exquisite; all of the ingredients being locally sourced and dishes created fresh to order ensuring the high standards of the cafe remain so. Sandwiches, Panini, bagels, the choices are almost endless and there is certainly something for every taste and preference.

The cafe is open between 8.30 am and 4.30 pm Monday to Saturday and is closed on Sundays. There is no disabled toilet but there are access facilities.

Market Place, Great Dunmow,
Essex CM6 1AX
Tel: 01371 874321 Fax: 01371 876642
e-mail: starrrestaurant@btinternet.com
website: www.the-starr.co.uk

Advertising itself as a 'Restaurant with rooms', **The Starr** manages to supply warm and comfortable accommodation along with simply stunning food to create a memorable dining experience. This timber built 15th century inn is owned and run by Terry and Louise George, who have been in the local area for more than 25 years, they are therefore well placed to provide expert guidance on local attractions and points of interest. The knowledge gained over the years includes a good understanding with suppliers; the George's are able to ensure that only the best of local produce is delivered and used by the excellent chefs.

Set in the bustling market place of Great Dunmow, The Starr is a traditional looking building complete with quaintly uneven walls and a black and white paint job set off nicely by the many colourful window boxes. Inside is just as full of charm, with plenty of exposed beams and uneven ceilings throughout the dining areas and into the bedrooms. The main buildings holds the dining area and the conference rooms whilst there is an old stable block to the rear which has been tastefully renovated into accommodation. Eight individually decorated rooms are available for hire and each have their own selling points; the Pine room has a corner bath with his and her marble washbasins, and the Oak room boasts a four poster bed and a free standing Victorian bath. Other options include the Blue room, the Poppy room and the Brass room; you are sure to find a purely individual room unlike any standardised hotel chain.

Serving food from Tuesday to Sunday lunchtime, the restaurant has several a la carte menus with a variety of mouth watering options; during the week there is the standard luncheon menu or a set 3 course market lunches for just £19.50. The Starr also offers a 5 course tasting menu alongside the dinner menu, which is perfect for a group who are just a little peckish. Sunday is a more traditional lunch with a choice of 7 or 8 starters and main courses. For any with dietary requirements, the chef team are more than happy to cater for specific needs. There are also two conference rooms that can be used for that important business meeting or special occasion; the Oak room is slightly smaller than the Market room, although both can be used simultaneously.

**Swan Lane, Margaretting Tye,
Essex CM4 9JX
Tel: 01277 840478
e-mail: liz@thewhitehart.com
website: www.thewhitehart.com**

Owner Liz Haines and her team of friendly staff have established **The White Hart** as one of the best pubs in the whole region. The pub is a traditional Essex weather-board building, consisting of a large single bar and an extensive family room/conservatory. The rural setting lends itself to a number of excellent walks which makes it a popular choice with ramblers, cyclists and tourists. The pub is located on Swan Lane; a grade II listed street running from Stock to Galleywood & Margaretting. The frontage is always adorned with flower baskets and boxes and the gardens are beautifully maintained all year round. Inside the bar area is heavily beamed with a vaulted ceiling and a wood burning stove, a welcome source of warmth on cold winter days, all of

which adds to the cosy, traditional ambience. An extensive collection of beer and champagne bottles decorate the shelves around the bar and the walls are festooned with old pictures (some of the pub in days gone by, and others of agricultural scenes) and pub and brewery memorabilia.

There is always a fine selection of excellent real ales. Liz, ably assisted by Barry Mott, the cellar man, keeps an enviable cellar with house beers coming from local champion brewer Mighty Oak (Oscar Wilde Mild and IPA) and regional stalwart Adnams (Best and Broadside). Apart from this selection, which would get the majority of pubs a fair write up in the pages of GBBG, Liz always has a minimum of 3 to 4 other guest ales serving. All are poured directly from the barrel in the tap room behind the bar. They have recently been awarded Chelmsford & Mid-Essex CAMRA Pub of the Year as a result of their achievements in this area.

The White Hart has an excellent reputation as a really good place to eat. The long standing Chef Ting Sayer puts the emphasis on using only quality produce sourced locally when available. Food is available 7 days a week with a wide range of meals and snacks. A selection of 'Daily Specials' are featured on a huge blackboard that hangs over the fireplace in the main bar.

Two key events during the year are a stunning Summer Beer Festival in June with over 60 beers, ciders and perry in a marquee that could put the Chelsea Flower Show to shame (in size if not flora and fauna!!); and a smaller winter Beer Festival over the last weekend in October. Liz has recently added B & B facilities to the already wonderful establishment; two en suite rooms are available for hire at very reasonable rates.

7 Warley Street, Great Warley,
Brentwood CM13 3LB
Tel: 01277 217107
e-mail: info@thekilnshotel.co.uk
website: www.thekilnshotel.co.uk

Often referred to as Brentwood's best kept secret. **The Kilns Hotel** is a splendid 3 storey story Queen Anne house, grade II listed with an early 18th century brick façade that masks elements that date back as far as the 16th century. Whilst the exterior captures that olde worlde appearance of that era, the interior has been completely renovated to the highest standards producing a beautiful contemporary boutique style hotel. Each room has its own individuality with comfort and relaxation in mind.

Just off junction 29 of the M25, the Kilns is situated just 3.5 miles from Brentwood and Upminster town centres in the conservation village of Great Warley, which has a number of country pubs, national trust parks, golf courses and historical buildings such as the Parish Church of St. Mary the Virgin; with its renowned Art Deco interior. The Kilns is only 30 minutes from the metropolis of London and approximately 3½ hours from Paris via Ebbsfleet International train station, which is approximately 26 minutes away with regular trains travelling to Europe. Well placed geographically, The Kilns is also conveniently located within easy access to Stansted Airport to the North West and London city to the east, both approximately 30 minuets drive. London Gatwick airport is 44 miles and London Heathrow Airport is 58 miles.

The Kilns is privately owned and is managed by Luke Bonnett who is available most days and is likely to be the one who will greet you upon your arrival and will then confidently leave you in the capable hands of his helpful and friendly staff. The owners hotel policy is expressed in its company motto which reads *"Your comfort is our pleasure"* and you can be sure that during your stay you will receive the very best the hotel has to offer.

The Kilns boasts 15 excellent rooms which are decorated and furnished to a high standard. Each room is centrally heated and has modern en-suite shower or bath rooms, with hot water on demand. All the rooms are bright, elegant and comfortable and are fully equipped with wireless internet, digital TV, in-room telephones and tea and coffee making facilities. House keeping can provide a laundry service upon request.

In addition to the beautiful guest rooms there is also the splendid, cosy and intimate White Napkin lounge bar and restaurant. There is an air of sophistication in these two rooms with a mixture of contemporary and classic furnishings. The bar and dining room are open to guests and public all year round. The crisp chic of the dining room creates a sense of freshness, but the fine food, good company and seamless service guarantee to give each meal a more intimate feel. The bar serves a good selection of wines, spirits, beers, soft drinks, teas and coffees to accompany a careful selected menu of the finest seasonal produce.

This can be extended for other services, as the Kilns hotel is also available to be hired for private functions and is particularly popular with wedding parties, corporate events and family reunions – please ring for details.

Whatever the occasion; a romantic break away, a family get together, or simply a comfortable nights stay for the discerning business man, the Kilns hotel is the perfect choice.

87 ESSEX MARINA BAR

Essex Marina, Wallasea Island,
Rochford, Essex SS4 2HF
Tel: 01702 258936

The Essex Marina can be found on the River
Crouch, in the heart of an area of outstanding
natural beauty; just 7 miles from Southend and
an hour's drive from London, Essex Marina
attracts visitors from all over the south-east.
Ever busy, the marina is well served by the
Essex Marina Bar, where all of the marina's
visitors go for a cold pint, well cooked meal and
a gossip with the local sailors. Thoroughly
modern and contemporary, yet charming and
full of character, the bar overlooks the river
Crouch and the balcony is one of the finest
places to spend a summer evening!

Inside the decor is tastefully done, with oak floors and sofas
creating a cosy atmosphere that is perfect for relaxing in. Debbie
Knight is the manager and her experience has been key in
promoting the bar's appeal to the boat owners, members of the
yacht club, passengers from the ferry and the other hundreds of
people who pass through every week. The Marina Bar also serves
great food all week long, including the popular roast dinner on
Sundays.

88 THE ROSE & CROWN

Minnow's End, Great Waltham,
Chelmsford, Essex CM3 1AG
Tel: 01245 360359
e-mail: roseandcrown268@aol.com
website:
www.roseandcrowngreatwaltham.co.uk

Licensees Richard and Kate welcomes visitors
to the **Rose & Crown** with warm smiles, a fine
variety of real
ales and a
country menu
featuring local
produce,
traditionally
cooked. This
is definitely a
place for real
ale enthusiasts, with familiar brews from Sharps
and Nethergate Doombar joined by weekly
changing guests from local breweries.

The bar is open for food and drink from 12
– 2 at lunchtime and 6 -9 every evening and all
day Saturday and Sunday. TV racing in the snug
is a Saturday treat for racing fans.

HIDDEN PLACES GUIDES

Explore Britain and Ireland with
Hidden Places guides - a fascinating
series of national and local travel
guides.

Packed with easy to read information
on hundreds of places of interest as
well as places to stay, eat and drink.

Available from both high street and
internet booksellers

For more information on the full range
of *Hidden Places* guides and other
titles published by Travel Publishing
visit our website on

www.travelpublishing.co.uk
or ask for our leaflet by phoning
01752 697280 or emailing
info@travelpublishing.co.uk

89 COMPASSES INN

Littley Green, Chelmsford CM3 1BU
Tel: 01245 362308
e-mail:
compasseslittleygreen@googlemail.com
website: www.compasseslittleygreen.co.uk

No Jukeboxes, no music – just real fire, real ale, real food, a real welcome and real conversation. That's the motto of Joss Ridley who owns Compasses Inn, a delightfully picturesque country Inn situated in the quiet rural hamlet of Littley Green, ideally located for visitors from Chelmsford, Felsted, Braintree, Great Dunmow, Little/Great Waltham and Great Leigh's race course.

This traditional wood panelled and stone floored country pub promises a night in the slow lane, with real ales from Essex Breweries drawn by hand from the well stocked cellar. The speciality of the house, the Essex Huffer (a large traingular bap generously filled with various local ingredients), is available every lunchtime and evening. The pub is open Mon-Wed noon to 3pm and 5.30pm to midnight and Thurs-Sun noon to midnight. In the summer months this can all be enjoyed from one of the two

finely kept gardens, ideal for families and children to play in, where the original slate roofing and red brick country style can be admired at leisure. The relaxed atmosphere and rural environment make a perfect spot to sit back and enjoy the simpler pleasures.

90 THE HOT PLATE CAFÉ

10 High Street, Maldon CM9 5PJ
Tel: 01621 850504
e-mail: thehotplatecafe@aol.co.uk

Maldon has the distinction of being the second oldest town in England, this port plays host to, among other things, the mud race, the world's heaviest man and a winter torchlight carnival! Providing excellent home cooked food and snacks for the many visitors is **The Hot Plate Café**. Ideally situated on the high street, this café is ably run by Wendy and Chris and welcomes everybody; children, locals and tourists alike. Newly opened, the contemporary décor incorporates traditional beams and a brick construction fireplace to create a modern, bright and airy feel to the place. The grade II listed building boasts a glass frosted shop front which creates a great spot to sit a while and watch the world drift past as you enjoy a home made snack.

The food is all made fresh to order using the best of locally sourced produce and the menu is full of goodies. Popular favourites include the wonderful home made shepherds' pie, bread and butter pudding and the all day breakfasts. The café is open for breakfast and lunch all week long, between 8 am and 4 pm.

112 Station Road, Burnham on Crouch,
Essex CM0 8HR
Tel: 01621 786496
e-mail: trevor@theoystersmack.co.uk
website: www.theoystersmack.co.uk

Built in the 1800's, this smart building sets the scene for this extremely popular and high quality inn; oozing charm and character as you approach, the large sash windows and pitched roof create a good impression that doesn't go away. Burnham on Crouch is a lovely modern and contemporary town and **The Oyster Smack** fits in perfectly amongst the friendly streets, impressive townhouses and the busy yacht marina. The Oyster Smack is owned and run by Trevor Howell; a professional chef who trained at Westminster College whose CV includes working with Jamie Oliver in his first restaurant and at Gordon Ramsey's 3 Michelin star winning establishment as a pastry chef.

Inside the newly refurbished dining room is decorated to perfection, classy and timeless, the neutral decor provides a brilliant backdrop to this truly special dining experience. Wooden floors, high quality furniture and linen tablecloths all create an elegant feeling that has the Oyster Smack's reputation increasing every week. Accommodation takes the form of nine en suite rooms, all individually and expertly decorated and guaranteed to provide a warm and comfortable night's sleep. Reasonably priced, the tariff includes a fine breakfast in the mornings and the long running, and at quiet times there is a popular, special offer for dinner, bed and breakfast.

As you would expect from a place where the owner has such a good chef pedigree, the food at the Oyster Smack is spectacular; whether you are just popping in for a snack or a full three course meal as a special occasion. The bar menu features those pub classics that everybody loves; ham, egg and chips, liver and bacon on mash and battered fish and chips are just a few examples. The coastal location means that Trevor can take full advantage of fresh seafood and the Galley restaurant menu utilises these to full effect. Sumptuous examples include monkfish wrapped in pancetta, fillet of sea bass on creamed leeks and market fish of the day accompanied by seasonal garnish. Describing the menu as the best of modern British food, Trevor sources the finest of local ingredients to provide the a la carte menu that has put the Oyster Smack on the map.

Church Street, Histon, nr Cambridge,
Cambridgeshire CB24 9EP
Tel: 01223 233930
e-mail: susieatthekingbill@tiscali.co.uk

The **King William** is a 16th century coaching inn at the top of the village of Histon. The exterior has a very distinctive appearance, with smart white paint, a vast buttress chimney at one end and a steep tiled roof. Inside, exposed brick or plastered walls, original beams and log fires contribute to a very appealing, traditional ambience, and there's a pleasant area for enjoying an alfresco drink outside in the courtyard.

This is Susie Lees second pub; she is passionate about the classic appeal of an English country pub and has made this a popular meeting place for the local community. It's also a delightful escape from the bustle of Cambridge and a good spot to take a break on a journey along the busy A14 (leave at J32).

The drinks list is headed by Greene King IPA, Abbot Ale and St Austell Tribute along with a selection of bottled ales, and there's a happy hour between 5 and 7 on selected drinks.

All the food is prepared and cooked on the premises, and the daily changing blackboard menus make appetising reading: pie of the day (perhaps steak & kidney or chicken & mushroom), warm smoked mackerel salad; gammon with egg or pineapple; chicken with black bean sauce; tandoori chicken; cheese, mushroom & onion pasta; spicy potato wedges; and some scrumptious desserts to finish with a flourish. Senior Citizens' lunchtime specials are served Monday, Thursday and Friday. Opening times are 11.30 to 3 and 5 to 11 (Fri and Sat until midnight Fri, Sat and Sun all day).

Ramsey Road, St Ives,
Cambridgeshire PE27 5RB
Tel: 01480 463122 Fax: 01480 300706
e-mail: mail@slepehall.co.uk
website: www.slepehall.co.uk

Starting life as a Victorian girls' boarding school, **Slepe Hall** is a Grade II listed building offering high standards of service, comfort and cuisine. The best Victorian features have been preserved, sitting happily with the up-to-date comfort and amenities.

The 16 bedrooms, from singles to family rooms, are in individual in style and character: some traditional, some modern, several with very splendid four-poster beds. All have en suite facilities, satellite TV, telephone with modem point, radio-alarm clock, tea/coffee tray and hairdryer. Relaxation is the name of the game throughout this friendly hotel, in the bar, in the lounge or in the pleasant south-facing patio and garden.

Slepe Hall provides a good choice for diners, there is a specially designed family restaurant, AJ's offering an extensive cooked to order children's menu with soft ice creams, non alcohol cocktails and milk shakes. Some dishes are time-and-trusted favourites such as steaks, sausages & creamed potatoes,

liver & bacon, roasts from the carvery and lasagne (meat or vegetarian). Other dishes are more modern or more exotic in style, like chicken, pork & herb terrine, tagliatelle with mint & basil pesto and Thai fish cakes.

As well as very comfortable guest accommodation for both leisure and business guests, Slepe Hall caters admirably for meetings and conferences, with facilities for any number from 2 to 20, and for special occasions. Three rooms are licensed for civil ceremonies, with room for up to 60, and the Brunel Suite, tailor-made for functions, has a private entrance, its own bar, cloakrooms and space for up to 200 guests. The hotel has secure parking for 70 cars.

St Ives has plenty to attract the visitor, including the Portland stone statue of Oliver Cromwell, the beautiful parish church and the fascinating Norris Museum. Close by are Wilthorn Meadow, a Site of Natural History Interest, and the Holt Island Nature Reserve. And the Great Ouse provides some wonderful riverside walks. St Ives is very well connected to the main road network, with the A1, A10 and A14 all just a few minutes' drive away.

93 THE WHITE SWAN

Elsworth Road, Conington,
Cambridgeshire CB23 4LN
Tel: 01954 267251
e-mail: sarah_bleet@hotmail.com

Just 10 miles north of Cambridge is **The White Swan**, located near the A14, it is the perfect place to stop for an excellent meal and drink. Ably managed by Sarah with her son and daughter, this family run pub oozes charm and character with a warm and friendly atmosphere. The pretty 17th century

inn has a lot going for it; a well stocked bar with an open fire, a large dining area and a games room, complete with billiards and darts. Quality home made food is served all week long, there is a large garden, including a secure children's play area and there is ample parking.

96 CHILL OUT

Thorney Road, Guyhirn, Wisbech,
Cambridgeshire PE13 4AD
Tel: 01945 450996

The Chillingworth clan are keen to welcome you to **Chill Out**, a family run restaurant that stops at nothing to ensure every dining occasion is a special one. Now one of only a few non-chain restaurants on the A47; Chill Out is a great place to sample a truly unique meal. Inside the 70+ cover dining area has been well decorated to create a warm and cosy atmosphere that is intensified by the excellent service. Available for private functions in the evening, the sumptuous menu ranges from all day breakfasts to Sunday dinners and from pizzas to sandwiches.

 find**SOMEWHERE**.co.uk

For people who want to explore Britain and Ireland

Specialist Shops

Our easy-to use website contains details and locations of places to stay, places to eat and drink, specialist shops and places of interest throughout England, Wales, Scotland and Ireland.

Places to Stay:	**Places to Eat and Drink:**	**Places of Interest:**	**Specialist Shops:**	**Gardens:**
Hotels, guest accommodation, bed & breakfast, inns, self-catering accommodation	Restaurants, pubs, inns, cafes, tea rooms	Historic buildings, gardens, art galleries, museums, nature parks, wildlife parks, indoor and outdoor activities	Fashion shops, art and craft shops, gift shops, food and drink shops, antique shops, jewellery shops	Garden centres and retail nurseries

283

37 High Street, Earith,
Cambridgeshire PE28 3PP
Tel: 01487 841405 Fax: 01487 740822
e-mail: enquiries@theriverviewinn.co.uk
website: www.theriverviewinn.co.uk

The builders of **The Old Riverview Inn** certainly got the location right when it was constructed back in the 19th century, set in the picturesque village of Earith on the northern banks of the Great Ouse River. Situated on the A1123 between Cambridge and St Ives, the Old Riverview Inn makes the ideal base for those looking to explore the fenlands of Cambridgeshire and beyond. Built as a coaching inn, hospitality is certainly the name of the game at the Riverview and the current hosts do not disappoint. The black and white frontage is clean and well kept; covered in hanging baskets that provide bursts of colour during the spring and summer months, the exterior entices guests in with alarming ease. Inside the story is much the same; lazy dogs sleep by the open fire, a colourful parrot greets you as you enter the door and the smiling staff top off the warm and welcoming atmosphere.

Cliff and Wendy are your gracious hosts and their success has included the purchase of a sister pub, **The Crown Riverside Public House** which a stone's throw from the Riverview Inn. Split into two halves, the Crown has a traditional pub on one side and a more contemporary **Chill Out Bar** that has proven very popular with locals and visitors alike. As the two properties are merely 100 yards apart, they are able to provide the same menu at both with all of the food expertly prepared at the Riverview Inn. Creating fresh and contemporary dishes with hints of traditionalism, the experienced chefs utilise the best of locally sourced ingredients to provide a broad and well thought out menu that truly offers something for every palate.

Just to top things off, the Old Riverview Inn also boasts six very comfortable, en suite rooms for hire. Fully kitted out with all the modern amenities at very reasonable rates, the Old Riverview Inn makes a great place to stay whilst you enjoy everything Cambridgeshire has to offer.

For the more adventurous traveller, Cliff and Wendy also own a 25 foot, four berth boat that has become very popular. After a half hour tutorial, the keys will be handed over and you can enjoy a couple of days exploring the beautiful countryside of Cambridgeshire. This holiday opportunity is perfect for a small family or couple.

Tourist Information Centres

CAMBRIDGESHIRE

CAMBRIDGE
Wheeler Street, Cambridge, Cambridgeshire CB2 3QB
e-mail: tourism@cambridge.gov.uk
Tel: 0906 586 2526

ELY
Oliver Cromwell's House, 29 St Mary's Street, Ely,
Cambridgeshire CB7 4HF
e-mail: tic@eastcambs.gov.uk
Tel: 01353 662062

PETERBOROUGH
3-5 Minster Precincts, Peterborough,
Cambridgeshire PE1 1XS
e-mail: tic@peterborough.gov.uk
Tel: 01733 452336

WISBECH
2-3 Bridge Street, Wisbech, Cambridgeshire PE13 1EW
e-mail: tourism@fenland.gov.uk
Tel: 01945 583263

ESSEX

BRAINTREE
Town Hall Centre, Market Square, Braintree,
Essex CM7 3YG
e-mail: tic@braintree.gov.uk
Tel: 01376 550066

CLACTON-ON-SEA
Town Hall, Station Road, Clacton-on-Sea,
Essex CO15 1SE
e-mail: emorgan@tendringdc.gov.uk
Tel: 01255 686633

COLCHESTER
1 Queen Street, Colchester, Essex CO1 2PG
e-mail: vic@colchester.gov.uk
Tel: 01206 282920

HARWICH
Iconfield Park, Parkeston, Harwich, Essex CO12 4EN
e-mail: harwichtic@btconnect.com
Tel: 01255 506139

MALDON
Wenlock Way, High Street, Maldon, Essex CM9 5AD
e-mail: tic@maldon.gov.uk
Tel: 01621 856503

SAFFRON WALDEN
1 Market Place, Market Square, Saffron Walden,
Essex CB10 1HR
e-mail: tourism@saffronwalden.gov.uk
Tel: 0179 952 4002

SOUTHEND-ON-SEA
Pier Entrance, Western Esplanade, Southend-on-Sea,
Essex SS1 1EE
e-mail: vic@southend.gov.uk
Tel: 01702 215620

SOUTHMINSTER
1 High Street, Southminster, Essex CM0 7AA
e-mail: southminster@one-place.org.uk
Tel: 01621 774239

WALTHAM ABBEY
2 Highbridge Street, Waltham Abbey, Essex EN9 1DG
e-mail: tic@walthamabbey.org.uk
Tel: 01992 652295

NORFOLK

AYLSHAM
Bure Valley Railway Station, Tourist Information Centre,
Norwich Road, Aylsham, Norfolk NR11 6BW
e-mail: aylsham.tic@broadland.gov.uk
Tel: 01263 733903

BURNHAM DEEPDALE
Deepdale Farm, Burnham Deepdale, Norfolk PE31 8DD
e-mail: info@deepdalefarm.co.uk
Tel: 01485 210256

CROMER
Prince of Wales Road, Cromer, Norfolk NR27 9HS
e-mail: cromerinfo@north-norfolk.gov.uk
Tel: 0871 200 3071

DISS
Meres Mouth, Mere Street, Diss, Norfolk IP22 3AG
e-mail: dtic@s-norfolk.gov.uk
Tel: 01379 650523

DOWNHAM MARKET
The Priory Centre, 78 Priory Road, Downham Market,
Norfolk PE38 9JS
e-mail: downham-market.tic@west-norfolk.gov.uk
Tel: 01366 383287

GREAT YARMOUTH

25 Marine Parade, Great Yarmouth, Norfolk NR30 2EN
e-mail: tourism@great-yarmouth.gov.uk
Tel: 01493 846345

HOLT

3 Pound House, Market Place, Holt, Norfolk NR25 6BW
e-mail: holtinfo@north-norfolk.gov.uk
Tel: 0871 200 3071

HOVETON

Station Road, Hoveton, Norfolk NR12 8UR
e-mail: hovetoninfo@broads-authority.gov.uk
Tel: 01603 782281

HUNSTANTON

Town Hall, The Green, Hunstanton, Norfolk PE36 6BQ
e-mail: hunstanton.tic@west-norfolk.gov.uk
Tel: 01485 532610

KING'S LYNN

The Custom House, Purfleet Quay, King's Lynn,
Norfolk PE30 1HP
e-mail: kings-lynn.tic@west-norfolk.gov.uk
Tel: 01553 763044

NORWICH

The Forum, Millennium Plain, Norwich,
Norfolk NR2 1TF
e-mail: tourism@norwich.gov.uk
Tel: 01603 727927

SHERINGHAM

Station Approach, Sheringham, Norfolk NR26 8RA
e-mail: sheringhaminfo@north-norfolk.gov.uk
Tel: 0871 200 3071

SWAFFHAM

The Shambles, Market Place, Swaffham,
Norfolk PE37 7AB
e-mail: swaffham@eetb.info
Tel: 01760 722255

WELLS-NEXT-THE-SEA

Staithe Street, Wells-next-the-Sea, Norfolk NR23 1AN
e-mail: wellstic@north-norfolk.gov.uk
Tel: 0871 200 3071

WYMONDHAM

Market Cross, Market Place, Wymondham,
Norfolk NR18 0AX
e-mail: wymondhamtic@btconnect.com
Tel: 01953 604721

SUFFOLK

ALDEBURGH

152 High Street, Aldeburgh, Suffolk IP15 5AQ
e-mail: atic@suffolkcoastal.gov.uk
Tel: 01728 453637

BECCLES

The Quay, Fen Lane, Beccles, Suffolk NR34 9BH
e-mail: becclesinfo@broads-authority.gov.uk
Tel: 01502 713196

BURY ST EDMUNDS

6 Angel Hill, Bury St Edmunds, Suffolk IP33 1UZ
e-mail: tic@stedsbc.gov.uk
Tel: 01284 764667

FELIXSTOWE

91 Undercliff Road West, Felixstowe, Suffolk IP11 2AF
e-mail: ftic@suffolkcoastal.gov.uk
Tel: 01394 276770

FLATFORD

Flatford Lane, Flatford, East Bergholt, Suffolk CO7 6UL
e-mail: flatfordvic@babergh.gov.uk
Tel: 01206 299460

IPSWICH

St Stephens Church, St Stephens Lane, Ipswich,
Suffolk IP1 1DP
e-mail: tourist@ipswich.gov.uk
Tel: 01473 258070

LAVENHAM

Lady Street, Lavenham, Suffolk CO10 9RA
e-mail: lavenhamtic@babergh.gov.uk
Tel: 01787 248207

LOWESTOFT

East Point Pavilion, Royal Plain, Lowestoft,
Suffolk NR33 0AP
e-mail: touristinfo@waveney.gov.uk
Tel: 01502 533600

NEWMARKET

Palace House, Palace Street, Newmarket,
Suffolk CB8 8EP
e-mail: tic.newmarket@forest-heath.gov.uk
Tel: 01638 667200

SOUTHWOLD

69 High Street, Southwold, Suffolk IP18 6DS
e-mail: southwold.tic@waveney.gov.uk
Tel: 01502 724729

STOWMARKET

Wilkes Way, Stowmarket, Suffolk IP14 1DE
e-mail: tic@midsuffolk.gov.uk
Tel: 01449 676800

SUDBURY

Town Hall, Market Hill, Sudbury, Suffolk CO10 1TL
e-mail: sudburytic@babergh.gov.uk
Tel: 01787 881320

WOODBRIDGE

Station Buildings, Woodbridge, Suffolk IP12 4AJ
e-mail: wtic@suffolkcoastal.gov.uk
Tel: 01394 382240

Towns, Villages and Places of Interest

287

K

Kedington 128
   Church of St Peter and St Paul 128
Kelvedon 143
   Feering and Kelvedon Museum 143
Kelvedon Hatch 169
   Kelvedon Secret Nuclear Bunker 169
Kentford 131
   Gypsy Boy's Grave 131
Kersey 109
   Church of St Mary 109
   Kersey Pottery 109
   Water Splash 109
Kessingland 94
   Africa Alive! Wildlife Park 94
Keyston 206
   Church of St John the Baptist 206
Kimbolton 207
   Kimbolton Castle 207
   St Andrew's Church 207
King's Lynn
   Assembly Room 46
   Caithness Crystal Visitor Centre 47
King's Lynn 45
   Church of St Margaret 46
   Clifton House 46
   Custom House 46
   Greyfriars Tower 47
   Guildhall 46
   King's Lynn Arts Centre 46
   Old Gaol House 46
   Red Mount Chapel 47
   St George's Guildhall 47
   St Nicholas Chapel 45
   Town Hall 46
   Town House Museum 46
   Tuesday Market Place 46

L

Langford 183
   Museum of Power 183
Langham 24
   Langham Glass & Rural Crafts 24
Langmere 12
   100th Bomb Group Memorial Museum 12
Lavenham 110
   Church of St Peter and St Paul 110
   Guildhall 110
   John Constable 110
   Little Hall 110
   The Priory 110
Lawshall 122
   Church of All Saints 122
   Lawshall Hall 122
   Wishing Well 122
Laxfield 78
   Country Fair 78
   Laxfield & District Museum 78
Layer Breton 139
   Stamps and Crows 139
Layer Marney 139
   Layer Marney Tower 139

Leigh-on-Sea 177
   Leigh Heritage Centre 177
Leiston 81
   Leiston Abbey 80
   Long Shop Museum 81
   Sizewell 81
Lessingham 37
   Sutton Windmill 37
Leverington 219
   Church of St Leonard 219
Levington 104
   Trimley Marshes 104
Linford 174
   Walton Hall Museum 174
Linton 201
   Bartlow Hills 202
   Chilford Hall Vineyard 201
   Church of St Mary the Virgin 201
   Linton Zoo 201
Litcham 45
   Village Museum 45
Little Baddow 181
   Blakes Wood 181
Little Barningham 16
   St Mary's Church 16
Little Braxted 181
   Church of St Nicholas 181
Little Clacton 149
   Church of St James 149
Little Downham 192
   Church of St Leonard 192
Little Easton 160
   Church of St Mary 160
   Easton Lodge 160
Little Maplestead 147
   Round Church 147
Little Paxton 207
   Paxton Pits Nature Reserve 207
Little Thurlow 128
Little Walsingham 56
   Augustinian Priory 56
   Clink in Common Place 57
   Franciscan Friary 57
   Holy House 56
   Shrine of Our Lady of Walsingham 56
   Walsingham Shirehall Museum 57
Littleport 192
   St George's Church 192
Lode 197
   Anglesey Abbey 197
Long Melford 124
   Holy Trinity Church 124
   Kentwell Hall 125
   Melford Hall 124
Longthorpe 214
   Longthorpe Tower 214
Loughton 165
   Corbett Theatre 165
   Epping Forest 165
Lound 93
   Church of St John the Baptist 93

Lowestoft 91
   Claremont Pier 92
   Lowestoft & East Suffolk Maritime Museum 92
   Lowestoft Museum 92
   Mincarlo 91
   Oulton Broad 92
   Pleasurewood Hill 92
   Royal Naval Patrol Museum 92
   St Margaret's Church 92
   War Memorial Museum 92

M

Madingley 199
   The American Cemetery 199
Maldon 182
   Combined Military Services Museum 183
   Hythe Quay 183
   Maeldune Heritage Centre 182
   Maldon District Museum 183
   Moot Hall 182
   Plume Library 183
   St Giles the Leper Hospital 183
Manningtree 156
   Manningtree Museum 156
   The Walls 156
March 216
   Church of St Wendreda 216
   Dunhams Wood 216
   March and District Museum 216
   Nene-Ouse Navigation Link 216
Margaretting Tye 169
Mendham 100
Mendlesham 75
   Church of St Mary 75
Mersea Island 152
   Mersea Island Museum 152
   Mersea Island Vineyard 153
Middleton 80
Mildenhall 131
   Mildenhall & District Museum 132
   Mildenhall Treasure 132
   St Mary's 130
Milton 199
   Milton Country Park 199
Mistley 155
   Mistley Quay Workshops 155
   Mistley Towers 155
Monks Eleigh 109
Morston 23
Moulton 131
   Packhorse Bridge 131
Mountnessing 169
   Mountnessing Post Mill 169
Mundesley 35
   Maritime Museum 35
Mundford 39
   Lynford Hall 39
Mundon 184
   St Peter's Way 184

TRAVEL PUBLISHING ORDER FORM

To order any of our publications just fill in the payment details below and complete the order form. For orders of less than 4 copies please add £1.00 per book for postage and packing. Orders over 4 copies are P & P free.

Name:

Address:

Tel no:

Please Complete Either:

I enclose a cheque for £ _____ made payable to Travel Publishing Ltd

Or:

Card No: Expiry Date:

Signature:

Please either send, telephone, fax or e-mail your order to:
Travel Publishing Ltd, Airport Business Centre, 10 Thornbury Road, Estover, Plymouth PL6 7PP
Tel: 01752 697280   Fax: 01752 697299   e-mail: info@travelpublishing.co.uk

	Price	Quantity		Price	Quantity
HIDDEN PLACES REGIONAL TITLES			**COUNTRY LIVING RURAL GUIDES**		
Cornwall	£8.99	....	East Anglia	£10.99	....
Devon	£8.99	....	Heart of England	£10.99	....
Dorset, Hants & Isle of Wight	£8.99	....	Ireland	£11.99	....
East Anglia	£8.99	....	North East	£10.99	....
Lake District & Cumbria	£8.99	....	North West	£10.99	....
Lancashire & Cheshire	£8.99	....	Scotland	£11.99	....
Northumberland & Durham	£8.99	....	South of England	£10.99	....
Peak District and Derbyshire	£8.99	....	South East of England	£10.99	....
Yorkshire	£8.99	....	Wales	£11.99	....
HIDDEN PLACES NATIONAL TITLES			West Country	£10.99	....
England	£11.99	....			
Ireland	£11.99	....			
Scotland	£11.99	....			
Wales	£11.99	....	**TOTAL QUANTITY:**		
OTHER TITLES					
			POST & PACKING:		
Off the Motorway	£11.99	....			
Garden Centres & Nurseries	£11.99	....	**TOTAL VALUE:**		

HIDDEN PLACES GUIDES

Explore Britain and Ireland with *Hidden Places* guides - a fascinating series of national and local travel guides.

Packed with easy to read information on hundreds of places of interest as well as places to stay, eat and drink.

Available from both high street and internet booksellers

For more information on the full range of *Hidden Places* guides and other titles published by Travel Publishing visit our website on

www.travelpublishing.co.uk
or ask for our leaflet by phoning **01752 697280** or emailing **info@travelpublishing.co.uk**

THE HIDDEN PLACES OF
THE LAKE DISTRICT AND CUMBRIA

THE HIDDEN PLACES OF
THE PEAK DISTRICT AND DERBYSHIRE

THE HIDDEN PLACES OF
DEVON

 findSOMEWHERE.CO.uk

For people who want to explore Britain and Ireland

Places to Visit

Our easy-to use website contains details and locations of places to stay, places to eat and drink, specialist shops and places of interest throughout England, Wales, Scotland and Ireland.

Places to Stay:	**Places to Eat and Drink:**	**Places of Interest:**	**Specialist Shops:**	**Gardens:**
Hotels, guest accommodation, bed & breakfast, inns, self-catering accommodation	Restaurants, pubs, inns, cafes, tea rooms	Historic buildings, gardens, art galleries, museums, nature parks, wildlife parks, indoor and outdoor activities	Fashion shops, art and craft shops, gift shops, food and drink shops, antique shops, jewellery shops	Garden centres and retail nurseries

READER REACTION FORM

The *Travel Publishing* research team would like to receive reader's comments on any visitor attractions or places reviewed in the book and also recommendations for suitable entries to be included in the next edition. This will help ensure that the *Hidden Places series of Guides* continues to provide its readers with useful information on the more interesting, unusual or unique features of each attraction or place ensuring that their visit to the local area is an enjoyable and stimulating experience. To provide your comments or recommendations would you please complete the forms below and overleaf as indicated and send to:

The Research Department, Travel Publishing Ltd,
Airport Business Centre, 10 Thornbury Road, Estover, Plymouth PL6 7PP

Your Name:

Your Address:

Your Telephone Number:

Please tick as appropriate:

Comments ☐   Recommendation ☐

Name of Establishment:

Address:

Telephone Number:

Name of Contact:

READER REACTION FORM

COMMENT OR REASON FOR RECOMMENDATION:

Index of Advertisers